IMMIGRATION REALITIES

IMMIGRATION REALITIES

Challenging Common Misperceptions

ERNESTO CASTAÑEDA AND CARINA CIONE

Columbia University Press

New York

Columbia University Press
Publishers Since 1893
New York   Chichester, West Sussex

CENTER FOR
LATIN AMERICAN
& LATINO STUDIES
AMERICAN UNIVERSITY | WASHINGTON, DC

The Immigration Lab

Library of Congress Cataloging-in-Publication Data
Names: Castañeda, Ernesto, author. | Cione, Carina, author.
Title: Immigration realities : challenging common misperceptions / Ernesto Castañeda
    & Carina Cione.
Description: New York : Columbia University Press, 2024. | Includes
    bibliographical references and index.
Identifiers: LCCN 2024011651 | ISBN 9780231203746 (hardback) | ISBN 9780231203753
    (trade paperback) | ISBN 9780231555210 (ebook)
Subjects: LCSH: Emigration and immigration—Social aspects. | Immigrants—
    Social conditions—United States. | Immigrants—Social conditions—Great Britain. |
    United States—Emigration and immigration—Government policy. | Great Britain—
    Emigration and immigration—Government policy. | Mexican-American Border
    Region—Defenses. | European Union—Great Britain.
Classification: LCC JV6225 .C42 2024 | DDC 305.9/069120941—dc23/eng/20240522

Cover design: Noah Arlow
Cover image: Alamy

Dedicated to our families and to immigrants, now and then

In memory of Winifred Irwin and Abelardo Tinoco

CONTENTS

ACKNOWLEDGMENTS

First and foremost, we thank Eric Schwartz for his unwavering support and patience throughout the years it took to complete this book. Thanks to Jennifer Crewe, Alyssa M. Napier, Marielle Poss, and everyone at Columbia University Press for bringing this book to the public. We also thank the proposal and manuscript reviewers for their support and high-quality feedback and to Ben Kolstad and team for their speed and attention to detail during the production process.

We also thank the three cohorts of first-year students enrolled in the Complex Problems seminar "Borders, Migration, and Globalization," who identified important arguments and wrote papers regarding common myths that breed anti-immigrant sentiments. They include the fall 2017 cohort of Chloe Bambara, Anthony Baron, Jack Boone, Citlali Castillo, Molly Dee, Lauren Ferrier, Alyssa Hugel, Daniela Jallath, Minwoo Kang, Samantha Liptak, Bailey O'Donnell, Veronica Robertson, Grace Shanahan, Amber Shemesh, and Emilia Turrisi; the fall 2018 cohort of Kayla Baldie, Samuel Blodgett, Alexzandria Burns, Alyssa Bursie, Gabriel Cabanas, Sage Coates-Farley, Chase Dexter, Josephine Flanagan, Emily Fontaine, Gabriela Garcia-Astolfi, Ariel Krysmalski, Samantha Lord, Gavin Meyer, Anupama Paul, Juan Pelaez-Barboza, Joseph Rose, Timothy Ryan-Liss, and Nikolaos Theodoratos; and the fall 2019 cohort of Alexander Aurin, Brandon Buckley, Adaire Criner, Kylie Anne Doyle, Lulia Fitiwi, Jackson Goldstein, Maya Gutierrez, Calvin Hendren, Julia Herold, Zachary Hill, Philip Lacava, Dahlia Linowes, William McCormick, Paulina Mendoza, Rebecca Moran-Scoratow, Jackson Rabold, Arpad Sarkozy de Nagy Bocsa, and especially Claire Whitman and Madelyn Hagins, who helped even after the class was over. Nonetheless, the conclusions and views presented in this book belong only to the authors. These students bear no responsibility for any positions or errors. Thank you to the CORE and Complex Problems staff and faculty at American University for encouraging a novel approach to inquiry-based teaching and inspiring students to get their feet wet in the process of conducting social science and policy research. It was not easy, but this book proves that it is possible and worth it to do so.

Thanks to Jessica Chaikof, SteVon Felton, Erin Foley, Clara Garcia, Madelyn Hagins, Daniel Jenks, Ariel Krysmalski, Dulce Lara, Amber Shemesh, Karissa Stanio, Yas (Rose) Taury, Madison Shomaker, Makenna Lindsay, and Claire Whitman for their valuable assistance and input throughout the various phases of editing. We are indebted to Ali Chaudhary, René Flores, Yossi Harpaz, and Amelia Tseng, whose perceptive and honest feedback helped sharpen our case.

Thanks are due to Alejandro Portes, Patricia Fernandez-Kelly, Cecilia Menjivar, Phil Kasinitz, Nancy Foner, Robert Smith, David Cook-Martin, David Fitzgerald, Silvia Pedraza, Susan Eckstein, Douglas Massey, Asad Asad, Rawan Arar, Celia Lacayo, Van Tran, Maria de Jesus and many others for the inspiration from their work and for their constant encouragement to get the knowledge of the immigrant research field to a wider public. We are also grateful for our extensive network of colleagues, collaborators, and benefactors at American University: Mike Murphy and the faculty in the Department of Sociology; the Immigration Lab; the Sociology Research and Practice MA Program; the Center for Latin American & Latino Studies; the Metropolitan Policy Center; the Center for Health, Risk & Society; and the Transatlantic Policy Center. We extend our gratitude to Eric Hershberg, Derek Hyra, Garret Martin, Michelle Egan, Kim Blankenship, Gay Young, Linda Aldoory, Max Friedman, Scott Bass, Peter Starr, and Vicky Wilkins.

Last, and certainly not least, the deepest thanks to our families and friends. Ernesto thanks Lesley, Alexander, and Ernesto III for their patience and love during the many years it has taken to write this book and others. Thanks to Joann for taking care of Georgia. This book also took shape and was finished in the community where I live. Neighbors have been a support and inspiration.

Carina is grateful to her family and close friends for their advice, laughter, and understanding of the regular missed calls or unanswered texts throughout this process. She also extends special thanks to Yonata Negatu, whose relentless support, encouragement, and words of wisdom have been immeasurably helpful and valued.

IMMIGRATION REALITIES

IMMIGRATION REALITIES

INTRODUCTION

Immigration as a History of Exclusion and Homemaking

This book addresses commonplace beliefs about international migration that, although often touted in the media and everyday conversations, are incorrect. Immigration is a politicized topic in the United States and other countries. In the headlines, the political right and left alike state with hype that there are record-breaking numbers of migrants seeking entry at the U.S.-Mexico border, despite the fact that globally, the percentage of people who change residency due to war, political or religious persecution, poverty, or lack of opportunity is not at an all-time high and is not unmanageable for receiving countries. Indeed, only around 3.5 percent of the world's population lives in a country different from the one in which they were born.[1]

Dialogue about immigration consistently alarms native-born populations, especially because of certain harmful stereotypes about immigrants of color who migrate from Latin America, Africa, and Asia. They are portrayed as criminals, freeloaders, victims, or geniuses by popular media. These inaccurate generalizations of entire immigrant populations may help accentuate ethnic and racial differences and cause native-born White people to feel threatened.[2] This process breeds distrust and heightens the danger for immigrants of color, who are singled out for their "otherness" in historically majority-White societies and used as scapegoats for social and economic problems. Throughout the following chapters, we reference research that disproves popular but false beliefs about immigration so that the public can critically engage with diverse information and thus better understand the topic.

Most observations made in the media take the point of view of native-born and local residents, many of whom harbor misconceptions that immigrants are dangerous, commit crimes, and drain welfare resources. Because of this, most discussions in much of the world today frame immigration as a problem. In this book, we address the assumptions that create negative connotations of immigrants and immigration. We go one step further by contextualizing immigration in relation to other social processes, political campaigns, and changes in economic policies and briefly place these phenomena in a historical perspective. Therefore, this book is an interdisciplinary overview of some of the latest and most relevant research addressing empirical questions about migration. To cite all the published research conducted by the thousands of experts who dedicate their lives to the study of immigration would be an impossible feat. Nonetheless, we support our arguments with numerous reliable sources that, of course, rely on previous work themselves. While we could not include analyses of all the important works in sociology, the broader social sciences, or policy analysis, we explore topic areas where there is a large consensus among different types of publications from various years and disciplines.

This book will increase readers' knowledge about the myths we cover and their ability to critically analyze and engage with information regarding immigration. It is also important to clarify that this book is not a guide to obtaining an immigrant visa or winning an asylum case, nor is it a discussion of the minutia of immigration law, which is comprised of systems of ever-changing laws, regulations, and practices that dictate who is allowed to migrate and how. This is intentional because understanding and studying migration purely from the perspective of immigration law often does not account for the social dynamics that unfold outside of immigration courts. Migration is a human story, and while immigration laws matter and impact individuals, migration is also about experiences that go beyond the law. This is not to say that immigrants have a proclivity for ignoring the rule of law or committing crime but rather that survival transcends political borders and designs. The recent obsession that states have with controlling who crosses their international borders and flies into their airports is an invention of the last few decades, and it should not limit how we think analytically about international migration.[3] It is an utterly inaccurate and dangerous idea to assume or expect that all people living inside the boundaries of a country or territory share the same ethno-racial background, religion, or culture.[4] His-torically, this has rarely been the case, and it is surely not so today. Nonethe-less, the assumption creates high levels of cruelty and exclusionary systems that eventually use force to try to turn that idea of homogeneity into a reality. Nations, or nation-states, are a political project, not a neutral reflection of the distribution of populations across the world.

Before we begin our discussion, it will be helpful to define some terms. In this book, *migration* refers to the movement of individuals, families, or groups of people across space. Migration is the most general term and encompasses *inter-nal migration*, or people moving within a political unit. For example, internal migrants are the hundreds of people living in California who move from San Francisco to San Diego, as well as the millions who move to different states in the United States of America and the hundreds of millions of Chinese who relocate to different Chinese provinces.[5] Migration also encompasses the twin processes of emigration and immigration. *Emigration* is the process of leaving one's place of birth, while *immigration* is the process of arriving at a new place of residence. In this book, migration refers to both processes and mobility in general, whether or not it is done with visas and other permits.

WHY READ ABOUT ACADEMIC RESEARCH ON IMMIGRATION?

As renowned scholars have noted,[6] much of the knowledge gathered by U.S.-based and international academics across the social sciences has not profoundly impacted public debates about immigration. In some cases, scientific findings are cherry-picked and presented tendentiously. We address this issue by out-lining cutting-edge immigration research by multiple scholars from various disciplines and backgrounds so the public can be better informed, inoculated against misinformation, and able to demand more practical policies from their elected officials.

Conversations about migration can be controversial. The topic has become highly politicized, and people often have strong opinions based on idiosyn-cratic personal experiences, prejudicial views, and false assumptions spread by politicians and pundits. However, the average person often does not have—nor *can* they have—all the facts at hand to conceptualize migration from an objective yet empathetic perspective. Academic literature has much to offer to the public's understanding of the complex process of contemporary international migration. Nonetheless, the relevant scientific research is often locked behind paywalls, research specialization, and discipline-specific jargon that most readers find cumbersome and hard to understand.[7] There are many illuminating books on aspects of the migration experience to and from particular places, as researchers tend to focus on distinct case studies; they often avoid making generalizations about common processes. In contrast, this book summarizes relevant research findings around common myths for readers who may not be familiar with contemporary migration or border studies. Each chapter centers around a specific misconception and can be read as a stand-alone piece or together with the others.[8] The chapters contain relevant and up-to-date knowledge about the realities of migration that is presented so as to make it engaging and accessible to non-experts. Here, we describe how each chapter is framed around common questions and how the realities revealed through research shatter common misconceptions.

CHAPTER OVERVIEWS

1. Is the U.S.-Mexico Border a Dangerous Place?

The U.S. southern border region is regularly portrayed as a dangerous, lawless place in the media and in popular discussions.[9] It is geographically distant from the political, cultural, and media centers of Washington, D.C., and New York City, which contributes to the detached and uninformed nature of the myth that the border region is unsafe. We refer to secondary data, published research, expert interviews, and original survey data from 1,152 residents of El Paso, Texas, to show that U.S. border cities are very safe for White Americans because of low crime rates, heavy border surveillance, and a strong U.S. Border Patrol presence. Conversely, Black Americans, Latin citizens, immigrants, and asylum seekers disproportionately suffer from physical and psychological violence, detainment, deportation, and family separation at the hands of the state and its authorities on the ground. Minorities are not always safe in the border region or protected by legal entities.[10]

In terms of homeland security, the situation in the border region does not threaten the country's safety. Instead, it raises concerns for human security because it is a relatively poor and neglected region in terms of services and human and political rights. Latinos living or visiting there are under constant threat of categorical and political violence. For example, in 2019, a self-declared White nationalist perpetrated a mass shooting outside the Cielo Vista Walmart in El Paso, killing people for "being Mexican," an act that we discuss in chapter 1 and elsewhere.[11]

2. Would a Border Wall Keep Undocumented Immigrants Away?

Chapter 2 discusses the technological, physical, and ideological border barriers in the United States—specifically, their enforcers, their economic impact on taxpayers, and the damage they have caused in the lives of Hispanic immigrants, border residents, and U.S.-born citizens. We cite work by scholars to show that "walls won't work"[12] and that most border residents oppose building a wall.[13] Deterrence does not work in the long term and causes much unnecessary suffering. Migrants will continue making the journey to the United States, despite the dangers that await them in the north, and for multiple reasons, undocumented immigration will not cease. Given that most drugs are either smuggled through or cleared by corrupt border officials at legal ports of entry, a taller and stronger physical barrier will not be effective in curbing black-market trade.

3. Are Immigrants More Likely to Commit Crime?

The stereotype of the "criminal immigrant" dates to the beginning years of the United States as an independent country, and the White, Anglo-centric values on which the nation was founded remain strong undertones in political discussions about immigrants today. However, our data on El Paso, as well as crime data released by the FBI and published in research studies reveal that foreign-born individuals tend to commit fewer crimes than native-born Americans.[14] Border cities are safer than nonborder cities of comparable size.[15] Also, neighborhoods with higher percentages of immigrants tend to have less crime, meaning that their presence may be a form of protection.[16]

Substance use is legally conflated with criminal activity, and much like the current "crimmigration" system conflates immigration with law-breaking behavior, this has allowed for the mass incarceration and detainment of U.S.- and foreign-born people of color. Yet foreign-born Hispanics in El Paso have lower rates of reported illegal substance use than the U.S.-born, and Hispanics overall rarely tend to use illegal substances and suffer from substance use disorders in Texas and the broader United States. We also found that El Paso Hispanics who visit Mexico often use drugs less than those who do not, despite stereotypes that frame Latin people as drug mules, users, or traffickers.[17]

4. Do Immigrants Avoid Learning English?

Language abilities and accents are signifiers of individuals' cultural identities. Native-born people often comment on immigrants speaking foreign languages in public places and interpret this as a sign that immigrants do not want to learn English and integrate into their new community.[18] Nevertheless, that is not the immigrants' intention. The evidence shows that immigrants face barriers throughout the process of language acquisition and acculturation, including the lack of time and places for adults to study English and prejudice in the classroom for children learning English.[19]

We propose possible policy interventions to help in this process such as the expansion of state-level linguistic integration projects. Immigrants' desire to learn the local language has not changed. What has changed is their willingness to accept being shamed for speaking their native language in public and to refrain from speaking their native language to avoid this shaming. However, as in the past, immigrants, their children, and their grandchildren predominantly learn and speak English over time.

5. Are Immigrants Disproportionately Dependent on Welfare and Other Government Programs?

Another common point of debate is whether immigrants are motivated to migrate to specific regions in the Global North so they can depend on social welfare for the rest of their lives. In 1924, quotas were set in the United States to limit immigrants from southern and eastern Europe because they were thought to be "public charges" who would drain welfare resources. Yet current research as well as studies dating back to 1911 show that immigrants and ethnic minorities in the United States are less likely to use welfare programs than other groups, even when they are eligible for these benefits.[20] Current stereotypes about low-income Black, Asian, and Latin people and their perceived overuse of welfare have led to stringent state and federal policies that go so far as to restrict the size of eligible families. Chapter 5 analyzes how this misconception has influenced political and legal decisions and the economic well-being of foreign-born people in the United States, United Kingdom, Ireland, Australia, Denmark, and Sweden.

6. Are Remittances a Drain on the Host Economy? Should We Tax the Money That Migrants Send Home?

Recent immigrants commonly send money to their families in their places of origin. These transfers, referred to as *remittances*, add up to billions of dollars annually. There is a widespread inaccurate belief among native-born populations in different places that remittances drain economic resources from popular immigrant destinations. Because of this, they call for a remittance tax, but laws aimed at collecting portions of remittances as taxes have been rejected. If such taxes were imposed, remitters would stop using banks and formal channels to send money abroad and instead choose to remit via informal channels.

Most scholars studying remittances agree that taxing remittances would be not only ineffective and burdensome to implement but also unethical, since remitters have already paid taxes on their wages; remittances are simply a portion of their earnings they are sending to close family members abroad. Many development practitioners have framed remittances as foreign aid capable of igniting economic development in the Global South, and we outline competing arguments in chapter 6.[21]

7. Is the Number of Refugees Unmanageable? Is There a Refugee Crisis?

How can refugee destinations work with sending and transit countries to make the process safer and more orderly? The 2015 European "refugee crisis" and other mobility events emphasized in Western media are a social construction that frames refugees as social problems. The "crisis" discourse focuses on infantilizing, criminalizing, or blaming refugees for national issues instead of addressing the root causes of displacement: imperial histories that extracted resources from colonies and later from people from former colonies through migration.[22] Contemporary neocolonial conditions continue in many postcolonial countries: for example, Haiti and former colonies in Africa were forced to send annual payments to France in exchange for their independence. We actively reframe the idea of a refugee crisis as the continuation of Western violence imposed on the rest of the world and as a lack of accountability among countries in the Global North.

Chapter 7 draws on work conducted with refugees and asylum seekers in the United States and Europe. It provides a more nuanced description of who refugees, asylum seekers, and displaced people are, why they are legally considered such, and what challenges and institutional procedures they face, such as xenophobic stereotypes in the media, the asylum application process, and "pushbacks" against migrant boats in the Mediterranean and against those seeking to cross the U.S.-Mexico border.

8. Is There a Link Between Globalization and Migration?

Chapter 8 looks critically at the theoretical and rhetorical connections drawn between economic globalization and increased international migration. We point out that although these processes are related, they are mainly independent of one another. Nevertheless, the way that trade agreements, globalization, and the emergence of the European Union were sold to the public inferred that borders open to goods and services, the global village, and a cosmopolitan outlook were inherently intertwined phenomena that had never existed without one another. We provide a brief overview of times when economic globalization existed without increasing or halting international migration.

Furthermore, the effects of the 2007–2008 economic crisis and the stagnation of the middle class have resulted in a backlash against free trade as well as against foreign individuals and cultures. The United States has experienced a new wave of isolationism partly because the public and policymakers do not fully understand the differences between these two processes. This chapter elaborates on these differences by analyzing the literature on globalization and migration flows and the recent political rhetoric criticizing free trade, the North American Free Trade Agreement (USMCA), and the EU.

9. Will the Decision to Leave the European Union Stop Immigration to the United Kingdom?

Proponents of Brexit linked the UK's membership in the EU with increases in immigration and refugee resettlement. Prior to the 2016 referendum on whether to leave or remain in the EU, Brexit campaigners gained support by spouting myths about immigrants and promising to stop immigrants who were undocumented or otherwise framed as undesirable if the UK revoked its EU membership. Although the UK's decision to leave the EU has allowed Parliament to institute new border procedures and place entry restrictions on European immigrants, the rates of immigration from the rest of the world have not decreased.

Chapter 9 explores how the country's exit from the EU will affect immigrants and temporary migrant workers living in the UK as well as the many British people living in the EU. As we predicted when drafting this book, immigration has not decreased post-Brexit. Rather than returning to their home countries, many migrants have simply changed their legal immigration status, but the Settlement Scheme and the new process to claim documented immigration status have caused uncertainty and unnecessary chaos. The Brexit deal has also left loose ends that have led to trade difficulties with Ireland and to growing dissatisfaction among citizens in Scotland, both of which have implications that we discuss in the chapter.

10. Do Immigrants Integrate into Host Societies? What Lessons Can We Learn About Immigrant Integration from Different Cities and Countries?

It is common for mayors and the media to frame group asylum as a threat to cities after conflict and crisis abroad, but such an action most often turns into a future bonanza. Chapter 10 uses research on immigrant integration in New York, Paris, and Barcelona, as well as research conducted in El Paso and Washington, D.C., to discuss policies and practices that better integrate immigrants and improve relations between natives and newcomers. Here, we discuss the role of civil society, local initiatives, and immigrant organizations. We also define and discuss common terms, such as *assimilation*, *social integration*, and *belonging*, and provide a model for how cities can better welcome, integrate, and benefit from immigrants.

EL PASO DATA

In 2011 and 2012, Ernesto Castañeda directed a survey of 1,152 Hispanics in El Paso and an oversample of undocumented and homeless individuals. The median age of the sample was thirty years of age. The sample was stratified and purposefully oversampled the undocumented and marginally housed. In order to ensure the trust and safety of these populations and include them in the survey, the recruitment and surveying process was not household-based. Hundreds of local university students conducted the surveys. They had previous knowledge of the area and partly used their personal connections to identify hard-to-reach populations and to increase trust and data reliability. The project was supported by a grant from the National Institutes of Health (Award Number P20MD00287-04 from the National Institute on Minority Health and Health Disparities NIMHD) through the Hispanic Health Disparities Research Center at the University of Texas, El Paso. The project received approval from the university's institutional review board, and no identifying information was collected. The sample was weighted to reflect the homeless population in the city, which we calculated to be around three thousand.

The city of El Paso is located in the westernmost part of Texas, bordering New Mexico to the west and Ciudad Juárez, its sister city, directly to the south. El Paso and Juárez are divided by the now often dry Rio Grande but connected by a small number of bridges and streets that function as legal ports of entry. In the 2010 Census, the decennial census closest to the time when the data were collected, El Paso County had an estimated population of over 800,653 people, 83 percent of whom identified as Hispanic or Latino.[23] Given the important presence of Latin people in El Paso, their views and experiences are key to understanding the dynamics in this border city. We have published works using these data in academic journals, and a forthcoming book written alongside colleagues employs findings from this survey to address health disparities and the Hispanic and immigrant health paradoxes. Across the following chapters, we include El Paso as a relevant case study and an example to bolster our assertions. The data complement the arguments in many chapters and are similar to findings in studies conducted in different cities and by researchers from multiple disciplines. The El Paso data are not meant to carry all the evidentiary weight in disarming the myths discussed— they are simply relevant data points gathered from an original study.

The terms Hispanic, Latino, and Latinx all result from the immigration experience in the United States and are geographically specific. For instance, in this survey of 1,152 people in El Paso conducted in 2011,[24] 28.9 percent of respondents self-identified as Hispanic, 26.4 percent as Mexican, 22 percent as Mexican American, and 13 percent as American (table 0.1). Fewer than 3 percent identified as each of the remaining categories: foreigner, binational, Latino, Chicano, White, Native American, and other (see table 0.2). Thus in the tables in this book we often use Latin because it does not include the gendered ending of the Spanish Latino or Latina and is more general than Latine or Latinx without excluding those populations, and because most people from Latin America prefer the term Latino to Hispanic.

TABLE 0.1 Sample demographic characteristics

	Percentage
Gender	
Male	42.9%
Female	57.1%
U.S. legal citizenship status	
Citizen	78.9%
Resident	15.2%
Undocumented	3.4%
Work/student visa	2.5%
Education	
Less than high school	14.6%
High school/GED	23.3%
Tech/1-2 years college	28.3%
College and more	33.8%
Household Income	
Less than $10,000	21.6%
Between $10,000 and $20,000	19.9%
Between $20,001 and $30,000	15.8%
Between $30,001 and $40,000	11.8%
More than $40,000	30.9%
Immigrant generation	
First	26%
1.5	15.3%
Second	34.6%
Third	14.6%
>Third	9.5%
Marginally housed	1.3%

Weighted sample total N = 525,321

TABLE 0.2 How do you classify yourself?

Hispanic	28.9%
Mexican	26.4%
Mexican American	22.0%
American	13.0%
Latino	2.7%
Chicano	2.4%
Binational	2.0%
Other	2.0%
Foreigner	0.4%
White	0.2%
Native American	0%

CHAPTER 1

THE SOUTHERN BORDER IS SAFE, BUT BORDER ENFORCEMENT MAKES IT UNSAFE FOR MANY

Many U.S. politicians have argued that building a border wall is essential to keep criminals and undocumented immigrants out of the United States. However, existing research unequivocally reveals that immigrants are not coming to the United States to commit crimes and that a wall does not entirely stop migration. Further, people who live around the border say they feel safe. In this chapter, we explore why many believe the U.S.-Mexico border is unsafe and why the federal government chooses to focus so much of its time, money, and resources on the region.

One's individual identity largely determines their security at the U.S.-Mexico border. A U.S. citizen or a lawful permanent resident with a green card living in the border region experiences relative privilege, as official data show that border cities are among the safest places in the country.[1] Unfortunately, this is not the case for some migrants, who are among the region's most targeted and vulnerable individuals. Undocumented migrants—whether adults or children—face threats of state, vigilante, and gang violence as well as the risk of injury, kidnapping, dehydration, starvation, apprehension, abuse by U.S. Border Patrol agents, and deportation by U.S. Immigration and Customs Enforcement (ICE).[2] Minors and Indigenous and trans people face even more risks. Over time, measures to "secure" the southern border have had unintended consequences. The militarization of border authorities disrupts foreign relations and trade and throws ecosystems into an imbalance.[3] This border security system fosters an environment where human rights violations and state-sponsored violence against vulnerable people are a part of border officials' everyday jobs.

U.S.-MEXICO BORDER RELATIONS

Unequal Power Dynamics and U.S. Hegemony

Following the elaboration of the Monroe Doctrine, U.S. colonialism and hegemony shaped the nature of the United States' relationship with Mexico.[4] The unwarranted invasion and annexation of Mexican territory sparked the Mexican-American War in the 1840s and propelled U.S. borders farther west.[5] Since then, no open warfare has occurred between the neighboring countries. Mexico poses no threat and often cooperates with U.S. border enforcement procedures.[6] Despite these countries' strong economic partnership and the United States' hegemony over its southern neighbor, some U.S. politicians have insisted that the border area is unsafe for U.S. citizens. The anthropologist and border expert Joe Heyman notes that neither the Mexican nor the U.S. government poses "any military threat to the other" after working together for the past century to establish peace at the border.[7] The binational relationship has been mutually beneficial for each country's economy, resulting in the development of a vibrant transborder life in the region. However, the United States' decision in 2001 to fortify the southern border has created barriers to this transborder life and the coexistence between communities that have thrived for decades.[8] Heyman asserts that, by exerting its dominance through an excessive border security presence, the United States "insults" its southern neighbor and treats it "as a threat rather than a partner."[9]

Following Heyman's logic, Laura Velasco Ortiz and Oscar Contreras describe the U.S.-Mexico border at present as the "greatest structure of inequality in the modern world."[10] Power is not equally distributed between the two countries: the United States' superior resources and military power give it the upper hand. People and capital are constantly crossing between the two nations, but skewed power dynamics can be observed in the differences in surveillance and control of human mobility on the U.S. and Mexican sides. Although it is possible for American citizens to cross into Mexico whenever they wish, attempting to enter the United States without the correct documents has proved either costly or deadly for an increasing number of people. Even if migrants successfully cross the border, their stay may be only temporary. To date, the Department of Homeland Security has deported thousands of people— mainly to Mexico, Central America, and the Caribbean, where they may have no family or social ties.[11] Many are forced back into the same circumstances from which they fled in the first place.[12]

The border infrastructure is expensive and does not deter immigration. Nevertheless, it serves other functions. A vast private industrial complex is profiting from the idea that border walls are necessary, being the only way to "control" immigration. The resulting portrayal of wall building and patrolling as essential creates their own public support and justification. The illusion of the desirability of walling generates profit, especially for private prisons and those working in this sector.[13]

The Importance of Immigrant Labor and Mexican Goods to the U.S. Economy

The United States and Mexico are important trade partners. In 1994, the North American Free Trade Agreement (NAFTA) created a regional bloc that linked the economic fates of the United States, Mexico, and Canada and that continues with the renegotiated U.S.-Mexico-Canada Agreement (USMCA) of 2020. The nations involved in these agreements are economically dependent on one another. Without a porous border, the U.S. economy would suffer from the consequences of stalled trade. The estimated over $1.5 billion in exports that cross the southern border every day would disappear, along with over one million jobs that support this trade.[14] Closing the border long term to goods, services, and people would have dire effects on entire metropolitan pockets in the Southwest. We saw this partially unfold during the COVID-19 pandemic. The border was open to trade and goods, but the United States was effectively closed to noncitizens. Local businesses, employers, and families suffered because of this.[15]

Maquiladoras, assembly factories located along the Mexican side of the border, employ over one million Mexican nationals.[16] After NAFTA took effect, the number of these factories in Ciudad Juárez skyrocketed because the agreement cut tariffs and encouraged more trade. The growth in maquiladora manufacturing in Juárez made the city the largest in the state of Chihuahua and the source of 50 percent of that state's economic activity between 1999 and 2004. Most maquiladoras in the border region are owned by U.S. or other foreign corporations and exclusively manufacture goods that are immediately exported north. In this way, the demand for goods in the United States drives maquiladora manufacturing, and its workforce plays a vital role in the well-being of the American economy.[17] However, by 2009, the number of maquiladora workers in the city had declined,[18] as much of the foreign investment went to

China, although some later moved closer to U.S. shores after the pandemic. However exploitative or unfair, these factories are a prime example of what Heyman describes as "cross-boundary economic integration" that creates a symbiotic relationship between the two countries.[19] The long lines to cross into the United States also hurt the regional economy and U.S. citizens, both would be helped by more agile crossing.

Pia Orrenius, a senior economist at the U.S. Federal Reserve Bank of Dallas, shows that immigration provides serious economic benefits. There is a ripple effect on economic growth that begins when immigrants enter the labor force. Their participation is beneficial to American workers because it expands the U.S. economy and increases its GDP by anywhere between $36 and $72 billion in one year. As a result, the incomes of both foreign-born and native workers increase. Further, immigrants supply labor where a market needs it at any given time, significantly reducing labor shortages.[20] Migrant workers are crucial in the revitalization and stabilization of any economy, and the United States is dependent on their labor to continue growing; yet they are often underpaid and overqualified and fall victim to exploitation and wage theft.[21]

Transborder Lifestyles

Similar to Americans who live in one state and work in another, people living at the border spend time in the United States and Mexico for many different reasons. Millions of people have responsibilities, connections, and relationships with families, friends, employers, and health care providers in both countries. Others enjoy traveling and spending their weekends at popular vacation spots across the border, such as the beach neighborhoods of Tijuana.[22]

Adalberto Aguirre Jr. and Jennifer Simmers argue that the border is more than just a territorial line because it "identifies a sharing of geographical, cultural, and social space between two neighbors."[23] Many people, including students, work-ers, tourists, truck drivers, and families, lead cross-border lives.[24] Thousands of students live in Mexico while attending schools and universities in New Mexico, Arizona, California, and Texas. The cost of living is lower on the Mexican side of the line, and some students whose families have been deported prefer to live near their loved ones. Every weekday morning they ride public transportation and join the queue of workers and other students who pass through legal entry checkpoints to attend classes in the United States.[25] San Ysidro, a U.S. port of entry located just north of Tijuana, is considered one of the world's most active border checkpoints. An estimated seventy-six thousand cars and trucks and over twenty thousand pedestrians pass through daily.[26] There are people who, for example, "begin and end their day in San Diego, with a trip to Tijuana to have lunch with family[,] or who live south of the border but travel every day through San Ysidro to work in the U.S." They live their daily lives in both the United States and Mexico and regularly cross the border at legal entry points.[27] The same is true for people living in the border region of Switzerland and France, where crossing that international border is as easy for Europeans as crossing state lines is for anyone in the United States.[28]

Drastic increases in security and surveillance carried out by the U.S. government have created difficulties for people who cross the border frequently and have intensified transborder stigma.[29] Although plenty of American and Mexican nationals still go about their travels, the heavier presence of border control and immigration authorities can discourage and scare even legal travelers.[30] It is common for students with nonimmigrant visas or legal permanent residency in the United States to feel anxious or confused during their commutes now that border surveillance has intensified.[31] Since 2016, more people report feeling scared of the implications of a border wall for their education and forgo deeper questioning by border officials as well as longer waits at checkpoints.[32] Rates of entry into the United States for tourism, business, and other legal purposes flattened or decreased when border closures were temporarily implemented following the September 11, 2001, attacks on the Twin Towers and the Pentagon.[33] Americans unfamiliar with the region stopped interacting with it after President Felipe Calderón initiated Mexico's War on Drugs.[34] Exotic getaways in northern Mexico were suddenly associated with fears of being kidnapped by drug traffickers or caught in cartel gunfire.

Intimidation, surveillance, and weaponry at legal U.S. entry points might give the illusion that the United States and Mexico are two distant realms. However, border residents and researchers know that life is shared on both sides of the border. The futures of border sister cities such as Tijuana and San Diego are inextricably tied together because they are part of one larger community.[35] As Heyman argues, despite the imposition of a political boundary, the existing intimate human relationships on the ground will always connect Mexico and the United States.[36]

SAFETY IN EL PASO, TEXAS

El Paso, a city in west Texas, lies on the U.S.-Mexico border. Data from the FBI's Uniform Crime Reports were used in ranking it the safest city in the country with a population over 500,000 in 2012 and the sixth safest city overall in 2019.[37] El Paso has been rated as highly safe for the past two decades, even before policies to build a border wall or heavily police the border were implemented. With funding from the National Institutes of Health, we conducted a survey in El Paso in 2011–2012 that provided insights into crime, safety, and security. The study revealed that the overwhelming majority of residents feel safe or very safe living in El Paso,[38] even with foreign-born neighbors. Roughly half of the respondents also said that they visit Ciudad Juárez, and around half of these said that they do so often.

The same survey revealed that 42.4 percent of people who moved to El Paso did so hoping to have "a better life." It would be counterintuitive to invest effort and time in relocating to a city that experiences high rates of violence. Seeking to create "a better life" includes living in a safe place and maintaining that community's safety.

TABLE 1.1 Why did you move to El Paso?

Better life	42.4%
Economy	28.9%
Family	8.9%
School	4.6%
Other	15.20%

TABLE 1.2 How safe do you feel in El Paso?

Very safe	66.7%
Safe	30.4%
Not safe	2.9%

TABLE 1.3 How safe do you feel in your neighborhood (by nativity)?

	U.S.-born	Foreign-born
Very safe	70.3%	61.5%
Safe	26.8%	35.5%
Not safe	2.9%	3.0%

TABLE 1.4 Do you ever go to Juarez?

Yes	40.3%
No	59.7%

TABLE 1.5 Where do you seek medical treatment?

United States	67.9%
Mexico	16.7%
Both	15.4%

TERRORISM AND CRIME AT THE BORDER

Immigrants Are Not Terrorists or Criminals

The contemporary focus on border entry restrictions, immigration policy, and deportation has been coupled with a rise in rhetoric that criminalizes foreign-born people, going so far as to call them "thugs," "terrorists," "rapists," and "animals."[39] Throughout his presidency, Donald Trump was especially critical of undocumented Latin American immigrants and regularly referred to them in dehumanizing terms. This racist language is more than just offensive—it is fabricated purposely for short-term political gains and distorts the perception of immigrants by portraying them as essentially different and as subhuman.

These are not the only unfounded allegations that have been made against the Hispanic community. Claims made by President Trump and fellow immigration hard-liners that thousands of terrorists have been apprehended at the border and that many have sneaked into the United States are either false or misleading.[40] The former White House chief of staff Mick Mulvaney stated that authorities "had arrested 17,000 criminals at the southern border" in 2018.[41] Lori Robertson from FactCheck.org disproves Mulvaney's allegation by referencing data supplied by CBP. That year the Border Patrol apprehended "6,259 'criminal aliens' "—immigrants with previous criminal convictions—along the border. Almost half of them were considered "criminal" only because they had attempted to cross into or reenter the United States illegally, and only 3—or 0.048 percent of those apprehended—had previous convictions for homicide or manslaughter. An additional 10,572 "criminal aliens" were encountered and refused entry by CBP's Office of Field Operations at the 328 U.S. ports of entry it oversees. Although CBP didn't provide the number of encounters for specific ports of entry, it is likely that Mulvaney's "17,000 criminals" included people who tried to enter the United States through ports of entry that were not on the southern border.[42]

Ultimately, immigrants are overwhelmingly *not* criminals. They are often victims of crime and underreport such abuse because they fear interaction with law enforcement. This is only one of the many facets of life as an immigrant that policymakers and politicians typically overlook. Ignorance, negative stereotypes, and xenophobic language are seeds that will grow into more hate unless collective action is taken to dismantle the people, processes, and institutions that plant them.

Can Terrorists Pass Through the Southern Border?

Linking border security to terrorism plays on people's greatest fears and traumatic experiences, but it is a faulty connection. CBP's focus expanded after 2001
to include foreign terrorists, such as members of al-Qaeda, in addition to undocumented Mexican and Central American migrants.[43] These border security
reforms fueled the desire to build physical fences along the U.S.-Mexico border.

During a resurgence of restrictive immigration policy under the Trump
administration in 2017, the United States began conflating immigrants from
"special interest countries"—those nations with "a tendency to promote, produce, or protect terrorist organizations or their members"—with suspected terrorists. These countries are often in regions associated with known networks
of Islamist extremist organizations, but the list of special interest countries has
changed many times in the last decade.[44] This power to restrict immigration was
taken to the extreme in the 2018 travel ban, colloquially known as the "Muslim
Ban," which placed stringent restrictions on travelers, refugees, and immigrants
with origins in Muslim-majority nations.[45] Trump also toyed with considering
Cuba and Venezuela to be sponsors of terrorism and with designating drug cartels as terrorist organizations. On January 11, 2021, the Trump administration
designated Cuba as a state sponsor of terrorism without any empirical basis.

Based on existing research, these concerns are misplaced, and there is no crisis
related to terrorists entering the United States illegally through the southern
border. Between 2001 and 2018, all but two foreign terrorists who were active
in the United States entered the country legally through a port of entry on the
border with Canada. In fact, until 2020, only a handful of blacklisted individuals had legally entered the country via either the northern or the southern border.[46] Furthermore, despite the alarm surrounding special interest immigrants,
the Department of Homeland Security (DHS) and the American Immigration
Lawyers Association report that less than 1 percent of those apprehended by
the Border Patrol from 2007 until 2017 were people from special interest countries.[47] Absolutely no terrorist violence has been carried out by special interest
immigrants who have entered the country through a U.S.-Mexico legal port of
entry, and almost all terrorists who have committed violent attacks have entered
the United States legally through airports or are U.S.-born citizens.[48] Further,
evidence does not support the fears that undocumented Hispanic immigrants
will commit terrorist acts. While foreign-born terrorists do indeed exist, a list of

those who planned to or did commit terrorist attacks in the United States from 1975 until 2015 shows that only one was Mexican.[49]

Given this history, it is reasonable to conclude that while dangers exist at the southern border, much like anywhere else, the entry of terrorists disguised as migrants is not one that merits intense concern at this time. Information regarding the nature of immigrants has been miscommunicated and manipulated, and influential politicians from both major parties cite incorrect statistics and contribute to the spread of genuinely fake news.[50] Increasing physical security on the U.S.-Mexico border will not directly decrease dangers in the country, and increasing immigration enforcement will not end undocumented immigration. This can be done only if the structural factors that prompt migration are addressed and the U.S. legal immigration system is reformed.

White Supremacists Constitute the Majority of Recent U.S. Terrorists

Statistically, domestic White supremacists and other right-wing extremists pose a more significant threat to Americans than foreign-born terrorists. The Anti-Defamation League's Center on Extremism reports that Islamic extremists caused only one violent incident in 2019, whereas domestic White supremacists perpetrated multiple large-scale assaults. Forty-two extremist-related deaths occurred in the United States in 2019. While none resulted from domestic Islamic extremism, three U.S. sailors were killed in an attack on the Pensacola Naval Air Station carried out by a foreign-born Saudi student. The remaining deaths were attributed to other forms of domestic terrorism: 81 percent to White supremacy, 5 percent to antigovernment extremism, and 5 percent to incel and other right-wing extremist conspiracy groups, such as QAnon.[51]

African American, Jewish, and Latin communities were targeted in four of the five terrorist attacks in 2019. One of these tragedies, the mass shooting carried out by a White supremacist at a Walmart in El Paso on August 3, was the third most deadly attack by a U.S. citizen since 1970. The shooter killed twenty-two people and injured twenty-four more—they were almost exclusively Hispanic.[52] Eight of the victims were Mexican nationals. The shooter was racially motivated, and he circulated the contents of an anti-immigrant manifesto online through a conspiracy-driven chat room shortly before he committed the heinous act.[53]

Federal security has prioritized international terrorism since 2001 but has failed to adequately address the growing number of domestic terrorist attacks on schools, universities, churches, shopping centers, synagogues, and mosques that target marginalized communities and younger Americans. White supremacist terrorism is not confined to the United States, and similar shootings unfolded in 2019 at a mosque in Christchurch, New Zealand, and a synagogue in Halle, Germany. Furthermore, the young man who carried out the El Paso massacre said he was directly influenced by the manifesto written and published online by the Christchurch mosque shooter. Hate and White nationalist ideologies are transnational phenomena. The leaders of New Zealand and Germany swiftly denounced the horrific events that occurred in their countries, and New Zealand passed legislation banning semiautomatic weapons. Further, after the shooting in El Paso, the president of Mexico, Andres Manuel Lopez Obrador, argued that much of the danger faced by Mexican nationals occurred because of the unregulated and open sale of arms in the United States and that this "indiscriminate sale of weapons" needed to be controlled.[54] Still, President Trump failed to address gun control in a speech following the El Paso Walmart attack and instead denounced violent video games and the internet to deflect the blame from guns.[55]

Implementing stricter gun control legislation and regulations is one way for the U.S. government to counter domestic terrorism. However, the role of racially motivated attacks and the mounting political violence bred by far-right extremists is neglected or overlooked by many.

Fewer Crimes Are Committed in the Border Area

The U.S.-Mexico border is a predominantly safe place for White U.S. citizens. Crime rates in border cities and suburbs are lower than those in the rest of the country, ensuring that most White Americans have little to worry about.[56] This is partially because migrants, both with and without papers, are aware of xenophobic sentiments and take particular care to abide by the law. They avoid interactions with the police in order to preserve their immigration status. McAllen, Texas, located next to the Mexican city of Reynosa, was ranked as the seventh safest city in the United States and experienced no homicides in 2018.[57] The former CBP commissioner David Aguilar has described border communities as safer than those farther inland.[58]

In 2017, border counties had average violent crime and homicide rates of 347.8 and 3.4 per 100,000, respectively. According to the FBI-compiled data, these were significantly lower than rates in nonborder counties and in fact in the entire country that year. Border counties tallied 33.8 percent fewer homicides, 2.1 percent fewer property crimes, and 8 percent fewer violent crimes than did the United States as a whole.[59] The lives and well-being of people with U.S. citizenship, particularly European Americans, are not disproportionately threatened in the U.S.-Mexico border region. In fact, it is safer to live there than in plenty of other U.S. towns and cities. Federal drug and firearm convictions in southern Texas were 14.4 percent and 8.4 percent lower than the national averages in 2019, respectively. The same year federal convictions in Texas's southern and western regions related to child pornography, sexual abuse, money laundering, robbery, and fraud/theft/embezzlement were also much lower compared to convictions across the entire United States.[60]

The violence occurring in some areas of northern Mexico remains concentrated in those places and has not permeated to the U.S. side—despite widespread assumptions. According to a survey conducted in Ciudad Juárez in 2010, 95.37 percent of residents considered the city to be a little safe or not all safe, whereas in our separate survey, 97 percent considered El Paso to be safe or very safe (see table 1.3).[61] The homicide rate in Juárez at the time was 229 per 100,000, and over 230,000 people migrated to El Paso as a result.[62]

RISKS OF CROSSING THE BORDER

During the 2012 presidential debates, Mitt Romney suggested making life more difficult materially and psychologically for undocumented people so they would "self-deport" or opt to move back to their countries of birth. But prior to that, in 1995, the government had adopted the philosophy of prevention through deterrence in its programs to reduce illegal immigration, based on the assumption that increasing the difficulty and pain of crossing the border outside of ports of entry would make people not try.[63] These programs have made the crossing increasingly deadly for prospective immigrants who cannot qualify for visas, family reunification, or asylum.

The prevention through deterrence programs established by DHS concentrate border enforcement resources (personnel, fences, cameras, towers, motion sensors, floodlights, helicopters, and drones) at ports of entry and the surrounding urban and populated areas, allowing the areas between official ports, consisting mainly of rivers and deserts, to serve as "natural" deterrents. Thus, migrants were

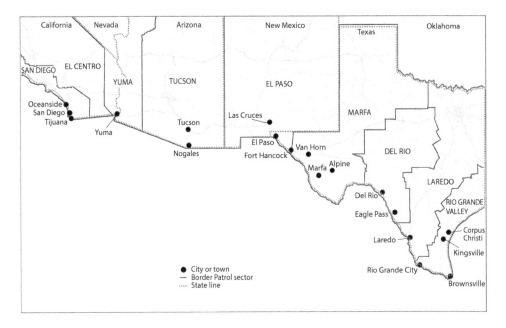

1.1 Map of southern Border Patrol sectors

deflected from El Paso and San Ysidro to what the Border Patrol refers to as the Tucson Sector, which covers 262 miles of the border from near the California/ Arizona state line to the Arizona/New Mexico state line, and the Rio Grande Valley Sector, since one of the busiest Border Patrol sectors in the Southwest (see figure 1.1).

The Migration Journey

Those who make the migratory journey are exposed to a set of unique risks that can endanger their psychological and physical health and well-being. The Mexican border at present has been called the "most violent border in the world between . . . two countries not at war with one another," and those who bear the brunt of the bloodshed are Central Americans and others fleeing political, economic, and social disorder in their home communities.[64] The strengthening of border security since the 1990s through CBP's prevention through deterrence approach has pushed migrants into dangerous terrain, like the rural desert, as they attempt to cross into the United States.[65] Most deaths are thought to occur on the Arizona side, where the terrain is uneven, rough, and vast.[66] Apprehensions rose to over 700,000 per year in Arizona as they declined in California and Texas.[67] Consequently, the probability of "finding dead Mexican bodies along the border joining Arizona and Mexico is so high that the area is known as 'The Devil's Highway.' "[68]

The Mexican-U.S. border can be deadly for migrants who dare cross it, seeing that they must battle "Mexican and American assailants and kidnappers after their money; heat, sun, snakes and cacti after their bodies; armed American vigilantes after their freedom; and Border Patrol agents after their records."[69] Large numbers of migrants succumb to dehydration and heat stroke, highway accidents, and the strong currents of the Rio Grande.[70] Enrique Morones, the founder of Border Angels, estimates that over eleven thousand people died in this area between 1994 and 2003, the most common cause of death being lack of water.[71] Some are cramped in small compartments for hours while being smuggled.[72] Thus, buffing up border security did not stop illegal migration but pushed migrants to forge new routes away from border cities and towns and through treacherous areas, exposing them for longer periods to the desert.[73] Because of this, migrants are increasingly dependent on the knowledge and guidance of *coyotes* to cross the border. Most coyotes used to be trusted neighbors who were approached by migrants needing help based on recommendations and word of mouth, but as border crossing has gotten harder and more profitable, other actors have come to play this role, including transnational smuggling networks and organized crime.[74] The high demand for coyotes also increases the likelihood that migrants will suffer abuse or death at the hands of inexperienced guides who profit from this flourishing market.[75] In 2018 alone, 222 bodies were retrieved in the Arizona desert, although it is common knowledge that many are swallowed by the hostile landscape and never unearthed.[76] The summer of 2005 was the deadliest recorded thus far for migrants at the U.S.-Mexico border: at least 472 people were found dead in Arizona and New Mexico.[77] One area along the border has even been given the nickname of "ankle alley" due to the incredible number of people who emerge from it with orthopedic injuries.[78]

The environment is not the migrants' only threat. They are frequently tricked or forcibly kidnapped by organized criminal bands that sometimes disguise themselves as local law enforcement.[79] Jeremy Slack documented multiple testimonials of migrants kidnapped and held for ransom or tortured and forced to work for cartels.[80] On top of this, extortion and corruption negatively impact

Central Americans traveling to the United States: migrants should expect to pay $1,200 to $1,500 on average to bribe Mexican or U.S. authorities during their journey. Still, these informal taxes pale in comparison to the total average amount that people tell us they have to pay coyotes to cross the border, which, according to recent arrivals interviewed in 2023, ranged from $7,000 to $10,000.[81]

No matter the consequences, however, migration does not stop. More robust border surveillance cannot prevent undocumented migration because the situation is bad enough in their home countries that they decide to embark on the extremely dangerous journey to the United States.[82] The reasons driving people to migrate are so urgent and time-sensitive that migrants are willing to risk their lives. Therefore, to minimize the likelihood of death, sickness, and family separation for migrants, the U.S. government cannot depend on the restrictive border policies currently in place. More humane policies could be implemented without risking national security.[83] When ethics and empathy are not used to guide immigration policy, migrants suffer as a result.

Migrant Deaths

Migration-related death, tragically, dates back many years. Between 1993 and 1997, over sixteen hundred migrants were reported dead by the U.S. and Mexican governments. However, migrant deaths are commonly undercounted, as many victims' bodies disappear along the Rio Grande and are cast out to the Gulf of Mexico, are hidden by human smugglers who fear prosecution and liability, or are simply never discovered in the vast desert landscape. States and counties in both nations also report deaths differently. Some localities require physical evidence, like a skull or spine, or a death certificate verifying a person's identity. Others need families of the departed to become involved, which happens infrequently, since many cannot afford burials abroad or the proceedings that accompany them.[84]

Human Rights Violations

On November 25, 2018, the United States shut down the San Ysidro port of entry at the southern border. Migrants had been protesting the slow U.S. asylum process that morning, and the protest quickly turned into hundreds of migrants crowding the border entry area, with some individuals attempting to cross.

In response, CBP agents fired tear gas at the protesters to drive them away, which escalated tensions between the two sides. Many waiting at the border, including children and pregnant women, suffered injuries and fainted from the tear gas. The protesters had peaceful intentions and hoped to influence CBP to open the border to more asylum seekers.[85]

Border Patrol agents have a history of violating human rights and using lethal force against immigrants and Hispanic local residents. The data on murders and physical harm committed by Border Patrol agents are not available to the public, so their involvement in migrant deaths is unknown and their accountability is questionable. However, even in the absence of official federal records, local organizations and journalistic outlets were able to document seventy-seven CBP-related deaths between 2010 and 2018.[86] Among them, one of the most well-known cases is the brutal killing of José Antonio Elena Rodriguez, a sixteen-year-old Mexican boy fatally shot ten times in the back on October 10, 2012. Lonnie Swartz, the border agent who shot José Antonio, was on the lookout for two smugglers reportedly trying to cross the border fence that separates Nogales into U.S. and Mexican cities.[87] Swartz was indicted by a federal grand jury and faced charges of second-degree murder and voluntary and involuntary manslaughter in two separate jury trials in 2018. Swartz's attorney argued that José Antonio tossed rocks at the fence, supposedly causing Swartz to "fear for his life" and fire sixteen rounds at the minor.[88] Swartz was acquitted of second-degree murder and involuntary manslaughter; prosecutors declined to pursue the remaining charge in a third trial. Neither DHS nor the Border Patrol has taken responsibility for the murders of José Antonio and scores of other Hispanic immigrants at the border.

José Antonio's case is emblematic of border authorities' ability to operate outside legal and constitutional boundaries. The Border Patrol occupies the top tier in the realm of U.S. law enforcement and surveillance, which explains why Swartz faced no retribution for violating José Antonio's Fourth and Fifth Amendment rights. As Todd Miller explains, the "Border Patrol can do a warrantless search on anyone who is within one hundred miles of U.S. coastlines and land borders. These Homeland Security officers have federal, extraconstitutional powers that are well above and beyond those of local law enforcement."[89] Border Patrol agents are thus protected and can search and detain any of the over 200 million people living in the U.S. border and costal zones if they so wish.[90] Border Patrol agents also jeopardize the safety and well-being of migrants because they destroy humanitarian aid. Dehydration is one of the most common causes of health complications and death for migrants. Volunteer groups and nonprofit organizations that place plastic containers of water in the desert landscape for migrants have filmed border agents kicking the water over and pouring it out into the sand.[91] It is estimated that border authorities vandalized more than 3,586 gallons of water between 2012 and 2015, snatching away help for thousands of individuals suffering from dehydration and exhaustion.[92]

CBP employees are required to refer to the *Use of Force Policy, Guidelines, and Procedures Handbook* to reduce and address situations where migrants are injured, killed, exploited, or unrightfully detained by agents. Despite the agency's supposed efforts to curb migrant suffering, a University of Houston study revealed that the only decrease in migrant deaths occurred in the late 1980s when legal status was granted to more than two million undocumented immigrants.[93] Whether or not border officials abide by the guidelines set by the *Handbook*, it is clear that the most effective way to save migrants from the perils at the border is to create wider legal pathways, welcome them into American society, and grant them access to citizenship. Doing so would also save the federal government billions of dollars in expenditures on surveillance, weapons, patrols, and inevitable lawsuits.

Mistreatment of Unaccompanied Children Seeking Asylum

Children might travel to the U.S. border for reasons similar to those of adult migrants, like reunifying with family and escaping violence in their home communities.[94] They arrive alone or with siblings but often without guardians or adult family members.[95] Unaccompanied migrant children are not an uncommon sight for border officials. In 2019, CBP apprehended an estimated 73,235 infants, toddlers, children, and adolescents from Guatemala, Honduras, El Salvador, and Mexico.[96] They make the perilous and exhausting trek north to flee dangerous home environments or to move in with relatives or parents in the United States. Many are sent by their guardians, who are desperate to get the children to safety but either cannot make the journey themselves or are denied entry.[97] Some asylum seekers who may or may not have passed their credible fear interview and who are awaiting either a hearing date with an immigration judge or a decision by U.S. Citizenship and Immigration Services were subject to being returned to

Mexico until further notice under the "Remain in Mexico," and Title 42 policies, while the children on their own could be admitted.

Some parents who are stranded and struggling in refugee camps on the Mexican side of the border send their children to the border fence because the United States cannot legally refuse to admit minors under the Trafficking Victims Protection Reauthorization Act (TVPRA).[98] This does not always work, as some children are, like many adults, either denied entry outright or deported back to their home country after being labeled "not at risk for trafficking."[99] In 2019, it was common for unaccompanied children to be denied the opportunity to apply for international protection by border officials at multiple ports of entry along the border.[100] This violates TVPRA and the international obligations of the United States as a party to the 1967 Protocol Relating to the Status of Refugees.[101] Additionally, under the 1997 *Flores v. Reno* decision, unaccompanied minors cannot spend more than twenty days in federal detainment and are guaranteed safe supervision, proper amounts of food and water, emergency medical care, and separation from detained adults. Although U.S. law requires that these minors be granted entry, 93 percent of Mexican children under the age of fourteen who sought U.S. asylum from 2009 until 2014 were refused entry and deported back to Mexico.[102] When this happens, U.S. border policy and its enforcers effectively prohibit asylum-seeking minors from living in safe conditions based on their identities, and these children will suffer the consequences of cruel political decisions made by one of the wealthiest countries in the world.

In Tijuana, some accompanied children sleep in shelters or on the streets with their guardians, while unaccompanied children live on the streets, in shelters, or in child protection centers. The report "Blocked from Safety: Unaccompanied Children Along the U.S.-Mexico Border," published by the nonprofit Kids in Need of Defense (KIND), addresses the repercussions of denying migrant children entry to the United States. Many children interviewed had been waiting in Tijuana for months in hopes of gaining such entry. KIND discovered children suffering "in unsafe and extremely dangerous conditions, afraid, confused, and in deteriorating mental health" during the wait. One child had begun self-harming, one had stopped eating, and another disclosed that they were experiencing suicidal thoughts.[103] Out of desperation, many children try to take matters into their own hands. A Central American migrant girl once fled a shelter to cross the border with a smuggler and was never heard from again. Similarly, a boy revealed that he could no longer wait in Tijuana and would risk crossing the border alone or with a smuggler.[104] Without consistent shelter and vulnerable to violence, migrant minors who are refused entry to the United States resort to desperate measures to cross the border. While U.S. border authorities are not ignorant of the dangers that migrant children face, they still carry out inhumane border policies that sentence innocent minors to unfathomable psychological, physical, and emotional pain and even death.

Not all unaccompanied migrant children who are provided shelter at the border are safe when in the custody of ICE and DHS. In 2016 and 2017, Kiera Coulter and colleagues surveyed ninety-seven recently deported unaccompanied Mexican minors and discovered that migrant children commonly experienced physical and verbal abuse while detained by CBP. Seven percent recounted instances of physical abuse, such as beatings, and an additional 7 percent said they were physically threatened with a weapon. More than half reported being treated with disrespect, such as being degraded through curse words and foul names. Fifty-seven percent disclosed that, in addition to subjecting them to this cruel behavior, Border Patrol agents did not screen them about escaping violence or persecution and therefore never gave them the opportunity to explain their reasons for migrating to the United States or to apply for asylum. Children who *were* screened experienced pressure from border guards to sign forms that they could not read or understand and were not explained to them.[105]

The ACLU obtained thirty thousand pages of records from DHS that disclosed details of complaints filed against CBP authorities alleging abuse in migrant holding centers between 2009 and 2014. These records revealed a disturbing and toxic culture of psychological and physical torture among agents. Migrant children as young as thirteen years old were subjected to gruesome beatings. There were multiple accounts of agents ignoring children's pleas to loosen the metal handcuffs that bound them—in response, one agent made them tighter, causing the child to bleed.[106] Authorities also assaulted children with Tasers, which issue an electric shock that causes muscle contractions. Agents are permitted to use a Taser only if a migrant threatens other people, but children who were not resisting arrest or displaying any use of force were shocked.[107] This research corroborates the common finding that U.S. border officials are continuously compromising the lives of migrant children and failing to uphold standards set by the national government and the international community.

A Rise in Apprehensions of Migrants

Migration flows are generally considered to be relatively constant, although migration may increase in some decades and decrease a bit during others. For example, there was an overall decline of nearly one million unauthorized immigrants living in the United States between 2010 and 2018. The number of apprehensions of migrants from Guatemala, Honduras, and El Salvador sharply increased by 187,000 between 2010 and 2018, but inward migration flows stayed around the same from 2014 to 2018.[108] *Apprehension* can lead to various punishments, like capture by ICE or the Border Patrol, detainment, federal trial, entry refusal, or deportation.[109] In addition, CBP reported a sharp decline in encounters (which include apprehensions and expulsions) with unaccompanied children, families, and individuals attempting to cross into the United States in 2020 because of the COVID-19 pandemic. There was an uptick in 2021 partly because Remain in Mexico ended and minors seeking asylum were once again admitted. The end of Title 42 also resulted in an increase of encounters not because of the policy itself but because the border reopened to asylum seekers and because the counting methodology changed from apprehensions to encounters. Nonetheless, the introduction of the CBPOne app to make appointments, regional offices, and new programs for people from Cuba, Nicaragua, Venezuela, and Haiti did not result in the increases that many warned about.[110]

On the other hand, asylum seekers who do not meet the definition of a refugee according to the 1967 Protocol Relating to the Status of Refugees are deemed "inadmissible" and are often refused entry into the country.[111] As discussed in the previous section, all unaccompanied minors seeking asylum and facing credible fear of returning to their home countries are guaranteed entry into the United States under international law and TVPRA.[112] However, Border Patrol officials are in control of admissions, and immigration court judges often require that both children and adults provide "physical proof of persecution in their countries."[113] Unaccompanied children have been turned away at legal entry points by border agents, violating the principle of non-refoulement and the 1967 protocol.[114]

CBP Detention Centers

The border region is safe for White citizens, but the reality for immigrants and all Hispanics is quite different. While the right to mobility is a universal human right, national governments that categorically identify people as "illegal" deny them what Hannah Arendt calls "the right to have rights."[115] Any refusal to process asylum claims and any prolonged detainment of asylum seekers violate the United Nations' Universal Declaration of Human Rights adopted in 1948 and its Convention and Protocol Relating to the Status of Refugees. The latter document specifies that "refugees should not be penalized for their illegal entry or stay. . . . The seeking of asylum can require refugees to breach immigration rules."[116] However, the horrid treatment migrants have received in the United States is a denial of their human rights.

Detention centers have been used by both conservative and liberal administrations to hold immigrants since 1996.[117] The detention centers controlled by CBP are notorious for their inhumane conditions and horrific behavior toward migrants and asylum seekers. Migrants are subjected to intensely derogatory insults and denied medical care, even if they are children, pregnant women, or people with chronic conditions. Detainees, including children, are sometimes molested by CBP authorities and illegally placed in cells where agents know they may be brutalized by other detainees.[118] Migrants are also refused hospitable living conditions and often get sick because of the cold temperatures and nutrient-poor meals. According to a DHS report released in June 2019, migrants were forced into standing-room-only cells with no showers or laundry facilities.[119] These facilities were designed to hold people for up to three days, but migrants were being kept for much longer periods—even for months. The DHS report also disclosed that ICE officers were given the option to use force against detainees who refused to return to said cells. After the release of the DHS report, the then House of Representatives speaker Nancy Pelosi called it "a shocking window into the dangerous and dehumanizing conditions that the Trump administration is inflicting on children and families at the border."[120] In 2020, a federal district court in Arizona ruled that the conditions at the Tucson detention center were unconstitutional and punishable by law.[121]

At least seven children have died in CBP custody in the past decade. Doctors note that some children have life-saving medications withheld from them, while other children, including infants, are released after developing serious health problems.[122] Some medical professionals disclosed in the DHS report that they were surprised more migrant children have not died, given the terrible conditions in detention centers.[123] Most migrants venture to the United States in search of safety and a better life. Nevertheless, they are confronted with violence and framed as enemies that must be kept out.

Gender-Based Violence

In addition to fatal exhaustion during the trek across the desert, the deadly currents of the Río Bravo/Rio Grande, apprehension by Border Patrol agents, confinement in ICE detention centers notorious for their squalid and abusive conditions, and possible deportation, those who make the journey to the United States are vulnerable to gender-based violence. The U.S.-Mexico border region can be a dangerous place for migrant women, girls, and noncisgender persons. Danger looms from many sides: there have been accounts of sexual violence at the hands of some of the individuals who smuggle immigrants across the U.S.-Mexico border, drug traffickers, and border officials.[124] Authorities and the immigration system do not always protect those at risk either. In fact, asylum seekers are often denied entry or not allowed to stay and are deported, which further endangers them.

This is not explained through the racist concept of *machismo* or hegemonic masculinity. Disappearances and femicides in Juárez are directly related to internal migration by unaccompanied poor Indigenous women and young girls in response to the growth of the maquiladoras—industrial sweatshops—and rural displacement post-NAFTA. Many of the femicide victims are female-presenting Indigenous people from rural parts of southern Mexico who come to the *frontera* looking for work because NAFTA's obliteration of Mexican corn production has pushed them off their land and made subsistence farming unfeasible. Prevention through deterrence and the illegalization of drugs keep many vulnerable people trapped in Mexican border cities while emboldening organized crime. Therefore, this violence is a side effect of the border buildup and U.S. trade policy that favors offshoring to Mexico.[125]

Feminicide, commonly referred to as *feminicidio* in Latin America, refers to a male individual killing a woman or femme person on the basis of gender and having impunity because of a structural context of patriarchy and misogyny.

Feminicide can occur during migration northward to the United States.[126] A comprehensive study conducted from 2009 to 2015 found that 23.5 percent of cisgender women and 55.2 percent of transgender people migrating north from Central America and Mexico experienced psychological, physical, and sexual violence. Many felt they would have been killed if they had fought their abusers. Thefts, beatings, and kidnappings were also frequent, and perpetrators included people from the local communities, crime groups, and law enforcement authorities looking to extort vulnerable migrants.[127]

Ciudad Juárez and the city of Chihuahua have grappled with their own feminicide crises, which made international headlines in the early 1990s.[128] The kidnapping, abuse, mutilation, and murder of women, especially those who were migrants from the south and often Indigenous, went ignored in the border state of Chihuahua by most of Mexican civil society until 1993. Grassroots feminist activist organizations began to crop up like dandelions across Juárez to protest national and state authorities' unwillingness to address this major problem. Fourteen groups banded together to form La Coordinadora de Organizaciones No Gubermentales en Pro de la Mujer (The Coalition of Nongovernmental Organizations for Women), which demanded protection of women at the local level, proper investigation of their cases, and appropriate legal action.[129] In 2008, researchers found that most information concerning feminicides in Mexican and U.S. border cities has never been empirically investigated by either government.[130] As exemplified by the situation in Ciudad Juárez, the lives of Brown women are jeopardized by narcos, the Mexican government, men who walk the city, and U.S. border authorities that deport asylum seekers back into this violent fray.[131] These individuals and institutional entities are immediate threats to the safety and well-being of migrant women, girls, and femmes in northern Mexico and borders around the world.

Human and Organ Trafficking

Human trafficking is a form of gender-based violence. The International Labor Organization estimated that 99 percent of sex trafficking victims in 2017 were women and girls.[132] Internationally and internally displaced women and children residing in border cities are in danger of trafficking, sex tourism, and sexual exploitation at the hands of organized crime groups. Some pedophiles and traffickers will frequent the border to exploit and coerce vulnerable migrant women and children. Victims who do not comply are faced with threats of involving law enforcement, which could lead to deportation and family separation.[133]

Exploitative industries exist on both sides of the U.S.-Mexico border. Annually, an estimated twenty thousand women and children are trafficked across territories or fall victim to trafficking by their smugglers. Many of those who are considered high-risk have little to no formal education, reside in low-income communities, are homeless, lack familial support, or have histories of previous abuse. Despite the insidious nature of their crimes, traffickers are rarely brought to justice because they hide their whereabouts and move from place to place quickly. In their research, Jim Walters and Patricia Davis discuss a couple that conducted a trafficking operation based out of Nashville, Tennessee, by promising to provide jobs in the restaurant industry for young girls from rural Oaxaca. However, upon their arrival, the children were brutalized and exploited in brothels across the southeastern United States.[134]

Mexican and Central American migrants also fall victim to organ trafficking. Siddharth Kara recalls interviewing a migrant woman who was staying in a shelter in Nuevo Laredo while he was conducting ethnographic research at the U.S.-Mexico border. After being arrested by local police and handed over to the Zetas (the organized crime organization in charge of the region), she witnessed a doctor examining eight migrants who were then taken away. Soon after, they returned in pain after having an organ forcibly removed, and one of them eventually succumbed to their wounds and died.[135] Others have recounted dangerous situations that occurred on their migration journey, finding themselves at one point "on makeshift operating tables in hotel rooms where their organs were harvested."[136] Americans experiencing renal failure will pay illicit organ brokers up to $300,000 for a new kidney that they believe is sourced from a willing donor living across the border. Hospitals in Mexican northern cities, like Tijuana and Monterrey, perform the transplant operations, as do what brokers refer to as "private clinics" on the U.S. side. There is nothing random about this abundance of human organs concentrated in one area of the country when the U.S. health care system cannot keep up with the need for transplants. The demand in the north is partially met with a black-market supply of organs stolen from living migrants who often die from lack of postoperative care.[137] Transplant teams at hospitals across the United States. are aware of this problem, but in the words of a nurse working in McAllen, Texas, doctors "want to save lives"—that is, American lives.[138] Suspicious activity is mostly ignored as long as the organ is healthy and the donor is said to have consented. Here, it is made clear that migrants are regarded not only as less worthy of belonging in the United States than citizens but also as less worthy of enjoying life itself.

CONCLUSION

In the last few decades, immigration has taken center stage in political debates, and the overall safety of the U.S.-Mexico border has been put into question. However, U.S. border cities are some of the safest in the country, and U.S. citizens living in urban areas or away from the border are not endangered by inward migration. At most, people who own houses and ranches along the border may occasionally have people pass through their property. The main nuisance may come from the federal government trying to build walls, barriers, and buffer zones through their land. Immigration is the lifeblood of the border region and is not a threat to U.S. cities along the border. It allows for population growth, economic prosperity, and cultural exchange. Much of the region is populated by Mexican Americans and Native Americans, many of whom have low average incomes. Border counties have a concentration of Mexican Americans and a high percentage of poverty.[139] Although the cost of living is low, they have less wealth and live in worse conditions than most White populations in other parts of the United States. There is underinvestment in the region. Residents of border counties in Texas often feel that neglect from the state government in Austin is a bigger issue than immigration.[140]

While White U.S. citizens need not worry, Latin citizens and undocumented immigrants are in constant fear of deportation and suffer disproportionately from harsh border policies. Strict immigration laws, like Arizona's "Papers Please" measure and Florida's Senate Bill 1718, have made it common practice in some jurisdictions to openly racially profile, intimidate, and follow people who look "illegal."[141] Law enforcement agencies, such as local police forces, ICE, and CBP, are permitted to stop any Latin people who are traveling, working, living, or migrating in the southern border region and demand to see proof of citizenship or legal immigration status.[142] This is also a regular occurrence for members of Native American communities like the Tohono O'odham, who have resided in U.S.-Mexico borderlands since before the United States was even claimed as a British colony. ICE officers threaten tribal members and searches their vehicles without warrants.[143] Adalberto Aguirre Jr. and Jennifer Simmers argue that this discrimination is the result of the criminalization of the "Mexican" body. The U.S. public is conditioned to perceive Latin people in or migrating to the United States as disruptive to mainstream White, Eurocentric, and English-speaking society and culture. Ultimately, they are framed as a danger to the Eurocentric American way of life.[144] Media reports, coupled with the application of expensive military and border security technology, give the impression that the border is fighting the clutches of Hades. The narrative is incredibly distorted, presenting the United States as a victim of a heinous crime when it is actually the reverse. The actors that need protection are the migrants who are refused entry, deported, arrested, and killed simply for being migrants. We have shown how the U.S. side of the border is safe for almost everybody except undocumented migrants, the very same people whom some blame for making the border dangerous.

CHAPTER 2

BORDER WALLS DO NOT KEEP
IMMIGRANTS OUT OF A COUNTRY

For when security is made the only absolute and everything is brought under it, we will end up with a social environment that is more akin to tyranny than to democracy; we will end up with an obnoxious bureaucracy underpinned by fear and arbitrariness. Nowhere is this more evident than at the border, where the security apparatus has become nearly unbearable. Border security agents are the cops, the investigators, the adjudicators, the judges, the jury, the executioners, and there is hardly any ability for anyone to appeal. . . . They have all the power.

Tony Payan, *The Three U.S.-Mexico Border Wars*

The longest partial shutdown of the U.S. government in history—35 days—took place after President Donald Trump and Congress failed to establish a budget for the 2019 fiscal year. Thousands of federal employees were furloughed before it ended in January 2019. President Trump demanded $5.7 billion to continue building a wall at the southern border—but Congress refused to grant his request in the budget that eventually passed, and the president acquiesced, ending the shutdown.[1] Only about a month after the government reopened, Trump declared a "national emergency" at the border so that he could bypass Congress this time around, obtaining $3.7 billion for the border wall project. He justified the declaration by saying "We're talking about an invasion of our country . . . with drugs, human traffickers, with all types of criminals and gangs."[2]

Politicians from both sides of the aisle condemned the move, which many believed to be outside of the law and an abuse of power. The governors of New Mexico and California called off National Guard troops that were ordered by the Trump administration to patrol the border, claiming that the extra security was not only unnecessary but also solely a political move.[3] Will Hurd, a Republican congressman (2015–2021) whose Texas district reaches from San Antonio to El Paso, disapproved of the wall, calling it "the most expensive and least effective way to do border security."[4] President Joe Biden rescinded the emergency declaration just hours after his inauguration on January 20, 2021, and redirected the funds back to Congress.[5]

The U.S. border region is safe from a national security perspective, but it is not safe for migrants and other minoritized communities from a human security perspective. This chapter explores and deconstructs the common misconceptions behind the purpose, function, and efficiency of a U.S.-Mexico border wall. We begin by providing insight into the historical and ideological debate on the construction of a southern border wall and explaining the social realities of that border region. Then our discussion shifts its focus to the dynamics of the border region in terms of the ways that federal and local policies are implemented. We present an overview of the U.S. actors that occupy the border and operationalize border policy there as well as the impacts of such policies—for example, the use of probable cause—on the individuals and legal processes involved in migrant detainment, deportation, and asylum seeking. Expanding on this, we clarify how the H-2 visa program, which appears favorable for migrant workers, truly benefits U.S. employers far more.

The chapter continues with a rebuttal to commonplace arguments and approaches to immigration policy that support zero-tolerance policing of migrants, such as "prevention through deterrence, deterrence through enforcement." We highlight how the currently low migration rate, repetitive and unceasing nature of migration, protests of border residents, legal entry status of most immigrants, and regularity of drug trafficking at legal entry points are strong justifications for halting any new plans for a border wall. We move on to weigh the wall's economic, human, and environmental costs against the ideological isolation, assertion of dominance, and intended security it presents. Finally, we close the chapter with recommendations for alternative mechanisms for integrating migrants into U.S. society in such a way that violence and danger are minimized and U.S. taxpayer funds are allocated more effectively.

BUILDING THE WALL

The idea of a border wall gained traction in policy discussions as a supposed solution to undocumented border crossings in the second half of the 1980s, when then President Ronald Reagan's administration built a section of the wall.[6] President Bill Clinton then adopted an even more aggressive approach after he was elected in 1992, funneling billions of dollars into new fences and barriers that separated urban neighborhoods in El Paso and San Diego from their neighboring Mexican cities and intensifying border security at those sites.[7] Indeed, U.S. Border Patrol initiatives like Operation Hold the Line and Operation Gatekeeper filled the cities of El Paso and San Diego with immigration authorities to create a human barrier that blocked migrants from entering.[8] Soon after, President George W. Bush followed Clinton's approach and continued strengthening the U.S.-Mexico boundary well into the first decade of the twenty-first century.

2.1 View of El Paso and Ciudad Juárez from El Paso hills

Source: Ernesto Castañeda.

The idea behind these operations was that physical barriers and a strong Border Patrol presence would dissuade migrants from crossing without papers, prevent the flow of drugs into the country, and reduce the total immigration rate. This was not the outcome—for multiple reasons. Drug cartels continued to import products, and at the same time, new and militarized operations in southern Texas, Arizona, and California forced migrants into increasingly dangerous territories. This Clinton-era model of border surveillance and apprehension resulted in fewer urban crossings but more migrant deaths as their guides, or *coyotes*, struggled to lead them safely through the unforgiving desert terrain.[9]

Indeed, the rate of immigration via the southern border has decreased twofold since 2010—but not because of the physical or technological walls that have been installed by U.S. Customs and Border Protection (CBP).[10] Rather, the demographic shifts in the migrants' countries are more responsible for this change. New inward migration flows from Mexico to the United States have decreased since 2008,[11] partly due to Mexico's aging population, declining birth rate, and decreasing rural population.[12] Central America is not big enough to surpass the stream of migration previously produced by Mexico in the long run.[13]

It is evident that security strategies that combined physical barriers and increased border personnel did stop migration.[14] People, including those aware of the newly developing security situation, still took their chances and made the journey to the United States. The government's efforts were superfluous, and yet similar strategies are employed at the southern border today. More than just a physical blockade, the U.S. border wall has become a symbol of the country's "tough" approach to undocumented immigrants and its vigilance in guarding whiteness rather than a tool that actually decreases migration flows and drug trafficking, the reasons commonly used to justify it.[15] Neither a barricade nor a greater or stricter Border Patrol presence will be effective in the way that supporters anticipate in solving the problems that politicians and policymakers have associated with the U.S.-Mexico border.

Physical Realities of the Border Region

What does the border actually look like? The answer fluctuates depending on where you are. The line dividing the United States from Mexico stretches from the Pacific Ocean to the Gulf of Mexico, separating the U.S. states of California, New Mexico, Arizona, and Texas from the Mexican states of Baja California, Sonora, Chihuahua, Coahuila, Nuevo León, and Tamaulipas.[16]

2.2 Natural landscape, West Texas
Source: Ernesto Castañeda.

2.3 Factory in West Texas
Source: Ernesto Castañeda.

2.4 Border view from Tijuana toward the Pacific Ocean
Source: Ernesto Castañeda.

The border is home to diverse communities, landscapes, and ecosystems. On either side of the border, you might come across Native American reservations, bustling cities, college towns, tropical beaches, and nature reserves. In Arizona, the San Pedro River Valley teems with wildlife. The area encompasses grasslands, mountain ranges, and lush forest spots that are home to hundreds of animal species. It is also a refuge for nearly four hundred types of migratory birds.[17] However, desert plains, with their dry air, hot sands, and brutal temperatures, dominate the westernmost section of the border region. In Texas, manufactured physical boundaries are supplemented by the Rio Grande, a river that snakes along the border and acts as a natural barricade. Although these sections of the U.S.-Mexico border are geographically different, many of them share something in common—miles of wire fencing and concrete wall.

According to 2021 figures, a physical barrier consisting of concrete wall and steel and wire fencing stretches for about 771 miles out of the 1,989 total miles of shared border with Mexico.[18] The remaining unfenced areas stretch through

2.5 El Paso suburbs
Source: Ernesto Castañeda.

mountain ranges, the Rio Grande, and desert sands, all of which provide a deadly natural shield.[19] According to agents and townspeople, migrants try to cross whether or not there is a wall.[20] The Department of Homeland Security (DHS) and its prevention through deterrence initiative, which we expand on later, purposefully push immigrants into perilous regions, which has caused the number of deaths to increase. Supporters of the border wall see a higher death rate as a marker of success: it means that policies put in place to decrease undocumented immigration are working, ignoring the tragic human costs.

In El Paso, a Texas border county, conflicting border politics are on full display. A YouTube video released by Business Insider in 2019 tracks CBP agents in the El Paso region as they guide migrants through the asylum-seeking procedure and process their information. The agents are not seen using violence; instead, they are shown as humanitarians, speaking Spanish to the migrants in a rational and calming tone.[21] The agency even hosts festivals and has agents march in the annual El Paso Thanksgiving parade to establish a good reputation with the community and encourage kids to work in law enforcement.[22] This image that border authorities curate fails to show the vastly different and nuanced reality of CBP's purpose and actions. Its attempts to appeal to locals in the southern border region are not always met with open arms, as many people living in El Paso and other border areas are all too familiar with the harm that the agency has done.

LAW ENFORCEMENT AT THE BORDER: THE HUMAN AND ECONOMIC COSTS

Federal and state policies prioritize security and entry protocols at the U.S.-Mexico border that address the border wall, agent patrols, surveillance technology, deportation operations, asylum processing, legal proceedings, visa checking, interviews with border crossers, and determination of peoples' abilities to enter based on foreign relations with their country of origin. The responsibility for carrying out border security falls mainly on CBP, a branch of DHS, the mammoth agency created in 2003 to manage all domestic threats. CBP's main tasks are operating border crossing ports, monitoring the entire U.S.-Mexico border, and apprehending offenders. It is a law enforcement agency and not a humanitarian organization.

The goals and operations of border agents have changed since the first U.S. Border Patrol was established in 1924.[23] Historically, it was a comparatively tiny part of the Department of Labor, staffed with only a few hundred employees who enforced brand-new documentation requirements set forth by the National Origins Act.[24] Now their presence is all-encompassing. In 2018, 19,555 agents were guarding the entire perimeter of the United States.[25] This includes 8,000 miles of land at the southern and northern borders as well as the oceans along southern California, Florida, and Puerto Rico. Typically, 90 percent of agents are dispatched to the southwest border region to act as "America's shield" against undocumented immigrants.[26] On occasion, state National Guard troops are authorized to indirectly support operations in the southern border region.[27] When a group of around eight thousand migrants traveled to the border to petition for asylum in late 2018, the federal government sent at least 2,100 National Guard troops to southern Texas to block the migrants from entering.[28]

Seeking Asylum

Before the 2000s, most migrants were Mexican nationals immigrating predominantly to fill a demand for labor in the U.S. agriculture, meatpacking, and domestic care industries, to name a few.[29] While some people still move in search of economic opportunity, many attempting to cross after the 2008 economic crisis have been asylum seekers or people trying to reunite with their families in the United States. Increasingly, they are from Central and South America rather than Mexico and may be as young as ten years old. Asylum seekers do not look to cross the border undetected but instead turn themselves in willingly to CBP to ask for asylum.

The border wall should be irrelevant for asylum seekers because U.S. and international laws recognize the right of persecuted individuals to seek safety abroad under the 1951 Convention Relating to the Status of Refugees.[30] The legal proceedings to obtain asylum, however, are slow. Around 320,000 citizenship applications were backlogged in the district courts in 2020 because of immigration policies and refugee entry caps put in place by the Trump administration.[31] One of these, known as the Remain in Mexico policy, or Migrant Protection Protocols (MPP), forced individuals and families to await their hearings in makeshift camps in northern Mexico instead of in the United States.[32] The asylum process is complex and often difficult. Refugees and asylum seekers must demonstrate that they meet the statutory definition of a *refugee*[33] and are not subject to an exception or a bar.[34] Asylum seekers thus bear the burden of proof to establish that they meet the criteria to be considered refugees in order to be officially recognized as such by the United Nations and any national government. In order to do this, they must provide evidence that they are outside of their country of nationality and are "unable or unwilling to return . . . owing to a well-founded fear of being persecuted for reasons of race, religion, nationality, membership in a particular social group, or political opinion."[35] What is necessary to show "credible" fear of death, violence, and imprisonment related to one's identity and "valid" justification for fleeing is subject to interpretation by CBP agents at the border.[36]

Additionally, immigration judges and U.S. Citizenship and Immigration Services (USCIS) can broadly interpret the characteristics of a protected social group. This gives national leaders wiggle room to exclude certain immigrants from permissible criteria and thus deny their petitions for asylum or adjustment of status, even if they are genuinely afraid of persecution. Opponents of the excruciatingly complex standards required to obtain asylum in the United States were outraged at the unprecedented 2018 Supreme Court ruling that upheld the Trump administration's travel ban aimed at persons from several named countries. Attorney General Jeff Sessions used this decision to leverage his authority to make the process of granting asylum even more difficult for judges and petitioners. Such immigration policies effectively wiped away protections for survivors of gang conflicts and domestic violence.[37]

On July 16, 2019, the Department of Justice and DHS published a rule that further limited the number of asylum seekers by rendering them ineligible if they failed to seek protection in a third country.[38] For several months after this rule was passed, asylum seekers whose cases otherwise fulfilled the criteria for refugee status were not allowed to have their cases reviewed by judges. Instead, they were automatically transferred into removal proceedings because they had not applied for asylum in Mexico or a Central American country after initially fleeing their home country. Around the same time that this new standard was passed, the MPP was forcing Central and South American asylum seekers to wait in Mexico while their asylum requests were processed by immigration courts. This exposed them to various dangers and violence, such as kidnapping and extortion, as discussed in the previous chapter.[39] Furthermore, immigration judges could take into account the "country conditions" of an immigrant's home country so as to contextualize their fear of persecution according to legal criteria. Because of this, those seeking asylum from Iran, Venezuela, Yemen, Somalia, Syria, Libya, and North Korea were subjected to "additional scrutiny" and "enhanced screening and vetting requirements" or were barred from obtaining nonimmigrant visas altogether.[40]

Because of the Trump administration's stringent new policies, the number of asylum seekers permitted entry into the country dropped to thirty thousand in fiscal year 2019, the lowest ceiling count for refugees in the preceding forty years. Migrants' willingness to leave home and make the perilous journey to the United States should fulfill the requirements for refugee status in this instance. Sadly, thousands are turned away or deported each year, including people who were raised in the United States or who have children who are U.S. citizens. Sometimes this occurs because immigrants are unaware that they can file an appeal for legal representation, which can otherwise be costly, although being supplied with a lawyer rarely guarantees a win in court.[41]

The U.S. Supreme Court has previously worked to align U.S. law with the Convention and Protocol Relating to the Status of Refugees, which outlines protections for asylum seekers.[42] Nonetheless, we do not always see this alignment occur. Policies that focus on aiding migrants, facilitating family reunification, and creating pathways to citizenship are not always prioritized. Funds are instead used to pay for military surveillance technology, physical barriers, detention centers, and border agents, which traumatize families and individuals daily and do not provide a feasible long-term approach to handling U.S. immigration.

The H-2 Visa Program

There are solutions to migration-related issues other than building a wall. For example, many undocumented Mexican laborers working on U.S. farms during harvesting season would prefer to return home to Mexico during the off-season instead of remaining in the north. Regardless of this preference, they realistically cannot leave because the militarization of the border has made the journey to and from Mexico dangerous, unpredictable, cumbersome, and expensive, so these laborers opt to stay in the United States, instead arranging for their families to migrate to reunite with them.[43] If a pathway to quicker naturalized citizenship was opened for them, this would not remain a problem. The federal government has engaged with this dilemma on a surface level, but the proposed fixes have not created a solution for migrant workers. The H-2 visa program, housed in the U.S. Department of Labor, grants legal U.S. entry to temporary workers. Migrants working in agriculture apply for an H-2A, while all others are limited to the H-2B visa. The number of H-2 visa holders has tripled since the early 2000s, enabling migrant workers to travel on legal terms.

The H-2 program is far more self-serving for the U.S. economy than it is helpful for migrant workers. In *Undocumented: How Immigration Became Illegal*, Aviva Chomsky explains that workers are not protected from the penalization of their transborder movements or labor exploitation under the H-2 program. Employers and landlords have a history of abusing migrant workers with fake visa processing and transportation fees, meager wages, and squalid working and living conditions.[44] Under the Bracero program, a guest worker program initiated between Mexico and the United States during World War II, migrant workers were permitted to cycle across the border to provide needed seasonal labor from 1942 until 1964. The United States terminated this program once the migration corridor had been established. Scholars and civil rights activists also shed light on employers' inhumane and exploitative behavior that the government enabled.[45] The H-2 program is fundamentally no different than the Bracero program in that migrant workers are temporarily allowed to work in the United States and are technically considered "illegal" if working outside that program. This arguably gives employers more power and discretion to fire workers while the workers' labor benefits U.S. companies.

A "Deportation Regime"

Border security became one of the federal government's top priorities after the Immigration Reform and Control Act of 1986 (IRCA) was passed during the Reagan administration.[46] The law was disguised as a welcoming hand to immigrants because it offered millions of unauthorized individuals legal status. What is less widely known is that it also reinforced the perceived need to stem and control immigration and established what Todd Miller calls "the legal blueprint for a deportation regime that would only become more massive."[47] After the IRCA was passed, the annual number of deportations skyrocketed from around 2,000 to over 400,000 during President Barack Obama's administration.[48] This policy not only sought to physically expel migrants but also pushed them so close to the fringes of society that they would have no choice but to leave. To this day, any employer found to be knowingly hiring undocumented workers can be fined or criminally prosecuted.[49]

Since U.S. Immigration and Customs Enforcement (ICE) was created during the establishment of DHS, enforcement of immigration policy has continuously expanded. ICE agents carry out arrests, immigration raids, and deportations, and the agency's national presence has intensified quickly. It has become notorious for its checkpoints, searches, apprehensions, and raids in American communities, including in coastal South Carolina, southwestern Detroit, upstate New York, and central Mississippi.[50] ICE is a far-reaching federal tool that applies border policy and stretches the dynamics of the border region into nonborder and noncoastal regions of the United States. In this way, the border wall transcends its material nature and acts as an ideological representation of popular anti-immigrant sentiments. Although ICE agents are stationed across the country, they implement border policy and are products of the myth that a border wall is necessary to protect U.S. citizens.

"Prevention Through Deterrence, Deterrence Through Enforcement"

The IRCA was the first of many restrictive laws that altered how immigrants lived and were perceived by the American criminal justice system. Moreover, it paved the way for the implementation of the border policy of "prevention through deterrence, deterrence through enforcement," introduced in 1994 by President Clinton.[51] This policy built on the IRCA by openly declaring war on immigration. It espoused the beliefs that immigration poses the greatest danger to the U.S. way of life and that migrants are American citizens' competitors for resources. To alleviate the fabricated dangers that undocumented immigrants pose, prevention through deterrence focuses on (1) militarizing the security infrastructure in and around urban border areas, thus forcing border crossers into more remote and dangerous locations where they are less likely to make it through alive, and (2) strictly enforcing immigration law and apprehending immigrants in the border region using Border Patrol agents, technology, and a border wall.[52]

In practice, prevention through deterrence occurs on the land, in the sky, and at sea. Legal ports of entry along the southern border have also become militarized through the use of advanced technological tools like X-ray sensors.[53] Agents are heavily equipped with Marine Corps–grade M4 rifles, stun grenades, and tear gas.[54] CBP conducts surveillance at ports of entry and along the rest of the border through communication towers, helicopters, and mobile police units that travel across the landscape using systems of roads and stations.[55] At the same time, unmanned Predator B drones patrol from the sky, picking up movement with radar sensors and video surveillance.[56] Nonetheless, rural areas are difficult to police constantly, even with newer technologies and physical barriers. Subsequently, migrants and *coyotes* have found ways to bypass them.

Putting prevention through deterrence into action involved deploying surveillance technology, building a security wall, hiring more border agents, and closing the ports of entry in densely populated places.[57] To do this, the federal government poured funding into CBP and ICE. In the 1960s, the budget for border security was little to nothing. Funds slowly increased to $1 billion in 1995 and have rapidly grown since then.[58] More than $324 billion has been spent on border buildup since the establishment of DHS, the bulk of which finances border operations and immigration enforcement.[59]

CBP receives more funding than the FBI, making it the largest and most expensive federal agency.[60] In 2021 alone, CBP requested over $18.2 billion from the federal government for surveillance technology, immigration databases, and aircraft. It set aside $15.5 million for a single Army helicopter and an additional $13 million for aircraft sensors, both of which are large amounts of money for seemingly superfluous items. Additionally, it planned to dedicate some of this money to building eighty-two more miles of border wall and 200 more surveillance towers. The rest was to be used to train 876 more border agents, hire 300 more border staff, construct new facilities, and maintain those facilities already in place.[61] The intent to carefully allocate money for border security is rarely explicitly stated by DHS or CBP, and in the 2021 budget, they merely claimed that they would "safeguard" the public's tax dollars from being wasted or abused.[62] However, an oversight exercise found much waste and duplication of efforts.[63] Taxpayers contributed $46 million for each mile of new border wall from 2016 to 2020.[64] Aid-focused tactics that provide migrants with basic care and legal support during asylum proceedings have received little attention or resources compared to military-like field arrangements. Only one of the new facilities proposed in the 2021 budget was to provide such care and support— a Humanitarian Care Center in Rio Grande, Texas.[65]

By 2014, an estimated ten thousand migrants had died at the border since prevention through deterrence took effect, and many others had incurred psychological trauma and physical injuries from heat stroke, exhaustion, dehydration, starvation, violence, and abuse. One out of ten unauthorized migrants caught crossing the border is a victim of physical abuse, and one out of six experiences aggression of some kind from CBP.[66] There are several reports of abuse at the hands of the CBP.[67] Any migration curbed in the past by prevention through deterrence has been at the expense of the lives and well-being of migrants.

In *The Shadow of the Wall: Violence and Migration on the U.S.-Mexico Border*, Jeremy Slack, Daniel E. Martínez, and Scott Whiteford[68] discuss the mediocrity of the physical and technological walls at the border. CBP agents are trained to combat violent enemies, but neither immigrants nor *coyotes* are typically violent. On the contrary, both want to remain undetected and fly under the radar. The existing training methods for Border Patrol officers should focus more on search-and-rescue tactics and emergency care for ill and injured people. By pushing immigrants into treacherous terrain, "deterrence" is nearly akin to a death sentence. CBP is aware of this, but instead of managing the flow of migrants, it readies its agents for war against them.

Probable Cause

The federal government grants border agents an extraordinary degree of legal authority. CBP's official website explains that, under the Immigration and Nationality Act and the Code of Federal Regulations, officers have the power, even without search warrants, to "board and search for aliens in any vessel within the territorial waters of the United States and any railcar, aircraft, conveyance, or vehicle" located within one hundred miles of the border.[69] This legal power—which requires agents to have *probable cause*, a belief based on facts that it is probable a person has violated or is violating immigration or federal laws, before taking action against them—is another way they act as extensions of the border wall. CBP officers have full discretion to arrest and search someone and their belongings based on pure speculation. This increases the likelihood of Hispanics being racially profiled in the border region, much like New York City's stop-and-frisk policy disproportionately targeted neighborhoods populated by immigrants and people of color.[70]

The use of force by Border Patrol agents has sharply increased since the application of probable cause and prevention through deterrence. At least 133 people have been killed in encounters with agents since 2010, and many of them were American citizens who were accidentally shot during gunfights, struck by border agent vehicles on the street or in their cars, or wrongfully and violently apprehended.[71] In 1997, U.S. Marines shot and killed Esequiel Hernández Jr., a teenager and U.S. citizen living in the Texas border town of Redford who was tending to his herd of goats when agents approached and shot him from a distance.[72] At least half of the fatal shootings carried out by Border Patrol agents have come under public scrutiny because of suspicious autopsy reports, witness testimonies, and injuries (or lack thereof) sustained by agents. There is currently no oversight council to review these events, and any progress made in the past toward building a review board has been stalled. An advisory council set up by CBP in 2013 recommended that the agency hire 350 internal affairs investigators and create a high-level position to manage disciplinary and misconduct cases once they occur. As of 2019, only fifty investigators had been hired, and there were no open councilor positions, which were intended to bolster the CBP commissioner's handle on corruption and misconduct cases.[73] Border agents' extraconstitutional powers, along with CBP's lack of structure for disciplinary measures, its aggressive prevention through deterrence enforcement measures, and its increasing use of force in unwarranted searches by officers, threaten U.S. citizens and migrants alike.[74]

WHY THE BORDER WALL IS INEFFECTIVE

The Purpose of the Wall Is Exclusion, Not Security

As we pointed out earlier, the border wall is more than just a physical barrier. It is a representation of state authority, sovereignty, and autonomy to the international community. Physical structures are built in order to differentiate a state from its neighbors, who may be viewed as inferior.[75] This has been and is currently being carried out by countries besides the United States. Israel now has barriers separating it from Egypt, Lebanon, the West Bank, and the Gaza Strip to stop neighbors, particularly Palestinians, from entering freely.[76] Hungary erected fences along its borders with Serbia and Croatia in 2015 to "protect" the historically Christian country from migrants, most of whom were escaping the Syrian civil war.[77] Xenophobic border policies are being disguised as valiant attempts to shield civilian populations from an enemy, but they cannot do so unless migration comes to a full stop.

On the social and political planes, walls are built to try to contain, control, and preserve human populations. In doing so, the state controls those living within and outside its borders, maintains the construction of "illegality," and monitors migrants.[78] In the case of a U.S.-Mexico border wall, national security is not the only goal. The border wall is also tied to a symbolic effort to draw a line in the sand territorially and therefore to formally self-isolate. Countries like the United States create walls because of internal exclusionary ideologies as well as the perceived need for extra security that comes from political fearmongering. The border wall will not achieve its proclaimed purposes; instead, it will sow discord in the lives of immigrants.

Most Immigrants Enter the United States Legally

Contrary to popular belief, a border wall is unnecessary because most immigrants enter the United States legally. The narrative and visuals of immigrants

2.6 Border monument in Tijuana, Mexico
Source: Ernesto Castañeda.

climbing walls, swimming across rivers, and hiding in cars to cross the border are legitimate but do not apply to the majority of migrants and refugees. From 2010 to 2018, an estimated 66 percent of immigrants became undocumented by entering legally and overstaying their visas, whereas 34 percent crossed the U.S.-Mexico border illegally.[79] A more recent cross-sectional analysis indicates a similar trend: 42 percent of undocumented persons in 2019 had overstayed their visas.[80] This adds up to about 4.5 million, or two out of every five undocumented immigrants, who have entered the country with permission.[81] Still, they may be hunted down by ICE instead of CBP agents.

Migration Will Not Stop

History has shown that if people want something badly enough, criminalizing or outlawing the act or object will not successfully stop them from practicing or obtaining it. In the same way that Prohibition did not curb alcohol consumption and police cannot prevent crime from occurring, a border wall wastes money and resources in a fruitless attempt to stop immigration.

In southern California, a border wall installed in the mid-2000s did indeed result in a reduction of unauthorized crossings in that area. But this was because migrants, in order to avoid the wall and new strongholds for border agents, simply moved eastward to cross through rural parts of Arizona, New Mexico, and Texas.[82] This is one of the immediate intended effects that prevention through deterrence and border wall operations had on migrants. Border authorities purposely put fences and steel barriers in high-traffic areas in order to direct migrants into more dangerous natural environments and thus "deter" them from entering the United States.[83] In this way, CBP guides migrants into a trap where the climate kills or maims them. Some now make the journey through parts of the border region where a wall is impractical or geographically impossible due to factors like mountain ranges or the Rio Grande. Researcher Jason De León conducted an experiment by laying the bodies of three recently slaughtered pigs in the Arizona desert to observe the speed at which they would decompose—pigs "have long been the preferred proxy for a human body in forensic experiments."[84] Their corpses were swallowed by the dry sands within just a few days, proving that the same could occur to human corpses.

The construction of a border wall and the intensification of border policing have literally killed people.[85] Thousands of migrants have died. The exact number of deaths cannot be accurately calculated, but approximations are tragic. Between 1994 and 2000, when sweeping immigration reform and the prevention through deterrence approach were enacted, migrant deaths increased by 474 percent, and the leading cause of death changed from accidents to preventable causes, like hypothermia, dehydration, and heatstroke.[86] Brad Jones states that since 2001, just "in the Arizona-Mexico borderlands itself, nearly 4,000 people have lost their lives. . . . On average, about every two days migrants' remains are found."[87]

The nonprofit Border Angels estimates that in the past twenty-seven years, over 11,000 people have died attempting to cross the border.[88] CBP claims to make efforts to prevent migrant deaths and to mold the border into a safe space for everyone.[89] Nevertheless, the assumed need for increased safety measures implies that the region is fundamentally unsafe, which has been disproven. Rob Guerette suggests a harm reduction strategy to save migrant lives while managing immigration because a supposed restriction on immigration through increased security is counterproductive and cruel.[90]

The dangers migrants face at the border are not enough to stop them from arriving and to bring migration to a halt. While border walls and stringent immigration policies dissuade and delay the entrance of some immigrants, they do not deter them from trying in the first place. Barriers do not change the circumstances in migrants' home countries, which are the root causes of emigration. Therefore, they cannot stop migrants from seeking asylum or attempting to cross over.

The Current Rate of Migration Is Low

For years, the rate of undocumented border crossings, particularly by those from Mexico, has been relatively low compared to its peak in 2000. Central American immigrants have increased the interactions of immigration authorities with people at the border,[91] but this is unlikely to last in the long term. Data from the U.S. Census Bureau's American Community Survey suggest that 5.3 million undocumented immigrants left the United States between 2010 and 2018.[92] The number of undocumented Mexicans decreased by 23 percent, as did that of undocumented Ecuadorians, whose numbers dropped by 36 percent. On the other hand, the Guatemalan, Salvadoran, and Honduran populations have experienced rapid growth since 2014, with rising numbers of minors applying for asylum at the border.[93] Political unrest since 2014 has led to a 164 percent surge in unauthorized Venezuelans, but the undocumented Central and South American community in the United States steadily diminished for awhile, with the most notable declines being in traditional destination states such as California, New York, and Illinois.[94]

In 2015, border agents caught 26,500 migrants trying to cross illegally near San Diego. However, this number does not come close to the 629,656 apprehended in 1986.[95] Despite headlines in conservative media outlets, the number of migrants who are smuggled across the border by coyotes was lower than in previous years. Due to this, as well as other factors, many Border Patrol agents do not consider the extension of the wall necessary in order for them to perform their jobs well. In 2016, one Border Patrol agent stated confidently to journalists that they "manage with what they have now," and agent Wendi Low disclosed that the current enforcement methods are keeping illegal crossings at a "near all-time low" and that the current scenario "works perfectly for [them]."[96] Even CBP agents believe that continuing the construction of a border wall is taking deterrence too far. Crossings, apprehensions, and encounters go up in certain months and years but they also go down.

Drug Trafficking Occurs at Legal Points of Entry

The federal government has repeatedly cited drug trafficking as a part of the crisis at the border that a wall could solve. Drugs trafficked across the border—whether illegal like cocaine, heroin, and methamphetamines or legal like tobacco—have created demand in both countries.[97] However, most drug trafficking occurs at official points of entry, not in remote areas, making a wall unlikely to deter this type of criminal activity.[98]

As Dudley Poston points out, "Most illicit drugs don't enter the U.S. via people sneaking across the border."[99] A study conducted by the Brookings Institution found that most drugs aren't smuggled into the United States by illegal border crossers, and a Drug Enforcement Administration report declared that "Mexican drug cartels bring the bulk of their drugs over the southern border through ports of entry via trucks, passenger vehicles and tractor-trailers."[100] (These findings contradict the stereotype that undocumented immigrants are equivalent to drug mules, which we examine in the following chapter.) Christopher Wilson, a Global Fellow at the Wilson Center, agrees that the border wall will not reduce drug smuggling. He argues that heroin and cocaine, among other drugs, travel into the United States through formal ports of entry, earning the industry $1 million a minute.[101]

Border security cannot rush to implement severe rules at ports of entry, despite the discretionary power granted to them by probable cause, because imposing strict transborder access regulations has backfired in the past. Federal forces thought that organized crime groups would be iced out and stagnate if their strategies were no match for U.S. surveillance. However, these groups just adopted more-sophisticated smuggling methods, including "producing networks of scouts, lookouts and bribery infrastructures to sidestep the human element" of border authority.[102] It is also difficult to eliminate instances of drug trafficking and smuggling because drug cartels are active and operate in both the United States and Mexico. A full border wall will not eliminate this market because large amounts of money flow back and forth and provide for people on both sides of the border.[103] One of the major differences is that, unlike in Mexico, corruption on the U.S. side is often concealed, and even a small amount of corruption can have a forceful impact.[104] In some cases, agents on both sides work jointly with organized crime. For example, U.S. border officials have permitted drugs and migrants to be smuggled, sold green cards, and provided valuable insider information to cartels. Therefore, corruption within the institutions of power that govern the border renders a wall inadequate, especially if its keepers commit offenses.[105] According to Ruben Garcia, the director of Annunciation House, an immigrant shelter in El Paso, actions taken to put corrupt CBP agents in prison have helped battle cartels and drug traffickers.[106] Border Patrol agents are relatively well paid, and these jobs offer a path into the middle class for many Mexican Americans, but corruption still ensnares a few agents.

People Living in the Border Region Do Not Support the Wall

Border residents living within 350 miles of the U.S.-Mexico border are the least likely to support building a border wall.[107] By comparison, many who live far from the border see it as a violent and dangerous place and therefore support aggressive border policies. In El Paso, which is predominantly Hispanic, many students and workers who cross the border regularly were extremely concerned by Trump's attempts to shut entry points from Mexico. In fact, so many students cross the border bridge linking the city to neighboring Ciudad Juárez that authorities have assigned them their own pedestrian lane, and when border agents crack down on security at crossing points, traffic lanes slow.[108]

A Border Wall Is Not Cost-Effective

Despite relentless calls, "many experts question whether building out the wall . . . is worth the cost."[112] DHS estimates that the metal barrier will cost the United States a minimum of $21.6 billion after accounting for labor, materials, machinery,

Gerardo Pozas, a border resident, moved to El Paso from Ciudad Juárez in 1997 to attend high school and later became a U.S. citizen. Like many others, his decision to move did not diminish or erase his strong ties with his birthplace.[109] According to survey data gathered by Castañeda in 2011–2012, 59.7 percent of immigrant Hispanics living in El Paso at the time visited their hometowns (table 2.1). Conversely, about the same percentage of people reported that their family and friends travel to visit them in the United States. Most interview respondents were from northern and central Mexico and often crossed the border to visit loved ones or had siblings and/or parents who went back to visit. Transborder travel and relations are an important and common part of life for El Paso residents that a thirty-foot steel wall would forever change. During the Trump presidency, a thirty-five-mile-long steel mesh that runs directly east of El Paso was reconstructed and threatened to cut people off from travel routes.[110] Border residents benefit from cross-border travel because it allows for the temporary reunification of families, stimulates local economies in the region, and supports business owners who conduct their work across the border.

Some of the Hispanic El Paso respondents crossed only a few times per year, but over 40 percent had an active transborder life: 19.3 percent crossed often to visit family, 15.8 percent crossed up to seven times a week, and 10 percent crossed once a month. Therefore, an enhanced border security system risks intimidating potential authorized border crossers, like relatives of U.S. citizens, and denying entry to legal U.S. residents and visa holders who are required to prove their status with specific documents. If, for whatever reason, border

TABLE 2.1 Transnational activities

	Yes	
Do you go back to your hometown to visit?	57.9%	
Do your parents go back to their hometown to visit?	49.7%	
Do your siblings go back to your hometown to visit?	49.9%	
Do people from your home country visit you?	58.0%	
Do you ever go to Ciudad Juárez?	40.3%	
Are you afraid of being detained by U.S. immigration authorities when you go back and forth to Ciudad Juárez?	6.9%	

	United States	Mexico	Both
Where do you seek medical treatment?	67.9%	16.7%	15.4

agents are not satisfied with the evidence that is provided to them or act out of prejudice, they are permitted to block people from returning to their homes and lives in the United States. About 7 percent of the respondents in Castañeda's survey who traveled to Ciudad Juárez feared potential detainment by U.S. border authorities. This fear is justified when we look at different variables in the data-set. For example, 9.9 percent of Hispanic individuals had been unjustly detained by police, and 15.9 percent had recently experienced discrimination. These stress-ful situations reinforce feelings of exclusion and "otherness" that stick in the psyche and transform a person's sense of safety. Research on stress shows that this is especially true if their experience is traumatic or violent because, as the situation unfolds, the stress response is triggered. In turn, it informs the brain to associate people and certain somatic elements involved in the event with a threat to survival in the future.[111] Whether survey respondents had a negative experience with law enforcement in the past or not, a sizable proportion of the Hispanic population in El Paso perceived border control as a threat.

land seizure legal fees, and inevitable lawsuits.[113] However, a report issued by Democrats in the U.S. Senate projected a maximum cost of $70 billion for con-struction and an additional $150 million each year for maintenance.[114] Constant repairs are also expensive. In 2018, CBP spent $4.84 million per mile just in repairs, and to mend the 9,287 breaches in pedestrian fencing that occurred from 2010 until 2015, taxpayers unknowingly paid an average of $784 per breach.[115] In this way, Hispanics, who constitute the largest ethno-racial minority in the United States, and other taxpayers are forced to pay for the expulsion of their relatives, friends, and acquaintances.

In addition to the material wall, other facets of immigration enforcement and border security are burning through dollars. In 2010, the government spent $17.1 billion on border enforcement, which has been criticized by many for being "overkill."[116] Funds spent on ICE have increased by 103 percent since its inception, and the CBP budget has tripled since 2003, jumping from $5.9 to $17.7 billion in 2021.[117] A border wall also has consequences for Americans' total incomes. President George W. Bush signed the Secure Fence Act of 2006, which spurred the construction of more fencing at the border. Supporters rejoiced, believ-ing it would benefit low-skill American workers, since fewer migrants could now "steal" jobs. Immigrant labor brings down the cost of goods and services, increases corporate profits, and has small effects on wages. Some estimated that the effects of the border wall and a decrease in immigration resulted in a minor $.36 increase in workers' annual income between 2007 and 2010, while high-skill workers lost $4.35 annually. They also estimated that the further buildup of the wall stopped about 144,256 foreign-born workers from earning money in the United States. For each migrant lost, U.S. GDP fell by $30,000, equaling a loss of over $2.5 billion.[118] In the end, the economy suffered from having a smaller immigrant presence.

Other similar operations have resulted in negative consequences. The Western Hemisphere Travel Initiative (WHTI) was created in 2009 with a primary purpose of establishing an advanced documentation system that would require sophisticated paperwork, such as NEXUS travel documentation, in order to cross either the U.S.-Mexico or the U.S.-Canada border. This initiative aimed to stop trafficking and smuggling operations, but it failed to do so and instead caused financial strain in border regions. Many legitimate businesses and individuals that rely on transborder land travel are now struggling, while the black markets involved in contraband and human smuggling have found new ways to pass the safeguards in place. Moreover, the goals of the WHTI are not in line with the actual improvement of border security. While one goal may have been genuine improvement, this approach has not worked in the past. When nearly all transborder travel was suspended throughout the country after 9/11, the economic aftershock was staggering. The United States relies on Canadian and Mexican industries, but the money passing through both borders is being interrupted by the increased documentation measures instituted by the WHTI. This endangers relations between the United States and its northern and southern neighbors, limits trade, and restricts transborder business.[119]

The Environment Will Suffer

Ecologists fear for the fragile environment that stretches along the U.S.-Mexico border. These borderlands are home to some of the most diverse habitats, ranging from woodlands and temperate forests to lush wetlands, and to at least sixty-two endangered species of animals and plants.[120] A 2014 study shows that physical barriers leave small and large mammals vulnerable to isolation and extinction. For example, fencing in Arizona hurt the local environment but resulted in few differences in the movement of migrants. Structures erected in the vulnerable coastal regions of California and Texas and the Madrean Sky Island Archipelago in Arizona already interfere with species movement through different habitats and will certainly do so in the future.[121] In these habitats, a wall ruptures a shared landscape, effectively "severing a vital link" that has serious consequences for the homes and movements of wildlife. The natural migration routes of certain insects, birds, and animals are crucial for their survival, but the wall creates an unavoidable physical interruption. The structure of an ecosystem may change with an absence of or decrease in interactions between different types of organisms. Surveillance tools like CBP vehicles, drones, aircraft, and artificial night lights disrupt migration and habitat. Other natural processes that may suffer from the intense border authority presence are species circulation, pollination, and fertilization.[122]

The federal government fails to address the effects of the border wall on the environment and ignores any suitable alternatives despite warnings from environmental experts. In its statements on potential environmental concerns related to the border wall, DHS inaccurately described the southern border region as only an arid climate. It also failed to consider the impacts on wetlands, which comprise a considerable portion of the region and its surrounding areas, and disregarded how a physical barrier would affect endangered species that either live in or migrate through the U.S.-Mexico region.[123]

CONCLUSION

Border walls were used by ancient empires, like the Holy Roman Empire and the Han dynasty, to assert their dominance in a region and keep unconquered people out.[124] Lynn Stephen writes that "while it is clear that the construction of walls does not stop people from coming," walls reproduce "the notion of a fixed border" and also remind us about their social salience and the ebbs and flows of political domains, as the walls do not demarcate permanent political borders.[125] Border areas range from open areas to lines in the sand to militarized zones like those in Berlin after World War II and the Demilitarized Zone between South and North Korea.

Formal immigration policy should match the lived realities experienced by border residents rather than political talking points, and lawmakers must recognize how closely intertwined the Mexican and U.S. communities are. People cross borderlands on a daily basis for work and family reasons, and the United

States and Mexico are also economically interdependent. Restricting people's access to either side has dire consequences for their finances, education, businesses, and careers. Embracing the borderlands as an area of exchange and relaxing strict immigration policies would ensure inclusivity, safety, and economic well-being for U.S. citizens, migrant workers, and CBP agents who work at the border. Instead of using the border wall as an ideological weapon against its southern neighbor, killing and maiming migrants, and wasting taxpayers' money, the United States should provide a safe and well-defined path to citizenship for immigrants of all backgrounds and statuses. The country's legal process for seeking asylum and obtaining a visa has resulted in long waiting times. At the same time, deportation proceedings occur more expeditiously to ensure that individuals who travel to the United States unsanctioned or who prolong their stay are deported after being apprehended.

Furthermore, the U.S. government should divert some of its resources to ensure that its citizens are taken care of and have access to necessities before spending billions of dollars on a barrier that does not achieve its intended purpose. In their research on the border, Susan Forster-Cox and colleagues note that many small rural towns struggle to obtain and sustain essential items, clean and stable water sources, homes with working electricity, and safe roads. Due to the poor living conditions, there are "more than 325,000 hospitalizations and 5,000 deaths annually" on the U.S. side of the border alone.[126] The authors further describe a project aimed at improving living conditions for people residing in the border region and find that after years of operation, the project's efforts have significantly improved the lives of people in the area. The United States would do well to take this type of approach instead of infiltrating border communities with unnecessary numbers of agents and resources that it uses to project force. Funds used for militarizing the border could be reallocated to national programs aiming at reducing inequality or to domestic infrastructure projects. The government also has an opportunity to engage in cross-border innovation and cooperation alongside the many nonprofit organizations and local powers that already work toward that goal.[127] Given the interdependence of the U.S. and Mexican communities, investing in economic, educational, and social development initiatives could positively impact residents in ways that border security cannot.

Immigration across the U.S.-Mexico border is an omnipresent subject of debate in the media. Due to all the news coverage and attention from politicians, the real characteristics of the region and its people have been watered down with rhetoric that alludes to lawlessness. This rhetoric also stirs an "Us vs. Them" attitude toward immigrants, who are said to spread crime, steal jobs, and take advantage of U.S. resources. Media outlets incite fear, convincing Americans that immediate and drastic action is required to turn the situation around. The need to "secure" the southern border contributes to the mass hysteria and ignores the fact that, as Kristian Ramos explains, the region "has long been a positive space for commerce, trade, and the movement of labor."[128] To say that a wall is necessary at the border disregards the ecological, social, and economic complexities of the region.

CHAPTER 3

IMMIGRANTS COMMIT LESS CRIME THAN NATIVE-BORN PEOPLE

Cristhian Bahena Rivera, a twenty-four-year-old undocumented immigrant living in Iowa, was arrested and convicted for the murder of a young woman named Mollie Tibbetts in 2018. The tragic case made national news, and right-wing politicians seized and used it as a broad justification for strengthening border security and entry requirements for immigrants.[1] They claimed that stemming immigration is vital to protecting the country because immigrants, like Cristhian, come with the intent to commit crime, are naturally aggressive, and bring the violent baggage of their home countries.[2]

Contemporary discussions about immigration are heavily based on fearmongering and stereotypes that have conflated immigrant illegality and crime.[3] There is a pervasive misconception that immigration status and nationality are determinants of someone's propensity for violence and crime. The nearly eleven million undocumented immigrants living in the United States are commonly blamed for a whole range of issues, especially violent and petty crime and, to a degree, the underground drug trade.[4] Because of this false belief, nonimmigrants think that immigrant neighborhoods need to be intensely policed, unaware that surveillance worsens living conditions and results in the disproportionate incarceration of immigrants and people of color. President Donald Trump's 2016 presidential campaign is best summarized by his now infamous comments regarding Mexican immigrants: "When they send their people, they aren't sending their best. . . . They are bringing drugs. They are bringing crime. They're rapists. And some, I assume, are good people."[5] The popularity of similar sentiments begs the question: Do immigrants *really* commit more crimes than U.S.-born people?

Research overwhelmingly shows that immigrants in the United States commit fewer crimes than their U.S.-born counterparts. After reviewing conviction rates among people of similar economic, demographic, and legal backgrounds, we argue in this chapter that immigrants do not engage in more criminal behavior than their native-born counterparts. First, we outline evidence supporting the conclusion that immigrants are less likely to commit crime or use drugs in their host countries than native-born people; this is due to many factors, such as more severe legal consequences for themselves and their families and cultural attitudes surrounding drug use. We also emphasize that because immigrants are victimized by the criminal justice system, they cannot rely on the police and often do not report crimes committed against them.

Then we discuss how xenophobic environments, exclusionary narratives, and stringent immigration policies negatively impact immigrants' abilities to integrate. Social science research suggests that the degree to which immigrants are constrained in the political and economic spheres in Europe and the United States influences their likelihood of committing crimes, among other things, which intensifies the need to cultivate welcoming environments. We also address claims that immigrants are particularly prone to use drugs by recounting how Nixon's War on Drugs, the drug trade, and political instability in Mexico have strengthened prejudiced associations that link Latin people with drugs in the United States. Next, we provide a brief historical overview of discourse regarding immigrants, crime, and drugs as well as the punitive actions taken against them as a result of changes in U.S. immigration policies and the use of discretion by local authorities in sanctuary jurisdictions. Crime is not a clear concept; rather, it is shaped by the racial biases of a given sociohistorical moment. Building on this, we highlight biased social and legal phenomena that contribute to misleadingly high rates of immigrant detainment, including racial profiling and mass incarceration.

IMMIGRANTS COMMIT FEWER CRIMES THAN NATIVE-BORN AMERICANS

Increases in Immigration May Lead to Decreases in Crime

Early theories about immigration assumed that young immigrants, who comprised most of immigrant inflows, would be more likely to commit crimes because of their age, race, and ethnic identity. Nevertheless, there is no direct evidence of an overall positive association between immigration and crime rates.

Instead, immigration might help to *prevent* crime. Recent declines in national crime rates have coincided with spikes in immigration in the United States.[6] From the late 1990s into the 2010s, the United States experienced an extreme drop in violence not seen since the 1960s. Also between the 1990s and 2018, the number of Mexican and Central American migrants moving into the country increased, and the total immigrant population rose from 7.9 percent to 13.7 percent,[7] thus returning to numbers common at the turn of the twentieth century. Undocumented immigrants increased from 3.5 million to an estimated 11.2 million. Despite the increase in immigration, however, violent crime and theft rates plummeted.[8] Crime became less common as the undocumented immigrant community expanded.

With these trends in mind, it is possible to conclude that immigration either has no connection to crime or acts indirectly as a shield against criminal activity.[9] The decrease in crime during this period could be attributed to the changing age structure of the U.S. immigrant population in the late 1990s and early 2000s. The proportion of young people at that time was declining, and younger people have a higher propensity to commit crime. Immigrants tend to be younger than the local population, so according to connections between age and criminality, immigrants would be more likely to commit crimes. Nevertheless, studies linking strong immigrant presence to low crime rates date back to the 1990s and range from local investigations to nationwide analyses.[10] For instance, between 2007 and 2016, criminal activity decreased on average in metropolitan areas across the United States that experienced increases in undocumented immigration. Their property crime rates either remained unchanged or decreased. Increases in undocumented immigration also correlated with a decrease in violent crimes.[11] The same trend occurred in San Diego between 1960 and 2010. Over the years, whenever the border city saw an influx of immigrants, there were fewer homicides.[12]

Some areas of the United States are considered new immigrant destinations where large groups of foreign-born people tend to settle. In the early 2000s, researchers found that the 194 cities and towns across the United States where immigrant residents had increased by 150 percent or more over ten years all saw massive decreases in crime.[13] One such place was Chicago, where Mexican Americans were proven to commit fewer violent crimes than nonimmigrants living in the city. The rate of violence in 2006 was lowest among first-generation Mexicans, whose likelihood of committing violent crime was 45 percent lower than that of third-generation Mexicans.[14] Immigrant communities' low crime rates are partly attributed to the presence of shared ethics and "strong social controls"—including community, solidarity, and cohesion—in immigrant neighborhoods, given that most recent immigrants are likely to cultivate immigrant trust networks whose members police one another's behavior and provide support when necessary.[15] Latin immigrants also have fewer documented psychiatric issues and problems with violent behavior, which may partly explain why they are four to ten times less likely to be involved in violent or criminal behavior.[16]

The Southern Border Region Has Lower Crime Rates

The border states of California, Arizona, New Mexico, and Texas are home to millions of Hispanics.[17] If the myth that foreign-born people are more likely to be criminals were true, predominantly immigrant-populated counties would exhibit higher crime rates. However, on average, counties along the U.S.-Mexico border that are home to many Latin immigrants have lower crime rates than the rest of the country. According to the FBI's Uniform Crime Report for 2017, homicide, violent crime, and property crime rates along the border were significantly lower than national averages and averages in nonborder counties (table 3.1).[18]

The border region experienced 33.8 percent fewer homicides than the entire country, 2.1 percent fewer property crimes, and 8 percent fewer violent crimes in 2017. Your chances of being a victim of crime are much lower as you get closer to Mexico, so claiming that there is a crisis at the southern border but not across the rest of the country is misleading. Data from 2000 to 2018 show the El Paso's murder rate per 100,000 people was lower than the rates for Texas and the United States as a whole.[19]

TABLE 3.1 Crime rates per 100,000 people by U.S. region, 2017

	Violent crime	Property crime	Homicide
Border counties	347.8	2,207.1	3.4
Nonborder counties	378.6	2,256.4	5.2
All U.S. counties	377.8	2,255.2	5.1

Source: FBI Uniform Crime Report, 2017.

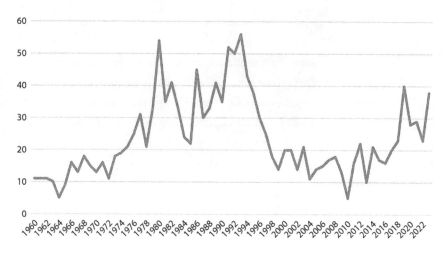

3.1 Number of murders in El Paso, 1960–2023
Source: El Paso Police Department and FBI Crime Statistics.

Crime rates were low in areas of the United States with large immigrant populations even before the federal government increased its border militarization. Despite being a large city, El Paso had an annual murder rate that never exceeded fifty-six (1993), although it usually reached double digits (figure 3.1). Nearly the same number of homicides occurred in El Paso in 2017 as in 2001, 1985, and 1975.[20] The absolute numbers are not that different across decades, and in many ways, they have declined in the last decades even as population has increased. It is also important to note that the forty murders in 2019, a relatively high number for the city, include the twenty-three fatalities caused by a White nationalist shooting at shoppers outside Cielo Vista Mall's Walmart.

Immigrants in Texas Are Less Likely to Be Convicted of a Crime,
Despite Racial Profiling

Right-wing politicians and policymakers who insist that migrants bring crime with them would know they are making false claims if they looked at the demographics of U.S. prison populations. Because of the biased nature of the criminal justice system, we know that it is not only "criminals" who get locked up and that Brown and Black people are overrepresented among imprisoned people. Still, there are proportionally fewer immigrants in federal, state, and local prisons than U.S.-born people: immigrants constitute over 13 percent of the U.S. population but are 5.6 percent of overall inmates.[21] While noncitizens comprise 22 percent of federal prisoners, many are imprisoned because their undocumented status, an immigration law violation, was tried as a felony offense. In other words, a large portion of these people are in prison for being immigrants and have not committed any other crime. Additionally, in 2018, Mexican immigrants composed one-quarter of the U.S. immigrant community and slightly more than half of all unauthorized immigrants.[22] Immigrants who are convicted of violent crimes, like homicide, often must serve their sentence in the United States before being deported,[23] so the smaller number of foreign-born people in the U.S. prison system is not a result of immediate deportation.

Texas is the only U.S. state that offers a record of crimes broken down by citizenship status, and, therefore, claims cannot be made about immigrants' crime rates on a national scale without looking at independent research. The necessary state-level data are not easily accessible. According to the data that we do have from the Texas Department of Public Safety, since 2010 native-born American citizens have been convicted of federal crimes at an incredibly high rate compared to both undocumented and authorized immigrants.[24]

Texas has a large Hispanic population: nearly 40 percent of people in the state identify as Hispanic.[25] Historically, this population has Mexican and Native American origins. More Central American immigrants, however, have settled in Texas in the past few decades. Most immigrants living in the state now have origins in Mexico (51 percent), India (6 percent), El Salvador (5 percent), Vietnam (4 percent), and Honduras (3 percent).[26] The inward flow of Central Americans has not significantly worsened crime rates because immigrants living in Texas generally commit fewer crimes. From 2011 until 2017, U.S.-born Texans were convicted of crimes at a rate of 1,797 per 100,000. In contrast, undocumented immigrants were convicted at a rate of 899 per 100,000, while authorized immigrants had the lowest rate, 611 per 100,000 (see figure 3.2). Undocumented immigrants also had a 7.9 percent lower conviction rate for sex crimes and a 77 percent lower conviction rate for theft/larceny than native-born Americans throughout the same period.[27]

In general, Hispanic people commit considerably fewer federal crimes involving violence, theft, assault, drugs, or sex than non-Hispanics. In its 2019 *Crime in Texas* report, the Texas Department of Public Safety outlined federal arrests according to ethnicity.[28] Non-Hispanic Texans committed more of these types of

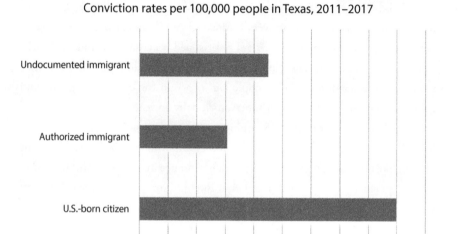

3.2 Conviction rate per 100,000 people in Texas, 2011–2017
Source: Created by the authors with data from Nowratesh, "Criminal Immigrants in Texas."

federal crimes, and especially assaults and thefts, than Hispanic people (table 3.2). Even though the data do not distinguish between U.S.- and foreign-born Latin people and do not provide the respective percentages, the comparison is still useful because the majority of immigrants in the state are Hispanic, and around that time, close to half of the state was Hispanic.

TABLE 3.2 Arrests according to ethnicity in Texas, 2019

Crime	Hispanic	Non-Hispanic
Murder	213	511
Rape	990	1,177
Robbery	1,928	3,881
Aggravated assault	9,669	17,631
Burglary	3,275	5,767
Theft	19,311	39,003
Other assaults	28,553	50,558

Source: Texas Department of Public Safety, 2019.

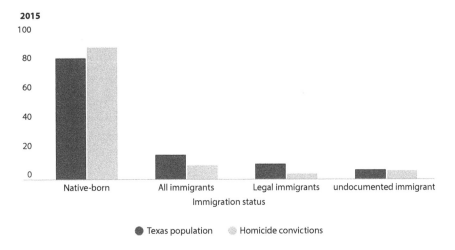

3.3 Share of Texas population and homicide convictions by immigration status, 2015

Source: Nowratesh, "Criminal Immigrants in Texas," with data from the Texas Department of Public Safety, the American Community Survey, and the Center for Migration Studies.

Both undocumented and legally residing immigrants committed fewer crimes than U.S. citizens in the state of Texas in 2015. The undocumented community had 56 percent fewer convictions than U.S.-born residents, and legal immigrants had 85 percent fewer convictions.[29] According to figure 3.3, U.S.-born people committed more homicides *and* were overrepresented in the total number of homicide convictions, further corroborating our argument. It is essential to note that figure 3.3 includes federal immigration violations, which must be considered when assessing undocumented people's crime rates.[30]

ECONOMIC AND SOCIAL CONSTRAINTS IMPACT IMMIGRANTS' RELATIONSHIPS TO CRIME

Migrants Are Likely to Be Victims of Crime, Not Perpetrators

It is clear by now that immigrants are at an extreme disadvantage when it comes to living in the United States. Hispanic communities face police brutality, detainment, stigmatization, and employment exploitation. Shockingly, more Hispanic men are killed by police than White men: in 2015, 12 percent of the U.S. population was Hispanic, and yet 33 percent of fatal police shootings targeted a

Hispanic person.[31] The "criminal immigrant" myth frames foreign-born people, particularly immigrants of color, as perpetrators of crime when they actually fall victim to unlawful arrest, murder, and deportation more often than White citizens and immigrants.[32]

If immigrant youth experience abuse or crime, they often do not report it to the police, especially if they have had a negative experience with law enforcement or are not U.S. citizens.[33] For undocumented people, interacting with state

In El Paso (figure 3.4), a Hispanic-majority city, up to 2,400 Border Patrol officers monitor the community in addition to the local police force. Hispanic residents in the area have reported negative experiences with law enforcement.[36] These sentiments were echoed in the survey data we collected in El Paso in 2011–2012. Nearly 10 percent of Hispanic people surveyed felt that they had been unjustly detained by police. Fully processed federal convictions brought against residents were sparse, although one-third of those convicted were undocumented immigrants who were likely being punished for their immigration status.

3.4 View of the El Paso/Juárez metroplex

Source: © Ernesto Castañeda 2013.

Prejudice and racism also appeared to be prevalent issues in El Paso. About 16 percent of Hispanic residents, including immigrants, experienced recent discrimination at the time of the study, and 12 percent believed that the color of their skin affected their lives. It was also very common for immigrants who had been convicted previously or who had experienced run-ins with law enforcement to report experiencing recent discrimination and unwarranted arrest. This supports evidence of the damage that racial profiling causes in people's lives and the added burden of racism for Hispanic immigrants of color in the United States.

TABLE 3.3 Discrimination experiences (by nativity)

	Foreign-born	U.S.-born
Experienced discrimination in the last five years	19.2%	13.5%
Your skin color affects daily life	8.2%	14.4%

authorities could have drastic consequences, even in some sanctuary jurisdictions. Immigration without documentation is punishable by imprisonment and deportation. Therefore, immigrants typically strive to avoid interaction with law enforcement as much as possible.[34] If undocumented immigrants, and even authorized immigrants, are victims of a crime, they probably will not report it.[35] It is hard for them to rely on the U.S. justice system when the law considers them "illegals" or outsiders.

Crime and Financial Insecurity Are Exacerbated in Unwelcoming Societies

It is useful to compare experiences across various countries to understand local dynamics. The context of immigrant reception and integration, culturally and economically, is far different in France than in the United States.[37] French scholars have found associations between immigration and crime—but only when immigrants are in dire economic situations. A study by Yu Aoki and Yasuyuki Todo used national French census data from 1999 to examine crime and immigration. Unemployed immigrants were more likely to commit crimes than unemployed French nationals because they faced more adversity than French nationals, who had better access to public spaces and services, had greater religious acceptance, and faced less discrimination in the job market.[38] There was a significantly positive association between immigration and crime when immigrants were struggling economically, but this was not the case when immigrants had stable living situations.

Aoki and Todo concluded that "policies that improve the economic circumstances of immigrants may go a long way to lowering crime rates" as opposed to incarceration and deportation.[39] People may commit crimes based on the expected gain compared to other alternatives. Given that they are discriminated against in the workplace, job market, and other spheres of life, unemployed immigrants in France feel alienated and excluded from mainstream French society and experience hopelessness.[40] In this challenging context, some turn to crime. A positive correlation between immigration and crime in France in 1999 might also be explained by its restrictive immigration policy, significant barriers to entry in place for immigrants, and absence of legal and public encouragement to permanently settle in the country.[41] Since native-born French and government actors rarely welcome immigrants into mainstream society, economic, cultural, and political integration resources are lacking. Poor integration policies also have an impact on drug use. In 2005, approximately 16 percent of the Swedish population consisted of first- or second-generation immigrants. Immigrant youth from other Nordic countries tended to use alcohol and illicit drugs more often than native-born Swedes of the same age group, contrary to what researchers have discovered in the United States. On the other hand, behavior varied among ethnic and racial communities. Non-European immigrant adolescents, especially girls, drank less alcohol than their Swedish-born and European immigrant counterparts.[42]

What does this mean for the United States? How does this explain low rates of immigrant violence and crime exposure? Ernesto Castañeda found that how immigrants are received in much of the United States and in European cities influenced their ability to make money.[43] In New York City, immigrants could find work regardless of immigration status. Having a job, a place to live, and enough money to support or eventually start a family creates hope and belonging. As a result, economic integration is intertwined with social integration: individuals—regardless of race, ethnicity, class, or immigration status—are less likely to turn to crime when their economic needs are within reach. Even low-paying jobs are insufficient to sustain a family in expensive coastal cities. Therefore, the solution to crime is not to build a wall or detain immigrants but to build opportunities and stability.

IMMIGRANTS ENGAGE WITH DRUGS LESS THAN NATIVE-BORN AMERICANS

Drogas y Narcos

One of the largest concerns of the U.S. government regarding crime is the drug trafficking industry. While drugs and money do cycle across the border, it is wrong to assume that all those involved in the supply of drugs are Hispanic migrants. In coordination with the U.S. government, the Mexican government has declared a total war against drug cartels. Their success has been limited, though, as hundreds of thousands of Mexicans, including journalists, students, and politicians, have been killed as a result of cartel-related violence. Mexican cartels have dominated the illegal drug trade since the collapse of the major Colombian cartels in the mid-1990s.[44] At that time, cartels had operated in Mexico for decades without any major violence due to "an unwritten pact that criminal organizations had with some members of the 70-year ruling party, the Institutional Revolutionary Party (PRI.)"[45] Because of this, the PRI could punish cartels that fell out of line without inciting mass violence. However, the opposition party took control in the early 2000s, thus ending the agreement and relinquishing the power to keep cartels in line. This reached a head in 2006 when Felipe Calderón declared war on the cartels and deployed the military to stamp them out violently. After this decision, homicide rates jumped due to a combination of factors, including political decentralization, retaliatory wars, and the splintering of cartels. The new system of more localized political control established by Calderón also failed to address corruption, and the Peña Nieto administration that replaced Calderón's was notoriously ineffective in deescalating conflict between drug trafficking organizations and regulating crime in general.[46]

The continued corruption of the police, military, and political structures in Mexico has made the cartels very powerful and influential; in many cases, they work with police and military officers to dispose of enemies or opposition. These coalitions have created an environment rife with crime: despite government deployment of massive security forces and assistance from the United States via the Mérida Initiative, the national murder rate reached 25 per 100,000 people in 2017.[47] To this day, the demand for drugs in the United States remains pervasive and unrelenting, perpetuating the violence and instability occurring south of the border. Vast quantities of heroin, methamphetamines, fentanyl, and marijuana are smuggled north to appease American consumers. Most trafficking occurs at ports of entry right under the noses of U.S. Customs and Border Protection (CBP) officials.

Cocaine, Marijuana, and the Drug Trade

The United States is home to gangs like MS-13 and 18th Street, but it would be inaccurate to conflate these with transnational cartels. Cartels usually manufacture and smuggle drugs into the United States and outsource the retail trade to local gangs, according to the Drug Enforcement Administration (DEA) in its 2016 *National Drug Threat Assessment*. Instead of directly holding territory as cartels do in Mexico, U.S.-based organizations tend to control markets indirectly using local gangs.[48]

Most of the heroin, opium, and cocaine presently consumed across the Americas is produced in and exported from Mexico, Colombia, and Guatemala. Between 2013 and 2016, however, poppy cultivation in Mexico tripled, "reaching a record of 32,000 hectares in 2016."[49] Increases in heroin and opium production have historically been linked to growing rates of intravenous drug use and HIV prevalence in Tijuana and Baja California.[50] Perhaps due to this surge in production, Mexico also reports the highest incidence of use of these drugs in all of Latin America. The opium epidemic, which has had disastrous effects on communities in the United States, has begun to affect Mexico in the same way, especially in the northern states that sit closer to the border. This phenomenon has led to recommendations that the two nations collaborate to tackle the epidemic more effectively. This could hopefully lead to a practical compromise and a more secure border area, which benefits both countries.[51]

A video issued by the FBI in 2010 titled *Crime on Southwest Border* sheds light on the attitudes that border authorities have toward the border and the approaches they employ to combat drug trafficking. The FBI and CBP overwhelmingly refer to the border with negativity and paranoia, insisting that the region is a dangerous and crime-ridden place where physical barriers have the potential to be effective, especially in urban areas. They emphasize the importance of fighting corruption within the ranks of border officials, as it poses a serious issue. The DEA's El Paso Intelligence Center aids with border security, and the FBI stated in the video that they work together to curb the drug trafficking industry in the region.[52]

Marijuana and cocaine are drugs that are also commonly associated with Mexico. The majority of cocaine is produced in South America and must travel through Mexico to reach its destination in the United States. Conversations involving cocaine at the U.S.-Mexico border almost always reference cartel violence and the drug trafficking industry.[53] Meanwhile, it is well-known that cannabis is grown across multiple Mexican states.[54] Cannabis production has been one of the primary targets for federal eradication efforts. In 1975, U.S. and Mexican forces sprayed massive amounts of the pesticide paraquat on cannabis fields so that Americans would stop buying from Mexican producers, and since the 1970s, legislation regarding the medical and recreational use of cannabis has changed drastically.[55] Many U.S. states, as well as the District of Columbia, have decriminalized or legalized recreational marijuana. While efforts to relax laws on marijuana use benefit White Americans, they do not change harsh policies for immigrants seeking entry into the country. CBP agents can inquire whether immigrants have ever used or worked with marijuana. If an immigrant answers yes or if it is discovered that they have used marijuana through drug testing at ports of entry, entrance to the United States is automatically denied. While this cannot be used to revoke one's citizenship, it is generally used to disqualify applicants for entry.[56] Interestingly, most of the cannabis consumed in the United States is now grown domestically.

Immigrants Are Less Likely to Smuggle and Traffic Drugs

Because Mexico is a source of drugs for American consumers, political groups and media outlets have devised harmful stereotypes that conflate Latin immigrants with drug mules, smugglers, traffickers, or users. As a result, Hispanics and the U.S.-Mexico border region are usually included in discussions about the international drug trade, which is sensationalized and celebrated in popular television shows like Narcos, The Bridge, Queen of the South, and Breaking Bad as well as films like Scarface and American Made. The presence of Latin people, regardless of documentation or immigration status, has instilled fear of lawlessness in non-Hispanic White individuals partially because of the prejudiced belief that most, if not all, Hispanics are involved in drugs and crime.[57] We now consider drug-related convictions and instances of substance use disorder to illustrate the glaringly fabricated nature of this stereotype.

Like the other facets contributing to the impression of a criminal immigrant, the belief that immigrants traffic drugs at higher rates than U.S.-born people is untrue. In 2018, the U.S. Sentencing Commission found that 77 percent of federal drug trafficking convictions were against U.S. citizens. Immigrants are arrested for drug trafficking and smuggling less than in the past, as the share of convicted undocumented immigrants dropped by 5 percent between 2012 and 2018. American citizens are also more likely to smuggle.[58]

Drug traffickers who do business in Mexican border towns often battle each other over valuable drug-trafficking routes. Indeed, they pose one of the greatest safety threats for Mexican nationals and Central American migrants. Drug smuggling is also becoming tied to the migrant smuggling industry.[59] Human traffickers, many of whom increasingly work jointly with drug cartels, intimidate, kidnap, exploit, and kill migrants on their journey north.[60] Sometimes they torture migrants, giving them no choice but to join cartel operations and work in the trafficking industry. Other times they command Central American and Mexican migrants to smuggle drugs into the United States and threaten to hurt these victims' loved ones if they refuse or later defect.[61] Thus, recent immigrants may smuggle drugs across the border without any criminal intent. Smuggling is also a desirable occupation for multiple reasons. It is a profitable and in-demand service that offers steady income, protection, and a way for vulnerable people to improve their lives. Some migrants who are tired of being victimized by local gangs and kidnapped for ransom might decide to engage in criminal activity, whereas others might choose to avoid getting involved.[62] It is generally more common for U.S.-born people to be caught smuggling and trafficking illicit drugs on the U.S. side, but we cannot discount the active decisions that migrants make because of the environmental constraints they experience.

Substance Use

The United States' War on Drugs was declared in 1971 when, amid the civil rights and anti–Vietnam War movements, President Richard Nixon imposed severe consequences for people purchasing and selling marijuana, heroin, cocaine, and other drugs. Two years later the DEA was created to lead the fight in the "war."[63] Nixon's decision was entirely political: he aimed to turn the American public against the civil rights and antiwar activists by associating these groups with drugs. John Ehrlichman, who acted as Nixon's counsel and as assistant to the president for domestic affairs, admitted in a 2016 interview that the scheme was not grounded in fact.[64] It was intended to silence and incarcerate activists by spreading lies about their drug use and conflating their political and social goals with criminal activity.[65]

What is happening right now at the U.S.-Mexico border is a result of the declaration of the War on Drugs and has serious consequences for Black and Latin immigrants. Similar to the Black people and antiwar activists who were said to be wrapped up in drugs, immigrants arriving at the southern border are stereotyped as *traficantes*, dealers, gangsters, smugglers, or substance users.[66] Furthermore, Central American immigrants who are caught with drugs are punished more severely than White Americans. Wealthy White adolescents who overdose on heroin have been framed as victims of Mexican cartels and immigrant smugglers. In a case in Plano, near Dallas, sixteen White teenagers arrested for selling heroin and marijuana received little jail time or probation despite being charged with conspiracy to murder. The thirteen Mexican dealers involved in the same case were sentenced to twenty years to life in prison.[67] In this way, immigrants, particularly Hispanics, are used as scapegoats nationwide. White U.S. citizens use substances more often than noncitizens, creating a market demand for drugs, and yet they avoid blame and harsh prison sentences.[68] Instead, noncitizens are associated with substances. This approach is useful to the government because it garners support for immigration enforcement, border security, deportation, detention, mass incarceration, and maltreatment of immigrants.

First- and Second-Generation Immigrants Are Less Likely to Use Drugs

Despite what federal policies insinuate, native-born Americans are more at risk of substance use disorders than immigrants with origins in Africa, Europe, Latin America, and Asia.[69] U.S.-born people have the greater proportion of lifetime substance use disorders related to alcohol, marijuana, stimulants, sedatives, tranquilizers, opioids, and heroin when compared to first- and second-generation Mexican immigrants. Mexican immigrants are three times less likely to be diagnosed with alcohol use disorder than White Americans, and White Americans are twice as likely to use cocaine in their lifetime as Hispanic immigrants.[70] In general, immigrants struggle with cannabis, cocaine, and opioid addictions less often than U.S.-born people.

Adolescents as a group are at high risk for developing substance use disorders. It is common for people to try drugs for the first time as teenagers, although first-generation immigrants have been shown to partake far less often than their U.S.-born peers. In a 2007 study, about 40 percent of immigrant youth had never tried any illicit drug before.[71] Of course, adolescents can always change their minds and experiment with drugs in the future. It may be that immigrant teenagers are less inclined to do so at a younger age because they are living with family or because they hold certain cultural beliefs about substance use. In their survey of 2,635 eighth- and tenth-grade students in Massachusetts, Susan Blake and colleagues found a connection between the recency of immigration and students' substance use behaviors, as native-born youth smoked marijuana and drank alcohol more often than their immigrant peers.[72]

U.S. Acculturation Increases the Likelihood of Substance Abuse

Immigrants *do* use drugs and alcohol, even if they statistically use them much less than U.S.-born people. Children of immigrants are more likely to try drugs than their parents, which Samuel Garcia claims is related to a cultural shift that occurs for immigrants who arrive in the United States at a younger age or are born in the United States.[73] Kids and teenagers are generally more familiar with U.S. culture than their parents and older family members, and this may be why U.S.-born Mexican Americans are more likely to use substances than their foreign-born counterparts.[74] First-generation immigrants report significantly fewer substance use disorders than later generations, hinting that acculturation in the United States may lead to more experimentation with drugs or more openness to disclosing substance use behavior.[75]

A person's environment significantly influences their drug use, and an increase in the acculturation of a child or their parents can increase the likelihood of illicit drug use. The probability of a Latin youth being surrounded by substance use at home is lower than that of a U.S.-born child. In one study, Hispanic people were less likely to use alcohol during pregnancy if they lived in an area with low levels of U.S. acculturation.[76] For instance, girls who migrated to the United States when they were younger than thirteen had more opportunities to use alcohol than those who migrated when they were older. This suggests that living in the United States exposes immigrants to more opportunities to use alcohol and illicit drugs, depending on age and gender.[77]

Cultural Perceptions of Substance Use

Immigrants' lower rates of drug and alcohol consumption can be explained to some extent by cultural beliefs surrounding these substances. Because of Mexico's ongoing struggle with cartels, Central American and Mexican immigrants have harsher opinions about drug use than people born in the United States.[78] They commonly consider drug use to be a great risk to their well-being and general health: 63.4 percent of Hispanic immigrants in El Paso thought that illicit drugs

El Paso is a prime example of a city that has benefited from Mexican immigration. Although it borders Ciudad Juárez, at times one of the most dangerous cities in Mexico, it is one of the safest communities in the United States for citizens and authorized residents. As illustrated previously, Hispanic people in the region commit fewer crimes than people of other ethnicities, and Hispanic immigrants have even lower crime rates. In 2012, immigrants were convicted of fewer felonies and reported having fewer problems with the law than U.S.-born Hispanics, according to our survey data. Of respondents, 9.9 percent felt they had been unjustly detained by the police, but this perception was higher for the U.S.-born (12.9 percent) than the foreign-born (5.6 percent). Those who had been convicted of a felony were much more likely to feel they had been victims of discrimination in general and that their skin color had an effect on their opportunities. (See tables 3.3 and 3.4.)

Acculturative shifts in drug use were also noted in our El Paso survey. Foreign-born Hispanics drank less alcohol and used smaller quantities of drugs. Overall, 5.5 percent of foreign-born Hispanics in El Paso reported using any illicit drugs compared to 11.1 percent of Hispanics born in the United States. However, both of their rates of drug use are comparatively low.[81] Perceptions of drugs also

TABLE 3.4 Experiences of Hispanics with law enforcement in El Paso
(by nativity; self-reported)

	Foreign-born	U.S.-born
Was convicted of a felony	0.9%	3.9%
Had run-ins with the law	9.8%	16.9%
Was unjustly detained by police	5.3%	12.9%

(continued on next page)

(*continued from previous page*)

changed over generations. Although first- and 1.5-generation immigrants were the least likely to use drugs, they considered drugs to be more problematic than U.S.-born Hispanics of later generations (table 3.5). Most of the drug use across generations involved marijuana.

TABLE 3.5 Drug use by generation

Do you use*	First	1.5	Second	Third	Fourth+	Overall
Any illicit drugs	4.4%	6.5%	11.5%	13.1%	8.1%	8.8%
Marijuana	4.4%	5.6%	9.2%	13.1%	6.7%	7.7%
Cocaine	0%	0%	4.4%	0.9%	1.4%	1.8%
Heroin	0%	0%	0.7%	0%	0%	0.3%
Meth	0%	0%	1.1%	0%	0%	0.5%
Spice	0.5%	0.8%	0.7%	0%	1.3%	0.6%
Perceive use as a problem	10%	5.5%	4.9%	0.1%	2.6%	5.4%

*Significant at $p > .001$

were a problem in their lives compared to 36.6 percent of U.S.-born Hispanics who thought the same. Parents tend to demonize the use of drugs, so many children of Latin immigrants abstain from drug use, try them fewer times, or go to great lengths to hide their behavior from family. This may partially explain why Latin immigrants have the lowest rates of marijuana, heroin, LSD, and cigarette use over the course of their lives compared to White immigrants, U.S.-born Whites, and U.S.-born Hispanics.[79] We also found less use of illegal substances among more recent immigrant generations in El Paso.[80]

Drugs and Alcohol Can Compromise Life in the United States

The consequences for being arrested on drug- or alcohol-related charges are severe for all immigrants regardless of legal status. Possession of nearly any substance intended for personal use is a deportable federal offense that can leave immigrants stripped of their green cards or visas.[82] A court can even order the deportation of an immigrant who is arrested for being under the influence of a federally banned substance. Immigrants are more cautious out of fear of the harsh repercussions that immigration laws entail. Their concern is reflected in the research, as undocumented immigrants do not drive drunk as often and are less likely to be arrested for drug and alcohol offenses than the native-born American population.[83] Drunken driving and drug arrests have declined in areas where immigrant populations are rising, which implies that immigrant neighborhoods are safer for children and pedestrians.[84]

WHY DO PEOPLE THINK THAT IMMIGRANTS COMMIT MORE CRIME?

John Burnett of NPR reported that in 2018 seven out of ten Republican voters in Texas believed that all undocumented immigrants should be deported immediately regardless of whether they have committed a crime.[85] Many of them in fact *do* think that immigrants are criminals. According to a 2020 study, many White Texans believed that immigrants either traffic or sell drugs, cheat on their taxes, vote illegally, or commit serious crimes. They also considered immigrants from White-majority European countries to be less of a threat than foreign-born Hispanics, Libyans, and Syrians.[86] These perceptions further racialize Hispanics and Muslims, encourage exclusionary social narratives, and inspire hate crimes against members of these categorical groups.

One major issue contributing to the criminal immigrant stereotype is how crime rates are reported. Statistics can be oversimplified, inflated, or presented without proper context so that numbers look menacing but do not actually tell a true story.[87] This has been done where U.S.-born Hispanic incarceration rates are conflated with *immigrant* Hispanic incarceration rates and where petty crimes and misdemeanors are not categorized differently from actual imprisonments and convictions. That is, in the statistical data, someone who was arrested on suspicion of vandalism or theft is treated the same way as someone who was convicted of homicide. This faulty reporting without background information or details fails to account for some basic yet serious differences. Another reason people believe immigrants commit more crime is found in the demographics of immigrants. Many migrants are young men between the ages of fifteen and thirty-five who are looking to work and intend to send money to their families abroad or establish a home in the United States to escape violence. Because younger men constitute the majority of criminal perpetrators in the United States, people assume that immigrants contribute to the problem.[88]

As we continue, it becomes clear that these ideas about immigrant criminality are bogus and are repeated to distort public perceptions about immigrants.

Some researchers and academics do support a closed U.S. border. Researchers have used multiple hypotheses in the past to justify and guide their work on immigration and crime. One of these is the importation model, which is based on the belief that immigrants consciously choose to migrate to a specific country only to commit crime.[89] This framework is used to justify the deportation of noncitizens with criminal offenses and to explain networks of human and drug trafficking, organized crime, gang violence, and terrorism. Other early theories associated immigration with "social disorganization" or "disorder," believing that the poor conditions in which immigrants live upon arriving in their host country push them to become angry and commit crimes to make ends meet and express their spite.[90] The same sentiments are echoed in the broken windows theory, which became popular after Rudy Giuliani implemented it while mayor of New York City in the late 1990s. Broken windows, panhandling, graffiti, and abandoned buildings are considered signifiers of crime in an urban neighborhood.[91] The New York Police Department became stricter, cracking down on petty theft and minor crime and instituting invasive surveillance methods, like stop-and-frisk, to proverbially "fix the windows" and bring crime rates down in neighborhoods predominantly populated by people of color and immigrants.[92] These actions succeeded in erasing visible elements of nonWhite and immigrant cultures from the streets but led to the arrest of millions of people for minor offenses, some of which were not even punishable by jail time.[93] The broken windows theory has informed aggressive policing techniques domestically and internationally from Lowell, Massachusetts, and Albuquerque, New Mexico, to communities in Australia.[94] Tough-on-crime policies guided by the broken windows theory and similar frameworks are effective tools of mass incarceration that funnel taxpayers' dollars into criminalizing poverty, vacant housing, and urban disinvestment.

Unlike the previous theories, the bias model posits that the criminal justice system and other power structures systemically discriminate against immigrants. It asserts that Latin immigrants, and other racial and ethnic minorities and immigrant groups, are thought to commit more crime only because they experience more suspicion, racial profiling, surveillance, policing, and punishment than U.S.-born White people. Any statistical overrepresentation of racial, ethnic, or immigrant groups is not the result of actual significant differences in behavior but rather the product of a discriminatory criminal justice system.[95] The fact that immigrants are specially targeted and still underrepresented among those convicted shows the low levels at which they commit criminal acts.

IMMIGRANT CRIMINALITY AND U.S. IMMIGRATION POLICIES THROUGH THE YEARS

Despite the many different theories that are used to infer connections between immigration and crime, researchers and politicians have long disputed misconceptions about immigrant criminality. In multiple periods of U.S. history, federal policies that discriminate against specific groups of immigrants have been implemented. In 1875, the Page Act blocked Chinese women from immigrating to the United States because they were stereotyped as sex workers, initiating the era of ideological, political, and cultural "gatekeeping" that continues to this day.[96] This policy was later extended through the Chinese Exclusion Act of 1882, which banned all Chinese labor immigration for ten years and barred Chinese immigrants from naturalized citizenship.[97] Anti-Chinese sentiments continued to flourish while new hostilities toward different populations of immigrants also gained traction. From the 1880s until the 1930s, there was widespread discrimination against large groups of Polish, Italian, and Armenian immigrants arriving at New York's Ellis Island and California's Angel Island. To curb the inflow of people, the U.S. government passed a wave of anti-immigration laws, including the 1924 Immigration Act, which restricted the number of immigrants permitted entry from these countries. Nonimmigrants and people with western European origins publicly condemned Asian, southern European, and eastern European immigrants as criminals who brought violence and un-American values.[98]

The Federal Immigration Commission, or Dillingham Commission, was a federal committee formed in 1907 that recommended the exclusion of immigrants because of their perceived violent nature. Ironically, in studies conducted in 1911, the commission found no connection between immigration and crime. It could not empirically support its own claims, despite still attempting to do so by making vague statements about Italians and violent crime.[99] Likewise, the Wickersham Commission addressed the myth concerning Latin immigrants in 1931, only to discover that popular opinion had everything backward: people born in the United States committed more crimes than people born in Mexico.[100] Contemporary scholars were skeptical of these early studies, which appeared biased, and reanalyzed the data used by both commissions. When looking at incarceration rates, their findings were not different than those published earlier. In 1910, 3,000 foreign-born White people served time in prison compared to 10,119 native-born individuals. According to the Wickersham Commission data, rates of arrest for "serious" offenses were about the same among foreign-born Whites, Mexicans, and native-born people.[101] Policies prejudiced against immigrants decreased a bit after this especially intense era of xenophobic legislation.

Some view the Immigration Act of 1965 as introducing colorblind immigration policies. However, the drafters intended to favor and increase northern European immigration. The law also imposed severe restrictions on legal migration from Mexico.[102] In practice, it reopened the door to migration from Asia and Africa. Then, the early 1990s saw an upheaval of immigration and refugee policy reforms that eerily echoed those from nearly one century prior.[103] The 1996 Illegal Immigration Reform and Immigrant Responsibility Act (IIRIRA) played a major role in revamping anti-immigrant policies. It broadened the types of deportable crimes, made undocumented immigration a federal crime, and locked migrants awaiting court hearings in detention centers.[104] Once again, this time under the direction of President Bill Clinton, the U.S. government actively targeted immigrants and portrayed them as a danger to U.S. society.

Sanctuary Cities

A transnational movement emerged in the 1980s that challenged the U.S. government's decision to close the border to thousands of Central American asylum seekers.[105] Initially a faith-based campaign, it was labeled the *sanctuary movement* because religious leaders across the country declared churches to be sanctuary spaces where Latin migrants could seek various forms of assistance.[106] Soon entire communities and local governments adopted the same ethical concerns and welcoming approach as churches in the sanctuary movement, and, eventually, many states began to pass laws that officially declared the land within their borders a "sanctuary" for immigrants, asylum seekers, and refugees.

Since then, the discourse on immigrant crime has commonly included debates about sanctuary jurisdictions, which are cities, counties, or states where local law enforcement chooses not to cooperate with federal immigration authorities, does not report people's immigration status, and enacts relatively pro-immigrant policies.[107] Sanctuary cities vary in their openness to immigrants, and local jurisdictions have independent control over their criminal justice system and its resources. They have full discretion over their own law enforcement agencies and do not have to comply with federal authorities' requests that, in the end, cost local departments money, time, and effort. These communities also aim to establish stronger internal bonds by lowering the incidence of unlawful arrests, discrimination, and racial profiling. Sanctuary legislation can foster trust and communication between law enforcement and community members, especially those who normally refrain from calling the police out of fear of deportation or discrimination.[108] Depending on the extent of the sanctuary policies, undocumented immigrants may be penalized less often for their immigration status and may feel less afraid of communicating with state authorities. Latin citizens of many ethnicities have been shown to report crimes more often in sanctuary jurisdictions, which improves public safety.[109]

Opponents believe sanctuary cities are crime hot spots because of local law enforcement's limited surveillance of undocumented residents and minimal cooperation with federal agencies like U.S. Immigration and Customs Enforcement (ICE). In the past, national leaders have proposed legislation banning sanctuary localities from receiving federal funds as punishment for their sanctuary status.[110] However, there is no statistical evidence that undocumented immigrants bring violent crime to sanctuary cities. Research shows that sanctuary cities have the potential to be safer than nonsanctuary localities.[111] Crime trends in 107 U.S. cities revealed that localities that had recently adopted sanctuary policies saw reductions in robberies, and a larger presence of undocumented Mexican immigrants coincided with fewer murders in those cities.[112]

Racial Profiling and Unlawful Detainment

As discussed in chapter 1, federal law enforcement underwent a massive reorganization following the attacks on New York City and the Pentagon on September 11, 2001. The country built up national security and border defenses and imposed further restrictions on immigration. At the same time, xenophobia surged with refreshed malice. Muslim Americans and immigrants were depicted as enemies of the state by literature, entertainment, and the media, inspiring discrimination and hate crimes.[113]

New methods to strengthen the border were put in place during this time, like the "probable cause" policy, which gives CBP agents the power to search vehicles without a warrant and stop anyone whom they consider suspicious.[114] Naturally, allowing officers to stop, search, and arrest people at their discretion has led to the racial profiling, unlawful arrest, and deportation of countless immigrants and even U.S. citizens.[115] Adding more surveillance to immigrant communities under the belief that they are plagued by crime is a clever excuse for law enforcement to widen its deportation regime. Using probable cause as justification, local police and ICE can target immigrants while assuming the guise of community protectors. This policy also gives the impression to noncitizens that immigrants are criminals, since they are arrested often. However, these policies are counterproductive and ineffective. Each year there are new accounts of Americans being wrongfully detained or removed from the country by ICE. Between 2007 and 2015, 818 citizens were arrested and placed in detention centers.[116] The battles ensuing between individuals and immigration authorities are long-winded, arduous, and nerve-wracking, and detainees must make their case while being locked up.[117] When he was eighteen years old, Francisco Erwin Galicia was held in a Texas detention center for one month before authorities decided his Social Security card, ID card, and birth certificate were real. Francisco's Latin identity and his little brother's lack of an ID aroused suspicion among Border Patrol agents at a driving checkpoint.[118] Proving your citizenship once does not save you from experiencing suspicion or wrongful detainment either. For example, in a span of sixteen years, one naturalized U.S. citizen was detained and tried three times by ICE.[119]

Immigrants who face civil or criminal charges also do not have the same resources that are available to citizens. Everyone facing charges in a U.S. court has the right to seek counsel from a lawyer. If a citizen seeks counsel but cannot afford to hire someone, they are appointed an attorney by the court. However, these services are not available for immigrants in deportation proceedings.[120] Across the 1.2 million removal cases carried out from 2007 until 2012 in the United States, 63 percent of people went to court without legal representation.[121] In San Diego and El Paso, immigrant Hispanic adolescents will often remain in jail until their court hearing, unlike other detainees who have the funds to pay bail or do not have detainers[122] issued against them due to their racial/ethnic identity.[123] There are cases where former green card holders, foreign-born military veterans, and even citizens are deported with little legal recourse.[124]

Probable cause, overpolicing, and immigration authorities' extraconstitutional powers terrorize Hispanic communities. People are harassed, brutalized, and arrested on racially charged and false pretenses. Immigrants are locked away in detention centers because of their immigration status and because of a criminal justice system that criminalizes their existence.

Crimmigration and Mass Incarceration

One of the purposes of walls and main entrance gates in medieval cities such as Paris was to collect taxes from traveling merchants.[125] So the state's emphasis on people crossing to ports of entry was initially related to trade, customs, and taxation. Besides commercial cargo, the emphasis at airports, ports, and border entries has shifted from customs to citizenship and visa controls. The development of mass international tourism and free trade agreements have been part of this shift. Identity checks and document stamping is a new processes that in practice can hardly be universal. One misunderstanding about U.S. immigration law, common since at least the 1980s when the terms *wetback* and *illegal* came to be used more frequently, is that entry outside of customs posts (*aduanas*) is a criminal offense; instead, it is a civil offense. Criminal law deals with actions where a wrong is committed against the state or the larger society, whereas civil law generally deals with injuries to private parties, such as individuals and corporations. In the United States, immigration law has been traditionally considered civil law, and immigration cases are decided by administrative judges rather than citizen juries. Nevertheless, these cases are being increasingly dealt with through punitive legislation.[126] So while immigration violations are technically considered civil violations (the way breach of a contract would be), they are nonetheless sometimes treated punitively (the way a crime would be). The purposeful criminalization of immigration infractions, "crimmigration," aims to exclude and largely targets Brown and Black men.[127]

There are three major consequences of crimmigration that should be emphasized. First, because of this arrangement of civil law with criminal consequences, immigrant detention is considered a nonpunitive action when in fact it is no different from criminal incarceration. But unlike regular imprisonment, immigrant detention forces people to forfeit due process and other basic constitutional rights. Second, after the passage of the IIRIRA in 1996, people can be subject to double punishment: a permanent resident might serve a criminal sentence by being imprisoned for years but then, despite having served that sentence, be eligible for deportation. Deportation is technically not considered punitive—even though it obviously is. So essentially immigrants are liable to get punished twice for things that citizens would get punished for only once. Third, what is considered a misdemeanor in criminal law (like marijuana possession) is considered a felony in civil law. As a result, the very same crime might be considered a misdemeanor or a felony depending on citizenship status, which has implications for a person's likelihood of getting deported.[128]

Ultimately, arguments portraying immigrants as more dangerous than native-born Americans are used for political reasons. Crime rates within the immigrant population are overstated because immigration itself became criminalized in the 1990s. Upon the passage of the IIRIRA, federal immigration enforcement authorities began receiving more funding and obtained new powers to incarcerate and try immigrants living in the United States.[129] Younger Hispanics, particularly Mexican immigrants, were targeted because of their growing presence in the country. Now, due to the 1996 reforms, a migrant who is arrested for being undocumented is counted as a "criminal" because immigration has increasingly entered the realm of federal criminal law. This, of course, contradicts the traditional conception of immigration courts and offenses as civil, not criminal. Elizabeth Cohen accurately sums up the phenomenon of illegality: " 'Illegal' or 'undocumented' immigrants were not invented by a line in the sand or a wall around the country. They came into being through the enactment of laws that make some immigration legal and some illegal."[130] The rise in arrests and convictions among noncitizens resulted from changes in policy and law that discriminate against Latin American immigrants—not from their propensity to commit more crimes.

The criminalization of drug use and the declaration of the War on Drugs were also major political moves that negatively impacted entire communities of color, including immigrants. For example, both undocumented and authorized immigrants arrested in the United States for drug trafficking or homicide are now immediately deported to their country of origin after serving their full prison sentence. Together these policy changes helped pave the way for an era of mass incarceration that hit Black and immigrant populations hard.[131] Hispanic immigrants are disproportionately scrutinized and arrested because of immigration status and racial and ethnic background. Crime statistics, unfortunately, do not account for the reality that many immigrants are incarcerated simply because of their immigration status. Nonetheless, the research has shown that large immigrant populations account for fewer crimes or play only a small part in their increase. Even though the cards are systematically stacked against them, immigrants commit fewer crimes than U.S.-born people, and these findings further exonerate foreign-born people from the criminal immigrant myth.[132]

CONCLUSION

Immigrants, particularly those from Mexico and Central and South America, are commonly said to bring violence with them when they cross the southern border, which insinuates that they are criminals who will corrupt American society. Nonetheless, throughout this chapter, we have shown studies and statistics that make it clear that immigrants are considerably less involved in criminal behavior and drug use than the U.S.-born population. For example, crime rates among the undocumented in Texas are lower than for other groups.[133] This is not because fewer immigrants are entering the country or because local police departments or federal immigration authorities have been lax in policing the area.

How immigrants are received by a country, state, or neighborhood crafts how they build a life within and interact with their host societies. The environment in a host country is more instrumental in increasing or reducing crime than people's racial demographics or immigration status. This can be misconstrued in statistical data that portray high rates of immigrant arrest and detainment by not accounting for immigration offenses. The crimmigration system in the United States finds undocumented immigration equally as heinous as violent crime, and noncitizens are disproportionately incarcerated because of aggressive policing tactics, like stop-and-frisk, in immigrant and low-income neighborhoods.

Given the hostility toward immigrants in the United States, they often avoid engaging in crime, communicating with local authorities, and calling the police. Immigrants are aware that the criminal justice system rarely favors them, and individuals or their family members might lose the lives they have built in the United States if they are caught using drugs or doing anything illegal. Even immigrants with green cards can be deported for committing a crime and can always be imprisoned or fined if they get into trouble with the law. This is not to say that immigrants will become violent in welcoming communities where they are not criminalized; rather, research on sanctuary cities exhibited decreases in robberies and homicides. The same can be said for drug use, as acculturation to U.S. social standards and practices is the primary factor that raises the likelihood of drug use in children of immigrants.[134] Cultural attitudes about drugs in fact protect against the development of substance use disorders among immigrant groups,[135] despite stereotypes that frame Latin immigrants as drug smugglers, traffickers, or mules.

Additionally, the assumption that foreign-born people are lawless and the unwarranted scrutiny they face from law enforcement because of this stereotype reinforce their exclusion from mainstream U.S. society. Ultimately, even if an immigrant is not a criminal, they are still treated as such. The use of *illegal alien* instead of *undocumented person* when referring to someone without papers perpetuates a negative impression of immigrants, and even those with legal documentation or naturalized citizen status are stereotyped as "illegal" because of their physical or cultural characteristics.[136] Andrea Gómez Cervantes describes the implicit association of a Latin person with undocumented immigration status as the "racialization of illegality," pointing out that Latin immigrants navigate this stereotype differently, depending on their ethnic identities and phenotypes.[137] People's physical characteristics are not the only facets of their identity that dictate their perceived illegality. English proficiency and accents are also heavily scrutinized and rouse discrimination, which we examine in the following chapter.

CHAPTER 4

IMMIGRANTS WANT TO, AND DO, LEARN THE LOCAL LANGUAGE

There are billions of bilingual and multilingual people globally, and one in five people over the age of five in the United States speaks a language other than English at home.[1] Multilingualism, especially bilingualism, is common in Europe, Africa, Asia, and other regions of the world. Nevertheless, in the United States some monolingual English speakers are unfamiliar with the challenges and rewards that come with mastering another language. English is the current lingua franca for business, science, popular culture, and the arts, and people of all nationalities often use it to communicate. It is considered an official language in an array of Caribbean, African, Polynesian, Mediterranean, and western European countries and is spoken fluently in many others across Scandinavia and Asia. It is a privilege when the common global language also happens to be your own native tongue since and it is unnecessary to learn a new language to interact in the international arena. If you speak English, you will probably have no problem ordering a coffee in Copenhagen, Berlin, Milan, Taipei, or Buenos Aires. But what is it like for non-English speakers, who do not have this advantage, and why do some Americans think immigrants refuse to learn English?

Immigrants in the United States are consistently criticized for speaking their native languages. Some native-born people in countries around the world go so far as to label immigrants as national security concerns if they cannot speak the dominant language.[2] While many immigrants learn how to speak the local language well, others struggle to learn due to various social, economic, and legal factors that influence their proficiency levels. In this chapter, we establish that immigrants *do* want to learn the local language. In doing so, we explore their incentives to learn by outlining existing evidence and contextualizing the postmigration adjustment process within important historical and sociocultural trends. In many places, current cultural environments and institutional practices negatively affect language learning, which in turn may adversely affect immigrants' mental health and physical well-being. We review various reasons why immigrants might struggle to learn or speak English, including broader trends that influence linguistic assimilation and structural barriers that migrants face when learning local languages. We close out the discussion by analyzing the impact of limited English proficiency on immigrant communities in the United States.

WHY MIGHT IMMIGRANTS NOT LEARN ENGLISH?

The United States is widely known as a hub of immigration. Often called a "melting pot," it appears inclusive because it is home to a diverse population. In some respects, this is true. In 2017, the U.S. foreign-born population surpassed 44.4 million residents, or 13.6 percent of the entire U.S. population, and included immigrants from nearly every country in the world.[3] Still, the quantitative data do not show the humans behind these numbers, along with the hardships they endure on their quest to integrate into mainstream American society. Language is a major element of integration and one of the most difficult shared obstacles. It is not unusual to feel embarrassed, nervous, or ashamed throughout the language-learning process, and people will opt to live in communities where they can communicate in their native tongue without experiencing anxiety or such negative emotions. However, those communities offer fewer opportunities to practice and pick up new English vocabulary.[4] Immigrant communities are important sources of protection, support, and cultural continuity where non-English-fluent immigrants can avoid discrimination, enjoy rich social lives, and build social networks in their native languages. These pockets of society, typically called immigrant enclaves, do not reflect any collective stubbornness or unwillingness to learn English.[5] Extensive research with different immigrant cohorts has revealed that structural factors rather than personal choices often shape immigrants' reasons for learning minimal English, if any at all.

In this chapter, we focus on Latin immigrants and the language barriers they experience. In the United States, Latin people make up the majority of the national immigrant population. In 2015, they constituted 63 percent of English language learners (ELLs), although Spanish-speaking immigrants tend to learn English at a lower rate than other immigrant groups.[6] Gender, sexual orientation, age, family relations, social connections, immigration status, and socioeconomic background all influence Latin immigrants' need and urgency to learn and retain English. Reading and writing proficiency in one's native language also matters, an important nuance often forgotten when considering immigrants' English abilities.[7] For example, those who cannot read and write in their native language are more likely to learn a new language more slowly than those who already have those skills. Some Latin immigrants with low levels of formal education worked as children or experienced a lack of opportunity in their countries of origin, thus compromising their early reading and writing comprehension in their native language.[8] Furthermore, some immigrants speak only Indigenous languages, such as Mixtec, Nahuatl, Quechua, or Ixil Mayan, and cannot communicate with monolingual English speakers *or* many Spanish speakers. The Latin diaspora is incredibly linguistically and culturally diverse.

A wide range of factors must be accounted for to understand why immigrants might not learn what is considered "enough" English. Someone's access to resources, like formal language classes, books, technology, and learning time, shapes how quickly and proficiently they might learn English. Ingrid Piller expands on this, describing how an immigrant's proficiency in a new language is predicted by "level of education, aptitude, [English] teaching program, language proximity or access to interactional opportunities."[9] It should also not be overlooked that language acquisition is a lifelong process that occurs mostly in early childhood and that language competence is an ever-fluctuating and conditional capability.[10] We typically do not master our native language until we are older. We are always learning new vocabulary and grammar, especially throughout childhood and adolescence. Even as adults, we are constantly gaining knowledge about different phrases, words, pronunciations, and dialects, so it is important to practice empathy, patience, and humility with people who are learning a new language later in life.[11]

The true value of the melting pot boils down to how open and welcoming U.S. society is to other people and cultures as well as the degree of "Americanization" that immigrants are expected to undergo. The United States has historically emphasized assimilation and pressured immigrants, oftentimes violently, to abandon their native cultural identities, languages, values, and practices for those of a White and western Europeanized society. This institutionalized exclusion of "non-American" identities only intensifies during periods of heightened nationalism and xenophobia and has previously warped government policies.[12] Throughout the 1990s, Congress voted on multiple amendments intended to ban the use of all languages except English in schools, government, and social services.[13] Those supporting the legislation wanted to force immigrants out of crucial political conversations by reducing their representation and making community resources more difficult to access. Lately, a shift has occurred, as seen through sentiments and policies that favor intercultural integration. Allowing immigrants to retain their cultures and languages while simultaneously gaining fluency in their host society's norms is becoming more conventional, although the prejudiced misconception that immigrants should become monolingual English speakers remains prevalent in the United States.

IMMIGRANTS DO STRIVE TO LEARN ENGLISH

There are native English speakers who fear that English is endangered by the strong linguistic presence of Spanish and other immigrant languages, which is not a novel sentiment. When a new immigrant group grows in numbers and visibility in any given place, native-born communities interpret the immigrant community's presence as a threat to their own cultural identity.[14] What gets lost in translation is that different cultures can thrive while near one another and that immigrants also strive to be part of the larger national community.[15]

Despite the difficulties and negative stereotypes imposed on them, in general immigrants *do* learn English. Moreover, they *want* to learn and put great effort into transitioning into American society and adopting local values because immigrants in the United States are typically aware that they will fare better economically and socially if they learn English.[16] An extensive 2015 report proved that a large portion of the foreign-born population already speaks English: 66 percent of immigrants who spoke their native language at home also spoke English well.[17] People also prepared themselves for the language shift before they migrated. About 38 percent of recently authorized immigrants had taken English classes before arriving in the United States, and almost all immigrants aimed to improve their knowledge of English before leaving their homes by looking through U.S. media products or newspapers.[18] Indeed, the utility of English has made it the most widely studied language in the world.[19] Present-day immigrants and their children are learning English more quickly than their predecessors. In 2013, 89 percent of U.S.-born Hispanics were proficient in English compared to 72 percent in 1980.[20] Non-English-speaking newcomers have more incentives to learn than previous generations, partially because of today's stringent requirements for high English proficiency in higher education and the job market. As Lucy Tse writes, "English fluency is a badge of prestige, a membership card for entry into the mainstream."[21] Speaking the dominant language is also advantageous because it helps families avoid social isolation, maintain financial stability, and communicate more easily with health care providers and schoolteachers.

Julie Dowling and colleagues interviewed a group of Mexican immigrants living in Texas and found that all, but especially the women, viewed English proficiency as extremely important. The authors describe how "English acquisition does not need to be forced by ballot initiates, legislation, or judicial rulings" because immigrants are already aware of the benefits of learning the local language.[22] Most immigrants arrive in the United States already believing that knowledge of English is required to succeed.[23] English proficiency opens new doors to economic success, community relations, cultural fluency, and the exchange of knowledge and information. It encourages integration and a sense of belonging so that people feel at peace with their postmigration transition. This general need to integrate and belong is also seen in immigrant communities in other English-speaking countries. For example, in Australia, improvements in their English skills have helped immigrants feel more confident and have positively affected their well-being.[24]

Because, or perhaps despite, the practical benefits of speaking English, bilingualism is common among Latin immigrants and their children. It was estimated in 2013 that nearly half of Latinos born in the United States were bilingual.[25] That same year about 56 percent of all people who spoke Spanish at home also spoke English "very well."[26] Patterns among third-generation individuals from immigrant families, however, are different: for numerous reasons, they often either lose or never gain the ability to speak their heritage language. Assimilation pressure, discrimination and bullying, and a lack of supportive multilingual education and public policy are important components in determining the language(s) that descendants of immigrants speak. Bilingual education is beneficial in this context because speaking more than one language has been proven to set people up for success in the economic, political, social, health, and educational arenas.[27] Being bilingual also benefits cognitive functions like verbal intelligence and cognitive flexibility and can even postpone the onset of certain symptoms of dementia.[28] Despite the benefits of multilingualism and bilingualism, many policymakers and education professionals in the United States rarely address or operationalize this vast field of research properly and are not interested in the survival of languages other than English.

IMMIGRANTS USED TO LEARN ENGLISH SLOWLY, IF AT ALL

Immigrants today are commonly accused of integrating more slowly and learning less English than immigrant groups that arrived in the United States in the past. Nevertheless, immigrants throughout history have rarely immediately abandoned their native language for English. Any unwillingness to relinquish one's native language is not a new phenomenon but a continuation of a historical trend. Language is a rich and important aspect of culture, and the right of minority groups to speak their own languages is guaranteed by provisions in international treaties, such as article 27 of the United Nations' International Covenant on Civil and Political Rights.[29] Western European immigrants who migrated in the nineteenth and twentieth centuries are currently glorified, which has led to the misconception that modern-day immigrants know less English. Immigrants with western and northern European origins who have resided in the United States for longer are referred to as "good" and "model" immigrants because they are thought to have immediately shed their cultural identities, abandoned their languages, embraced English, and succeeded in assimilating into American society. The reality is that for a long time, regional groups of German immigrants refrained from learning how to speak English.[30] Many who migrated in waves in the past were hesitant to let go of their native tongue, with German still being spoken in the home several generations after arriving in the United States. About thirty years after an upsurge in German immigrants, over 20 percent of those living in Wisconsin were still considered monolingual speakers of German.[31] Multilingualism lingered in these communities until World War I sparked anti-German sentiment and social pressures to prove their "American-ness" led them to stop speaking German.

Immigrants always take a while to master U.S. English.[32] It is easy for White Americans to reflect on earlier immigrants of western European descent and put them on a pedestal because fabricated stories about Germans' English abilities favor whiteness in a society that criminalizes nonwhiteness, especially among immigrants. Regardless of the similarities in their language learning trajectories, nonwhite immigrants are viewed as not being "ideal" because of their race or ethnicity, not because of their linguistic abilities.

FEWER NATIVE ENGLISH SPEAKERS ARE IMMIGRATING TO THE UNITED STATES

The U.S. Census Bureau issued a press release in 2014 that detailed rates of English proficiency among immigrants according to their country of origin and spoken language. At the time, about 44 percent of incoming immigrants spoke English "very well." In comparison, 13 percent spoke no English at all upon arrival. This information starkly contrasts with data on immigrants who arrived prior to 1980, when 63 percent of recent immigrants were proficient in English and only 6 percent spoke no English at all.[33] Some researchers might interpret these data as a downward trend in English learning until they consider immigrants' nations of origin.

Significantly fewer people from Canada, Germany, Jamaica, and the United Kingdom are migrating to the United States now compared to 1980. All four of these countries have high English fluency rates because English is either an official national language or one commonly spoken. Today, unlike in the 1980s, most immigrants are not coming from English-speaking regions. More are migrating to the United States from Venezuela, Nicaragua, Cuba, Mexico, Vietnam, China, and El Salvador.[34] Children raised in places where the general population is familiar with English tend to arrive with a better grasp of the language than those from countries where they were never exposed to it.[35] This discrepancy, and not immigrants' perceived inability or refusal to learn English, partially accounts for the shift in English proficiency among immigrants since that period.

THE CHALLENGES OF LEARNING ENGLISH

Wealth and Financial Barriers

Immigrants and refugees face unique hurdles during their English-language-learning journey. In addition to the natural difficulties of learning a new language, they might grapple with low income, employment discrimination, lack of educational access, few opportunities, cultural challenges, and questions about identity. Wealth and finances play an important role in determining an immigrant's access to English resources. Those who flee to the United States to seek asylum, especially those who make the journey northward from South and Central America, pay thousands of dollars for guidance to reach the border and are typically extorted along the way. They also run the risk of losing or being robbed of any precious belongings they have carried with them and may arrive at the border with little capital and few assets. Many depend on aid organizations to provide them with food, shelter, and care upon arrival.

University degrees, professional certificates, and years of career experience are often not considered with high regard, and sometimes not even formally recognized, by U.S. employers and institutions. Hence, immigrants have difficulty practicing in their fields of expertise until receiving U.S.-based training or education. Tutors and programs cost money, time, and effort, which must first be used to cover basic priorities like work, sleep, food, transportation, rent, childcare, and bills. Foreign-born people learn English at different rates, depending on their financial stability, responsibilities, and abilities to provide for their necessities.[36] Policymakers, politicians, and some of the American public demand that immigrants immediately learn English, but adequate support or infrastructure for ELLs is often lacking.

Gender Disparities

Across different ethnic groups, immigrant women in the United States tend to speak less English than their male counterparts. Somali and Hmong women living in Minnesota speak and read much less English than men, and the gender differences in English proficiency in the Mexican community are even wider than in other ethnic groups.[37] In one study, Mexican men spoke English at three times the rate of Mexican women, even though nearly half of the women had jobs that may have required English skills.[38] Older Korean women also speak less English than Korean men, which has been shown to negatively impact their health and restrict them when expressing their concerns to health care providers.[39]

Learning a new language can change one's sense of self within one's broader community, and this identity shift is often influenced by gender and related sociocultural norms.[40] For example, gender can predict English acquisition among adults in southern California's Latin immigrant communities. Men have more opportunities to learn English, as much of their work occurs outside the home and places them in situations where people speak English. In contrast, Latin immigrant women in southern California often work in their own homes or as domestic workers and housekeepers, occupations that do not typically require more than a basic knowledge of English nor provide many opportunities for language learning.[41]

Gender also impacts immigrants by way of traditional expectations and power structures. Some men feel threatened by women's English skills and frown on their choice to continue learning the language to a level of fluency if it is not immediately financially or socially necessary. Researchers have observed how many women would like to learn English but sometimes do not seek to advance their language skills because of gender norms, domestic pressures, fear of domestic violence, or the belief that it is too late for them to learn. Many mothers with roots in patriarchal cultures consider caring for the house and home to be their main job. Their work may be concentrated in spaces where their native language is spoken; therefore, they do not need to learn English as urgently as others in different fields. Also, given women's socially ascribed role as caretaker across cultures, an immigrant mother might feel more pressured than a father to preserve and transmit language and culture to the next generation. Separating themselves from the dominant English-speaking culture is also a way to maintain their cultural traditions.[42]

Age

It is well-known that immigrants who arrive in the United States at younger ages, especially as children, are more likely to become English proficient.[43] Linguists believe there may be many reasons for this, including how environmental factors and learning opportunities significantly affect adults' language learning. The notion of a "critical period" of age for optimal language acquisition, once widely accepted, is now greatly debated.[44] Nonetheless, age directly influences the success and speed with which immigrants learn English. At the turn of the twenty-first century, Minnesota experienced a rise in Hmong (predominantly from Laos), Russian Jewish, Somali, and Mexican immigrants. Using data from telephone interviews with nearly two thousand adults, Katherine Fennelly and

Nicole Palasz discovered that migrating at a young age was one of the best indicators of written and spoken English proficiency across all ethnic groups.[45] Likewise, non-English-speaking immigrants who arrive before the age of nine have a higher collective English proficiency than those who were older at their time of arrival.[46]

Socioeconomic Status and Access to Education Optimize English Proficiency Outcomes

Education is a central component of many immigrants' abilities to converse, read, and write in a second language. Highly educated immigrants are more likely to speak English well before and after migrating, providing a higher probability of obtaining better-paying jobs. The connection between education and occupation brings awareness of another layer of inequality regarding language learning. Around the world, people with college degrees generally make more money than those without them.[47] This is also true for U.S. immigrants in relation to English skills. ELLs have disproportionately lower incomes, have obtained less education, and work more dangerous, taxing, undesirable, or low-paying jobs than English speakers.[48] Limited English proficient (LEP) men typically work in the fields of construction, natural resources, agriculture, landscaping, maintenance, and food service, while LEP women often work in the service and care industries.[49] There are institutions like Skills and Opportunity for the New American Workforce and the Community College Consortium for Immigrant Education that help LEP immigrants develop their English and business communication skills.[50] The largest gap in the job market consists of middle-skill jobs that require more schooling than a high school degree but not necessarily a four-year college degree, and many immigrants fit the requirements if they become English proficient.[51]

Another facet of inequality is that low-income people have fewer educational opportunities because school is expensive. According to the Public Policy Institute of California, immigrants spend an equivalent of between $3,000 to $5,000 for English language classes in their home countries, online courses, or self-learning textbooks.[52] Immigrants from low-income regions and backgrounds speak less English upon and after arrival because of their socioeconomic status. Some native-born people fail to see that recent immigrants who are fluent or proficient in English have experienced privilege in some form or capacity that many others have not, which creates an imbalance in English proficiency levels. Researchers have seen these dynamics involving education, income, and English play out in distinct communities. In one study conducted in the Minneapolis–St. Paul area, having a college diploma was shown to be one of the best indicators of written and spoken English proficiency among four different immigrant groups from all over the world. Compared to immigrants who did not complete high school, immigrant college graduates were twenty-nine times more likely to speak English well and twenty times more likely to be proficient readers.[53] Similarly, in California older Latino and Asian immigrants who have significantly less formal education also speak limited English.[54]

In addition, the children of immigrants directly benefit from their family's education. Parents who have attended institutions of higher education and speak English are better able to help their children with homework, connect them to academic resources, and advocate for them. In a 2017 study, children of immigrant parents with a college degree performed better in school and adopted a new language more quickly than other students.[55] It is also likely that immigrant parents who speak English will expose their children to it, especially if they anticipate migrating to an English-speaking country, thus raising the likelihood of their children becoming fluent.[56]

Country of origin and class are also influential factors in people's abilities to speak, write, and read bilingually. In 2013, the Pew Research Center found that in the United States, Dominicans had the highest bilingualism rate (43 percent), while Mexicans had the lowest (34 percent).[57] This can be explained by socioeconomic background: on average, Dominican immigrants in the United States have middle-class incomes, while there are many Mexican immigrants who come from rural backgrounds with relatively little education compared to the greater U.S. population.[58] On the other hand, some immigrant groups receive more help in the form of federal and local government resources and programs than others. Well-settled and serviced refugees can integrate more quickly; for example, many of the Cubans who arrived after the Cuban Revolution were welcome, received papers and help. They took root in Miami and have fostered a multilingual environment to this day.[59] Also, well-serviced Somali refugees who resettled in the Minneapolis–St. Paul region reported extremely high rates of English proficiency after an average of seven years spent in the United States.[60] When immigrants and refugees are provided ample support and resources, they are successful in learning the local language.

In Immigrant Neighborhoods, English Is Not Always Necessary

Some immigrants initially opt to live in more isolated enclaves and operate most of their days in their local language, perhaps without learning much English.[61] First-generation immigrants tend to migrate to well-established immigrant communities where friends, family, or acquaintances from their hometowns might already live. Their preexisting social networks can be helpful in adjusting to U.S. culture and accessing the local job market, but they can also limit English exposure.[62] The social pressure to speak English is buffered when socializing mostly with Spanish speakers. A study by the Philadelphia Education Research Consortium found that kindergartners who spoke Spanish at home were more likely to fall behind in English development because they already had a way to communicate with family members and close friends. Similarly, several immigrants who moved from the Dominican Republic to the Washington Heights neighborhood in New York City, which is heavily Hispanic, did not feel the urgent need to learn English.[63] With such ease of communication, it is hard to justify spending money, time, and energy on the arduous language-learning process. Nonetheless, research on Chinatowns and ethnic enclaves shows that after arriving and spending some years in these neighborhoods most immigrants then leave to other more diverse neighborhoods.[64] So, ethnic enclaves are not the reason why some immigrants may have limited English even decades after living in the United States.

Immigrants Feel Afraid to Speak English with Native Speakers

In 1995, Bonny Norton Peirce conducted a study of immigrant women's experiences with learning English in Ontario, Canada. Students hailed from Peru, Czechoslovakia, Vietnam, and Poland and had a relatively high level of motivation to learn English, as they were originally part of an English as a second language (ESL) course that consisted of rigorous meetings and regular homework. All but one of the participants indicated that they felt comfortable speaking English to their friends, classmates, neighbors, and other immigrants. However, they all felt *uncomfortable* talking to people they considered to be of a higher status than they were, like bosses, customers, coworkers, teachers, doctors, and other fluent English speakers. The women said they fell silent and felt discouraged when people commented on their accents or when they did not know how to express certain words or phrases in English.[65]

Other immigrant groups have expressed the same fears. Older Russian immigrants are highly motivated to learn English, yet they still speak Russian with each other. They also crave independence, desiring to rely solely on themselves for English knowledge. Many older Russians go so far as to combine ESL classes with their own personal study of the language at home, yet they still feel ashamed for not having learned English in their youth and embarrassed in instances of miscommunication.[66] Even if immigrants are highly educated, motivated, and able, the acquisition of the English language is difficult because of the negative emotions associated with practicing their second language with fluent speakers. Experience with English typically increases as immigrants spend more time in the United States and establish community ties, although discrimination and bullying related to their heritage language and accents are a constant threat to their confidence, comfort, and feelings of safety.[67]

Linguistic Discrimination

Language discrimination creates barriers for immigrants who learn English and want to climb the employment ladder and secure high-paying jobs. Latin migrant workers living in North Carolina have recalled feeling powerless and discouraged when communicating with native English speakers because of their accents. Despite improving their English skills, they regard their accents as permanent hindrances to their ability to achieve professional mobility and get hired for the positions they want.[68] Some immigrants do not want to speak English with native speakers because their improper grammar or accent will expose and emphasize their foreign identity, and they may hesitate to socialize or talk on the phone with native English speakers. Accents can also cause misunderstandings between teachers and adolescent ESL students, making both feel uncomfortable.[69] Immigrant women in Canada who are motivated to learn and speak English say they have conflicting feelings because they are afraid of using the local language, yet they feel socially isolated and want to provide for their families. On occasion, these women avoid associating with Canadian-born people because in the past they have been disrespected, ignored, or made to feel uncomfortable by fluent English speakers.[70]

Up to 47 percent of Hispanic immigrants feel discriminated against because of their language abilities, which can deter them from practicing or learning further.[71] Older African immigrants have also described the negative turns that conversations take when U.S.-born Americans notice their accent. They are questioned about their ethnicity, stared at, laughed at, ignored, and considered less educated or qualified for a job. To avoid these types of upsetting and disrespectful interactions, some older Africans living in the United States avoid visiting places mostly occupied by native speakers or speaking with people they think might be prejudiced.[72] In this way, individual experiences with discrimination and xenophobia act as roadblocks that prevent immigrants from practicing and becoming more familiar with English.

No federal law designates English as the official language of the United States. Individual state governments, instead, have the power to institute their own official state languages, and English is now an official language—and usually *the* official language—in more than half of U.S. states.[73] In the past, some states have established English as the official language to convey a message of intolerance toward foreign-born communities. California's Republican governor Pete Wilson and conservative lawmakers pushed for the passage of Proposition 227 in 1998 to legally suppress bilingualism in classrooms in California.[74] While Republican presidential candidate Bob Dole was campaigning he proposed to formally adopt English as a national language. More recently, the governor of Iowa proposed the English Language Unity Act of 2019, which would have made English the official language of the United States.[75] There is no doubt that anti-immigrant sentiments have flourished since the 1990s, when a tidal wave of restrictive federal reforms cracked down on border entry and criminalized immigration. Since then, various presidential administrations have harbored and kept this malice toward immigrants alive. The Trump administration did so by enacting immigration laws that permitted entry to high-skilled, English-speaking immigrants while forcing thousands of Mexicans and Central and South Americans seeking asylum to wait in Mexico for months on end.[76]

Nationalist ideologies that seek to enforce an English-only cultural environment in the United States are heavily advocated for in the political arena and everyday life. The Pew Research Center surveyed two thousand people and found that 26 percent were bothered when speaking with immigrants who speak little to no English.[77] Negative attitudes toward languages other than English are also exhibited in after-school programs for immigrant children and adolescents. Two programs in San Francisco taught kids to "hold on to their roots" while ironically banning them from speaking any other language except English.[78] There have been reports that U.S. Immigration and Customs Enforcement agents patrol community-based education centers, libraries, and churches that offer English classes, which further prevents immigrants from taking advantage of English learning opportunities and leaves them feeling it is too unsafe to attend classes.[79] A xenophobic environment creates integration barriers for immigrants and is not conducive to English learning. The effectiveness of English-only policies is disproven by research showing that suppressing bilingualism hinders learning in the classroom because strength in one language helps in acquisition of a new one.[80]

Racism Affects Linguistic Perception

The difference between the narratives about "good" immigrants arriving in the 1800s and those about "bad" immigrants arriving today lies predominantly in race and ethnicity. The United States is more willing to accept White immigrants into the social fabric than immigrants of color and judges them less harshly. European immigrants in earlier migrations, while initially not considered White, came to be perceived as such over time.[81] White foreign-born people are regarded less often as outsiders than Latin, Asian, or Black immigrants because they fit the dominant racial/ethnic mold of Eurocentric U.S. culture. This perception also influences stereotypes about which immigrants do not speak English. "Foreign-looking" people—even fluent English speakers born in the United States—are often assumed not to speak English proficiently or at all, which systemically layers expectations about linguistic capability upon perceptions of physical appearance, exemplifying what Nelson Flores and Jonathan Rosa refer to as "raciolinguistic ideologies."[82] These attitudes permeate society, from individual interactions to powerful policies affecting crucial services such as education.[83]

In addition to being judged on their appearance, immigrants are assumed not to speak English based on their accents, even while many use English in their daily lives. This prejudiced perception is based on the misconception that in order to truly "speak a language," someone must do so exactly like an idealized native speaker. Linguistic repertoires are broad and flexible, and speakers use the range of languages at their disposal to communicate in any given context. It is common for multilinguals to bounce between languages, depending on those with whom they are conversing, and to use specialized vocabulary in different settings or situations. They can still communicate freely and get their point across without using "perfect" grammar. A good example of this is code-switching, or using more than one language in an interaction. While often criticized as "not speaking either language correctly," code-switching demands plenty of linguistic skill in both languages.[84] Bilingualism is traditionally viewed as a deficit instead of being celebrated, and this negative impression of bilingualism and multilingualism is racist. Latinos who were born in the United States and who are monolingual English speakers are often assumed not to speak English based on their physical appearances or last names.[85] When U.S. college students listened to the same recording of a standard American voice while being shown images of White and Asian faces, they reported that the "Asian speaker" had an accent and was difficult to understand, despite listening to the same voice throughout.[86] Meanwhile, second-generation immigrants face the same pressures and stereotypes with their heritage languages that they do with English and are criticized for not speaking their heritage language with native fluency.[87]

Prejudice Impairs the Language-Learning Environment

Immigrants experience a drastic language shock in a new country, and students endure this shock even more as they grapple with an unfamiliar school system and teaching methods, a new social scene, and exclusion and discrimination by peers and teachers.[88] Learning the dominant language is made even more difficult in classrooms where xenophobia and racism go unaddressed and may be explicitly overlooked by adults in charge. Students might not feel comfortable sharing ideas in English for fear that others will ridicule them for their accent or a linguistic mistake, not to mention the fact that the U.S. school system reinforces the misconception that ELLs are intellectually deficient because of their inability to speak the dominant language. As a result, these students are considered less capable and viewed as less academically engaged.[89]

There is also evidence that teachers are usually not adequately trained to work within a multicultural school context with children and parents of various racial, ethnic, and religious backgrounds.[90] Prejudices about immigrants or second language learners affect their abilities or efforts to assist children in ESL programs across education levels, and ELLs have also been physically abused for speaking Spanish in the classroom.[91] For teachers, an easy first step is to undergo the certification process for teaching ELLs, but a certification is not always a comprehensive solution.[92] At a structural level, preservice teacher trainings are unevenly distributed across states and regions in the United States and are generally not inclusive or comprehensive. Not only does this aspect of ESL education disadvantage ELLs, but it also further deepens learning disparities between all minority children and their White peers.[93] Successful second language learning occurs in a comfortable and welcoming environment where students are not penalized for using their mother language. If they feel safe to make mistakes and engage in conversation, then the learning process may also be seen as less of a burden and more of a collaborative journey involving ELLs, peers, and teachers.[94]

Lack of communication and understanding between adolescent social groups can breed negative stereotypes and drive even more space between young people of different backgrounds. Hispanic immigrant youth are perceived as an out-group, or "other," by White teenagers, who have been found to consider their Hispanic peers nearly invisible unless they are heard speaking Spanish because they notice the linguistic difference more than their other similarities. A study by Annette Daoud and Alice Quiocho documented that groups of White adolescent boys in a California high school felt annoyed and threatened by their Spanish-speaking peers.[95] This research finding speaks only to explicit hostility and negative behavior toward Spanish-speaking people. It does not account for implicit preferential treatment, like positive regard and friendliness, that people who consider themselves part of the same social group share almost exclusively with each other.[96] It also does not account for implicit bias built into high-stakes assessments and for misdiagnoses of Latin students as having special needs or lacking in language skills.[97] Someone who is not outwardly hostile to immigrants is not necessarily devoid of stereotypes about them and might never acknowledge their prejudice, which is why dispelling misconceptions about immigrants is so crucial in shifting the social narrative that schools and universities reflect. These social institutions are affected by public opinions and policies and generally echo the broader status quo into which immigrant students are expected to assimilate as quickly as possible.

IMMIGRANTS SACRIFICE THEIR NATIVE LANGUAGES, CULTURES, AND IDENTITIES TO LEARN ENGLISH

Throughout its history, the United States has advocated for the elimination of immigrant languages. Studies on acculturation show that learning English is often a "subtractive exchange," one that sacrifices the native language for English.[98] To be accepted into mainstream American culture and avoid harassment and exclusion, immigrants must relinquish core parts of their identities that "other" them.

Some immigrants give up their pursuit of English so that they can preserve their cultures but face backlash for that decision on multiple fronts. The United States is a "melting pot" not because of its sustained diversity but because of its erasure of native and immigrant identities, which are all boiled down into the same pale broth. In this way, English is more than just a tool for communication—it is a tool for proving your American-ness and your deservingness to live in the United States. Instead of continued English-language dominance, we advocate for fostering an intercultural environment that uplifts the country's rich quantity of immigrant cultures and languages. No need to worry; English is safe.

Generational, Cultural, and Linguistic Rifts

The vast majority of immigrant children in the United States pick up English as a substitute for their native language or as a valuable addition to their linguistic repertoire. Most second- and third-generation immigrants are either bilingual or monolingual English speakers. Although the likelihood of losing proficiency in a native language increases in a family with each child, grandchild, and great-grandchild,[99] there are practical and emotional benefits and advantages for bilingual children who maintain ties to their ethnic cultures. Older immigrants recognize that bilingualism can be a crucial bridge between younger generations of immigrants and their heritage culture and ethnic identity.[100] Still, when younger generations assimilate into the U.S. culture, the process can cause interpersonal and familial conflict. Younger generations' less-than-fluent heritage language speech might be seen as a rejection of their native culture rather than the natural product of their social and educational experiences.[101]

English fluency and regular use of English in both home and work settings increase with each generation, alongside the likelihood of native language loss. In 2002–2006, only 23 percent of first-generation immigrant adults reported English fluency, whereas 88 percent of second-generation individuals eighteen and older spoke English fluently.[102] Hispanic parents acknowledge the importance of learning English for a variety of socioeconomic reasons, sometimes prioritizing it over their heritage language. Still, some would like their children to retain their ability to speak their heritage language as a way of preserving their culture. In a 1986 report of a study she conducted, Grace Snipper described these views as a developing dichotomy: parents encouraged their kids to become "proficient enough in English not to be foreclosed from the economic reward system of the United States, but

The same process of English language acquisition is playing out in El Paso, where reading and speaking abilities among immigrants and their children varied greatly in our 2011–2012 survey. Among more than one thousand Hispanic respondents, the rate of monolingual Spanish use diminished with each generation of immigrant children while monolingual English use increased. People who had recently moved to the United States, like first-generation immigrants, tended to prefer speaking Spanish, whereas DREAMers, who moved to the country as children, either had better Spanish-speaking skills or spoke both English and Spanish fluently. Subsequently, a major shift occurred with second-generation immigrants, who were the most likely among all the generations to be bilingual and who had a 3 percent higher likelihood of speaking only English. This pattern in English use continued while bilingualism tapered off, with about one-quarter of later generations being bilingual.

Table 4.1, which details the main language spoken by respondents growing up, shows that 56.5 percent of them spoke at least some English growing up. Table 4.2 outlines the self-reported language use at the time of the interview by immigrant generation. Given El Paso's location and demographics, many people remain bilingual as they grow older, but their children's experiences are different. While many third-generation immigrants retain some conversational Spanish, more than half of them cannot read in Spanish (table 4.3). As table 4.4 shows, English-language television was preferred across generations by those who watch television.

TABLE 4.1 Which language(s) did you speak as a child or teenager?

Only Spanish	43.1%
Spanish more than English	19.7%
Spanish and English equally	16.3%
English more than Spanish	10.5%
Only English	10.0%

TABLE 4.2 Which language do you speak the most?

	Overall	First	1.5	Second	Third	>Third
Only Spanish	15.4%	46.5%	16.3%	4.7%	0.9%	2.7%
Spanish more than English	20.9 %	36.1%	34.0%	10.9%	7.8%	2.7%
Spanish and English equally	32.4%	15.0%	37.2%	46.5%	24.1%	22.7%
English more than Spanish	25.1%	1.2%	12.1%	33.2%	49.1%	50.7%
Only English	5.7%	0%	0.5%	3.5%	18.1%	21.3%

$p < 0.001$

(continued on next page)

(continued from previous page)

TABLE 4.3 Language people read in according to immigrant generation

	Overall	First	1.5	Second	Third	>Third
Only Spanish	15.6%	44.9%	16.8%	5.9%	1.7%	2.7%
Spanish more than English	10.4%	23.0%	17.7%	3.1%	1.7%	0%
Spanish and English equally	27.8%	22.4%	36.2%	33.6%	15.4%	16.0%
English more than Spanish	26.4%	7.9%	20.9%	37.1%	37.6%	28.0%
Only English	19.5%	1.8%	7.5%	20.3%	43.6%	53.3%

$p < 0.001$

TABLE 4.4 What kind of TV do you watch?

English	40.9%
English and Spanish	38.9%
Spanish	15.0%
Do not watch TV	3.9%

not assume the cultural aspects which would make them less Hispanic and more American."[103] They viewed the retention of Spanish as integral to their culture.

Prioritizing English to Achieve the American Dream

Immigrant parents understand that English fluency is essential to their children's success, so they often prioritize English over their native language and encourage their children to learn it as a vehicle for academic success and social mobility.[104] Parents and guardians also feel pressured to assimilate, internalizing English hegemony and colonial dominance as a survival tool.[105] This implicit message of linguistic hierarchy in the United States causes children to detach from their native culture. Many families abandon their heritage language at home, while others struggle to keep it alive. Furthermore, an English-only focus assumes that language learning is an either-or proposition, implying that heritage languages impede English language learning and cannot exist in the same space as the dominant language. This subliminal message is often reinforced by schools and institutions, with teachers and other experts erroneously conveying the idea that speaking their mother tongue will prevent children from successfully learning English.

Studying a second language does not necessarily mean that a person will lose their first language. Heritage language death occurs only in places where diversity is unwelcome.[106] Parents, families, and communities play an important role in children's and adolescents' propensities to abandon their native language, as they have a lower likelihood of doing so if strong cultural norms and family cohesion are present.[107] Social, economic, and political spheres that support diversity can encourage bilingualism and heritage language maintenance. However, bilingual and multilingual children often speak less of their native language or lose their native language fluency upon starting school in the United States. The younger they are, the more likely this loss will happen if bilingualism is not encouraged at home or in the classroom.[108] Because of the Eurocentric beliefs in U.S. institutions, it is common for second-generation immigrant students to feel like they belong at school only when they speak English or are learning to do so. Schools are also actively set up to promote English at the expense of heritage languages, including in ESL programs.

Immigrant children are influenced by outside and social pressures in addition to the cultural languages that their families speak and promote at home. Young people recognize that to fit into mainstream American society, they must alter their behavior or identity, including their linguistic identity. Lily Wong Fillmore, a linguist and professor emerita at the University of California at Berkeley, elaborates on the social exclusion of immigrant children:

> Language-minority children are aware that they are different the moment they step out of their homes and into the world of school. They do not even have to step out of the house. They have only to turn on the television and they can see that they are different in language, appearance, and behavior, and they come to regard these differences as undesirable. They discover quickly that if they are to participate in the world outside the home, something has to change.[109]

Even in bilingual classes, children recognize the institutional focus on English and gradually stop using their first language. This has present and future impacts on their personal and family lives. When a child breaks away from their native language, they also separate themselves from an essential method of communication with parents, grandparents, and other relatives. The loss of their heritage language can lead to a lack of intimacy in families and the disappearance of shared values between parents and children. Still, a child's "choice" to stop speaking their first language is not purely a question of individual agency because it takes place within the same hegemonic matrix of assimilation that their parents face, which prioritizes English at the expense of their home cultures and languages. In other words, prioritizing English is more of a rule than a choice.

Tseng found that discourses on individual agency that place the responsibility for heritage language maintenance on later-generation youth, without taking external systemic circumstances into account, can seriously undermine ethnic identity by branding them as "inauthentic" to their culture.[110] For example, immigrants from eastern Europe living in the United States struggle to maintain the native languages that help them keep in touch with relatives across the Atlantic. When children lose their heritage language in exchange for English, parents try to reawaken it by visiting their home countries and reaching out to family more often. These interactions and learning processes are limited, however, because the children are steeped in American culture outside their home.[111] This phenomenon applies to other immigrant groups as well. The share of Latinos who spoke Spanish at home decreased by 5 percent between 2000 and 2013, coinciding with rising numbers of U.S.-born Hispanics as a share of the country's Hispanic population. Rates of inward migration from Latin America also slowed during this time.[112] If fewer monolingual Spanish speakers are arriving in the United States and the children of Hispanic immigrants are speaking less Spanish, many families are losing their connections to their heritage language at once.

The Fight to Maintain and Celebrate Multilingualism

An effective and popular way to combat heritage language death is to promote bilingualism, which is a natural outcome of multiculturalism and migration and preferable to heritage language loss.[113] It is estimated that about 29 percent of immigrant Latinos and 49 percent of U.S.-born Latinos are bilingual.[114] Native language retention patterns vary greatly according to immigrants' ethnic communities. For instance, second-generation Iranians generally speak and understand Persian well and use it to communicate with family and Iranian friends, and yet their parents rarely expose them to reading materials in Persian.[115] An acculturative shift and a loss of heritage language fluency have been documented among young Malaysians, Vietnamese, Chinese, Filipinos, and other Asian Americans. In one U.S. community with 61 percent foreign-born Asian American students, only 21 percent spoke their native language better than English.[116]

Homes and communities are primary sites of minority language maintenance. It is not criminal or un-American for immigrants to prefer speaking their native tongue, especially at home, where they can communicate quickly clearly and teach their children.[117] In fact, this helps children and young adults by enabling communication with older generations, improving cognitive abilities, and creating more employment opportunities in the future. Saturday or Sunday schools and summer camps that encourage the speaking of heritage languages and cultural study are among the community spaces that tend to be sites of language maintenance. Community organizations, cultural centers, and places of worship similarly provide safe spaces where immigrants can gather, speak, and pass down their native languages and preserve their cultures.[118]

Bilingualism Yields New Dialects of English

There are hundreds of English dialects that are spoken around the world in India, South Africa, Ireland, Jamaica, and beyond. Among the most spoken dialects are North American, Australian, and British English, all of which are distinct. New English dialects are born from bilingual communities and add to the richness of the larger linguistic community.[119] Dialects such as African American Vernacular English and Latino English are complex linguistic systems with rich histories and cultural associations that are often misunderstood and judged as "incorrect" English, since they do not follow all the linguistic norms related to traditionally White dialects of English. The forms of Latino English spoken in areas of California, Texas, New York City, Miami, and Washington, D.C., have roots in Spanish-English bilingualism and have evolved into English dialects that are transmitted and spoken even by Latinos who do not speak Spanish.[120] For example, the English spoken by second-generation Hispanic immigrants in Washington, D.C., combines Spanish-influenced features with local African American Vernacular English.[121] These dialects are intimately linked to a sense of local Hispanic identity, though their speakers are judged negatively based on race and class stereotypes.[122]

LANGUAGE LEARNING IN EDUCATIONAL SPHERES

Barriers to Attending ESL Classes

One writer once compared the postmigration experience to "having a massive stroke, only instead of being sent to the hospital and getting help you have to go out and get a job."[123] Culturally competent and affordable language integration services are few and far between in the United States, and getting access to ESL programs is more complex than simply locating a school. Immigrants must first have the time and resources to attend classes even before determining whether the quality of the education is worthwhile and whether they can balance school with work and family responsibilities.[124] A young working mother seeking to take English courses needs to anticipate the cost of attendance, books, reliable childcare, and a stable mode of transportation as well as the effect on work-life balance. These factors might lead that mother to make the potentially economically sound decision to forgo ESL classes altogether to ensure that her family's short-term needs are met.

The good news is that more children and adolescents are involved in ESL programs now than ever before. The National Center for Education Statistics has published the policies outlined in the U.S. educational system for children learning English as nonnative speakers. These children are expected to enroll in language assistance programs, and many do: the percentage of ELLs enrolled in U.S. public schools increased from 8.1 percent (3.8 million students) in fall 2000 to 10.2 percent (5 million students) in 2018.[125] These rising numbers suggest an increase in the amount of students needing this support but also that the nation's educational systems are able and can be prepared to meet immigrant children's needs.

Dual-Language Immersion Model

ESL is not the only model of English language education. It is a transitional model that prioritizes learning English at the expense of heritage languages rather than supporting bilingual and multilingual development.[126] Dual-language immersion is an alternate model that seeks to address ESL needs while maintaining heritage languages and providing enrichment for students. In this model, students who speak Spanish (or another language) and English speakers attend classes in both languages in an immersion environment. This model provides more equitable education that promotes bilingualism and biliteracy, and its recent growth in popularity attests to the country's growing interest in diversity and multilingualism, particularly in light of the economic potential of multilingualism in the labor market. Nevertheless, dual-language immersion programs are neither perfect nor free from systemic inequality, as race and class privileges can manifest.[127] Guadalupe Valdés has warned that Latin children could become "resources" for the enrichment of middle-class White children, increasing the potential of the latter and not the former, and that dual-language immersion programs could center around the experiences of English speakers, much like ESL.[128]

Cross-Cultural Communication Between Parents and Teachers

Non-English-proficient parents are sometimes thought to be uninterested in their children's education if they do not attend parent-teacher conferences or school events. The truth is much more complex: they are often unable to be as involved as they wish and might be constrained by a strict work schedule or language barriers. Cultural beliefs about parents' roles in education and teacher-parent relationships also get lost in translation and are mistaken for general aloofness. Although some school districts distribute information in multiple languages, parents struggle to communicate with teachers. Some parents even avoid their children's school events because interpreters are not provided. Non-English-speaking parents rely on their children to act as translators at parent-teacher conferences, even though these students may not be entirely proficient in English themselves or may avoid conveying information about behavioral or academic problems to stay out of trouble with their caretakers.

Yan Guo has identified some simple and effective strategies for reducing these divides and incorporating parents of ESL students into school programs. Schools should provide interpreters for immigrant children and parents or employ bilingual staff to serve as intermediaries. Immigrant families also might feel more welcome to participate in their children's education if schools organized parents' nights with the help of interpreters or staff. Guo additionally recommends that teachers attend trainings to increase their sensitivity to the educational practices of different cultures and facilitate cross-cultural communication with ELL parents and students.[129]

California Proposition 227 and Segregated Schooling

Education occurs within the broader U.S. political landscape and is directly affected by public policy. In 2011, 37.6 million people communicated in Spanish at home; they constituted just about 66 percent of all speakers of languages other than English in the United States.[130] In regions with large populations of Hispanic migrants, like California and Arizona, prohibitive language strategies and policies historically allowed for schooling only in English. This made it almost impossible for immigrant Latino children to learn effectively. School districts in the Southwest addressed this issue by isolating ELL children in separate schools. The reasons given for this by and large fell into two categories: the practice was thought to be beneficial for these children because they could learn English and adjust to American culture in classes devoted exclusively to them, and it solved a problem for non-Hispanic children who were irritated by and prejudiced against their Latin peers. Language policies in these schools were eerily akin to those of boarding schools for kidnapped Native American children, where they were forcibly kept and "Americanized" in abusive and deadly environments. Similarly, in ELL-only schools, "Mexican-origin students were educated in English only, often being punished for the use of their home language."[131] In 1951, linguistically segregated education was ruled unconstitutional. The U.S. District Court of Arizona banned the separation of predominantly Mexican American ELL children and their White counterparts in the *Gonzales v. Sheely* case.[132]

The passage of the Bilingual Education Act of 1968 was another signal of positive change. In introducing the legislation in Congress, Texas Senator Ralph Yarbrough formally acknowledged the pressing language needs of immigrants, but implementation of the act resulted only in minor funding for some trial ESL teaching programs. In 1974, the U.S. Supreme Court issued a major court ruling on education for ELLs in the *Lau v. Nichols* case. The justices decided that providing ELLs with an English-only education violated the Civil Rights Act of 1964 because it negatively affected their ability to learn.[133] However, in the 1990s, not long after the educational improvements required by the *Lau* ruling went into effect, efforts arose to again segregate ELLs.

Proposition 227, which won the support of a majority of California voters in 1998, effectively eliminated most bilingual education across the state until 2016. It ensured that *all* students were learning in an English-speaking setting and that ELLs could receive only up to one year of bilingual instruction.[134] At the same time, the schools separated ELL and non-ELL children. ELL students remained in separate classrooms from their English-speaking peers but were not permitted to learn in their native language.[135] Proposition 227 became law amid a wave of proposed anti-immigrant policies: Proposition 187 limited public benefits like health care and public education for undocumented immigrants, and Proposition 209 ended the practice of affirmative action across institutions of higher education in California. At that time, over 25 percent of Californians were immigrants, and around 33 percent of Californian schoolchildren spoke a language other than English outside of the classroom.[136] Proposition 227 was rescinded in 2016, although there have been residual effects. Among other things, it was discovered that school districts' efforts to communicate with parents about educational objectives, curriculum changes, and other basic educational concerns were lackluster and relied heavily on the children to relay information between parents and teachers rather than communicating directly through formal and informal channels in other languages. Furthermore, despite the favorable ruling in the *Gonzales v. Sheely* case that ruled educational segregation in Arizona unconstitutional, Spanish-speaking students in Arizona frequently attend residentially segregated schools with poorer educational systems, little support from tax dollars, and fewer resources.[137]

PSYCHOLOGICAL AND PHYSICAL IMPACTS OF LIMITED ENGLISH PROFICIENCY

Speaking English may not be required in all employment and home settings, but communication between patients and health care providers *is* essential. It is becoming more common for researchers to consider limited English proficiency to be a risk factor for poor physical and mental health because language barriers impact an immigrant's access to quality health care. Older Latino and Asian immigrants who speak little English frequently do not have health insurance and are more likely to be disabled, suffer from type 2 diabetes, and display symptoms of mental disorders than immigrants who are proficient or fluent in English.[138] This may partially be a result of their difficulty in understanding doctors, deciphering the medical information available at doctors' offices, and reading instructions in English on prescription bottles. They might also feel less inclined to seek regular health care because of the language barrier and anticipated miscommunication, and so experience worse health outcomes. Avoiding care altogether is dangerous, as it can lead to the manifestation and aggravation of illnesses or pains that have gone untreated. English is a major advantage in some contexts and a necessity in others, something immigrants are fully aware of and must grapple with throughout their postmigration experience in the United States.

It should also be highlighted that migration- and acculturation-related stressors wreak havoc on immigrants' health. In 2013, African adults with limited English proficiency reported that their health worsened upon arriving in the United States because of higher stress levels and language barriers. Their rates of stress-based illnesses, like heart disease, even increased postmigration.[139] In fact, the entire integration process is a significant source of stress. Experiencing discrimination, being unable to communicate, having to learn a new language, and even not understanding road signs can cause disproportionate psychological distress. Immigrants with limited English proficiency constantly report higher rates of loneliness, social isolation, depression, and general frustration than U.S.-born people.[140] A 2019 study found that Korean immigrants who were more "separated" from U.S. society felt much more stressed and depressed.[141] Such feelings can potentially have long-term negative effects on immigrants' mental and physical health, while developing better English skills can bring some relief. Bilingualism and biculturalism offer a range of practical benefits that protect against health-damaging stress. Many second-generation immigrants who are bilingual and bicultural can navigate the different demands of both their family's heritage culture and the broader U.S. culture.[142] Bicultural second-generation immigrants exhibit better psychological health, closer family relations, and higher self-esteem than monocultural second-generation immigrants. This is also true for foreign-born adults and children of many different Asian, Hispanic, and Black diasporas.[143] Being able to communicate fluently with people in multiple cultural contexts improves your well-being.

CONCLUSION

The United States has always been multilingual. Even before colonization, the land was home to hundreds of Indigenous languages, and both European colonists and enslaved Africans later arrived speaking languages of their own. Spanish was spoken before English in the Southwest and Florida, which were colonized by Spain.[144] Before the French and Indian War and the so-called Louisiana Purchase, the French controlled a large part of what is now U.S. territory, and many people there spoke French. The French colonists forced out of what is now Canada by the British resettled in Louisiana and are referred to as Cajuns.[145]

Despite the country's multilingual history, the pressure to learn English weighs heavily on immigrants. Becoming proficient in a second language is not easy, and it is rarely a lack of interest that prevents immigrants from doing so. The process can take anywhere from two to ten years, depending on the learner's resources, ability, exposure, motivations, and goals. The accumulated adjustment stressors of finding employment, establishing a social network, getting health insurance and health care, enrolling children in school, and paying expenses are compounded by worries regarding English education. The combination of factors can become too much for individuals to balance, forcing them to prioritize their immediate well-being over long-term goals. Immigrants' difficulties are not self-imposed but rather the result of systemic obstacles that go unacknowledged. Nationalistic English-only discourses vilify and suppress sociolinguistic diversity. This way of understanding language, integration, and belonging is a form of cultural dispossession that negatively impacts multiple aspects of immigrants' lives and those of their children. They should not be expected to erase their home identities and assimilate into U.S. culture for the sake of White America's comfort and xenophobic traditions.

In the end, immigrants may not learn English for many different reasons. Further, some may speak English and still be judged to be nonproficient because they "look foreign," have an accent, or speak at a slower pace than a native-born speaker. The myth that immigrants do not want to learn English disregards the nuances of postmigration integration processes and reduces their learning outcomes to individual effort alone. Accepting it as true reinforces a culture of victim blaming, opens the door to discrimination, and worsens immigrants' fears and insecurities about integration.

CHAPTER 5

IMMIGRANTS DO NOT DEPEND ON WELFARE PROGRAMS MORE THAN NATIVE-BORN PEOPLE

Immigrants have been portrayed as disproportionate burdens on social assistance programs for centuries. Some people, including politicians, believe that their access to welfare programs should be limited in order to reserve these benefits for struggling native-born citizens.[1] Despite the ubiquity in mainstream media of the belief that immigrants exhaust welfare resources, the data on this topic show that immigrants have access to fewer types of public benefits and less financial aid.

One of the most recent consequences of this misconception was an income test instituted by the Trump administration that required immigrants to prove that they had "sufficient" expected income to enter the country.[2] People who qualified for green cards were barred from joining their families and spouses in the United States if they did not earn enough money annually because they were considered to be too much of a financial burden to U.S.-born taxpayers, or a *public charge*.[3] This Trump administration rule also reevaluated welfare assistance and rescinded it, in some cases, for couples making at least $20,575 per year.[4] Enforcement of the income test was temporarily blocked by a federal judge halfway through 2020 and then dropped completely by the Biden administration in early 2021.[5] The RAISE Act, which was rejected in 2017, was another failed attempt aiming to erect legal walls and block "undesirable" immigrants.[6] President Donald Trump argued that under the act, "they're not going to come in and just immediately go and collect welfare."[7] It was later uncovered that inaccurate research and misconstrued findings were used to justify the government's reasoning for such hostile regulations. Anthony Cave of the Center for Law and Social Policy noticed a false statistic in a press release regarding the RAISE Act that was issued by the Trump White House. To support its claim that over

50 percent of immigrants were on welfare, the release referenced data from a 2015 report published by an anti-immigrant lobbying group. Cave's analysis revealed that the bill and its sources had repeated caveats and bad-faith data issues, like an inaccurate definition of *welfare* that included individuals who did not receive welfare assistance but who had qualified for programs like free school lunches.[8] Then, shortly after the bill failed to receive a vote in the Senate, Trump staffers claimed that 55 percent of immigrants were on welfare. Again, they were wrong: the percentage they referred to applied to all households with an immigrant, meaning that U.S.-born children living in poverty were counted as foreign-born people under this framing.[9]

In this chapter, we demonstrate that immigrants place a lighter burden on most social services than their native-born counterparts after accounting for demographic and socioeconomic factors. We begin by contextualizing important trends in U.S. history as well as contemporary differences between immigrant groups and their use of welfare in relation to linguistic, legal, and economic advantages. We provide an outline of federal stipulations that dictate immigrants' access to social services, and building on this, we review the legal and social barriers that influence welfare use, including the Personal Responsibility and Work Opportunity Reconciliation Act, the public charge rule, and racial and ethnic stereotypes. We also explore the impacts that legal and social obstacles to public benefits have on immigrants' lives and follow this analysis with a discussion of immigrant welfare use in the European Union, Ireland, the United Kingdom, Sweden, Australia, and Denmark.

A BRIEF TIMELINE OF THE WELFARE MYTH

The debate regarding immigrants and their perceived strain on the welfare state began well over a century ago. In the late 1880s, many Americans of northern and western European ancestry regarded eastern European Jews and Italian immigrants as inferior and unable to integrate, and in 1924, the United States set quotas to curtail their arrival to the country.[10] This welfare myth has resurfaced repeatedly and has been refuted each time, including when it came back in the 1980s.[11] Studies conducted during that time agreed that immigrant families depended less on welfare than U.S.-born families of the same socioeconomic background. A National Bureau of Economic Research report from 1991 backed up its findings with evidence that only 16 percent of households on welfare at the time were immigrant households.[12] Rising welfare rates nevertheless spurred renewed paranoia about noncitizens' use of government aid. At that time, refugees and immigrants alike were entitled to Supplemental Security Income (SSI) and Aid to Families with Dependent Children (AFDC). Like today, refugees qualified almost immediately for public services;[13] however, immigrants became eligible only after three years of U.S. residence. Before welfare reform in 1996, immigrants were thought to cost the welfare state more than the native-born population, but studies supporting that conclusion conveniently bypassed the need to account for socioeconomic and demographic variables in their research.[14] Their comparisons were misleading and successful in fanning the fires that destroyed many immigrants' access to government aid.

THE U.S. WELFARE SYSTEM: MANY MOVING PARTS AND ELIGIBILITY REQUIREMENTS

Some newcomers integrate into the local job market more quickly than others because they have a leg up in terms of language, citizenship, and familiarity with the dominant culture. People hailing from U.S. territories like Guam, Puerto Rico, and the Virgin Islands receive a larger share of government services than all other immigrant groups, likely because they are considered U.S. citizens under the law and do not confront the same obstacles that other immigrants do in terms of legality and citizenship in the mainland United States.[15] Still, these protectorates are modern-day colonies where citizens are afforded limited government representation and fewer economic opportunities.[16] On the other hand, immigrants from Asia, Africa, and Central America access moderate amounts of welfare, whereas those from Australia, New Zealand, and Canada use the least because their home countries are high-income and English-speaking. Their English proficiency and financial stability increase access to occupations that pay high wages and offer health benefits. Citizenship brings similar benefits: after becoming naturalized citizens, immigrants from nearly all places in the world rely less on welfare payments except for Central and South Americans, who are likely to stay in underpaid jobs.[17] The status of U.S. citizen yields more fruitful employment and educational opportunities for immigrants. They become eligible for government jobs and, on occasion, lower tax payments as well as federal grants and scholarships needed to pursue higher education.

Since 1996, the federal government has relied on certain criteria that render an immigrant "qualified" or "unqualified" for welfare programs. Certain documented migrants—including lawful permanent residents, refugees, those granted asylum or parole for at least a year, Cuban and Haitian entrants, certain abused immigrants and their families, and survivors of human trafficking—had previously been granted the chance to qualify for welfare rights similar to those of local citizens.[18] However, reforms in 1996 changed this aspect of social services, and these immigrants no longer have equal access to welfare.[19] Children of immigrant parents born in the United States are citizens and remain eligible for benefits.[20] In contrast, all other noncitizens, including temporary visa holders and the undocumented, have always been ineligible for most federal benefits programs.[21] Undocumented people, along with DREAMers, H-1B workers, and other temporary workers, do not qualify for many federal public benefits, including SSI, Medicaid, Medicare, and food stamps. Their eligibility is limited to some emergency hospital visits and the Special Supplemental Nutrition Program for Women, Infants, and Children (WIC).[22] Mexicans, Central Americans, and Asians are most affected by federal bars on welfare, as they make up the largest undocumented populations in the United States.[23] Hispanics without immigration papers experience the most difficulties obtaining health care and make annual physician visits at very low rates.[24]

Today, immigrants can qualify for very few federal welfare programs, but many states have implemented their own programs to fill gaps in federal coverage. For instance, although undocumented immigrants do not have access to the Patient Protection and Affordable Care Act (ACA), also known as Obamacare, individual states have authority to provide health care.[25] Next, we break down how and why new constraints on immigrants' welfare use unfolded at the turn of the twenty-first century.

LEGAL BARRIERS TO WELFARE ACCESS FOR IMMIGRANTS

The Personal Responsibility and Work Opportunity Reconciliation Act

Provisions On August 22, 1996, President Bill Clinton signed the Personal Responsibility and Work Opportunity Reconciliation Act (PRWORA), which entirely changed how immigrants receive social benefits in the United States.[26] The act was part of a wave of anti-immigrant and border control policies that took the country by storm in the mid-1990s, altering almost all of noncitizens' qualifications for welfare eligibility and restricting their access to benefits programs. Lawmakers had become intimidated by a quick increase in program applications and sought ways to block immigrants, especially those who were undocumented, from being eligible.

A reduction in those eligible for program benefits occurred almost instantly. Immigrant families with legal status who arrived after August 22, 1996, had their eligibility for nutrition, health, and cash assistance services either temporarily or permanently revoked.[27] PRWORA hit immigrants the hardest in the health care and nutritional arenas. Medicaid, the National School Lunch Program, and the Supplemental Nutrition Assistance Program (SNAP), formerly known as the Food Stamp Program, were the three welfare programs most commonly used by noncitizens before the 1996 reforms cut them out of immigrants' safety nets.[28] Through PRWORA, authorized noncitizens were prohibited from receiving Temporary Assistance for Needy Families (TANF), SSI, and Medicaid, as well as from participating in the Children's Health Insurance Program (CHIP) until they had lived in the United States as lawful permanent residents for five years.[29] They were also barred from accessing SNAP benefits until they became naturalized citizens.[30] Only those who had worked in the country for at least ten years, who had been given asylum status, or who were serving in the U.S. military retained eligibility.[31] PRWORA was sold to the public as a way to promote immigrant self-sufficiency, a justification that does not align with the true intentions behind the act, since refugees, people with disabilities, and the elderly were previously the primary recipients of benefits.[32] The real motive was financial: cutting welfare spending on noncitizens would return $23.8 billion to the federal budget for other uses.[33] An estimated 44 percent of the savings generated by the reforms would come from reduced assistance to immigrants alone.[34]

PRWORA also killed two birds with one stone, as undocumented immigrants now had no legal pathway to welfare. Supporters of the act insisted that undocumented people chose not to pursue legal citizenship or residency and therefore did not want to participate fully in U.S. society. They claimed that immigrants came to the United States for free social benefits and exploited government aid by collecting support for their U.S.-born children. Consequently, members of Congress on both sides of the aisle profoundly agreed that noncitizens should not be entitled to welfare. Some believed immigrants did not hold "American" values, like independence, freedom, self-sufficiency, and hard work, and because of this, they were considered unworthy of federal and state aid.[35]

Since that time, a few previously banned programs have reopened to immigrants. Two consecutive laws reestablished some eligibility: The Balanced Budget Act of 1997 ordered that SSI and Medicaid be restored to authorized immigrants who had them before PRWORA passed. The Agriculture Research, Extension, and Education Reform Act of 1998 also renewed SNAP eligibility for minors, people with disabilities, and elderly immigrants who were receiving assistance before the 1996 reforms.[36] Then the 2002 Farm Security and Rural Investment Act reestablished food stamp programs for nearly two-thirds of immigrants who had lost eligibility.[37] Some in-kind benefits, like the National School Lunch Program, were made available to everyone regardless of immigration status.[38] In 2020, policies implemented to alleviate the socioeconomic damage of the COVID-19 pandemic also resulted in the expansion of school lunch programs and other benefits, making them practically universal to protect public health and reduce child poverty.

Long-Term Impacts PRWORA is upheld to this day and has had palpable, lasting effects. According to a 2016 study, an estimated 19 percent of Mexican immigrant families who suffered from food insecurity were not receiving nutrition benefits.[39] This adds to the list of immigrant integration and support programs that are underfunded and overlooked by the federal government, like accessible English language classes for both children and adults.

Barring immigrants from most federal social services shifted the federal government's responsibility to provide aid for immigrant communities to state and local governments. Now many states' social service nets have their own distinct eligibility criteria for authorized and undocumented immigrants categorized as working-age adults, elderly people, children, and refugees.[40] Some states even choose to bypass the five-year federal bar on benefits for immigrants to provide them sooner.[41] The allocation of control of welfare services to state governments also came with significant pressure to fulfill certain goals. For example, states had to enroll all single- and two-parent families receiving assistance in work participation programs. This change left an exposed loophole: programs that allocate state-sourced funds as opposed to federally sourced funds can have looser restrictions. States have the discretion "to design their own eligibility application forms, web portals, outreach materials, and language services," which are all crucial elements in making welfare accessible. These "loophole" methods sometimes provide routes of access that do not explicitly require citizenship.[42]

PRWORA impacted the lives of tens of thousands of people living in the United States and established strict guidelines for those just arriving. The proportion of naturalized citizens jumped from 40 percent to 45 percent nearly one year after it was enacted because immigrants were scrambling to keep their eligibility.[43] PRWORA enforced drastic adjustments in the social security net, increased the destitution rate, and pushed previous beneficiaries into low-paying employment. However, it failed to do what it initially aimed to do, which was to push unauthorized and low-income immigrants out of the country and deincentivize others from arriving. Because of these reforms, however, whether one is labeled by the government as an undocumented migrant, a refugee, a lawful permanent resident, or a citizen is critical to their economic well-being.

The Public Charge Rule

What the Rule Means for Immigrants On February 24, 2020, the Trump administration began enforcing an expanded version of the public charge rule, which first appeared in the Immigration Act of 1882. Unlike the previous rule, it banned nonresidents from obtaining public aid and barred them and their families from receiving government-sponsored support.[44] This extended version of the rule, first proposed in 2019, expanded the criteria for "inadmissibility," stating that immigrants who received more than one year of government aid during their time in the United States were to be denied a visa or green card. Refugees, asylum seekers, those with special immigrant visas, and victims of human trafficking, abuse, and gender-based violence were exempt from inadmissibility based on this criterion. On March 9, 2021, a year after the expanded rule went into effect, the Biden administration replaced it with the previous public charge guidelines from 1999; these remain in effect and limit entry into the United States.[45]

The administrative change initiated in 2020 lasted for only a short time but made it incredibly difficult for low-income families to immigrate by putting a time limit on their use of social services. The list of federal public aid programs that would be considered in public charge cases was expanded, adding food assistance, public housing, and Medicaid to SSI, TANF, cash assistance, and long-term medical care, which were already included.[46] Those living in the country had to rethink their finances in 2020 and temporarily forgo meeting their basic needs for the chance to obtain a green card or visa. Up to 26 million immigrants may have withdrawn from public benefits because they did not want to jeopardize their prospects for obtaining citizenship or because they feared deportation. Around 5 percent of the almost two million Black immigrants in the United States are thought to have been affected, as were over eight million children. These numbers do not include undocumented people who were already avoiding social programs due to fears of legal repercussions regarding their immigration status.[47]

Furthermore, the new public charge rule applied to people already reliant on government programs as well as those who would rely on them in the future. It disqualified almost 70 percent of annual green card seekers from collecting benefits and had serious consequences for immigrants' health and employment opportunities and for the economy as a whole. Immigrants are vital to long-term economic growth and fill employment voids in labor-intensive and dangerous occupational fields on which people rely, like food production, transportation, and agriculture.[48] Immigrants are also integral actors in the corporate sphere: almost 44 percent of all Fortune 500 companies in the United States were founded by a first- or second-generation immigrant. The New American Economy Research Fund estimates that if all immigrants affected by this law had left the country, the economy would have suffered at least a $164.4 billion loss.[49]

How Did We Get Here? The original federal public charge rule, drafted in 1882, denied entry to any immigrant who was "unable to take care of himself or herself without becoming a public charge."[50] Soon after, immigration authorities were legally empowered to deport any immigrant who was considered too dependent on public services. States went so far as to collect a head tax from each immigrant who traveled via ship to the United States to make up for the money spent on welfare services and the deportation of "paupers," "vagrants," "professional beggars," and people with disabilities, whom officials judged would struggle to find employment.[51] Hidetaka Hirota recounts the case of two young Irish immigrants who were deported to Ireland by the government of Massachusetts for being public charges, as they were considered too poor to live in the country. In the early 1800s, working-class Irish immigrants were slandered as "leeches" who drained public service and taxpayer funds, and nativist Americans campaigned to close U.S. borders so that "indigent immigrants" from Europe could not enter.[52]

Things have not changed much since then. In 1999, the policy was updated and given formal guidelines, and a *public charge* is now defined as someone "primarily dependent on the government for subsistence" via cash assistance or long-term aid.[53] The attempted 2020 reforms also set a goal similar to that of the rejected RAISE Act: forcing immigrants off federal welfare and intimidating others from arriving was estimated to save the government about $2.27 billion every year and decrease the funds put toward public aid over time.[54] By doing so, the country sent a very clear message about which lives it considers valuable and which are expendable. Wendy Cervantes, a policy expert, believes that the public charge rule represented "a blow to immigrants, their families, and whole communities . . . making families choose between providing for their kids—putting food on the table and getting access to basic health care—or risk being separated and not being able to legalize their status."[55] Ultimately, the public charge provisions reflect the history of xenophobia, a foundational element of U.S. immigration policy.

Reproduction Restrictions Targeting Low-Income Families

Welfare is also a reproductive issue. Immigrant child-bearers are among those most undermined by the 1996 reforms. Some immigrant parents hold off on having children because they do not qualify for government financial support or health care coverage.[56] After PRWORA, the childbearing rate in states with few or no welfare programs for noncitizens dropped by 47 percent.[57]

Control over immigrants' bodily autonomy was written into the provisions of TANF. One of the program's four stated purposes is to prevent and reduce out-of-wedlock pregnancies and restore "traditional family norms."[58] Feminists and potential beneficiaries of TANF criticized this legislative move, arguing that it targets low-income people. This provision weaponized social spending to practice eugenics and legislate who is permitted to have a family. A perfect example of this can be found in what some called the state "illegitimacy bonus." States were given monetary incentives to reduce the number of out-of-wedlock births without providing more abortion services. Alabama, the District of Columbia, and Illinois had each received at least $20 million by 1999.[59] The bonuses were awarded as follows:

> For each of the four years beginning in 1999, the five states that achieve the greatest decline in their ratio of out-of-wedlock births to total births, while holding their abortion rate to below its 1995 level, are to receive $20 million each. If fewer than five states qualify in any given year, each is to receive $25 million. Significantly, the bonuses are for reductions in out-of-wedlock births among all women, not just welfare recipients or teenagers.[60]

Conjoined efforts to lower birth rates while keeping abortion rates unchanged began with restricting aid eligibility for low-income communities. Thirteen states have established family caps that revoke welfare funding for recipients who have another child or seek a divorce.[61] Thus, a guardian's children who already qualify for services do not lose coverage, but the unborn child does not qualify. This can push a parent to obtain an abortion if they cannot care for their new child without government support. Additionally, some of the low-income people who are stopped from having children are simultaneously barred from insurance-funded abortion services. In Georgia, abortions are not insured under ACA health coverage unless the pregnancy is life-threatening or has severe health implications.[62] Child-bearers have no choice but to pay for an abortion out of pocket or follow through with the pregnancy and subsequently support the child without aid from the program. The de facto government control over immigrant child-bearers' bodies and reproductive liberties is an area of the welfare debate that is often overlooked. Furthermore, there have been many legal restrictions around reproductive health.

Citizenship Limitations and an Imbalanced Welfare System

Contrary to popular belief, reforms have significantly limited immigrants' access to welfare; utilizing government resources is difficult for them because so many have been deemed ineligible for public services in the first place.[63] In 2011, 32.5 percent of native-born American adults collected SNAP benefits. The same year 29 percent of noncitizen adults and 25.4 percent of naturalized citizens received the same benefits. All welfare programs, including SNAP, spend fewer dollars to provide for immigrants relative to U.S.-born people.[64] Immigrant children also use less welfare than their native-born peers, and a 2009 study found that U.S.-born citizens who collected welfare as children failed to graduate from high school and remained dependent on government aid as adults more often than immigrants from the same socioeconomic background.[65]

Limiting immigrants to fewer welfare options has created an imbalanced system in which noncitizens must rely on aid that is temporary in nature. Programs that deal with health and retirement, and thus yield long-term benefits, are reserved for native-born people. For example, U.S.-born adults accessed more SSI, Medicare, and Social Security benefits in 2016. Individually, they consumed an estimated $56 more in SSI funds, $610 more in Medicare funds, and $1,808 more in Social Security retirement funds than immigrants. Immigrants not only received less money from these programs but also were more often barred from access to the programs altogether. In the programs for which they qualified, the average immigrant only used $7 more in SNAP, $98 more in Medicaid, and $6 more in cash assistance. Overall, immigrants individually consumed fewer dollars in total benefits: about $2,363 less than each U.S.-born person.[66] A substantial difference in welfare payments is also visible when we zoom out to get a bird's-eye view of federal spending. In 2016, the U.S. government spent about $2.3 trillion on the welfare state, or roughly 60 percent of annual government spending. Of that amount, about 65 percent was set aside for Social Security and Medicare, both programs for which most immigrants do not qualify. The remainder of this funding—$800 billion—was spent on means-tested welfare benefits that disproportionately contribute to support for low-income native-born individuals.[67]

IF IMMIGRANT DEPENDENCE ON WELFARE PROGRAMS IS A MYTH, WHY DO PEOPLE BELIEVE IT?

Statistical Manipulations

Statistical methods can be altered to support false claims about welfare. For instance, families headed by an immigrant tend to be larger than those headed by a native-born person. Thus, immigrants generally have more U.S.-born children in their families who are eligible for benefits due to birthright citizenship. Reports conducted by anti-immigrant organizations are aware of this and will use the family as the unit of measurement instead of the individual to alter their findings. Analyses that compare individuals' welfare use rates are more accurate and do not make the mistake of generalizing the habits of large groups of people. Research that refers to individuals repeatedly shows that immigrants use less welfare altogether than native-born Americans, especially in the case of cash assistance and housing programs.[68]

Part of the myth that immigrants use more social services asserts that people purposefully migrate to countries with relaxed welfare requirements and liberal social security nets. In fact, the generosity of a country's or a state's welfare system barely influences immigrants' decisions on where to relocate. Instead, wages and employment opportunities are up to ten times more important. First-generation immigrants are also more drawn to cities with established immigrant populations where they can find social support and personal connections within the immigrant community.[69]

Racial and Ethnic Stereotypes

There are stereotypes and social narratives about immigrants and U.S.-born people of color in regard to welfare usage among different racial and ethnic groups. Immigrants experience distinct prejudices that shape welfare policy changes and discussions. For instance, Black mothers in the United States have been stigmatized as "welfare queens" and unfit caretakers since the seventeenth century. They are chastised as reckless caretakers who do not comply with the "correct" standards of child-rearing, which have been set by wealthy white parents. White politicians like Ronald Reagan have vilified Black welfare users and caretakers to garner support from white communities.

In contrast, Asian mothers are commonly judged as tough and overly tenacious in their parenting techniques. The stereotypical "Tiger Mom" places great significance on their child's educational and professional successes.[70] Compared to Asian mothers, Black mothers take similar approaches to parenting and equally regard education as imperative to their child's future well-being.[71] Black, Asian, and Latin parents all value higher education as a necessary pathway for their children's success more than white Americans.[72] Despite this, Asian parents' disciplinarian methods are praised or overlooked by white Americans, while Black caretakers' similar approaches are met with harassment. Black immigrants are the least likely to use welfare and yet receive the most criticism for accessing it, which is exemplified by hostile and fabricated sentiments about their parenting abilities. The "model minority" stereotype is another prejudiced impression of Asian Americans that may protect them from being criminalized for using government aid. Because of preconceived notions about "Tiger Moms" and about cultural pressures to perform well in terms of their social positions, people of Asian descent in the United States are presumed to be high-achieving individuals who no longer face structural barriers to success.[73] This is not a true representation of all Asian Americans and can have opposite effects, sometimes impairing students' educational achievement and adding stress to their lives.[74] Still, this stereotype protects Asian immigrants from being perceived as villains who exhaust welfare resources, while other immigrants of color are not.

Like Black people, Latin people are often erroneously lumped together into one homogeneous and generalizable group of people with similar beliefs and behaviors. The U.S. media reference Latin people in relation to poverty, welfare, and immigration—and rarely much else. This misperception has created a stereotype of all Spanish-speaking people as poor, foreign-born, and dependent on government aid. However, *Latin* is an umbrella term for an expansive and diverse collection of identities, experiences, and socioeconomic realities. In 2008, 25 percent of Mexican immigrants experienced poverty compared to 15 percent of South Americans, and there are U.S.-born and immigrant Hispanics who enjoy high levels of social mobility.[75] Prejudice toward racial and ethnic minorities regarding their use of welfare is based on historically racist American misconceptions that manipulate the public and the U.S. legal system and block certain immigrants from entering the country, and it affects many Latin, Asian, and Black immigrants today.

IMMIGRANTS DO NOT USE WELFARE MORE OFTEN THAN NATIVE-BORN PEOPLE

Immigrants' Welfare Use Is Typically Temporary

The postmigration adjustment period in the United States can be overwhelming. Immigrants juggle multiple needs: to learn a new language, find a job, move into a new residence, and establish a social network, among many other things. It takes time for immigrants' general security and finances to recover from so many changes. Proponents of xenophobic welfare policies believe that immigrants who need financial support when they arrive in the United States will never want to work after collecting welfare. They insinuate that noncitizens will remain poor for the rest of their lives, disregarding the fact that people predominantly migrate to earn money.

This way of thinking has other fundamental flaws. It assumes that being an immigrant is synonymous with collecting welfare, failing to consider that less than one-quarter of noncitizens live in poverty.[76] This mindset also implies that immigrants will receive government aid indefinitely. Many immigrants only temporarily rely on public benefits, eventually achieving higher financial standing. The financial gap between the average immigrant and the average U.S.-born citizen shrinks within approximately twenty years.[77]

Older Immigrants Do Not Exhaust Welfare Resources

The number of elderly noncitizens on SSI grew after passage of the 1965 Immigration Act, which abolished annual country-specific caps on the number of immigrants who could migrate to the United States. More immigrants were entering the country than in previous years, so the number of them receiving welfare also grew. In the 1990s, proponents of PRWORA were aware of this trend, as well as the relationship between age and welfare usage, and used this information to frame statistical research they conducted to garner support for the law. As a result, it is now much harder for older newcomers to qualify for government benefits. The revised public charge rule that took effect in 2020 also briefly excluded many older people from qualifying for a visa.[78]

In general, older people rely on welfare more than younger generations. As people age, they retire, develop health problems, require regular and comprehensive care, and become socially isolated.[79] Typically, the older someone is, the more benefits they use, and older immigrants in particular have been found to consume more SSI than immigrant individuals and families who are younger and of working age.[80] Those who arrive in the United States and who are older than fifty-five use more welfare than younger immigrants who migrate during their working years.[81] Post-PRWORA, elderly immigrants had more economic incentive to naturalize, as anyone who became a citizen could bypass the new welfare restrictions, and there was an overall increase in the number of people, including older immigrants, who were using government benefits after the act took effect.[82] However, the increase in the use of aid relative to age does not apply to noncitizens any more than it does to U.S. nationals of the same age and socioeconomic status. Vibeke Jakobsen and Peder Pedersen compared welfare use rates of both citizens and immigrants in Denmark and explained how extremely high poverty and disability levels among older Iranian, Pakistani, and Vietnamese refugees and migrants caused them to rely on government support more often. Danish-born people aged sixty and older earned much higher wages and received more nonstate pension funds.[83]

Immigrant Children and Welfare

Growing up is harder for children who must navigate various cultures in multiple spaces—their home, neighborhood, school, greater community, and social media. This adjustment process can induce financial and familial strain, and child welfare services might need to intervene. Children of foreign-born immigrants can be granted special immigrant juvenile status, which "provides lawful permanent residency to children who are under the jurisdiction of a juvenile court and who will not be reunified with their parents due to abuse, neglect, or abandonment."[84] However, undocumented children are still not eligible for federally funded foster care services. State or private welfare services are harder to come by and often result in high fees or require documentation of citizenship status. Change has yet to come in this area for child welfare agencies, which "have a responsibility to support legislation and regulations to ensure the well-being of youth . . . regardless of the dominant ideology and political climate surrounding immigration issues."[85] While trainings on and curriculum that center cultural sensitivity, language skills, and multicultural customs are being implemented, regular funding and more research are needed to support immigrant children.

More Latin children have been entering the U.S. welfare system since the 1990s. While this might be a result of a growing Latin population, it is also related to welfare reform and immigration policy. The percentage of Latin children who collected government aid rose from 10 percent in 1995 to 17.4 percent in 2005, likely because their parents' eligibility was temporarily or permanently revoked. Nearly 5.2 percent of Latin children with immigrant parents were involved with the child welfare system in 1999–2000, although not always because of allegations of mistreatment.[86] Children are processed into the child welfare system when their parents are deported or confined to immigration detention centers for indeterminable lengths of time. Even before the Trump administration's "zero-tolerance" policy was put into effect at the U.S.-Mexico border in 2018, more than one thousand children were forcibly separated from their parents because those parents did not fulfill the requirements for entry to the country.[87] These separations were illegal, and the U.S. government has not been able to reunite hundreds of these children with their families.[88]

Even Eligible Immigrants Do Not Apply for Benefits

Stricter eligibility requirements under PRWORA prevent many immigrants who temporarily need welfare services from even attempting to access such funding. The complexity of the application process for benefits often makes it confusing, cumbersome, and intimidating. Immigrants might not even start the forms, or they might never turn them in because of language barriers, administrative misinterpretations, and fear of interacting with state or federal organizations.[89] Now, fewer immigrant families use government assistance programs despite struggling with poverty more often,[90] even though Medicaid, CHIP, TANF, and SNAP could contribute to their economic stability, personal growth, and health.

PRWORA also created uncertainty about which programs were available to immigrants. Some states, like New York and New Mexico, redirected their own funds to provide immigrants with only food and cash assistance, while others opened up new local TANF, SSI, and Medicaid programs. On the other hand, states like New Jersey and Florida provided none of these services. The nonuniformity of welfare access can discourage noncitizens from applying when they are in fact eligible.[91] Immigrants' distrust of government financial systems also contributes to their hesitancy to apply for public benefits. Some have been reliant on faulty welfare systems in the past and have lost financial stability after these systems failed. The welfare systems in countries like Mexico and Guatemala, where emigration is common, are weak. These previous experiences can disincentivize people from joining another system and risking a similar fate.

While many U.S.-born children of undocumented immigrants are eligible for social services, their parents are unlikely to utilize them for multiple reasons. They might fear deportation and stay away from government entities. Some people do not want to be regarded as public charges. Even prior to the expansion of the public charge rule in 2020, immigrants of any and all citizenship statuses opted out of social services due to widespread anxieties that participation in welfare programs would hurt their naturalization process.[92] A recent report finds that even in New York City, which is a relatively immigrant-friendly city, immigrants were reluctant to use programs to which they were entitled after Trump's public charge proposals. Respondents shared that even if the Biden administration had rescinded these changes, they were afraid that using welfare programs could affect their immigration status in the future.[93] This hesitancy leads nonnative parents to use health care, cash assistance, and nutrition benefits at lower rates than U.S.-born families, even when their children are living in the country legally.[94]

Immigrants Pay More in Taxes than They Receive in Welfare Benefits

Noncitizens contribute equally to state and federal tax systems as U.S. citizens, and yet they are blocked from accessing SSI, Medicare, and other forms of federal aid that their taxes fund. In 2017, the Institute on Taxation and Economic Policy clarified that immigrants pay an estimated eight percent of state and federal taxes on their incomes compared to the top 1 percent of all taxpayers, who pay 5.4 percent. Undocumented immigrants pay up to $11.74 billion each year in state and local taxes.[95] Foreign-born people, especially those with lower levels of education, are less often unemployed than their native-born counterparts with similar backgrounds and taxes cannot be gathered from wages that are never distributed. In 2017, immigrants comprised 17 percent of the civilian labor force in the United States. They are essential in ensuring the country's economic functioning.[96]

This trend also applies to health insurance premiums. If more restrictions are put on immigrants' access to health care, the insurance market could flounder because the number of enrollees in private insurance would be drastically reduced, weakening the insurance risk pool. Between 2007 and 2014, immigrants paid private insurers more in premiums than they received in benefits *and* more in premiums than what native U.S. citizens paid for the same benefits. Immigrants "accounted for 12.6 percent of premiums paid to private insurers in 2014, but only 9.1 percent of insurer expenditures."[97] The average immigrant's annual premiums exceeded their insurer's health care expenditures by $1,123, whereas the average U.S.-born enrollee's annual premiums totaled $163 less than their insurer's health-care expenditures—and this was true even for those who had lived in the United States for ten years. Altogether, noncitizens paid a health premium surplus of $174.4 billion during that period, helping insurance companies earn more from immigrants than from native-born Americans.[98]

Medicaid is one of the most commonly used welfare programs provided by state governments. In 2017, about 5.3 percent of the approximately 13.3 million Medicaid recipients were immigrants on the path to U.S. citizenship. If all of these immigrants stopped using Medicaid, community health centers would lose anywhere between $346 million and $624 million, as well as 295,000 patients per year.[99] Legal temporary residents and undocumented immigrants are paying billions into a system they cannot fully access.

IMMIGRANTS USE WELFARE AT VARYING RATES IN DIFFERENT COUNTRIES

Welfare use varies greatly among nations, regions, and cities. Each government has its own policies that dictate the size and frequency of government-sponsored payments that different groups of immigrants receive. Trends in welfare usage in the United States are not guaranteed to apply in other parts of the world, so we will briefly explore whether the belief that immigrants drain welfare resources is legitimate elsewhere.

Like the distinct states of the United States, member countries of the European Union provide government aid at different levels to people living within their borders. Immigrants in these countries, except for Poland and Portugal, overwhelmingly struggle with poverty more often, and yet they do not receive more welfare. Non-European immigrants in twelve EU countries collect smaller or equal amounts of government support compared to EU nationals. In the remaining seven EU countries, the relatively excessive use of aid by immigrants is limited to unemployment and child-related benefits, while European immigrants and EU-born people usually obtain more welfare related to retirement, health, and disability.[100]

Ireland and the United Kingdom

In Ireland, welfare recipients must be considered "habitually resident" to qualify for certain government support programs, like pensions, cash assistance, and unemployment and disability payments.[101] Habitual residence, in the case of Ireland, is a flexible term. An applicant and the members of their household will likely be granted eligibility if the applicant presents proof of current residence and future intentions to remain in the country and if they are actively working or searching for an Ireland-based job.[102] EU migrant workers are exempt from providing evidence of habitual residence, whereas people who have been granted refugee status, temporary protection, or EU-imposed subsidiary protection can fulfill the requirements once their legal status is finalized. They are barred from all welfare programs until their status is made official.[103]

So, it does not come as a surprise that immigrants use social services substantially less than the Irish-born, including when they are unemployed.[104] Irish nationals received 10.8 percent more unemployment and disability payments in 2007 than eligible immigrants, and those from English-speaking countries generally collect more benefits than immigrants from other parts of the world. These gaps in welfare use result from the characteristics of Irish-bound immigrants: they are highly educated and have good employment prospects, and they have fewer children and do not collect as many child assistance benefits.[105] Patterns are different in the UK. Some argued that before Brexit, immigrants participated in government economic assistance programs more often than UK-born citizens.[106] Since its rift with the EU, welfare policies have drastically shifted to favor UK citizens and constrain the types of benefits that immigrants can claim.[107]

Sweden

Immigrants in Sweden do not collect welfare for prolonged periods, typically graduating out of it.[108] This was the case between 1990 and 1996, when the Swedish economy was struggling. Unemployment had jumped by 6 percent, and people went to the government for financial aid. Citizens and immigrants were receiving the same amounts in welfare, but an increase in the number of immigrants around that time caused an uptick in total usage. Immigrants were using social services more often while they constituted only about 10 percent of Sweden's population. After six years, all immigrants and refugees had become better economically integrated, and their rates of government aid use leveled out to that of native-born Swedes.[109]

Denmark

The welfare system in Denmark is structured so that access to pensions depends on how many years a person has lived in the country. Consequently, immigrants usually have smaller pensions. They need to reside in the country for at least three years to receive any pension at all and for at least forty years to qualify for a full state pension. Those eligible for a pension with less than forty years of residency receive a certain fraction of support, so that "31 years of Danish residency gives the pensioner access to 31/40ths of a full state pension."[110] This retirement rule applies to the many non-European immigrants above age sixty-five who arrived in Denmark as guest workers, family members, or refugees before 1974. Danish welfare is considered nearly universal for everyone over the age of sixty-four, but there is still a question of whether immigrants have similar access.

Foreign-born people, especially women, were collecting more welfare than Danish nationals in 2011. This is likely because their incomes were also much lower: native Danish men between sixty and sixty-four earned over 141,000 kroner, equivalent to $12,925, more per year than the highest-earning immigrant community at the time. Similarly, immigrant women who had the highest incomes of their demographic still trailed native Danish women by over 87,000 kroner, or about $9,630. Although immigrants and refugees received welfare benefits more often than native Danes, they received fewer kroner in benefits as they aged. Danish retirement and social security programs prefer granting coverage to people who (1) have resided in Denmark for more than twenty years, (2) come from dual-earner families, and (3) have not received long-term disability or sickness benefits. These are the characteristics that are typical of Danish nationals.[111] Thus, immigrants consumed more unemployment and disability funds, but they could not access programs that would guarantee their financial stability later in life.

Australia

The immigration policies implemented in Australia are founded on dominant Anglo-Australian social customs and beliefs. They operate within a binary understanding of immigrant deservingness, ensuring that immigrants who do not acculturate to the level that native-born people consider "enough" have fewer economic opportunities postmigration and consequently are more likely to rely on government welfare.[112] This is a way for governments to force immigrants to assimilate: if they do not abide by discriminatory customs, they are excluded from participating in the economic and social fabric of the country. China Mills and Elise Klein view this phenomenon, which occurs in Australia, the United Kingdom, and the United States, as a form of welfare deterrence. They call it "a human technology . . . that specifically operates to change human conduct" by cultivating certain shared sentiments among the public that individuals eventually internalize as part of their national identity.[113]

Within this cultural framework, English-speaking immigrants in Australia experience economic success more easily and quickly and therefore do not require as much public financial support as immigrants who do not speak English. Some groups of non-English-speaking immigrants, such as those from Turkey, Lebanon, and Vietnam, are more dependent on pensions and benefits than other immigrants because of their high unemployment rates.[114] While each country's results depend on its government's approach to immigration policy, high-income countries usually have more extensive welfare states and spend more on their inhabitants per capita. Economic immigrants and refugees tend to start at low-skilled jobs and, as a result, are relatively poorer than their native-born counterparts. Therefore, analyses of immigrant welfare use should compare immigrants to native-born populations facing similar economic conditions rather than to all nonimmigrants.

CONCLUSION

Immigrants generally consume less welfare than native-born people in multiple regional contexts. Legal and practical barriers—exemplified by PRWORA, TANF, and public charge regulations—prevent noncitizens from accessing social services. Most immigrants who qualify for aid rely on it for a brief period, not the rest of their lives. Even those who require extended support, like elderly immigrants, do not exhaust resources compared to U.S.-born people of their age. Furthermore, immigrants of color collect the least amount of government support and are misrepresented in their use of aid because of racial and ethnic discrimination. The stigmatization of Black mothers as irresponsible "Welfare Queens" carries a more negative connotation than the aggressive "Tiger Mom" stereotype attributed to Asian mothers. White America's more favorable attitudes toward Asian and White immigrant groups influence welfare usage disparities.

In 2011–2012, only 2 percent of the Hispanic residents in our El Paso sample were receiving unemployment benefits (table 5.1). The vast majority of these were citizens, while none were undocumented immigrants. Undocumented people did not receive workers' compensation, retirement pensions, or any type of public or private disability insurance payments. Instead, they accessed slightly more benefits from financial and nutrition assistance programs like TANF, general public assistance, and SNAP. These programs are temporary in nature, whereas retirement and disability benefits are typically long term. While 45.8 percent of the sample had served in the military or had family members who did, including many foreign-born and noncitizens, only 8.6 were registered with the Department of Veterans Affairs, and very few (1.5%) received VA disability benefits or workers' compensation payments (1.1%).

TABLE 5.1 Direct government support by immigration status in El Paso

	Citizen	Resident	Work visa	Student visa	Undocu- mented	Total
Unemployment benefits	2.2%	1.7%	0.1%	0%	0%	2%
Workers' compensation payments	1.4%	05	0%	0%	0%	1.1%
Veterans disability payments	1.7%	0.8%	0%	0%	0%	1.5%
Private disability insurance payments	0.6%	0%	0%	0%	0%	0.5%
Social Security Disability Insurance payments	4%	5.7%	0%	0%	0%	4.1%
Social Security retirement income	5.6%	4.9%	0%	0%	0%	5.2%
Supplemental Security Income (SSI)	4.3%	5.7%	0%	0.1%	3.7%	4.4%
Temporary Assistance to Needy Families (TANF)	0.5%	0%	0%	0.1%	3.8%	0.5%
General public assistance	1.1%	2.5%	0.1%	0%	3.8%	1.4%
Supplemental Nutrition Assistance Program (SNAP)	9.2%	20.6%	0.3%	0.1%	29.8%	11.4%
Financial aid grants	17.3%	7.4%	16.5%	15.3%	0%	15.2%

The myth that immigrants rely on government aid more often than U.S.-born people drives public sentiments, immigration and welfare policies, and the allocation of responsibility for care among state and federal actors. Asylum seekers and refugees are even frowned upon for using financial and nutrition programs when the purpose of government aid is to support those who cannot provide for themselves. Immigrants pay taxes, just like U.S. nationals, but they cannot always access the benefits to which they have contributed. They are not "stealing" from American citizens—to a certain degree, the opposite is happening. The tenacity of this myth is a cause for alarm. It has been disproved time and time again, but advocates of xenophobia and closed borders still manage to reenergize people's doubts and revive the misconception in political and media discourses. We must rely on research-driven findings, respect, and empathy to lead the country forward and make government support available for anyone who needs it.

Much of the apprehension against receiving immigrants, refugees, and asylum seekers is often related to aporophobia, a fear and dislike of poor people.[115] Many people think, often erroneously, that immigrants are among the poorest of the poor and that they will stay poor in their new country. International migration takes important resources, therefore the poorest of the poor cannot migrate. Furthermore, many immigrants come with significant savings and many others work hard, save, establish businesses, and experience social mobility. While not everyone can become rich, it is rare when immigrant families do not work to support themselves.

CHAPTER 6

REMITTANCES DO NOT DRAIN HOST COUNTRIES' ECONOMIES AND ARE NOT LIKE FOREIGN AID

The term *remittances* refers to the money transfers migrants make to loved ones living in their countries of origin.[1] They are commonly "intra-household transfers from members of a family who have emigrated to those who have remained behind," although they are sometimes also sent to friends and neighbors.[2] The ability to provide remittances is a key component in many people's decisions to migrate to a new country. In 2019 alone, one in seven people in the world was either sending or receiving remittances, amounting to approximately one billion people.[3] Remittances are the result of the international migration of workers who leave all or part of their nuclear family in order to supply them with a higher income.[4] They are relatively small amounts of money sent on a regular basis that are spent on valuable items and experiences; for example, they may be used to (1) cover main expenses of the nuclear family left behind, food and groceries, housing costs, clothing, and other common household expenses; (2) provide financial support for elders and the rest of the family; (3) repay debts or educational fees; (4) reimburse migration costs; (5) assist those facing economic turmoil and disruption; (6) buy gifts for relatives or friends; and (7) pay for health care, surgeries, and medicine.[5] On a macro level, poor local economies with limited job markets and low wages are fortified by remittances—but at the cost of widespread family separation.[6]

During his presidency, Donald Trump often complained that remittances are a burden on the U.S. economy, insisting that senders pay a tax that would contribute to the construction of a wall or physical barrier on the southern border. He was backed by anti-immigrant groups and individuals who believe that the country loses money because immigrants give part of their wages to their families and friends abroad instead of spending them in the U.S. economy.[7]

Others proposed a fine for each remittance sent by undocumented workers.[8] Although remittances are partially expatriated wages, immigrant-receiving societies need not worry about remittances hurting their local economies. Normally, remittances are relatively small amounts of money in relation to workers' income and their output, and most of the immigrants' wages are spent on housing, food, and other basic expenses in the country where they work, not to mention that U.S.-based employers financially benefit from immigrant labor. Migrant workers typically remit between $200 and $300 home every month, which represents between 15 percent and 30 percent of their monthly wages, and around 4 percent of their contributions to the firms that hire them.[9] A crucial point to highlight in the international conversation concerning remittances is that immigrants remit wages that have already been taxed by the national government. On top of taxes, they pay fees to often U.S.-based banks and remittance businesses in order to send payments abroad.

In this chapter, we provide evidence to disprove the myth that remittances drain and burden host countries' economies. We begin by outlining common arguments against remittances, particularly those from political speech, and subsequently contextualize important trends and demographic information regarding the characteristics of remitters, their reasons for remitting, and the share of wages they remit. We then review remittance policies and taxes proposed in the United States and consider the effectiveness and ethics of imposing further taxation on remittances, referencing international examples, studies, and statistical evidence to support our assertions.

GLOBAL REMITTANCE RELATIONSHIPS

Remitting is common in countries with abundant job opportunities and a moderate to high annual GDP.[10] The United States, the United Arab Emirates, and Saudi Arabia are among the top sources of remittances worldwide because their high-income economies attract immigrant workers from struggling countries. In 2020, India received the most remittance transfers, followed by China, Mexico, the Philippines, and Egypt.[11] Large sums of remittances are also sent from Hong Kong and Japan to mainland China, Spain to Morocco, Kuwait to Egypt, and Australia to multiple nations in Asia.[12] In the aggregate, millions of migrants sent an estimated $625 billion in 2017, $148 billion of which came from workers in the United States.[13] In 2023, global remittance flows are estimated to have reached $860 billions.[14] International students, foreign investors, and wealthy people living in the Global North for long periods may also receive remittances from abroad, thus bringing foreign income to wealthy countries.

Who Remits?

Immigrants with many backgrounds, education levels, jobs, identities, and national origins send money across national borders. Migrant workers, embassy employees, and people working for foreign companies remit internationally. In fact, some of the compensation provided for diplomats, embassy workers, expats, and the Social Security payments sent to U.S. retirees living abroad can be considered remittances in international accounting and may be included in official figures from national central banks.[15] Migrants have mixed success in the labor markets of receiving countries, as some get hired almost immediately, others eventually become highly successful, while others remain unemployed for extended periods while adjusting.[16] These financial outcomes are largely shaped by migrant workers' educational attainment, host language fluency, and legal status, among other things. Undocumented individuals, especially recent arrivals, are most likely to remit consistently, especially when their immediate family members stay in the former country of residence.[17] In contrast, immigrants with higher levels of education and income typically remit less often because they do not have their own families yet or they live with them.[18]

Differences in remittance rates among immigrant communities are dictated by elements of the receiving and sending communities. For example, Jorge Duany compared the ripple effects of remittances in Puerto Rico, the Dominican Republic, and Mexico. After analyzing data from the Latin American Migration Project and the Mexican Migration Project, Duany found that 34.8 percent of Puerto Ricans living in the United States sent remittances to relatives and friends compared to 66.5 percent of Dominicans and 76 percent of Mexicans. Puerto Ricans also sent less money: their monthly remittances averaged $84.80, whereas Dominicans and Mexicans remitted $192.00 and $376.00, respectively. Food and maintenance were the primary purposes for remittances in all three countries, but Puerto Rico was where the money was more often used to purchase consumer goods. In Mexico, the largest fraction of remitted money was spent for health purposes when compared to the other two countries.[19]

The variance in remittance rates depends on each country's welfare system, economic and social conditions, and migration rates. Puerto Rico has a more robust social safety net and higher levels of development than the rural parts of the Dominican Republic and Mexico.[20] Workers often look for employment in places with strong currencies that will go a long way in places with weaker currencies and a lower cost of living. As Puerto Rico is a U.S. territory, its economy is fully dollarized; this makes Puerto Rico a less appealing place to remit dollars than, say, Mexico, which, in 2023, had an exchange rate of around seventeen pesos to one U.S. dollar. U.S. borders are open for Puerto Ricans to come and go, making migration less risky than for Mexicans or Dominicans, and as U.S. citizens, Puerto Ricans have permission to settle and work freely in the mainland.

Reasons to Remit

Immigrants might have one or multiple reasons to send remittances. Many do this to continue their paternal, maternal, or filial duties, mainly as evidence of care for their loved ones and their belief that it is the moral course of action, particularly if their relatives might be experiencing hardships with work or illness. There are also instances where immigrants remit to their families or friends in exchange for a favor that had to be done in their home country, like taking care of a relative. In this case, the receiver is technically earning the remitted money as wages for a service provided. Immigrants commonly use remittances to repay people in their home communities for sponsoring their migration journey, to pay off loans, microcredits, or other debts, or to make loans to relatives or friends.[21] Remittances can also operate as a form of insurance for an individual or their family. Migrants might remit to prepare for emergencies or deportation.[22] They can also operate the other way around when the remitted money provides relatives with an insurance fund to protect them against income shocks or eventually to pay for their collective migration.[23]

Remittance Businesses

Migrants have traditionally been constrained in sending money from the country they work in to the country their family lives in for several reasons. First, small immigrant-sending hometowns, especially those in developing countries, might

In 2011–2012, about 11 percent of Hispanics living in El Paso remitted money to their communities of origin, as shown in table 6.1. Although their reasons varied, all were directly related to survival: just over half (55.5 percent) of remitters financially provided for food and basic necessities, while another 27.3 percent paid for health care and medicine. Similarly, almost 22 percent of Hispanics were part of families that remitted. Existing literature and the research conducted in El Paso suggest that remittances are crucial tools in ensuring the survival of migrant workers' families.

This survey also revealed who remits the most in the El Paso Hispanic community (table 6.2). Undocumented and resident-status men were most likely to send remittances at the time of the survey, and only 8.7 percent of remitters had been born in the United States. Remitters were more often first- and 1.5-generation immigrants, given that later-generation immigrants grow up in the United States and have fewer connections to their families' countries of origin.[24]

TABLE 6.1 Remitting behavior

Do you send money abroad?	
Yes	11.1%
Does your family send money back home?	
Yes	21.7%
For what purpose?	
Food and basic necessities	55.5%
Health care and medicines	27.3%
Education	6.2%
Birthdays	3.4%
Sporadic cash	2.1%
Holidays	1.4%
Emergencies	1.4%
House construction	0.7%
Church	0.7%
Business	0.7%
Other	0.6%

TABLE 6.2 Demographics of those who remit*

Undocumented	42.5%
Resident	24.4%
Citizen	7.3%
Visa	4.9%
Generation	
First	22.2%
1.5	17.6%
Second	6.9%
Third	1.5%
More than third	0%
Education	
Less than high school	23.3%
High school/GED	11.3%
4-year College degree or higher	8.2%
Technical school/Some college	7.8%

not have bank branches that process remittances or that are linked to the major money transfer businesses in the sending country. For example, a migrant worker can send money via Western Union (figure 6.1), but their family might not have a local bank that partners with that company. Second, some governments and

6.1 Migrant passing in front of a Western Union office in an immigrant neighborhood in Barcelona

Source: © Ernesto Castañeda 2008.

banks in cities that attract migrant workers have fees and/or strict requirements to open bank accounts. For instance, banks in Paris require many documents, including immigration papers, work permits, and letters documenting minimum guaranteed salaries. There has been a demand for personal couriers to travel back and forth between home and host countries for decades, all the while delivering cash, photos, gifts, and food.[25]

Multiple business models have appeared that help broker these transactions, moving money and sometimes packages from one place to another. Businesses through which people can send remittances often pop up in immigrant neighborhoods and become markers of immigration and ethno-racial diversity in urban spaces. While Ria, Western Union, and multinational banks are strong competitors, community-based businesses and remittance kiosks also constitute a portion of the market. These small family-owned businesses are more ingrained in their communities and have offices in immigrant-sending towns. Thus, they share local knowledge and social connections with people on both sides of a remittance transaction. The remittance market is also supported by chain migration, which we see play out when families reunify, immigrant enclaves blossom in the Global North, and neighborhoods adopt a particular ethnic character. People within the same social networks will likely share some information, resources, and opportunities that attract other immigrants to their community and its local economy.[26]

EFFORTS TO PENALIZE REMITTERS

Proposed U.S. Remittance Tax Policies

Two bills were proposed in Congress to tax remittances, one of which was the Border Wall Funding Act of 2017. This legislation, introduced in the House of Representatives, would have placed a 2 percent tax on all wire transfers of money to Mexico, all of Latin America, and the Caribbean. In turn, the funds collected from the tax would be funneled toward building a wall at the U.S.-Mexico border.[27] The other bill, the Remittance Status Verification Act of 2015, was proposed in the Senate and called for a 7 percent "penalty tax" on remittances for senders who cannot provide immigration documents demonstrating that they are in the United States legally. Neither bill was successful. As Jason Beaubien of NPR explains, taxes like these are a significant financial burden that would hurt those who are *receiving* money and not particularly those who are sending it.[28] They target immigrants who are undocumented but legally residing immigrants, as well as U.S. citizens who have family, friends, or loved ones living in foreign countries.

Furthermore, a tax on remittances would result in remitters being taxed twice and would therefore qualify as a double taxation of their wages.[29] Migrant workers and anyone who wants to remit would pay more taxes than a nonremitter. This is especially ironic, given that immigrants, especially undocumented immigrants and DREAMers, already contribute to a welfare system that they cannot fully access. In addition, remitters are required to pay the transmitting business a fee on most remittance transactions, the exception being online wire transfers.[30] Western Union and other services charge fees to send the money, make money on currency transactions, and pay taxes on their profits. Ultimately, any remittance tax is unnecessary and cruel because it intends to dissuade and punish migration and push undocumented immigrants out.

The United States is not the only country that has proposed additional remittance taxes. Similar debates and policies have been raised by the governments of Kuwait, Oman, the UAE, Bahrain, and Saudi Arabia, among others.[31] On the first day of 2018, the UAE introduced a value-added tax that aims to diversify the country's revenue and curb its dependence on oil. It levies an additional 5 percent general consumption fee on all goods and services, including remittances.[32] Saudi Arabia is another nation that has imposed a 5 percent remittance tax.[33]

Criminalization of Mexican Migrant Workers

Proponents of remittance taxes tend to demonize a subset of the remitting community: undocumented temporary Mexican laborers.[34] Mexico has received large amounts of remittances from the United States over the past decades. In 2017, over $50 billion in remittances was sent to Latin America from the United States, $30 billion of which went directly to Mexico.[35] Under the contemporary "crimmigration" regime, undocumented immigrants are considered illegal in all spaces, and their very existence in the United States is considered criminal by the justice system. Therefore, it is unsurprising that politicians and the public use Mexicans' remitting behavior as further justification for anti-immigrant policies. Some have proposed a fine for remitting while being undocumented.[36]

Although remitting is common, not all Mexican immigrants do so. Catalina Amuedo-Dorantes and Susan Pozo analyzed surveys of labor migrants who were voluntarily returning to Mexico from the United States between 1993 and 2000. They found, for example, that 34 percent of authorized immigrants and 37 percent of undocumented immigrants had sent remittances during their time in the United States. On average, documented migrant workers remitted 49 percent of their monthly earnings, leaving about half to use for themselves or save.[37] Even so, the criminalization of any Mexican migrant workers for remitting is unwarranted, as is the call for a formal remittance tax.

WHY REMITTANCES SHOULD NOT BE TAXED

Remittances Strengthen the U.S. Economy

The belief that remittances drain the U.S. economy ignores complex economic factors that are intertwined with remittances. Remitted funds boost U.S. exports by increasing foreigners' ability to purchase American goods.[38] In Mexico, "increases in per capita spending on individual resident household goods and services correspond closely to the pattern of remittance flows."[39] When people have more money, they purchase more electronics and other luxury goods that American companies manufacture or sell. Further, Texas, Arizona, and California are the states that export the most goods to Mexico, and the value of these exports increases with rising demand. Remittances may also impact exchange rates and facilitate international commerce.[40]

Remittances not only increase the ability to purchase U.S. products abroad, but they also serve as a key indicator of the contributions that remitters make directly to the U.S. economy. Most remitters, who are predominantly immigrants, enhance productivity and fill labor gaps in the United States. A report by the Center for Latin America and Latino Studies (CLALS) and the immigration lab at American University estimated that in 2022 alone, migrants who remit contributed at least $2.2 trillion to the U.S. economy, which is around 8% of the country's GDP.[41]

Immigrants who remit provide short-term support to the U.S. economy, helping to keep inflation low. They contribute to maintaining more youthful and economically active demographics in an aging population. Additionally, they fill labor gaps in key industries such as construction. The CLALS report also indicates that migrant workers are more responsive to changes in labor demands than native-born workers.

While CLALS's estimate of the contributions of immigrants is a good starting point, it doesn't fully encapsulate the substantial contributions of remitters. This estimate doesn't consider the economic growth stimulated by immigrants through their spending in the U.S., which creates demand and generates jobs. Moreover, it overlooks their human, cultural, culinary, and creative contributions. Despite these limitations, the estimate represents a step forward in painting a comprehensive picture of the significant contributions made by remitters to the U.S. economy and society. It reminds us that remittances are evidence of the important economic participation that migrants have in their new societies and they benefit more than the countries that receive remittances.

Taxing Remittances Is Ineffective

Taxing remittances has not been effective in reducing the amount of money transferred overseas and would not bring in significant amounts of money. In countries that have placed a tax on outgoing monetary transfers, like Gabon in 2008 and Palau in 2013, overall remittance amounts did not change significantly.[42] According to the IMF, "the revenue raised from a tax on remittances will be small relative to the revenue base of the country."[43] For example, a 5 percent tax levied on remittances sent from the Gulf Cooperation Council countries would bring in only an extra $4 billion, which is equivalent to 0.3 percent of their combined GDP.[44]

The 7 percent fee on remittances by undocumented immigrants that was proposed in the U.S. Senate would have generated an estimated maximum of $1 billion in tax revenue. The plan was to use that tax revenue to pay for a border wall, but estimates of the cost of a wall along the southern border range between $21 billion and $30 billion. A 7 percent tax would not begin to cover such astronomical costs and would ultimately prove to be inconsequential to the state of the economy. Because of this, the cost of imposing, administering, and enforcing this tax would likely exceed its expected revenue, rendering the entire situation incredibly impractical.[45]

While an extra remittance tax may seem like a minor change, it would have a greater impact than people may initially predict. It would place undue financial burdens on the family members to whom the money is sent.[46] Clearly, taxing remittances would raise the cost of remitting, reducing the amount that people in the home country ultimately receive with each transaction. Even a small tax can have a significant accumulated effect on the ability of families to support themselves. Imposing taxes on remittances not only violates workers' rights, as their wages have already been taxed, but it can also jeopardize the lives of those receiving remittances.[47]

Low-Income Remitters Would Pay More in Taxes

As countries around the world curate immigration policies that favor highly skilled immigrants, those who are less educated are more threatened by government proposals to tax remittances. Immigrants with little to no formal education remit proportionally more funds to their home countries than those who are more educated. On average, those who do not complete more than primary or secondary education send the most remittances, and those with lower incomes send larger portions of their weekly wages to families abroad.[48] Thus, any tax levied on remittances would have a greater impact on immigrants of low socioeconomic status and potentially harm their transnational families. In 2007, Riccardo Faini questioned whether low-, middle-, and high-earning migrant workers remitted different sums to their home countries. He challenged the belief that higher-skilled immigrants remitted more than those with fewer skills, arguing that while skilled laborers earn more, they use their funds to spend time in their home country and relocate their families to their host country. Faini developed a model using data from the World Bank to corroborate his hypothesis that skilled immigrant workers exhibited a smaller propensity to remit than low-skilled immigrant workers. Our data from El Paso, and comparable data from Paris and New York showed similar findings.[49] These findings debunk arguments that a remittance tax would mainly impact high-income workers who could afford the extra fee.[50]

A Remittance Tax Would Strengthen the Unregulated Informal Economy

Taxing the money that immigrants send to loved ones will not stop them from remitting, especially considering that families depend on their wages for survival. Instead, it may cause immigrants to turn to underground or newly created illegal avenues of money transfer and increase the global necessity of black markets. Previous research on migration has repeatedly asserted that informal pathways of money transfer would replace more formal methods of sending remittances if a tax was imposed.[51] It was further shown that regardless of the socioeconomic status of migrant workers, they will find more practical ways to remit if they are forced away from traditional mechanisms. A study conducted by Ariel Stevenson verified that a tax on migratory workers would bring in more government revenue without seriously impacting the economic positions of migrant workers. However, the conclusions of the study are incomplete because it failed to consider informal remittance channels, which only a couple decades ago dominated the distribution of remittances worldwide.[52]

Furthermore, demands for the government to closely monitor remittances are hard to fulfill. In the past, regulation of "informal" channels has led to certain unintended consequences, like denying people access to remitted funds.[53] An example of a historical remittance system is the *hawala*, which is used in the Muslim world to make transfers based on traditional accounting and bookkeeping methods in which the money does not actually move. Interest is not charged on the money in order to comply with Islamic practice. The United States and international bodies cracked down on the use of the hawala system after September 11, 2001, alleging that it could be used to finance terrorism. Instead, the World Bank, IMF, Inter-American Development Bank, and other regional banking bodies now push to "bankarize" immigrants. They encourage migrants to open bank accounts and remit through large transnational banks with headquarters in immigrant-receiving regions. Interestingly though, similar to hawala, banks and remittance businesses do not physically send money. Instead, they transmit information about the money received at point A to match a withdrawal at point B.[54]

People have always migrated and will continue to do so, sending remittances all the while. As is common throughout history, adding barriers to financial activities like sending remittances will result only in more unregulated transactions. Now and before, community members traveling back and forth bring money and gifts; some even make a living as personal couriers for many immigrant families in the same communities.

While statisticians try to account for remittance undercounts, it may be impossible to accurately measure the amount of remitted money and the frequency with which it circulates worldwide. Intermediary organizations and informal channels are sometimes utilized to send money abroad.[55] In fact, unregulated transfer mechanisms are oftentimes more "efficient and attentive" than official bank channels.[56] An immigrant's preferred remittance system depends on whether they have a bank account, their trust in banks and businesses, remittance fees, and the convenience and speed of delivery.[57]

Remittances Can Reduce Poverty

The contemporary interest in remittances is partially due to global policy efforts that aim to reduce poverty within neoliberal premises without making large commitments for foreign aid. Thus, framing remittances as development tools is central to showing that rich countries are providing financial assistance to developing countries and mitigating global poverty without committing significantly larger amounts of state funds.[58] Remittances to low- and middle-income countries have risen from around $75 billion in 1989, to $125 billion by the mid-2000s, and to more than $350 billion in 2011.[59] These are underestimations, given that unrecorded remittances also flow through informal pathways.[60]

In 2018, remittances were essential to the livelihoods of over 800 million individuals.[61] Dennis Conway and Jeffrey Cohen consider remittances, or "migradollars," as positive contributions toward home communities in Latin America.[62] Some Mexican families and households depend on global migration to produce remittances as a type of economic "survival strategy."[63] For lower-income families, remittances are a critical resource that ensures stability in the long run, and with the benefits they provide to those who receive them, they serve as a symbol of heightened social status and thus, as a local creator of inequality. Sometimes, their investments allow young migrant families to be able to afford much more than they could previously, therefore heightening status through a partial transfer of money from the Global North to the Global South[64]— but not without the frequent cost of family separation for long periods.

Remittances Contribute Foreign Currency

According to the World Bank, an estimated 270 million migrants worldwide remitted a combined total of $689 billion in 2019.[65] These funds are a lifeline for smaller economies because they are the most reliable assistance that people have during economic crashes, natural disasters, and political upheavals.[66] Remittances can aid entrepreneurship in countries where people struggle financially, acting as crucial initial capital for microbusinesses.[67] Remittance inflows benefit central banks by bringing borrowing costs in foreign currencies down. They also improve a country's credit rating. Some nations, such as Egypt, Nigeria, and the Philippines, would have very weak credit ratings if they did not receive remittances.[68] While risky to do so, some countries have used remittance projections as the basis for borrowing foreign currency abroad.

The agricultural labor force in many Latin American nations decreased during a wave of migration to the United States in the 1970s and 1980s, leading to a massive drop in their agricultural GDP. These countries changed from "agroexporting economies" to "labor-exporting nations."[69] During this time, remittances skyrocketed and became many families' primary source of stable income. Between 1980 and 2000, the remittances sent to Colombia alone increased by over $5 billion. Similarly, the Dominican Republic's GDP grew by about 12.5 percent from remittances alone.[70] At the macro level, remittances strengthen the national economy and lower the rate of poverty in some countries. However, those who frame remittances as a panacea often overstate the case or measure impacts mainly in the short term.[71]

Some researchers argue that although large remittance inflows into a country may appear to be beneficial, they may place that country at a long-term disadvantage.[72] From this perspective, some countries are ultimately more crippled than assisted by remittances. For example, many people in Jordan depend on remittances as a major source of income. At multiple points between 1972 and 2009, remittances accounted for over 20 percent of Jordan's GDP and reached around $2.8 billion in 2009. Remittances from Jordanian expatriates, three-fourths of whom reside in Saudi Arabia and the UAE, have been steadily increasing since the early 1990s. Rises in remittance inflows typically do not mean that migrants are earning higher incomes than before but rather that there are more workers living abroad.[73] As immigrant families reunite abroad or move back remittance flows decrease so emigration and remittances cannot continue to increase indefinitely.

DECEPTIVE PORTRAYALS OF REMITTANCES

Remittances Do Not Function Like Foreign Aid

Some economists and development workers deceivingly frame remittances as a new type of foreign aid. Clearly, remittances are more resilient and reliable forms of income for transnational families than international development aid or loans.[74] Throughout the financial instability of 2008 and 2009, remittance rates dipped no more than 5.2 percent.[75] At the same time, foreign direct investment (FDI) plummeted by 39.7 percent.[76] Foreign aid is important in supporting struggling economies and migrants should not be held responsible for creating economic development in their places of origin.

Researchers projected in 2020 that the global economy would experience the sharpest and most rapid decline in remittances the world had ever seen as a result of the COVID-19 pandemic.[77] The prediction did not come true, as remittances fell by only 1.6 percent.[78] Again, foreign investments and international development aid funds did not remain nearly as stable in the face of crisis. Remittances in 2020 outpaced FDI by $281 billion and development assistance by $361 billion.[79] Immigrants also remit their wages for extended periods. According to Robert Suro, 23 percent of migrant workers who have lived in the United States for more than twenty years still remit[80]—although this does not mean they will remit forever. Remittances end after families reunify at either location of the transnational household, and extended family members and friends either move or die. United Nations' reports point out that remittances make up "over three times the amount of official development assistance (ODA) and foreign direct investment (FDI) combined."[81] An estimated 50 percent of global remittances are sent to rural regions of the world, many of which are in the most need of aid.[82] For countries like Haiti, remittances are their largest source of foreign capital.[83] The GDPs of places with smaller economies, such as Moldova, Tonga, Guyana, and Haiti, depend heavily on remittances.[84]

In addition to providing for typical daily needs, remitted money can mean extra relief for victims of natural disasters. Haitian families receiving remittances from relatives working in the United States recovered much more quickly from a major earthquake in 2010 than those who did not. In the aftermath of the disaster, remittances surged 20 percent, totaling $360 million more than the usual annual average.[85] Remittances can cushion the tragic consequences of environmental disasters and provide direct support to those who are affected. David Henderson, a former economic adviser in the Reagan administration, argues that remittances are substantially more effective than foreign aid because corrupt governments cannot disrupt them.[86] He cites the example of the Congo, where President Mobutu used developmental aid in a way that Henderson describes as "yet another means to accumulate personal wealth."[87] Dilip Ratha and Sanket Mohapatra agree that people receiving remittances do not experience the bureaucratic barriers or problems that are associated with official aid.[88]

Some argue that remittances are a global transfer of wages that contribute to the 2030 United Nations Sustainable Development Goals, which include helping to eradicate poverty and hunger, establishing good health and well-being, supporting quality education, providing clean water and sanitation, bolstering economic growth and employment, and reducing inequality worldwide.[89] Thus, remittances have been wrongly called the "most significant and effective source of global development aid."[90] This is equivalent to saying that having a high-paying job is the best way to combat poverty, even if many people are barred from applying for these jobs. If policymakers and development experts truly believed in migration and the resulting decrease in global inequality, they would advocate for open borders for workers. What further goes unmentioned is the role that taxation and the public funding of universal programs and public goods have in decreasing inequality in welfare states.

Many researchers who have analyzed the links between remittances and economic growth believe remittances are a more stable source of income and benefits than development aid and loans.[91] But as we have established, remittances are sent to family and loved ones as support for basic needs and living expenses. Remittances should not be conflated with international aid. Remittances are private funds, and foreign aid consists of large monetary gifts from rich to poor countries to be used, for example, to alleviate poverty, fight pandemics, address humanitarian crises, or support public projects.[92] Migrant workers have worked to earn remittances before distributing them—the sacrifice represented by remittances furthers the economic precarity of the workers who send them, quite in contrast to money sent by the wealthiest countries and individuals in the world. Furthermore, immigrants who send these funds are doing so despite often being underpaid and suffering social exclusion, hate crimes, and deportation in the countries where they work. This money goes straight into the pockets of the intended recipients and not into the hands of a government entity that redistributes the funds. Also, remittance behaviors and uses are uniquely shaped by the human relationships that precede them.[93] It is difficult to argue that charities, nonprofit organizations, and government agencies share the same deep personal motivations to send money as individuals.

Remittances Help Children Attain Basic Education but Not Always Higher Education

Pakistan and El Salvador and other Latin American countries may experience higher long-term school retention rates and lower child labor rates as a result of labor migration and remittances.[94] The 2008 and 2009 Mexican National Occupation and Employment Survey, which tracks the employment of Mexicans who are twelve and older, revealed that rural Mexican families who received remittances generally lived in towns with less than 2,500 people, had poor health care, and experienced an overall lack of resources. The probability of a child going to school was significantly reduced during the remittance shortage caused by the 2008–2009 recession.[95] Children are pushed to work and therefore don't attend school when their families struggle financially. Remittances are a major source of income and enable children to get an education instead of earning money to survive. Nonetheless, most of these studies measure enrollment in basic education; remittances do not necessarily mean that children of immigrants who are left behind will go to college in their home country. While remittances help with basic education, they do not necessarily contribute to generalized upward social mobility through access to higher education and professional jobs locally, as many children of migrants drop out of school or reunite with family members abroad and thus cannot directly contribute to development in their place of birth.

Remittances Do Not Necessarily Promote Democracy

Many migrants do not sever their connections to their home countries. They participate in transnational communities and ultimately in a broader cultural exchange. Peggy Levitt proposed the term *social remittances* in 1998, defining it as "the ideas, behaviors, identities, and social capital that flow from receiving to sending country communities."[96] She identified three main types of social remittances: normative structures, systems of practice, and social capital.[97] Normative structures are the ideas, values, and belief systems of a culture that are exchanged, while systems of practice are the individual or group actions subsequently shaped by such norms. Remittance-led migration may also be driven by the desire to increase one's family esteem and social standing, or their social capital, in their community. Levitt's conclusions are based on her fieldwork with transnational communities in the Dominican Republic and in Boston's Jamaica Plain neighborhood.[98] Social remittances were exchanged when migrants returned to live in or visit their communities of origin, when family members visited migrants in their host communities, and when letters, videos, cassettes, and telephone calls were shared between migrants and family members.[99] Levitt and others argue that through these interactions, immigrants living in democratic and diverse societies may spread some of these ideas to less democratic and supposedly homogenous or race-blind contexts.[100]

We can think of examples of social remittances that immigrants send to their communities of orgin, but many cases show that this does not necessarily applied to democratic values. Many authoritarian countries have important diasporas and this has not always produced dedemocratization in their countries of origin.

Some argue that remittances raise the incomes of individual households and therefore undermine autocratic regimes, which can no longer easily garner support by providing goods for those in need. This can lead to the disintegration of electoral support for one-party dictatorships and to the promotion of democratization.[101] More remittances have been linked to greater government accountability in Mexico, but they have also been linked to government deterioration in parts of the low-income Muslim world with weak democratic institutions.[102] Aware that families are receiving migrant wages, governments can become increasingly corrupt and disincentivized to spend money on providing public services.[103] Remittances to low-income people can cause delays in the formation of a welfare state and lessen the pressure on authorities to provide services, infrastructure, and social programs to remote rural areas. Remittances delay the negotiations between rulers and the ruled and thus also delay democratization in the sense of expanding the rights and political voice of groups previously excluded.[104]

Recent developments show that remittances—or high income—do not protect against autocracy. Cubans and those living under other authoritarian regimes have received remittances for decades, and democratization has not occurred. Furthermore, there has been much dedemocratization in many countries in the Global North in recent decades.[105]

CONCLUSION

The dynamics around remittances are complex and require a multifaceted approach to be understood. Some researchers have discovered downfalls to remittances: for example, they may create a cycle of financial dependence for low-income nations that is unsustainable and ultimately harmful to those countries' intrinsic development. However, it is important to recall that remittances are necessary in the first place only when a nation is not financially providing for its people. The pressure to feed one's family is too great to wait until unemployment and inflation rates fall. Remittances are a portion of a transnational family's wage income sent across borders instead of being spent locally. It is not equal at all to foreign aid and most often is not like charity either. Some people remit to help those in need or to support local churches and organizations. Yet, the bulk of remittances goes to food, housing, and other basic needs of the rest of the nuclear family or other close relatives. Migrants' home communities may also experience the long-term effects of some "brain drain," or the emigration of part of a country's highly skilled workforce. It is difficult for economies to recover from hard times when many highly trained and educated young people find work elsewhere. Although migrant workers help to improve conditions in their home country by sending remittances to loved ones, some remit less money over time because they eventually allocate funds toward relocating their family to their host country.[106] They are also engaging in and contributing to a local economy different than that of their home country. Their new homes are often places with more opportunities where they can contribute and develop professionally than in their places of birth, so their move represents an overall personal and global gain.

Issuing a tax on remittances operates on the assumption that immigrant income will never be recycled back into the U.S. economy, but research shows that such recycling *does* happen already.[107] This tax would be regressive, as low-income workers are more likely to remit an important part of their wages to families abroad, while wealthier immigrants who move their families to their host country send less in remittances. These are major gaps that separate policy decisions and declarations from real-world processes.

CHAPTER 7

THERE IS NO REFUGEE CRISIS

Imperialism, decolonization, violence, natural disasters, instability, and poverty have uprooted people around the world for thousands of years. Early in the twentieth century, around the time of World War I, invasions and ethnic cleansing forced Serbians, Armenians, and Belgians out of their respective countries.[1] People fleeing the chaos of World War II, the 1956 Hungarian Revolution, the fall of the Soviet Union, the Cuban Revolution, the disintegration of Yugoslavia in the early 1990s, the invasions of Iraq and Afghanistan, genocide, and countless other tragedies became part of what Western countries refer to as refugee crises. The United Nations High Commissioner for Refugees (UNHCR) reported that in 2001 an estimated twelve million refugees—most with roots in Afghanistan, Macedonia, and Palestine—fled their home countries and could not return.[2] The year prior, the number of forcibly displaced Afghans had already reached 3.6 million, and, globally, more than 1 million people sought asylum in host countries.[3] Since then, conditions around the world have not significantly improved for refugees. In 2011, the outbreak of war in Syria and Libya forced millions of people to seek refuge in other countries, and in 2021, millions of people were still displaced internationally.

Organizations, websites, and thousands of articles refer to various crises. At this point, it seems that the modern world is drowning in crises. Labeling these distinct situations as crises is akin to keeping a window open during a thunderstorm and hurriedly wiping up the raindrops while never questioning how they got inside. Of course, as the storm continues, the rain pours in. One serious, systemic problem regarding displacement is the legacies of imperialism and current neocolonial relations.

This chapter is divided into four primary sections, the first of which expands on twenty-first-century global migration trends and the formal categorizations of migrants, refugees, asylum seekers, and internally displaced people. We then challenge the truth and usefulness of the term *refugee crisis*, analyzing how Western powers have supported its popularity to avoid taking responsibility for the root causes of conflicts in postcolonial regions. We further dissect international rates of refugee resettlement, particularly those of Syrian refugees, since 2015, alongside the exclusionary actions of certain countries that endanger migrants. Building on this, we distinguish how the rhetoric that blames, infantilizes, and criminalizes refugees works in conjunction with xenophobia, stereotypes, and fearmongering to support the myth of a crisis. We wrap up the discussion by calling for a shift in the status quo of how refugees and asylum seekers are framed in international discussions about migration and aided by organizations and governments. We provide recommendations for the different social, health, and political arenas in which policies regarding the treatment and allocation of refugees can be improved. In doing so, we address the need to rebuild countries that have experienced conflict, to uphold the Schengen Agreement in Europe, to provide mental health services for refugees, and in the case of the West, to acknowledge its role and benefit in the current postcolonial world order.

MIGRATION TRENDS AND STATISTICS

A *refugee* is defined as someone who has left their home country and cannot return due to a well-founded fear of violence and/or persecution related to any element of their identity or political opinion.[4] Daniel Trilling notes that the word has two meanings: the "legal meaning, in that it describes a person who is eligible for asylum under international law, and a colloquial meaning, in that it describes a person who has fled their home."[5] People who can no longer remain in their homes may be placed temporarily in refugee camps managed by UNHCR in developing countries and may eventually be relocated to host countries. Importantly, the criteria for being internationally recognized as a refugee are rigid, and other displaced people might be mistakenly referred to as refugees.

While refugees who meet the UNHCR definition fall under the jurisdiction of the UN, internally displaced people do not, and are not eligible to, receive most types of humanitarian aid offered by that organization. Internally displaced people are also forced to flee their homes, yet they remain within the same country, never crossing an international border. If they cross such a border, they have the option to seek asylum in a different country and may eventually meet the criteria to be recognized as refugees. Many, however, are formally referred to as asylum seekers, who request protection and assistance from a host country to which they relocate. Some asylum seekers do not meet the criteria that the international community requires to be officially recognized as a refugee, whereas others are simply waiting for their status to be determined.[6] Ironically, people who flee war, natural disasters, or famine are not formally considered refugee candidates until they apply for asylum in a host country. Many Central Americans and others do so at the U.S.-Mexico border, and it is becoming increasingly common for Venezuelans and Colombians to request asylum in Spain as they face economic crises, political dictatorships, violent protests, guerilla warfare, and the COVID-19 pandemic at home.[7]

In contrast, a stateless person is not a citizen of any country. Some populations may feel an ethnic affinity to one another but believe they lack a country of their own. For example, the 1916 Sykes-Picot Agreement divided West Asia into the nations of Syria, Iraq, Palestine, and Lebanon, leaving the populous Kurdish ethnic group spread across different political units. To dispute their political exclusion, large Kurdish populations declared themselves citizens of Kurdistan, an internationally unrecognized nation that spans portions of modern-day Iraq, Iran, Syria, and Turkey. Other stateless groups include the Uyghurs, many of whom live in the Xinjiang region in northwestern China, and the Rohingya, who are an Indigenous people from western Myanmar. Both are mostly composed of Muslims and have been persecuted by national authorities and refused citizenship in their countries of origin.[8]

In 2019, 79.5 million people were forcibly displaced worldwide, and 4.2 million were stateless. Since it is difficult to obtain precise counts, these numbers are ostensibly low estimates, and there are likely millions more who have not been recognized. The overwhelming majority of UNHCR-mandated refugees have origins in Syria, Venezuela, Afghanistan, Myanmar, or South Sudan. Many Syrian refugees are housed in Turkey, while others now reside in Lebanon and Jordan. The Rohingya population has been fleeing ethnic cleansing and violence perpetrated by the Myanmar government and military since 2017, escaping into the southern regions of Bangladesh.[9] Turkey, Colombia, Pakistan, Uganda, and Germany host the most refugees, partly because of their proximity to refugee-producing countries, international arrangements, and welcoming programs.[10] Despite the immediate need for new homes, only an estimated 107,800 displaced people have been formally resettled, representing a small fraction of the actual number of people who require help.[11] This large gap between those who seek resettlement and those who have received it reveals the extent to which the international community disregards the urgency of the needs of displaced people and demonstrates an overwhelming demand for more welcoming integration policies.

Wealthy countries have the means to help alleviate refugee suffering, but the United States has a complicated history in this regard. Since the 1980s, the numbers of refugees and immigrants permitted into the country annually have often decreased. Instead of prioritizing resettlement programs, national leaders opt to restrict the number of refugees they take in. Refugee and immigrant communities often experience limited access to labor markets, education, health services, and public goods in their host countries and are sometimes forced to work in shadow economies where they are vulnerable to exploitation. To ensure the long-term security and success of native-born citizens and refugees alike, the international community should prioritize policies that encourage cross-cultural understanding, provide support for newly acclimated residents, and extend opportunities to immigrants.

THE REAL CRISIS: UNMANAGED MIGRATION

The Number of Migrants and Refugees Is Manageable

Refugee resettlement and migration in general are not new phenomena: people worldwide are deeply familiar with the stories of those who had to leave their homes because of war, famine, or persecution in Europe, Latin America, and Asia throughout different historical periods and today. The United States has always experienced influxes of people. In 1948, after World War II displaced millions of people worldwide, the United States passed the Displaced Persons Act, which accepted 400,000 European refugees into the country and granted them visas. Similarly, over one million Southeast Asian refugees arrived in the 1970s and 1980s, most from Vietnam and Cambodia.[12]

Despite the regularity of migration spurred by conflict, the number of refugees at any given time in contemporary history is typically framed as unmanageable, posing too much of a burden on the international community. Of course, for one small country like Greece, accepting all the world's refugees and migrants would be incredibly challenging, if not impossible, in terms of state and local resources. However, Greece is not the only place to seek refuge; there are hundreds of other countries that are able to accept, resettle, and integrate immigrants into their societies. Many places in Europe are aging and losing population, and like towns in the Greek islands and countryside, they desperately need more people to stay viable.

Compared to native-born populations in Western countries, refugees are the minority by a landslide. The United States has accepted an estimated 3.1 million refugees since 1980, which averages about 77,500 refugees yearly, or 0.02 percent of the total country's population in 2021.[13] Similarly, months before Europe declared a refugee crisis in 2015, the total European Union population had reached 508.2 million.[14] EU member countries panicked and fought over how to handle the newcomers, settling on accepting 1.3 million, or a mere 0.26 percent of the EU population.[15] Millions more could, and should, have been granted asylum in wealthy European countries. Kenneth Roth describes what many call the current "wave of people" as "more like a trickle when considered against the pool that must absorb it."[16] To put this into perspective, roughly 340,000 individuals are estimated to be using irregular paths to enter Europe across the Mediterranean or through the Balkans. Compared to the over 448 million people who lived in the EU in 2019, this number is not as intimidating as it appears.[17] Given the wealth and development of most EU countries, accepting such a small proportion of people should not pose any serious difficulties.

The West Cries Wolf

According to Charley Yaxley, a spokesman for UNHCR, the actual crisis is that a few countries are handling "a disproportionate responsibility for receiving new arrivals," not that there is a relatively disproportionate number of arrivals.[18] Tom Miles highlights that since 2015, fewer people have made the migration journey to Europe every year. The flow of people into the EU decreased to 46,449 refugees and migrants in 2018. These data show that migration flows are not as dramatic as they are portrayed to be by news outlets and politicians. In fact, instead of focusing on the roots of conflict and conditions in countries that produce refugees, the media often discuss these issues only in relation to the movement of refugees. Leonard Doyle, a spokesman for the UN International

Organization for Migration, articulated the unwarranted emphasis on migrants and refugees clearly: "We consider it a political crisis, not a migrant crisis. We are concerned that the toxic narrative against migrants, to put it bluntly, be diminished, and people see migration for what it is. It's a necessary part of the modern world, provided it's managed. The issue is that people's perception is that it's out of control."[19]

It seems that the world has been thrown into a perpetual state of alarm about people on the move. National governments are playing hot potato with displaced people's lives and remain divided "about who should take responsibility for migrants crossing the Mediterranean" and landing on European shores.[20] Debates on this topic have, quite literally, divided the EU. The United Kingdom, a country that houses over 100,000 refugees, voted to exit the EU in 2016 partially in an effort to close its borders to migrants (see chapter 9). However, the chaos that has ensued in Europe is not attributable to refugees themselves; rather, it is countries' negative reactions to them, as many of them refuse to integrate refugees and immigrants within their borders. Instead of accepting the current situation and adapting to the temporary waves of migrants, the EU, the United States, Australia, and other countries around the world justify their increasingly conservative border policies by characterizing the situation as a crisis.

Violent Means, Violent Ends

The unceasing fabrication of refugee crises influences the public's political and social views on migration. The general Western population now perceives the flow of refugees *alone* as something that requires solving, but this attitude fails to acknowledge the root causes of migration and common patterns in human movement that all countries have witnessed. Migration cannot be "solved" because it is a timeless and constantly fluctuating phenomenon. The distinction between legal and illegal migration is a fictitious one. As referenced in chapter 2, border walls built by European and Chinese rulers temporarily kept enemies, refugees, and stateless peoples on the outside. However, in the long run, those walls did not permanently stop the movement of people.

Imperialism and the West Instead of trying to solve migration, it is imperative that we explore the historical and contemporary events causing people to seek refuge. High-income countries concentrated in the West, with histories of colonial expansion and domination, receive asylum applications from people with origins in regions of the world that were once split up and shared among colonizers, as decreed by documents like the Sykes-Picot Agreement. One could say that the modern world is defined by crises, violence, and displacement created by imperial expansion. The genocide of Native Americans and the capture of their territories, the kidnapping and enslavement of Africans, and the extraction of resources across Latin America—all crimes against the vulnerable—are victories for colonizing oppressors that shaped current international relationships and that perpetuate social and economic hegemony over the colonized.

Neocolonialism The suffering created by these historical events has in turn fostered unstable conditions among colonized populations that produce refugees. Hegemonic countries rely on instability to maintain power over postcolonial places to this day, although they operationalize domination via less explicit methods than earlier in history. A visible and relevant example is U.S. interventions in Latin America, which ranged from providing military power for coup d'états of left-leaning rulers to inserting multinational agricultural corporations in struggling regions.[21] By interfering with the economies and politics of rising postcolonial countries, the United States ensures that its own interests are immediately met while sowing further instability for its future benefit. This process of ongoing contemporary oppression of postcolonial countries is referred to as neocolonialism, which began appearing in discourse regarding postcoloniality, imperialism, and neoliberal capitalism in the early 1960s.[22] The term was used by Ghana's first president, Kwame Nkrumah, in 1965 when leaders of newly independent African countries were drawing attention to how their relationships with their colonial oppressors had not changed very much since achieving political liberation.[23] He pointed out that, despite their formal sovereignty, countries in postcolonial regions are still ruled by the economic markets, trade rules, political ideologies, and linguistic hierarchies of their colonizers and other high-income countries. Inequality is produced within and largely between countries.[24] Entire regions in Africa, Asia, and the Americas have been distinguished first as the Third World and now as the Global South by their past and present subordination and not simply by their low national incomes or levels of integration into the international market.

So why is it important to discuss neocolonialism in relation to refugees? Imperial states are now turning away migrants whose very displacement they are guilty of causing through previous or current military intervention.[25] Plenty of research on refugees and migration in general ignores the violent history of imperialism that set the stage for intranational struggles, political instability, economic hardship, and dependence on foreign aid and remittances. For instance, the United States has repeatedly intervened in the economy, political rule, and social structure of Guatemala, Honduras, and El Salvador since the 1900s.[26] It is no coincidence that those three countries produce some of the highest numbers of refugees in the world. It is especially ironic that the Western world fights the very conditions that it designed not too long ago and that the United States turns Guatemalan, Honduran, and Salvadoran asylum seekers away from its southern border.[27]

Creating a Crisis to Avoid Responsibility Countries in the West insist that they cannot manage the number of refugees and migrants seeking a new home in the world, but these governments *could* if they chose to do so. Displacement is a branch on the tree, but the centuries-old roots of imperialist ventures are what hold the overall structure in place to this day. Any "refugee crisis" is a socially constructed term that distracts from the actual problem: high-income and imperialist countries do not take responsibility for their violent actions because they benefit from the equally violent postcolonial world order. No so-called crises would permeate news outlets and public discourse if refugees, asylum seekers, and economic immigrants were welcomed into more Western nations at slightly higher numbers. It is these countries' unwillingness to provide proper aid, resettlement programs, and integration initiatives that has led them to cry wolf and declare refugee crises. By doing so, they reinforce the belief that refugees are problematic people, avoid international responses, and deny their responsibility for contemporary neocolonial conditions. This may be part of the neoliberal reduction of the welfare state, resulting in a lack of government programs for the public and an acceptance of decreased tax rates for the very rich (see chapter 8).

Refugee Resettlement Efforts Are Lacking

The Syrian civil war and subsequent conflict are often cited as one of the most pressing contemporary international humanitarian issues, and the outcomes have been horrific. Beginning in 2011, the conflict resulted in the displacement of an estimated six million Syrians, amounting to about half of the country's population. At least 100,000 people were killed over nine years, and this upheaval spurred what the Western world labeled the 2015 European refugee crisis.[28] In 2015, only an estimated 107,800 total refugees around the world were resettled in new countries through governmental processes. Millions of Syrians remain in a legal limbo, lacking formal resettlement and integration support but permitted to remain in different countries and refugee camps. While these numbers signify how severe and widespread the effects of the civil war were on Syrians, they represent cumulative statistics and do not account for population growth trends. Furthermore, in 2014, the number of forcibly displaced people had risen 50 percent since the beginning of the conflict three years prior. This was a result of the mass exodus of Syrians as well as host countries' reluctance to accept refugees.[29]

There are more informal and temporary types of resettlement that displaced people experience.[30] In 2019, a majority (86 percent) of all refugees were hosted in predominantly low-income Middle Eastern, African, and South Asian countries. Places closest to refugee-producing nations typically hold a large share of displaced people. However, sometimes these regions lack resources and should not be expected to be the sole providers of support.[31] Refugees might bide their time in these places and wait until they can return home or temporarily stop in a neighboring country before embarking on a longer migration journey. This pattern has held true in the case of Syria. Its neighboring countries, such as Lebanon, Egypt, Turkey, Jordan, and Iraq, have accommodated perhaps the largest populations of Syrian refugees. The UNHCR reports that there are, according to official registries, over four million Syrians who have found refuge in those countries as well as in North Africa.[32] Iraq and Lebanon have provided cash assistance and essential items and services to Syrians seeking asylum within their borders. Germany, Sweden, the UK, and the United States were the Western countries that first offered protection to Syrians through resettlement programs and committed to accepting additional refugees, albeit to varying degrees.[33]

In Europe, regional debates about refugee resettlement that began in 2015 soon coalesced into an international discussion because of the lack of resettlement options provided to Syrians and others impacted by the war. Although resettlements increased to almost 190,000 worldwide the following year, they were spread out among only thirty-seven host countries.[34] Clearly, the total percentage of displaced people is bound to rise year after year if most host countries institute an annual acceptance cap of 5,135 asylum seekers. After 2016, even fewer countries formally resettled refugees—around twenty-eight nations in 2018 and twenty-six in 2019.[35] The number of people permitted entry into the United States also nosedived because President Donald Trump's administration placed highly restrictive caps on refugees and immigrants. Shortly after, COVID-19 restrictions reduced international resettlement operations. Because of new stringencies, the number of formally resettled refugees declined to 34,400 in 2020.[36] New adult asylum seekers were banned from the United States under the Public Health Service Act, codified in Title 42 of the U.S. Code, due to supposed public health concerns about COVID-19 that could have been alleviated by imposing a mandatory two-week quarantine for immigrants.

Member countries of the UN had the chance to reform and grow their refugee resettlement schemes in 2016, but their compromises far surpassed their accomplishments at their meetings on the Syrian conflict at the organization's Geneva headquarters. Policies related to refugees and immigration slightly expanded for Syrian refugees in EU countries but ultimately produced very few new entry slots.[37]

Rethinking Climate Refugees While people adapt, and may initially move close by, a person who leaves their country for environmental reasons is not considered a refugee in the eyes of the UN. The fact that climate refugees are not regarded as such under international law is problematic because they are perpetually regarded as asylum seekers, and rising sea levels and the increasing occurrence of natural disasters caused by climate change will inevitably displace more people in the near future. Varying estimates agree that at least 200 million people will be displaced by climate change by 2050.[38] Increasing temperatures, rising sea levels, and more frequent and severe natural disasters will force people out of their communities. An increase in temperature as minimal as 1–2 degrees could create water shortages for up to 1.5 billion individuals, especially for the 50–60 percent of the world's population that depend on glacial melt from the Hindu Kush–Himalayas region in Asia.[39] It is still unclear how the international community will manage inevitable waves of climate change refugees when it still has not decided how to manage present migration flows.

Pushing Migrants Away from Safety

Fewer migrants made the dangerous journey across the Mediterranean after the first few years of the Syrian conflict, but more were dying in the process. In 2018, 139,000 refugees and migrants arrived in Europe, the lowest number since 2012. Nevertheless, one refugee died for every fourteen that arrived in Europe that same year.[40] Why was the death toll rising when fewer people were migrating?

Border and naval authorities who conduct surveillance of nearby seas have sometimes used their discretionary power to outright block migrants from entering a country. At times, border authorities in Greece, Libya, Malta, Turkey, and Italy have forced boats of migrants away from their shores and provided inadequate assistance or none at all.[41] Similarly, Rohingyas escaping ethnic cleansing in Myanmar were once stranded on cramped boats with limited provisions for weeks because Thailand, Malaysia, and Indonesia bickered over which country should offer them refuge.[42] Things became even more complicated when the spread of COVID-19 caused the impoundment of humanitarian ships that normally patrolled Italian waters so that workers could quarantine. Malta and Italy vowed to prevent most migrants from disembarking at their ports, declaring that the countries were unsafe. This meant that calls made to emergency rescue lines were either transferred to organizations in different countries or ignored.[43] Since September 2021, the UK has done the same, laying out plans and training personnel to block boats with migrants and asylum seekers from landing on its shores. These "pushbacks" would force the boats back to the points in France from which they originally embarked.[44] As a result, even when migrant flows are relatively low, migrants lose their lives because states close their doors and shores to them.

CONTEMPORARY ANTIREFUGEE ATTITUDES AND XENOPHOBIA

Conservative National Border Policies Are on the Rise

The international community must collaborate and take a collective interest in the allocation of refugees in order to ensure their safety and well-being. It should be a priority to save the lives of migrants, but past promises made by world leaders have not been fulfilled. Certain wealthy nations have avoided providing support to refugees. The UN reportedly "received less than half the funding" required to keep Syrian and South Sudanese refugees properly cared for in 2019, forcing many of them into exploitative labor markets.[45] Instead of building a collaborative plan, countries have chosen to hide behind border barriers and increase national security measures to curb the mobility of those in need. They have also made agreements with transit countries, such as the 2016 deal between the EU and Turkey in which Turkey agreed to hold and allow refugees to settle there.[46]

Kelly Greenhill argues that the EU's response to the needs of asylum seekers and refugees has been disjointed and counterproductive. Rather than properly helping displaced communities, it has bred insecurity and volatility toward refugees in host countries. Responses to refugees have varied considerably from country to country; Germany offers asylum under the Schengen border policy, whereas Poland and Hungary use highly restrictive immigration policies that prioritize domestic political interests over solidarity with refugees and collaboration with other EU members. Others, like Sweden, have not adopted the "hardline stances" that some of their neighbors have, although refugees and immigrants are framed as potential threats in places where they are also encouraged to resettle.[47] Some EU member countries fear that when ties between refugee communities and socially excluded local populations are strengthened, the groups will form a unit capable of challenging dominant political leadership and demanding change.[48]

Problematizing Refugees in Academic, Political, Media, and Public Discourses

As we explained earlier, the present number of displaced people *can* in fact be managed. One of the reasons why the number of refugees and migrants appears unmanageable is the language employed to describe them by the state authorities, media, academics, and researchers that have normalized the use of terms like *refugee crisis*, *refugee problem*, and *solution*.[49] Similarly, Amnesty International wrote that high-income countries were "treating refugees as somebody else's problem."[50] Hosting displaced people is regularly referred to as a burden that the members of the international community must share.[51] These words work *against* refugees, even when written by advocates and migration scholars in opposition to right-wing border policies, because they frame displaced people as alien, alone, incapable, or chaotic. This language portrays them as ontologically problematic, a viewpoint that the media, state powers, and politicians reinforce by associating them with suspicion and crime. In reality, they are people experiencing problems and are not fundamentally a problem themselves. Language is a powerful tool of coercion that has been employed against refugees and immigrant communities as a whole by structures of power that do not welcome immigrants into their borders.

The disintegration of Syria resulted in perhaps one of the most flagrant and striking displays of violence, ignorance, and xenophobia on the part of the rest of the world.[52] The constant spread of images of, and information on, the situation via the internet and the use of the term *crisis* to describe it birthed an international frenzy that simultaneously victimized, criminalized, and blamed displaced Syrians in news coverage and political debates. The same process unfolded in the United States after a crisis was announced at the southern border: immigrants from Mexico and Central and South America are regarded with similar pity, fear, and contempt. This rhetoric has immense consequences for asylum seekers on all fronts and is inherently antirefugee. Counterintuitively, it is used throughout Western literature, including on research regarding displacement and migration, and is key to understanding how the topic is framed and discussed.

The current numbers of incoming asylum seekers and immigrants are also labeled as out of control, an assessment further amplified in political debate because the persons arriving do not match the state's desired religious, racial, ethnic, or socioeconomic demographic. In the United States, which has a long history of favoring western Europeans, White immigrants are less likely to be considered dangerous than immigrants of color (see chapter 2). Meanwhile, Central American and Mexican migrants are regarded as a threat, and the fabrication of a border crisis has only worsened public perceptions about them. According to T. Alexander Aleinikoff, "Refugees are subject to more serious security scrutiny than any other class of immigrants," which shows that some in the international community truly regard them as dangers to the state instead of people seeking refuge. This intense vetting should assuage those who say some refugees are terrorists in disguise.[53]

Polarizing the Public

Recent migration debates in Germany, the second most popular destination for migrants among countries belonging to the Organisation for Economic

Co-operation and Development, have resulted in the sudden polarization of political beliefs about and attitudes toward immigrants and refugees. Former German chancellor Angela Merkel, a proponent of refugee integration, received backlash from conservative politicians and EU citizens for maintaining moderately porous borders and promoting her motto of "Wir schauffen das" (We can do it).[54] Since the declaration of a crisis, far-right politicians have gained greater approval throughout Germany and framed Muslims as a threat to its social order. On the other hand, massive civic movements practicing "welcome culture" have also stood in solidarity with refugees and offered them assistance. In the long-term, these refugees have allowed the German economy to grow and to recover from the economic effects of the pandemic.

In nearby Austria, Esther Greussing and Hajo Boomgaarden conducted a study on media coverage in six newspapers to distinguish any dominant patterns that might influence how the general public understands the arrival of refugees. Media outlets in 2015 regularly associated refugees with crime, terrorism, and illegality, focusing on the criminalization of asylum seekers by questioning their deservingness of "sympathy and support."[55] The authors discovered multiple narratives that related immigration to economic and national security threats, whereas fewer media providers adopted educational and humanitarian frameworks when discussing refugees. On the other hand, some presented them as naïve victims who have been dehumanized and infantilized.[56] A strong pattern of polarized attitudes and stereotypes was confirmed in all six newspapers, including during intense political, social, and economic periods. There were major issues with the media's representation of events, which can invoke prejudice, feed into anti-immigrant attitudes, and exaggerate the appearance of a crisis, given that the media are central to the public's interpretations of complex issues. Refugees are not invaders, nor are they helpless or primitive. An empathetic, complex, and politically neutral approach in the media is equally as important as providing information on the conflicts that produce refugees in the first place.

Stereotyping and Systematic Exclusion

Refugees experience migration differently than most migrant workers or students studying abroad. According to Alex Braithwaite and colleagues, refugees go through four resettlement phases: (1) segregation, (2) expulsion, (3) integration, and

(4) dispersion.[57] First, they experience segregation and expulsion by their home community, host country, and other nations that refuse to offer them asylum. They are often criminalized and negatively stereotyped as relatively inferior to native-born people, who in turn use these stereotypes to justify their exclusion and discrimination. Then refugees integrate, on varying levels, with their neighborhood communities or the broader host country.

Even in nations with high rates of resettlement, liberal border policies, and staunch supporters, not all refugees are welcomed with open arms. The *good refugee–bad refugee* binary complicates things and cultivates an idea that refugees must act a certain way and assimilate to a certain degree to be properly deserving of asylum. This binary is employed to "demarcate the 'deserving' refugee from the 'undeserving' migrant and play into fear of cultural, religious, and ethnic difference" and to create divisions between groups.[58] Governments may sacrifice some "so that others may live," with many of those sacrificed being refugees who are labeled as undesirable.[59] The process of refugee designation and resettlement often bestows more deservingness on some groups than others—namely, children, women, and the elderly. The granting of asylum is not neutral, as it favors groups in narrow categories and those who can provide evidence or credible testimony. In other words, many people escaping persecution are never offered legal asylum and may have to remain undocumented, in the shadows, and on the fringes of society.[60]

Outward indications of difference, including dress and skin color, can instigate native-born prejudice and discrimination against immigrants and refugees. As Katherine Jensen writes, "Asylum can be cruel. Rather than attenuate suffering, asylum also produces and legitimates it. It normalizes the suffering of those excluded."[61] In the Canadian province of British Columbia, 26 percent of Southeast Asian refugees were discriminated against based on their race.[62] Cubans cite similar experiences in the United States, as do Africans.[63] In a 2006 study, it was documented that more than half of Sudanese refugee respondents living in Nebraska had experienced racism, and 20 percent believed racism had hampered their access to proper health care.[64] Displaced people from Africa have been unjustifiably placed in subordinate social positions in the aftermath of slavery, and Africans resettling in Europe, Australia, and North America are particularly prone to experiencing racism and discrimination.[65] Levels of segregation and exclusion differ across immigrant communities and perceived individual identities but hurt them all.

Furthermore, a *refugee* is considered distinct from a *migrant* in the EU, and these terms impact attitudes and policies differently. Drawing from interviews of 215 migrants who traveled across the Mediterranean to Greece, Heaven Crawley and Dimitris Skleparis used the term *categorical fetishism* to describe how stereotyping entire groups of people as either only migrants or only refugees fails to capture an individual's unique relationship with migration and any changes in their status.[66] Interviewees discussed a variety of reasons for leaving their home countries. They fled conflicts, sought out jobs, and faced religious persecution. Many did not initially consider Europe their destination but had been turned away by other countries, and the dangerous journey was their last resort. It is essential to move beyond the stereotypes of refugee, migrant, and asylum seeker, as well as the formal confines of each official category, to truly understand the complexities of displaced people's experiences and the future of public policy and integration.

Instilling Fear and Resentment in the Public

Hungary, Poland, Denmark, the United States, and other countries that have essentially closed their borders to asylum seekers have not necessarily done so against the will of the public. Characterizing current migration and refugee moves as a crisis impacts how they are understood and what actions are taken by both national leaders and the public.[67] Migration is framed as a security issue instead of a humanitarian issue, which justifies governments' decisions to close their borders, purportedly in the name of safety. This way, government leaders mold citizens' reactions to produce their desired outcome. Negative attitudes toward refugees and immigrants, encouraged by the rise of alt-right ideology and political leadership, inhibit their protection, well-being, and ability to integrate.[68]

One of the primary obstacles to successful refugee resettlement is xenophobia. Migrants are subsequently excluded, leaving them with almost no alternatives but to take dangerous smuggling routes to cross territorial lines. These conservative policies kill two birds with one stone, as they also prevent refugees and immigrants from resettling successfully. This fuels the false perception of a crisis when the reality is much more complicated. Immigrants and refugees are people with agency and dignity and should be treated accordingly—not as "security threats, commodities or mere passive victims."[69] Dispelling myths that paint refugees and immigrants as such should be among the first steps taken by host countries. Doing so will ensure the natural development of a welcoming environment, diminish the effect of stress on migrants' physical and mental health, employ them in the labor market, and effectively incorporate them into the host country's social fabric.[70] Unfortunately, political parties that push nationalist agendas and advocate for conservative border policies have gained popularity across Europe and the United States. It is unknown whether such parties will pursue refugee integration in the near future.

SHIFTING THE STATUS QUO

In conclusion, framing migration as a crisis is largely part of a contrived narrative that is pushed by state and local actors that oppose immigration. This is not to say that the combination of violence, abuse, hardships, and deaths inflicted on refugees and migrants is not a severe and urgent issue—the problem is that the term *refugee crisis* is constructed and employed by Western countries for sinister reasons. While conflict in their home countries directly harms many refugees, other countries' reluctance to provide aid also harms them. European inaction and closed-border policies, especially following the Syrian civil war, resulted in avoidable migrant deaths and exposed the EU's lack of preparedness and concerted planning. The refusal to accept refugees and asylum seekers across national borders and to help them survive is only a continuation of centuries-long processes of subordinating colonized people. The welcome of Ukrainian refugees in many countries shows that other ways to treat those fleeing wars and invasions are possible. The case of Ukraine also shows how the imperial wishes of territorial expansion of some regimes are still present in the world.

Additionally, European xenophobia and anti-immigrant sentiments can be traced to how refugees are represented and the language used to characterize them. However, it is important to note that the so-called refugee crisis in Europe does not necessarily reflect the realities and statistics of migration: the number of refugees immigrating to Europe is not a high percentage of the receiving countries' populations and is therefore manageable. Most European countries are more than capable of mobilizing the resources required to address the humanitarian needs of migrants. Debates on immigration policy have created widespread political polarization across the EU, with many Europeans becoming fearful and resentful of migrants and refugees. Legal structures determine refugees' levels of deservingness, and the public also judges them based on vague and perfunctory information. Further, political narratives often ignore the complexity and nuances of migration, distracting people from the poor conditions and systemic discrimination many migrants face daily.

How can we address contemporary migration trends in a humane and effective way that minimizes the suffering experienced by migrants? First, aid programs should be expanded, so that nongovernmental organizations may build stronger ties with global citizens and federal programs to create a network of support for migrants. It is also important to broaden the number and types of pathways to citizenship, and the EU must recognize and uphold the Schengen Agreement. Furthermore, aid and resources should be directed toward migrants' countries of origin, and mental health should be prioritized as part of international aid and outreach toward migrants. Finally, Western countries must be held accountable for their role in creating the conditions that have led to refugee crises, especially in the context of colonialism and imperialism.

An important step that everyone must take together is to alter our language. We should stop using the term *crisis* and refer to events as what they truly are. Instead of publishing a headline about the "Rohingya Crisis," as plenty of news outlets and research institutes have, authors would be more accurate and helpful if they called it "ethnic cleansing by the Myanmar government against ethnic Muslims."[71] This way, human rights violations, rather than the refugees themselves, are framed as a problem. Academics, researchers, and supporters must also look closer at the language and phrases they use in discussions regarding refugees and immigrants. Self-acclaimed critical thinkers, influencers, and pundits should decrease their linguistic shortcuts, stop repeating the same sound bites about group asylum claims, and think critically and analytically about how we understand sovereignty, immigrants, and asylum seekers.[72]

Next Steps for the United States

The Western Hemisphere faces a situation similar to the one in Europe. Central and South Americans are migrating to the U.S.-Mexico border, Venezuelans are crossing into neighboring Colombia, and Bolivians are seeking refuge in Chile and Argentina because of economic insecurity, political instability, and rising violence. Amidst this, the United States has failed to provide proper support for refugees, especially between 2016 and 2020. Its actions (or lack thereof) prompted criticism from politicians, human rights advocates, and national security experts worldwide. The Trump administration enacted three consecutive travel bans in 2017 alone, one of which barred the entry of Syrian refugees. Refugees from Muslim-majority countries were temporarily blocked, and two of the bans involved suspending refugee resettlement programs for 120 days. There have been multiple accounts of refugees' requests for asylum being denied.[73] Some still make the trip, but there is ultimately no guarantee that the United States—or the EU, for that matter—will hear their cases, grant them asylum, or refrain from deporting them.[74] In 2018, shortly after the introduction of its travel bans, the Trump administration slashed annual refugee acceptance numbers to a cap of 45,000, thus reducing the rate of new arrivals to the lowest the nation had ever seen. Despite the already incredibly low cutoff, only 22,491 were admitted. President Trump further reduced the acceptance cap to 30,000 refugees in 2019, just over a quarter of the number of refugees permitted under President Barack Obama.[75] These stringent new policies, like the Migrant Protection Protocols/ Remain in Mexico policy, banned asylum seekers from awaiting their application decisions in the United States and caused additional harm to displaced people seeking refuge at the southern border.

Scholars have coined the term *crimmigration* to refer to the merging of the criminal justice and immigration enforcement systems, which has resulted in the mass incarceration and deportation of Hispanic and Black immigrants in the United States.[76] As shown in previous chapters, immigrants are criminalized and disproportionately targeted by law enforcement. Being undocumented often leads to arrest, to detention, and almost always to deportation to an immigrant's home country. Alternatively, they are sent across the border into Mexico to apply for and await legal entry into the United States. Crimmigration policy is based on the belief that all immigrants, even asylum seekers and refugees, do not belong in the United States, are unfit to live there, and/or harbor criminal intentions.[77] The United States has long been one of the leading contributors to international refugee assistance programs, including those of the UN and International Red Cross. Because of its large contributions, the country's resettlement policies influence how the issue is approached worldwide. The United States may reestablish itself in time as a supporter of refugees and immigrants, but it cannot do so if it uses unsupported claims of a border crisis to justify tearing families apart, racially profiling residents, and deporting immigrants.

The failures and dangers of isolationist domestic policy in the United States can inform how the country welcomes refugees in the future. If it is truly as powerful as politicians imply, the United States cannot be threatened by immigration and can develop helpful programs for refugees and immigrants. For example, making medical visas and care immediately available to all new arrivals was an automatic service on Ellis Island in the 1900s that should be reintroduced.[78] David Kampf recommends that the United States aim to resettle 200,000 refugees each year, funnel more resources into domestic and global aid, and encourage and collaborate with other nations so that humanitarian responses can improve collectively and effectively.[79]

Furthermore, educating medical professionals on cultural competency is one immediate way to improve the lives of refugees. Physicians need more training in cross-cultural communication and the health implications of trauma to be "prepared to navigate the verbal semantics and varied communication styles of non-Western patients."[80] To attain a more culturally informed health system, medical schools need to develop interdisciplinary curricula that cover topics in the fields of the humanities, global studies, and languages. Furthermore, to provide services for all refugees swiftly and successfully, students should be taught how to distinguish trauma and treat patients who are coping with daily distress and to be conscious of the role that discretion plays in treating immigrant patients.[81]

Next Steps for Governments Around the Globe

Welcoming refugees into host countries is the first basic step in supporting their survival and well-being. Amnesty International insists that there are many ways for nations to offer immediate help, starting with granting visas to reunify families and allowing migrants to enter without requiring specific documentation. This way, migrants would all be considered "legal," could not be discriminated against, and would avoid being judged as "undeserving" of asylum based on their status. Furthermore, the dangers that refugees face on their migratory journeys must be taken into consideration. This is another reason why offering care to immigrants and asylum seekers should be prioritized.[82]

In addition to making changes in political policy, nations should not forget that refugees struggle to meet basic needs, even with the help of refugee resettlement case managers and temporary financial support. Effective aid programs that provide education, health care, employment, affordable housing, language classes, proper nutrition, and access to technology must be developed, especially if countries go through with resettlement expansion. In 2015, the European Commission gave more than $3.5 billion in assistance to internally displaced Syrians and communities of Syrian refugees living in Iraq, Lebanon, Turkey, Egypt, and Jordan.[83] The UK and the United States were the top donors of humanitarian aid at the time but have not successfully involved other countries in a collective response. By doing so, current major donors could increase their donations while promoting the growth of new donors, such as the Gulf States.[84]

Next Steps for Nongovernmental Organizations and Global Citizens

Organizations like Doctors Without Borders and the International Rescue Committee, which created hospitals in refugee camps and provided resources to refugees in over seven countries, played a pivotal role in assisting with the Syrian conflict. Oftentimes, true success in distributing aid hinges on the mobilization of resources by, and collaboration between, different nonprofits. Nongovernmental refugee aid organizations that uphold relationships with other organizations and network with donors are most successful in helping their clients.[85] Moreover, as a Doctors Without Borders UK spokesperson once stated, "The force of public opinion makes a crucial difference."[86] The general public can help by gathering, online or in person, and demanding the prioritization and allocation of funds for state initiatives and organizations that support refugees and immigrants.

Economic assistance alone is not enough to address the needs of displaced communities and does not relieve countries of their responsibility to provide other forms of support. National programs should be proposed that uniquely support single-parent families, refugees with serious medical conditions, and survivors of torture, trafficking, and domestic abuse. Individuals who fit these criteria must not be turned away by national border authorities but instead should be prioritized by resettlement and integration programs, though not to the exclusion of other displaced people. Expanding available pathways to protection and citizenship is crucial. Nicole Ostrand believes this can be accomplished by implementing a humanitarian visa program that would permit private sponsorship for U.S. citizenship by nongovernmental organizations and provide asylum seekers with the ability to apply for protection through embassies or offices in or near their home countries.[87]

Conclusion: Crucial Collaborative Actions

Upholding the Schengen Agreement The European community would do well to recognize and uphold the 1985 Schengen Agreement and Dublin Regulation, which organized a gradual disintegration of border checkpoints and visas. Documentation was no longer deemed necessary to travel between member states to foster "the free movement of persons, goods, services, and capital" in a concentrated European market.[88] Giving up internal borders, however, meant that more attention and resources were allocated for surveillance along the external border surrounding the Schengen countries, allowing for the construction of a fence at the Greece-Turkey border in 2012 and the total closure of entry into Hungary in 2015.[89] Neither agreement offers explicit directions regarding the collective actions the EU should take, as acknowledged by German chancellor Angela Merkel, which is why nations have taken such varied approaches. Nonetheless, the Schengen space was established as one without internal borders, and increasingly conservative border policies have violated this facet of the Schengen Agreement by trying to restrict the movement of people from outside within the area.[90]

Rebuilding Nations from Which People Once Fled Refugees who finally return to their home countries are too often met with deplorable conditions. International aid should include initiatives that funnel resources into damaged communities in need of help and healing time. For example, migrants who are deported or who voluntarily move back to their communities of origin may once again be subjected to political, economic, and social instability in the region if a new leader transitions into power. Similarly, after the fall of a violent regime, a power vacuum leaves a nation vulnerable to further disagreement and conflict over interim policies and new leadership. At times like these, national governments and lower-level actors, such as organizations working to provide aid on the ground and local municipalities, should collaborate to deliver essentials like food, water, and health services.[91]

Prioritizing Mental Health Services in International Aid Programs When services are offered, mental health is normally not prioritized in the same way that physical wellness is. Displaced peoples and asylum seekers are at higher risk of trauma and chronic stress than nonmigrant populations, so it is equally important that they have access to mental health providers who are culturally and linguistically competent. More than half of Congolese refugee women participating in a research study said they had experienced violence either before or during their time in a refugee camp in Rwanda. One in four reported having poor mental health or mental health disorders, like depression, due to displacement and interpersonal partner violence.[92] Providing comprehensive humanitarian aid calls for an awareness that refugees' and migrants' circumstances render them vulnerable to traumatic stress and for the inclusion of mental health specialists when providing support on the ground.[93]

Increasing Accountability Ultimately, no change will last unless it directly addresses the causes of conflict in postcolonial and low-income countries: poverty, inequality, and domination by wealthier nations. For example, the lack of experienced leadership, reorganization, and sustainable institutions in the postcolonial era produced an environment in the Great Lakes region of Africa that displaced large numbers of people. Human rights violations, struggles for political and economic power, civil war, and ethnic persecution in low-income countries are rooted in histories of colonization and subordination. Refugee policies fail to consider these integral factors, ignoring "the dynamics of inclusion and exclusion that are a common feature in any context."[94] Ensuring that returning refugees have citizenship in their home country is essential, in addition to macrolevel changes to ensure that inequality, the politicization of identities, and violence, which were standard practices for colonial states, are not perpetuated in postcolonial conditions.

If there is war, violence, or suffering, people will, and have the right to, seek sustenance and safety elsewhere. It has never been reasonable to expect everyone to live and die in the same place they were born. The supposed solution that wealthy nations yearn for is not attainable because the "refugee problem" has been politically and mediatically constructed. The damage imperialism continues to inflict on the world has fueled instability and inequality and has fostered ideal environments for armed conflict. Ironically, colonizing powers now demand that their former colonies somehow find peace, shake their heads when more migrants arrive at their borders, and ignore their own role in causing the situation. The West must confront its gruesome history and take responsibility for its current violent monopolization of Indigenous communities, local economies, and political movements in regions around the world before moving forward. Welcoming immigrants is a straightforward way to begin repairing some of the historical damage done abroad.

CHAPTER 8

GLOBALIZATION AND MIGRATION ARE INDEPENDENT PROCESSES

T he effects of the 2008 economic crisis and the visible stagnation of the middle class resulted in a backlash against President Ronald Reagan's "trickle-down economics," or what many academics call neoliberal policies, which favor government deregulation, privatization, international trade, and foreign direct investment. The left has shown the many negative consequences of these policies, such as deindustrialization, growing inequality, and lower social and geographical mobility in the United States.[1] Movements like 15-M/Indignados in Spain and Occupy Wall Street in the United States organized to protest these policies.[2]

In some sectors, particularly on the right, the backlash has been against trade and immigration. The processes of economic globalization and international migration are related to, and yet largely independent of, one another. Nevertheless, early proponents of globalization celebrated the free flow of goods and capital along with the more frequent interaction among peoples and cultures in a world with no border walls. Thus, some of the backlash against neoliberal economic policies has been directed toward immigrants and foreign nations instead of the structures of power that uphold and encourage neoliberal economic policies, weakened welfare states, and growing inequalities. We do not mean to say that all critiques of neoliberalism or globalization are xenophobic or anti-immigrant; rather, some of the critiques on migration from the right have resulted from different conceptions of the United States and the role of white supremacy as well as from discontent with deindustrialization, cosmopolitanism, and the weakening of the manufacturing middle class. We are not arguing in favor of neoliberal economic globalization; instead, we are explaining how many people, including early proponents, linked globalization, mobility, and ethno-racial diversity.

In this chapter, we concentrate on disproving misconceptions that overstate the relationship between migration and the economic aspect of globalization, which is characterized by fewer barriers to the flow of capital, services, and commodities. We refute the idea that globalization functions like a construction crane that scoops up people, businesses, and jobs and drops them into other countries. By examining the reasoning behind this exaggerated connection between the two forces in the minds of many voters, we establish why globalization and migration are best understood as distinct and should be handled as such in both theoretical, political, and policy discussions.

WHY IS GLOBALIZATION THOUGHT TO BE A CAUSE OF MIGRATION?

The Rising Popularity of Globalization

Globalization is a term that is widely used yet rarely defined or described empirically. There is consensus that it is rooted in changes in economic policy, but its definition has grown increasingly expansive. It is a concept that is discussed in many contexts—technological innovation, migration, media, knowledge, and social change. As a result, globalization has become a polysemic term, constantly being molded and manipulated to take on different characteristics to the point of confusion.

Academic interpretations of globalization have varied throughout the years. An essential aspect of globalization agreed on by most researchers is the increase in international trade and capital investments as well as in the movement of ideas, tastes, and values.[3] Some theoretical definitions exaggerate the newness and degree of global interconnection. David Held framed globalization as a social and spatial shift made possible by advancements in technology, transportation, and travel that generated "transcontinental or inter-regional flows and networks of activity, interaction, and the exercise of power."[4] Similarly, Manuel Castells wrote that communication costs over long distances have decreased and have had important social implications. Some authors have extended these hypotheses to insinuate that technological advancements increase global migration.[5] According to this viewpoint, popular in the social sciences in the early 2000s, globalization is assumed to cause the spread of migrant networks that foster relationships across borders.[6] Nevertheless, people and information are different entities, and while most places in the world are open to Google and Facebook, they are not always open to international migrants. There have also been historical moment where the proportion of international trade has been very high even before the arrival of the internet or cellphones. Likewise communication technologies could not prevent the disruption of supply chains during the COVID-19 pandemic.

Entangling Economic Globalization, Free Trade, and Open Borders

The descriptions of globalization presented here aim to capture its essence, but we must be wary of the generalizations they invite, especially in the context of migration. It is easy to assume that economic globalization leads to a general increase in people moving around the world because the two concepts have been conflated. Scholars now use globalization as a framework to understand the migration of workers who fill labor shortages in the agriculture, care, and service sectors. However, as Charles Tilly argued, globalization is a process best understood as an increase in the consumption of goods produced far away compared to that of goods produced locally.[7] While cheap refrigeration and transportation can make it easier for food to travel longer distances within a country or across political borders, there is a limit to economic globalization. Most services, such as food preparation, haircuts, and car washes, must be conducted locally.[8]

Economic Globalization

The popularized framing of globalization entangles various phenomena, such as free trade policies, offshoring, the expansion of the internet, cosmopolitan identities, and international migration, in one concept. It has become an umbrella term used in discussions about free trade agreements, like the North American Free Trade Agreement (or USMCA), that eliminate tariffs on many imported goods and encourage investment in other national economies. Here, we define the deregulation of trade and the diffusion of neoliberal policies and ideology as economic globalization. To justify the connection between globalization and immigration, some social theorists, politicians, and pundits have linked economic liberalization to increased migration, diversity, and open borders. Although the concepts of migration and globalization appear to be apples that have fallen from the same tree, they have different tastes. If they are separate from one another, why do globalization scholars from various disciplines still consider them interdependent?

This conflation of many different processes was embraced for political reasons by the political left and right alike. Theorists oversell globalization, exaggerating the magnitude of the changes that the world has undergone to sell their work, just as politicians oversell globalization theories to advance neoliberal policies that favor capital over labor. Coining "globalization" enabled people to denote ongoing social change—yet it was also used to brand a policy project while its consequences were starting to unfold. Like a financial derivative, the concept of globalization packaged fragments of independent objects and branded them as a desirable investment. As with other derivatives after the 2008 recession, the globalization combo seemed less appealing after the shrinking of the middle class.[9] The backlash against free trade following the recession affected public perceptions of migrant workers and the manufacturing economy in the United States.

MIGRATION AND GLOBALIZATION ARE RELATED BUT INDEPENDENT

Globalization and migration are framed as two faces on the same coin, but in reality they are much different phenomena. Some argue that globalization is the defining feature of our time and associate it with large numbers of migrants moving from place to place. The United Nations' *International Migration Report 2017* states that it is "easier, cheaper and faster for people to move in search of jobs, opportunity, education and quality of life" than ever before, revealing the assumption that globalization goes hand in hand with migration.[10] In the previous chapter, we disproved part of this belief by highlighting that migrants and refugees were and still are produced by imperialist processes carried out by hegemonic countries in addition to conflict, poverty, inequality, and instability.

Some proponents of globalization argue in favor of the ability of people to move freely across national borders, as they see it as allowing the global supply of labor to distribute itself most efficiently according to demand. Others caution that a lack of protective trade policies and migration regulations puts the economies of certain countries at risk.[11] However, economic globalization and migration do not share a causal relationship because migration trends do not necessarily align with trade trends: periods of expanded international trade ebb and flow throughout history and do not correlate with waves of migration.[12] Migration has a reciprocal relationship with transnational social networks of families, friends, and communities, both creating and resulting from these relationships and social ties. Similarly, transnational corporations have a presence in multiple locations around the globe, acting as an economic network of employees and capital.[13] Because the global movement of people is not caused by the global movement of capital, resorting to protectionist economic policies does not itself decrease immigration. As discussed in the next chapter, the false belief that such policies would decrease immigration was an important driver of the United Kingdom's decision to leave the European Union. Pro-Brexiters hoped to reduce immigration by surveilling incoming immigrants more closely and doing away with the EU's internal open-border policy (see chapter 9).

Restricting Immigration Will Not Create Jobs for Native-Born People

Income and wealth inequalities have increased since the 1980s.[14] In the United States, the 1 percent of people with the highest earnings received about 20 percent of the overall total income in 2011, up from about 10 percent in the late 1970s.[15] Since the early 1980s, "the incomes of the top 5 percent of earners have increased faster than the incomes of other families."[16] However, rather than attacking the fiscal policies causing this growing inequality, many have blamed cosmopolitanism. Opportunistic politicians attack immigrants and ethnic minorities for supposedly lowering the wages and employment security of native-born people. But inequality and economic insecurity were brought up by neoliberal economic policies linked to globalization not by immigrants. Right-wing politicians have blamed them directly for deindustrialization and a decreasing standard of living among the white working class. However, they fail to mention that U.S. corporations and shareholders have been some of the largest beneficiaries of access to cheap labor at home and abroad.[17]

Former president Donald Trump vowed to "Make America Great Again," always insisting that Hispanic immigrants and Chinese manufacturers weaken the national economy. He highlighted the disparity between global trade and wealth for the average American, stating that "globalization has made the financial elite who donate to politicians very, very wealthy . . . but it has left millions of our workers with nothing but poverty and heartache."[18] Rather than attributing this to the economic system and probusiness policies, he used immigrant laborers as scapegoats, asserting that migrant workers "steal" jobs from Americans. He explicitly stated that in July 2015: "They're taking our manufacturing jobs.

They're taking our money. They're killing us."[19] Under this logic (or lack thereof), immigration must be heavily restricted, and deportations must continue in order to decrease unemployment, increase wages, and restrengthen the economy. However, punitive actions against Asian and Latin immigrants will not provide any of these benefits. Industries predominantly employing migrant workers, like agriculture, construction, and hospitality, require strenuous physical labor and sacrifice.[20] Immigrants are filling the labor gaps, and migrant labor has been proven to have no significant effect on native-born wages.[21]

Khalid Koser believes that the foundational link between globalization and migration lies in "developmental, demographic, and democratic disparities" that are growing alongside a higher demand for migrant workers. The inequality between various groups of people in various parts of the world contributes to migration and the creation of an hourglass economy with both high-paying and low-paying labor markets in global cities.[22] Still, migration is not only caused by poverty, but also results from aggressive recruitment: for example, the recruitment of Algerian guest workers to help reconstruct France after World War II, of Turkish migrants to fill labor gaps in Germany in the late 1990s, and of Mexican seasonal laborers under the United States'

Guest worker programs in the twentieth century, all of which relations were informed by preceding military interventions and colonial legacies and connections. Ending labor agreements is not enough to end migration once links have been made by thousands of employers and workers, and workers and family members move where work is. Where labor migration is not permitted, the growth of an underground migration industry further fuels international migration. Some countries respond to this by creating new economic sectors around immigrant policing, detention, and deportation, which Adam Goodman calls the "deportation machine."[23]

It is important to note that not everyone has the means to migrate or even wants to. It is much easier for those with the proper passports and money to travel as a tourist, study abroad, work remotely from an area with a low cost of living, or live in multiple countries throughout one's life.

The Endless Quest for Cheaper Labor

Capitalism encourages low selling prices and lower wages for workers. Businesses and consumers benefit from the labor of refugees, authorized immigrants, and undocumented people who are not given proper wages and benefits. Less money is spent on them, which therefore keeps consumer prices low and owners' pockets full. This is not an optimal or sustainable way of life for immigrants and society at large. It affects everyone's labor rights and pushes other businesses to hire the cheap labor provided mainly by immigrants and minorities.[24] This labor exploitation is a feature of capitalism that is not constrained by national borders. Historically, the only way to tame the excess of capitalism has been through legislation that protects labor rights: the eight-hour workday; the right to weekends, vacations, and sick days; and limitations on child labor, among other rights. Amnesty laws, like the one signed in 1986, are another way to uphold human and labor rights. That law allowed undocumented immigrants to obtain legal permanent residency, and proponents saw it as a way to enable them to leave exploitative employment relationships.

Multinational corporations look abroad not only for cheaper labor but also for weaker labor protections. The ability to offshore factories and outsource labor at all levels of the production chain is one of the drivers of global economic interdependence.[25] Cotton is picked in the southern United States, manufactured into clothing in Bangladesh, and sold at stores in China, a process that is the product of transnational ties and agreements forged by national governments, corporations, and companies. They do so to save and make money: manufacturing costs in other countries are significantly lower than in the United States, which reduces overall production fees. The process of offshoring has become a common framework for large businesses worldwide that are seeking to cut production costs.[26] It also facilitates the introduction of those products in the country that produces them.

GLOBALIZATION IS NOT A NEW PHENOMENON

Many scholars agree that economic globalization occurred long before the Industrial Revolution in the nineteenth century. Historically, companies have used raw materials from faraway lands and desperately sought markets abroad. In 1820, "café-goers would sip Chinese tea sweetened with Jamaican sugar."[27] While the term *globalization* may not have been used at that point in history, the concept was increasingly understood. Though it is difficult to pinpoint exact dates, economic globalization had already occurred long before the eighteenth century.[28]

The Silk Road, snaking its way from China to the Mediterranean, fostered the expansion of a transcontinental trade market.[29] That trade route existed for over a thousand years before other major globalization processes, like the colonization of the Americas and the transatlantic slave trade, began.[30]

According to Tilly and colleagues, globalization occurred in multiple distinct periods throughout history:

> During the half millennium since 1500, three main waves of globalization have occurred. The first arrived right around 1500. It resulted from the rapidly spreading influence of Europe, growth of the Ottoman Empire, and parallel expansions of Chinese and Arab merchants into the Indian Ocean and the Pacific. . . . We can place the second major post-1500 wave of globalization at approximately 1850–1914. . . . During this period, international trade and capital flows reached previously unmatched heights, especially across the Atlantic. . . . Migration, trade, and capital flows slowed between the two world wars. But as Europe and Asia recovered from World War II, a third post-1500 surge of globalization began. . . . During the early twenty-first century, the third wave of post-1500 globalization was moving ahead with full force.[31]

These authors do not mean to say that globalization comes in waves, like the effects of changes in the ocean or a force of nature producing waves following its own rhythm. Instead, they argue that there have been periods with high levels of globalization even before this term emerged. They also indicate that wars and epidemics have caused low levels of globalization in the past.[32] Thus, framing globalization as a novel process that emerged in contemporary history denies the existence of transnational economic exchanges that unfolded centuries before the term was officially coined. Globalization is not a destination or a one-way process; economies can also experience deglobalization.

MIGRATION FLOWS ARE STABLE

Around 3.4 percent of the world's population is estimated to live in a nation other than their nation of birth.[33] Contrary to the myth that globalization increases migration, this number has remained relatively consistent throughout modern history. Recent immigration data from 1960 to 2000 show no evidence of increases in the relative numbers of immigrants. Instead, immigrants' source countries, their permanent destinations, and the general direction of international movement change over time. In the twenty-first century, new migration hubs popped up in eastern Europe, the Gulf States, and Asia. The number of nations that produce immigrants and refugees is increasing.[34]

Migration patterns have fluctuated throughout history and will continue to do so in the foreseeable future. The current rates of immigration are not novel for the United States. In 2018, approximately 14.5 percent of the U.S. population was born abroad, roughly the same percentage as that found over one hundred years ago in 1910.[35] Until the mid-nineteenth century, most immigrants were coming from Europe, but in the last decades, most people are coming from Latin America and Asia.[36] After a decrease in the percentage of foreign-born people living in the United States around the world war periods, an increase followed the passage of the Immigration and Nationality Act of 1965. Otherwise known as the Hart-Celler Act, it permitted migrants of all nationalities to enter the country, prioritized family reunification, and raised the total annual immigration cap. This change in immigration policy, and not economic globalization, spurred a rise in asylum seekers and migrants.

Managed migration facilitated by government recruitment and training for specific labor industries and guest worker programs has also impacted migration numbers and patterns.[37] The number of temporary workers traveling abroad in the service and health care sectors has increased over the past forty years. The heavy recruitment of female nurses, domestic workers, and caregivers has resulted in the intended feminization of some migration flows.[38] Some of these programs have become so ingrained that the Philippines and parts of Latin America and the Caribbean have become human exporters. Their national governments support this exportation to alleviate unemployment and demographic pressures and to incentivize remittances. Additionally, this phenomenon is not limited to low-skilled workers. Many people leave their home countries to work or study in wealthier nations. Many university graduates from parts of Latin America and sub-Saharan Africa migrate to countries belonging to the Organisation for Economic Co-operation and Development, becoming an asset for the receiving countries.[39] However, when immigrants travel to work in another country, they are often overqualified for the jobs they can acquire due to discrimination, language barriers, or employers' refusal or legal inability to recognize foreign credentials.

CONCLUSION

While it may be attractive to draw broad conclusions about globalization, call it the defining feature of our times, and label it as a driving force behind international migration, the truth resists such simplicity. Some research suggests that there may be a correlation between the economic interdependence associated with globalization and an increase in migration among specific demographics, such as women employed as temporary domestic laborers.[40] However, data referring to the general global population do not support the conclusion that globalization drives migration.

As we have highlighted throughout this book, migration is an inherently human phenomenon, prone to changes that are influenced by local and national political, economic, and social conditions. It is important to remember that these factors are not inherently new, nor are they tied to the concept of globalization, given that they existed before our contemporary understanding of the concept became popular. Any vagueness regarding the term *globalization* must not be weaponized against migrants or their home countries. While globalization affects the economies to which migrants and natives contribute, a deeper understanding of the fundamental workings of globalization and migration preserves the awareness that they are distinct. Pinning the downfalls of economic globalization, such as shifting job fields and decreasing wages, on migrants, whose actions are more impacted by different forces, is an easy yet unjust response that fails to truly grasp the complexity of either process. In this way, migrants become global scapegoats. Nevertheless, wealth inequality between countries and individuals is true but relative deprivation is not what propels.

CHAPTER 9

BREXIT DID NOT AND WILL NOT HALT IMMIGRATION TO THE UNITED KINGDOM

I n the June 2016 Brexit referendum, the United Kingdom's voters shocked the international community by opting to leave the European Union. Much had changed since the first referendum about EU membership in 1975, when the clear majority wished to remain in the EU.[1] In the 2016 referendum, however, the vote was very close, with 52 percent of people participating choosing to leave the EU. Fewer than 30 percent of the "Stay" supporters were older than twenty-five, as the younger population overwhelmingly voted to stay in the EU.[2] The "Leave" supporters, mainly concentrated in the southern half of the island outside of the city of London, were concerned by misconceptions about immigration and trade.

In this chapter, we first explore the selling points for Brexit to understand how the change was deemed necessary by a slight majority of the population. We review social and political trends, including but not limited to xenophobia, isolationism, disagreements on EU policies, and misconceptions about immigrants, the popularization of which gave rise to Brexit. Subsequently, we examine some important components of the Brexit deal, including some of the UK's new immigration and asylum policies, the newly undocumented population, the effects on British expatriates in the EU, the ramifications for Ireland and Scotland, and the economic effects on the UK's economy and labor market. Finally, we use statistical evidence relating to migration trends to argue that Brexit will not reduce immigration into the UK. While the impact of Brexit is still unfolding, this chapter discusses some possible consequences for the UK and the EU in terms of international migration. It serves as a warning about the negative effects that can occur when policies that were intended to chase the anti-immigrant vote are actually implemented.

WHAT CAUSED BREXIT?

Although the UK was part of the EU for forty-seven years, it was one of the few countries that chose not to use the euro as their common currency. Several factors contributed to the growth of the anti-EU sentiments that primed the decision to leave, including economic competition and the fear of eurozone caucusing that might discriminate against EU countries that do not use the euro. In addition to economic competition, one of the most important motivators for leaving was British conservatives' qualms about the EU's immigration and shared border policies. Right-wing Brexit campaigners claimed that by relinquishing its relationship with the EU, the UK could implement more intensive border regulation and help stem immigration.

We evaluate Brexit's ability to fulfill the promises that Boris Johnson and Conservative, UK Independent (UKIP), and Labour Party politicians made to the public. We also explore how the exit from the EU will affect foreigners living in the UK and the many Britons living in EU member countries. Brexit will negatively affect immigrants living in the UK under temporary protected status, although many will simply change their legal immigration status rather than return "home." However, those most affected are the millions of UK citizens living legally in other parts of Europe, where they have enjoyed all the rights associated with citizenship, like health care, welfare, and public services, and are in danger of losing these benefits in the future. Consequently, Brexit is especially problematic for UK nationals seeking lower living costs in other EU countries, especially for those who cannot afford to live comfortably in the UK after retiring.[3]

Xenophobia Rampant in the "Vote Leave" Campaign

Led by Dominic Cummings, the "Vote Leave" campaign, which he cofounded with Matthew Eliot, was opportunistic and operated with an anti-immigrant agenda that fed off xenophobic and racist undercurrents. Its slogan "Vote Leave, Take Control" was motivated largely by what Jonathan Portes argues was false information fabricated by politicians that misled voters.[4] Some politicians created a negative frame around immigration, and there was a rise in hate crimes against them.[5] The "Stay" and "Leave" campaigns were starkly divided in their positions on the economy and immigration policy.[6] Supporters of the "Stay" movement did not believe the supposed economic gains outweighed the risks of leaving the EU. "Leave" supporters were less concerned with the economy and more motivated by immigration restrictions and the fear of losing "a distinct national identity" and facing a way of life characterized by from whiteness.[7]

The results of a study on differences among voters showed a country deeply divided along class, education, and geography. Anti-immigration and antimulticulturalism sentiments were profoundly more common in less educated voters, who were "in a more vulnerable position in the labor market."[8] On the other hand, those who voted to stay in the EU were typically highly educated young professionals living in more diverse urban areas like London.[9] Communities with the *lowest* concentrations of immigrants with EU origins were the most likely to vote to leave. South Staffordshire in the West Midlands had some of the lowest levels of EU migration in the UK, with less than 1 percent of the population born in mainland Europe. However, 78 percent of people in that area voted to leave. Of the twenty places with the fewest EU migrants in the country, fifteen voted to leave the EU. Regions that had experienced a sudden influx of EU migrants over the last ten years also tended to be in favor of leaving. In areas heavily occupied by EU immigrants, the opposite occurred. Of the twenty places with the most EU migrants in the UK, eighteen voted to stay in the EU.[10] It seems that EU immigrants were far less welcome in neighborhoods unfamiliar with their presence but that they were well accepted in the places where they have lived for a while in visible numbers.

Rising Tensions

The UK has shied away from prorefugee and proimmigrant resettlement and border policies before, so the consensus to "Brexit" does not completely diverge from historical actions. Britain's desire for economic isolation can also be traced back decades. The UK has a history of periods of isolationism, exemplified by the 1930s policy of "appeasement" when Prime Minister Neville Chamberlain looked the other way after Benito Mussolini invaded Ethiopia and Nazi Germany occupied much of Europe. In 1984, hardly a decade after being admitted to the European Economic Community (now the European Economic Area), Margaret Thatcher raised tensions when she advocated that the UK's financial contributions to the community be reduced. The UK also refused to align itself with certain group goals, like the adoption of the euro as a common currency. The EU was established in 1993, and over the following two decades, tensions between it and the UK continued to increase.

In 2010, a referendum lock was implemented that made it impossible for any new UK-EU policy or agreement to take effect in the UK without being approved by a popular vote. Party leaders across the spectrum agreed that the decision to leave the EU could be best made by hosting a referendum. Andrew Glencross points out that this is a product of British exceptionalism, or the belief that Britain is the superior European nation and need not subscribe to the same economic or political behavior as other EU member countries.[11] One year after the referendum lock began, David Cameron became the first prime minister to veto an EU treaty to safeguard Britain's financial interests. He then vowed to renegotiate the UK's membership in the EU if he won the next election. Upon winning the majority in the Conservative Party in 2015, Cameron laid the foundation for the Brexit referendum, trying to get ahead of competition from UKIP and the extreme right but without anticipating that Brexit would actually win at the voting booth.[12]

Disagreements on EU Policies

Originating from efforts to unify Europe in the years following World War II, the EU operates on the belief that countries that share commerce and foster economic relationships are less likely to instigate conflict. Member countries are expected to abide by certain conditions of membership that ensure that the EU is an "area of freedom, security, and justice" where "the free movement of persons is assured."[13] Citizens and immigrants in EU member nations have the right to move freely across internal EU borders to attend school, find work, travel, or settle down. Brexit supporters disagreed with this standard, pushing for more conservative policies and tougher immigration regulations. They believed that because immigration policy was agreed on by the collective EU and not the UK's singular national Parliament, exiting the EU would signify a return to true British "sovereignty" and "autonomy."[14] Before a deal was reached, there was speculation that the UK would adopt a position similar to that of Norway, which is not an EU member nation but still participates in the European Economic Area (EEA).

Boris Johnson blamed the country's partnership with the EU for economic stagnation, the British government's lack of funds, and an influx of migrants into English cities. Johnson promised that removing the UK from the interconnected EU economy would lower the number of migrants living in the country, allow it to "take back control" of its borders, and reverse what he called "the erosion of democracy" created by the EU.[15] Right-wing parliamentary leaders, including Johnson, became more popular and received public support as a result of their promises to lower immigration and refugee resettlement rates in the UK while still allowing the nation to remain a de facto participant in the EU single market.

The Welfare Myth

EU nationals are permitted to claim local welfare benefits in any EU country in which they choose to reside. This policy also extends to immigrants. Supporters of leaving the EU did not want migrants to receive government services; they believed these benefits should be reserved for citizens and claimed that the UK attracted the most migrants in all of the EU because it had "one of the most generous social security systems in the world."[16] However, that claim was disproved two years before the referendum was held.[17]

The UK does not have the world's most generous social security system, and welfare is not the main attractor of immigrants (see chapter 5). Studies have noted that welfare policy reforms passed in the UK before 2016 made claiming welfare significantly more complicated for ethnic minority immigrants.[18] Consequently, immigrants were already blocked from benefits programs. This claim is also shown to be false when other EU countries are considered. Italy and Spain received higher numbers of immigrants than Britain, Germany, and France between 2000 and 2014,[19] even when their welfare provisions were less generous than those in northern Europe. People migrate to the UK because of the labor market, not to collect benefits. Norway and the UK heavily depend on immigrants to fill jobs in the long-term care industry. Both countries have different social nets and similar immigration policies, which are elements that immigrants generally do not prioritize when choosing a destination country. Social networks and job availability in the UK's care industry are more important elements in the decision to migrate.[20]

The Argument That "They Steal Our Jobs," Again

A strong immigrant presence in the UK is a social and economic asset. Nationalism has fostered the false belief that immigrants drain the economy and take jobs from native-born Brits, much like the myths that exist in the United States surrounding Hispanic immigration. According to researchers, the UK was significantly more worried about immigrants than the rest of Europe around the time of the referendum.[21] This phenomenon is especially misguided and ill-informed, considering the UK had one of the largest shares of highly educated immigrants across the EU even before the referendum. Drawing data from the UK Labour Force Survey, the average educational attainment of immigrants had surpassed that of citizens in 1995 and has been growing ever since. Furthermore, although their presence has been shown to raise housing costs, highly educated immigrants contribute more to taxes than they receive in government assistance or benefits.[22]

The Perceived Need for Closer Surveillance of Refugees

EU migration policy is determined by the Common European Asylum System (CEAS), which has a standardized process for immigration that allows refugees and immigrants to obtain citizenship in their host countries. At the time of the 2015 influx of Syrian refugees, however, the EU was faced with the challenge of distributing refugees across member countries. Many governments refused to cooperate and instead enacted isolationist and exclusionary approaches to immigration. One of these governments was that of the UK, where conservatives argued that EU neighbors were unable to exercise restrictive border policies and were therefore responsible for the number of immigrants entering the country. Right-wing politicians also believed the EU's offers of asylum was responsible for terrorist attacks in Belgium, France, and Germany. Many of the EU migration hot spots and resources were located in the eastern Mediterranean,[23] and British conservatives used these events to argue that the country would be better protected if it implemented its own strict border surveillance. For instance, the "Leave" campaign gained votes by villainizing the UK's support for Turkey's request to join the EU. They framed Turkey's potential EU membership as an urgent security threat because of the number of immigrants that would gain free movement within EU territory, including the UK.[24]

THE BREXIT DEAL

Nearly five years after the 2016 referendum, the UK reached an exit agreement with the EU through the Trade and Cooperation Agreement (TCA).[25] Many UK residents and expatriates were in limbo during the negotiations, and many are unhappy with the outcomes of the negotiation. As we discuss here, the new laws are confusing, and they can change at any time. Our purpose is to indicate how many people born in continental Europe suddenly lost their status as "legal migrants." Such is the power of immigration legislation in England and beyond. This is also a reminder that an act of Congress can legalize millions of immigrants with the stroke of a pen.

New Immigration Policy

Many controversial decisions regarding migration and mobility were made in the Brexit deal. The UK opted out of Erasmus Plus, the EU-founded student exchange program that lets students move, study, and compete in sports at universities around Europe without extra cost. This is expected to stem the flow of educated young immigrants, who are precisely the type of immigrants that governments like to welcome.[26] On the other hand, the UK brought back its poststudy work visa, perhaps to make up for the loss of Erasmus. Students who pursue higher education can stay and search for work for up to two years after graduation.[27] Subsequently, a new points-based system was established to create a more uniform set of rules for EU and non-EU migrants. The system kept some features of the previous employer-driven system and eliminated entry routes for low-skill and temporary migrants.[28] Therefore, skill levels instead of nationality determine eligibility for entry. This system gives preference to high-income and well-educated migrants, which the government explicitly targeted in the first policy statement that addressed the change in the system. An individual needs to rack up a minimum of seventy points to live in the UK and apply for the Settlement Scheme, which we discuss in more detail later.

Table 9.1 lists the number of points that the government allots for each tracked characteristic. According to these numbers, an immigrant must fulfill at least four characteristics to obtain seventy points.[29] As shown in the table, income requirements were also instituted for EU migrants, with the most points awarded

TABLE 9.1 Characteristics of the post-Brexit points-based immigration system

Characteristic	Tradeable	Points
Offer of job by approved sponsor	No	20
Job at appropriate skill level	No	20
Speaks English at required level	No	10
Salary of £20,480 (minimum)–£23,039	Yes	0
Salary of £23,040–£25,599	Yes	10
Salary of £25,600 or above	Yes	20
Job in a shortage occupation (as designated by the Migration Advisory Committee)	Yes	20
Education qualification: PhD in subject relevant to the job	Yes	10
Education qualification: PhD in a STEM subject relevant to the job	Yes	20

Source: GOV.UK, "The UK's Points-Based Immigration System."

to someone who is already guaranteed employment that will earn them either at least £25,600 per year or the lower quartile of the current average national salary. For some occupations, the threshold is lowered to £20,480. Prospective immigrants' employers must also vouch for them on their Settlement Scheme applications.[30] Thus, any low-income migrant who is unemployed at arrival or is guaranteed to earn less than the required income cannot remain in the country. Exceptions are granted for unemployed people who (1) seek employment in an industry that desperately needs workers or (2) have earned a PhD in a field that is hiring.[31]

The EU Settlement Scheme

All EU, EEA, and Swiss nationals already living in the UK were required to apply to the country's new EU Settlement Scheme by June 30, 2021. Each person in a family had to apply separately. As of May 2021, the Settlement Scheme had received 5.6 million applications. When the deadline arrived, there were still at least 400,000 applications that had yet to be reviewed, over a quarter of which belonged to children.[32]

The Settlement Scheme sorts immigrants into two official status categories: settled and presettled. Settled status is reserved for people who have lived in the

UK continuously for at least five years and their children. Although some exceptions apply,[33] if settled status is granted, an applicant can remain indefinitely and apply for British citizenship.[34] It is the equivalent of the Indefinite Leave to Remain status under pre-Brexit immigration policy. Individuals will lose their settled status if they are absent from the country for more than five years.[35] Presettled status is for EU, EEA, and Swiss immigrants who have lived in the UK for less than five years. Once they have reached the five-year residency mark, they must apply again to the Settlement Scheme to obtain settled status.[36] A person with presettled status who does not apply again must leave the country or live undocumented. One of the most controversial elements of presettled status concerns children. A child born on UK soil to a settled parent is automatically a citizen. However, a child who is born on UK soil to a presettled parent is not: the family must apply on behalf of the baby, who is not eligible for settled status and citizenship unless one of their parents is.[37] All newborns and new arrivals are given ninety days to apply—what happens if they do not has yet to be seen.

Ongoing Debates About Welfare

Those with settled and presettled statuses mostly have the same rights to live, work, and study in the UK and move across its borders. However, their access to welfare is a different and much-debated story. Settled immigrants can access all welfare programs for which they are eligible, but presettled immigrants cannot.[38] The Court of Justice of the EU accepted the case of a Dutch and Croatian national with presettled status who was denied cash assistance by the UK's Universal Credit program. There is confusion and apprehension around the final decision, which has yet to be reached, and which will formally dictate the future of welfare access for people with presettled status."[39]

Post-Brexit debates over welfare do not come as a surprise. The UK grappled with renewed antirefugee sentiment before its citizens voted to leave the EU. A few months before David Cameron stepped down as prime minister, Theresa May, who later assumed the post, proposed that the country leave the European Convention on Human Rights.[40] Much like President Donald Trump, she expressed concerns over immigrants' welfare dependence despite research that proved her worries were misplaced.[41] As previously stated, people do not choose the UK as a destination country because of its social net. Leaving the EU will not stop refugees and labor immigrants from arriving; rather, the only result will be that they will not have the services necessary to integrate into society fully, thus perpetuating poverty and social isolation. Providing refugees access to such social services as health care, housing, employment, job training, language classes, childcare, and financial assistance is essential for their survival and integration into their host country.

In addition, there is also a long history of miscommunication across different divisions of welfare services. British immigration and welfare systems have been found to unlawfully refuse to provide proper support and to discriminate against immigrant families. Multiple instances have occurred in Newcastle, the borough of Barking, and Dagenham in East London.[42] Section 17 of the Children Act of 1989 codifies the duty to provide services for all children, including immigrants, and inevitably lends support to their guardians. This conflicted with the broader UK agenda to restrict immigrants' access to government services. As a result, there was a disconnect between the promises made by the national government and the actions of local authorities before the Brexit deal passed. For example, the local government in Newcastle attempted to unlawfully refuse Section 17 support to an immigrant family that was denied asylum in the UK.[43]

Following Brexit, Britain no longer needs to conform to EU immigration and welfare regulations. National and local authorities now set the criteria that immigrant families must meet to receive support, and they control the amount of funds available. The refusal of government services to foreign-born parents may grow more common with time.

Family Reunification for Asylum Seekers

When the UK was still a part of the EU, it could transfer asylum seekers to other member countries or receive them under the Dublin III Regulation. This could occur, for example, when a person seeking asylum in the UK had family members who resided in Denmark and wished to be reunited. While they were waiting in the UK, their asylum claim would be processed by Danish authorities instead. The same would happen when someone sought to reunite with family living in the UK but had first filed for asylum in a different EU country.[44] Essentially, national immigration authorities were able to request that a different country process an immigrant's asylum claim if the individual's family resided there. Brexit dissolved this pathway for all asylum seekers, and reunification applications remain open only to EU nationals who (1) have partners or children living in the UK who have refugee status, (2) have an adult relative or parent living in the UK who has refugee or settled status, or (3) share a personal or familial connection to someone living in the UK who has refugee, settled, or citizen status.[45]

Slightly different rules apply to non-EU asylum seekers because they are not included in the EU Settlement Scheme. According to the refugee family reunion policy, they must submit two applications for family reunification online and also apply for a visa at any visa processing center where they are located. The visa acts as entry clearance.[46] If a family member already resides in the UK, anyone in their family can migrate and apply for a visa afterward. People seeking asylum are exempt from the minimum income threshold rule, and a UK resident can sponsor their family members even if they receive welfare. Undocumented people, however, cannot sponsor anyone.[47]

Under the Dublin III Regulation, the EU held the UK partially responsible for processing asylum claims from other European countries. After Brexit, the international community has exerted less pressure on the British government to do so. The UK has vowed to respond to "take charge" requests from EU members, but it has omitted certain provisions in the updated policy that would have prevented the UK from missing response deadlines and turning migrants away on the basis of low income. Most asylum claims transferred to the UK in 2019 came from Greece, where resources for migrants are underfunded and poorly managed and often do not provide for travel for people getting their claims processed in different countries.[48]

The Newly Undocumented

Another consequential category for immigrants in the new points-based immigration system is that of undocumented. It includes any EU, EEA, or Swiss immigrant in the UK who did not meet the June 30, 2021, deadline to apply to the Settlement Scheme or did not qualify for a late application.[49] Presettled people who do not apply for settled status, those who are denied outright because of their criminal record, and those who simply never applied to the Settlement Scheme are considered undocumented, meaning that their presence is conspicuous and puts them in danger of deportation. The government has taken a lenient stance since the EU–UK Withdrawal Agreement took effect, sending out a twenty-eight-day notice to all who missed the application deadline and promising that their welfare benefits will not be revoked. Nonetheless, the transition process wreaked havoc for some immigrants who were being threatened with eviction because the government had not finished processing their applications.[50]

In addition, lack of communication between local municipalities and national authorities is causing inconsistency in the implementation of post-Brexit policy changes. The legal justification for deportation is also called into question because of the backlog in cases, and it certainly does not help that the UK Home Office has a poor track record related to wrongful deportation. In the 2018 Windrush scandal, thousands of Caribbean immigrants legally residing in Britain were wrongfully deported because they did not have printed proof of their status. Yasmeen Serhan writes that perhaps the biggest challenge "is ensuring that applicants have a valid form of identification, such as a passport," to vouch for themselves or family members.[51]

Ireland

Although Northern Ireland is no longer involved in EU trade or politics, the Republic of Ireland remains a member. In the TCA, the British government and the EU chose not to impose hard checkpoints at the Irish border, as doing so would violate the 1998 Belfast Agreement that ended the Troubles in Northern Ireland. Still, the EU requires that goods imported from non-EU countries be inspected, so items that cross from Britain or Northern Ireland into the Republic of Ireland must be accounted for and checked. The Northern Ireland Protocol was added to the TCA to avoid carrying out this process at the Irish border and potentially disrupting the peace. Checkpoints for goods bound for the Irish Republic are now located at ports in Northern Ireland. Unionists, who self-identify as British, are outwardly displeased with this change and resent that a new border has been drawn in the Irish Sea that differentiates Northern Ireland from the mainland. Port workers began receiving threats soon after the Northern Ireland Protocol was implemented, causing checkpoints to close temporarily and uninspected goods to cross EU borders.[52]

Scotland

The TCA and Withdrawal Agreement also raised questions for Scotland. All thirty-two of its council areas voted to remain in the EU, meaning that the region is being withdrawn from the union against its wishes.[53] Nicola Sturgeon, the first minister of Scotland, stated in 2016 that a separate referendum to decide on Scotland's independence from the UK will likely be held, and efforts toward such a referendum continue.[54] Scots already voted on independence in 2014, with a majority of people (55 percent) choosing to remain in the UK. Loyalist sentiments have further waned ever since, particularly due to Brexit and after the temporary installment of Boris Johnson as prime minister.[55] Indeed, the Scottish Parliament felt "consistently ignored by the UK government throughout the process of EU exit."[56] Whether the post-Brexit UK will remain truly "united" is uncertain, as its internal and psychological borders have deepened after sealing the agreements.

What Happens to UK Nationals Living in Europe?

Approximately one million British citizens living across the EU could need to return to the UK because of the TCA.[57] It banned the free movement of people across UK and EU borders, and UK nationals became subject to the same visa, health care, and residency regulations as all other non-EU visitors and residents. The Withdrawal Agreement sought to protect UK citizens from having the rug pulled out from under them. Any individual who was a lawful resident in an EU country before January 1, 2021, still enjoys most of the same rights and access to health care, education, work, welfare, and housing that they had before the TCA took effect. Even so, nearly all EU countries have required UK nationals to submit new applications for residence. In some countries, like Belgium, they are advised to travel with a residence card.[58]

Aside from these issues, most changes are minor. UK citizens will join the processions of non-EU nationals at the Customs checkpoints in any given European country, and EU citizens will do the same upon arrival in the UK. Dark blue passports have replaced the former burgundy version representing EU membership, but older passports are still valid for travel.

The Economic Consequences: Reduced Wages and Labor Shortages

Brexit created a multitude of questions that have yet to be answered. Confusion about the intricacies of the TCA and Withdrawal Agreement have left immigrants, businesses, and UK citizens speculating about the future, and employment and the economy are of particular concern. The UK relies on immigrant workers to fill labor shortages in important sectors like public services and production. The Confederation of British Industry, a nonprofit business interest group, has drawn attention to this in a report titled *Open and Controlled: A New Approach to Immigration After Brexit*, in which it urged the British government to continue allowing visa-free entry for EU citizens and to abandon plans to reduce net immigration.[59]

The "Leave" campaign attracted British-born people who were worried that high levels of immigration would negatively affect their incomes and job opportunities.[60] This is partially because the UK saw an increase in European immigration for about twenty years after the A8, a group of eight eastern European countries, joined the EU in 2004. Many of those who immigrated then are now returning to their countries of birth.[61] However, a stronger immigrant presence benefits wages because it increases productivity and overall national GDP. EU labor migration raised the pay of many British workers, especially those with lower incomes, by an estimated 3.5 percent between 1992 and 2017.[62] Despite what citizens might be told by those in power, it is *lower* rates of immigration from the EU that will result in a lower standard of living. A drop in immigration and foreign trade investment due to Brexit is predicted to lower UK wages across the board.[63] Indeed, the UK's economy has had the hardest time recovering from the pandemic when compared to those of other European countries and the United States. Immigrants' contributions strengthen the economy to such an extent that a reduction in migration will negatively impact British GDP. It will cause a roughly proportional economic decline, meaning that the more restrictive the immigration policies associated with Brexit are, the greater the harm these policies will cause to the economy. Such policies could trigger a shrinking job market, especially now that pathways for unemployed and low-income EU citizens have been blocked. Ironically, advocates for strict immigration have adopted such views under the pretense of protecting jobs for native-born citizens.[64]

The UK has found it incredibly hard to disentangle its economy from that of the EU. Companies and their employees are worried about the impact of the UK's withdrawal on their immigrant workforces.[65] Work is the main driver of EU migration to the UK, so restrictive labor migration policies are among the most important changes created by the decision to withdraw from the EU. The delayed trade agreement between the UK and EU bred uncertainty, negatively impacting individuals, companies, and the economy. In a survey of over 2,100 UK employers, more than half "had no knowledge of government plans for a post-Brexit immigration system," while only 7 percent knew what they considered to be "a lot" about proposed government plans in 2019.[66] Because of this, it was hard to prepare for the changes incurred by the TCA and Withdrawal Agreement. Many worry that there will be a shortage of low-skilled workers needed to fill jobs in key market sectors, and some businesses fear that Brexit will force them to move operations abroad.

The British government has shown no forbearance or concern for industries that predominantly employ low-skilled and migrant workers. Its policy statement on the points-based immigration system declared that businesses must "move away from a reliance on the UK's immigration system as an alternative to investment in staff retention, productivity, and wider investment in technology and automation."[67] Leaders are well aware of the immediate negative impact that this change will have on the economy. Even so, they offer no more than a recommendation to replace human labor with technology.

BREXIT WILL FAIL TO REDUCE IMMIGRATION

The UK's new immigration policy will reduce the total number of immigrants from the EU, given that it has established an EU-specific documentation system and drastically narrowed entry pathways for unemployed and low-skilled EU nationals. On the other hand, regulations for non-EU migrants did not undergo any serious changes because they were already using to a points-based entry system and the EU Blue Card scheme, which imposed minimum salary requirements and made an offer of employment necessary for entry into the UK. The UK's visa program also operated on points and employment.[68]

The population that has experienced the most drastic changes due to Brexit-imposed visa and immigration modifications is that of EU citizens, who were subjected to preexisting regulations that formerly applied only to non-EU nationals and who were stripped of their free movement and welfare benefits and had to obtain a visa to be able to work. Essentially, all incoming migrants were placed on an equal footing.[69] However, Brexit alone will not slash UK immigration rates or the number of immigrants living there. It is unlikely that most EU nationals will flee the UK and return to their home countries because of these changes. Assuming that each newly undocumented person will choose to leave before being apprehended by authorities would be historically uninformed.

But it will be less attractive for future new migrants from the EU. Furthermore, because of the relative flexibility of the EU Settlement Scheme, the number of EU citizens who are denied residency or will never apply is questionable. However, the effects of Brexit are still unfolding. It is possible that certain demographic groups may become targets for deportation or become newly undocumented en masse. The Roma, a migrant group that has suffered from structural exclusion across Europe, have expressed uncertainty and confusion about the Settlement Scheme application process.[70]

Inflow Migration from EU Countries Is Low

As a colonizer and former empire with a stable labor market, the UK is a popular destination for immigrants and refugees. In 2019, an estimated 14 percent of the British population was foreign-born, similar to the U.S. rate and significantly lower than those in Australia, Switzerland, and New Zealand.[71] Citizens of other EU nations can travel, live, and work freely among the member nations, while migrants from the rest of the world face much higher obstacles and scrutiny. The rate of EU immigration, particularly from central and eastern Europe, slowed down significantly after the eurozone debt crisis in 2012.[72] In 2019, shortly before a Brexit deal was reached, immigration to the UK from EU member nations hit its lowest point since 2009.[73] The number of EU immigrants has remained stable since 2018, fluctuating between 50,000 and 58,000 EU-born people, who are the immigrants that Brexit impacts the most.

Non-EU immigration has been rising each year, albeit very slowly in increments typically no greater than 177,000 people.[74] The foreign-born UK population exhibits extremely different characteristics than the UK-born population. About 70 percent of immigrants are people of working age with origins in Africa, Pakistan, the EU, Oceania, India, and greater Asia.[75] Brexit is projected to directly cut off the flow of European migrants but not that of other immigrant groups making up this larger and more diverse population. This trend is made clear in figure 9.1.

Lower postreferendum immigration rates may be a direct response to Brexit. The UK's Office for National Statistics found that more central and eastern European immigrants are exiting the UK than entering.[76] A significant cause of this is a broad emigration trend in which Polish and eastern European migrants are returning to their native countries. It is also possible that migrants are leaving the country for fear of having their immigration status revoked.

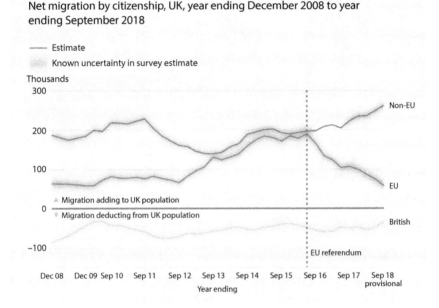

Net migration by citizenship, UK, year ending December 2008 to year ending September 2018

9.1 Net migration by citizenship, UK, December 2008–September 2018

Source: Migration Observatory, COMPAS, Oxford.

Given these circumstances, Brexit is not likely to motivate more people to leave than those who have already left or are doing so now. Migrants to the UK are also no longer primarily motivated by direct economic opportunity, as the numbers of international and EU migrant workers reached a five-year low in 2019. Instead, the largest portion of foreigners are pursuing higher education.[77] Although Brexit was sold to the public as a way to slow inflow migration, the changes will not be significant; while citizens of EU countries are no longer moving to the UK in large numbers, those from countries outside of Europe still are.

Rates of Asylum Applications Were Already on the Decline Before Brexit

The number of UK asylum applications has been declining steadily. Applications peaked in 2002 and grew only between 2010 and 2015.[78] In fact, asylum seekers now constitute a smaller fraction of immigrants than in the 1990s and early 2000s. This is not to say refugees and asylum seekers are not equally as deserving of residency and citizenship as migrant workers and reunified family members;

rather, the majority of immigrants moving to the UK at this time are not seeking asylum. Clearly, the decision to leave the EU was based on the urge to regulate and reduce immigration. The British government's goal is to shave the annual cap on immigrants permitted into the country from one hundred thousand to the tens of thousands.[79] What we have seen instead are important increases in immigration from the rest of the world, including high numbers of people moving to England while Johnson was in office.

CONCLUSION

This chapter began by contextualizing the factors that gave rise to Brexit, including xenophobia, disagreements on EU policies, and misconceptions about immigrants. Moreover, we reviewed important aspects of the Brexit deal, like the UK's new immigration and asylum policies, the effects on British expatriates in the EU, and the ramifications for Ireland and Scotland. We concluded by arguing that Brexit will not reduce migration into the UK. This is primarily because inflow migration from EU countries is already low and because regulations covering non-EU migrants, who make up an increasing share of inflow migration, have not fundamentally changed. In fact, Brexit will likely have wide-ranging negative economic consequences, including labor shortages, lower wages, and decreased GDP.

The desire for economic prosperity is common for many. However, it is important to reevaluate such desires if immigrants are used as scapegoats after economic shortfalls. Decades of dissatisfaction in the UK fueled by isolationism, xenophobia, and misconceptions about the effect of immigrants on British society ultimately led to Brexit. Although proponents of Brexit promised a better future for the UK, Brexit does not provide an instant remedy to Britain's qualms about immigration or economic inequality, nor does it prevent further xenophobia or isolationism. Eglė Dagilytė and Margaret Greenfields anticipate that the UK will still grapple with intense internal divisions and disagreements about immigration and the distribution of wealth after Brexit.[80] It is inevitable that the post-Brexit changes in immigration policy and entry requirements will force EU migrants and UK nationals to adapt. The vast number of applications that the government must handle and the effects that Brexit will have on immigrants' lives will make for a difficult transition in the coming years. Although a "hard" deal was reached in the last days of 2020, the long-term implications of Brexit are still unclear. The short-term impacts have not been promising, as employment rates, immigration, and economic growth have slowed since the referendum—because of Brexit and then the COVID-19 pandemic. The decision to exit the EU holds many unanticipated consequences.

This chapter reminds us that the antagonistic views many people harbor toward immigrants are not unique to the United States. Myths that immigrants "steal jobs" and "exploit social services" exist around the world. Our brief survey of the history that led to Brexit revealed that some of the most relevant factors are the belief in British exceptionalism, semi-isolationist economic policies, paranoia about the allocation of social services, and skewed notions about sovereignty and national autonomy. The chapter also demonstrates the inaccuracy of these views by looking at the purpose and impact of immigration in the UK. If we were to compare the costs and benefits of immigration for migrants versus those for the natives of the host country, the economic benefits reaped by natives due to migration would far outweigh the inconvenience of sharing cultural and social spaces.

History reveals that people migrate because of geopolitical insecurity, lack of safety, and issues that their local governments cannot immediately solve. The case for migrants is the same in the UK as in the United States: migrants contribute more than they supposedly "take." The arrival of migrants does not leave native residents with fewer social services. If anything, migrants render government aid programs more effective and accessible to the entire population of the host country because they alleviate labor shortages in both low- and high-skilled jobs, increase productivity, and increase GDP. The idea that technology and automation can resolve the demand for low-skilled labor is too simplistic.

CHAPTER 10

IMMIGRANTS CAN INTEGRATE WHILE MAINTAINING THEIR IDENTITIES

Popular discussions about immigration typically revolve around border security, immigration policy, and refugee admission caps, all of which dictate who is permitted into a country, how they obtain approval, and when and where they must enter. But what happens to refugees and immigrants after they have jumped through the many flaming hoops lit by the circus of national policies and authorities? How do they settle in a new home, find employment, learn the local language, and participate in their community? Social acceptance and resettlement services are crucial to the well-being of immigrants and their ability to thrive in a new country where the labor market, cultural and social norms, and stereotypes are all different. Policymakers often forget these tribulations, which leaves local leaders responsible for implementing effective programs and support systems for the foreign-born. For example, in the United States, there is a laissez-faire approach in which immigrants and their receiving communities must figure out how to integrate without formal help or explicit guidelines.[1] More effective approaches that guide immigrants toward achieving both the easily quantifiable and the subjective markers of integration are possible and necessary to foster belonging, community, and success among immigrants in their new countries.

IMMIGRANT INTEGRATION

Social Integration

Milton Gordon talked about different types of structural assimilation that allowed previously excluded groups to become part of "the mainstream," which before the 1950s meant WASP (white Anglo-Saxon protestant) culture.[2] Today one can also talk about partial integration in specific realms and not in others. An overall integration is what Ernesto Castañeda and others call *social integration*, which does not imply a cultural assimilation to the mores of the dominant group but rather suggests certain negotiations, two-way communication, and mutual influence. In the same vein, Mary Waters and Marisa Gerstein Pineau define *integration* as "the process by which members of immigrant groups and host societies come to resemble one another."[3] As time goes on, with each generation, immigrants become more integrated and more culturally familiar with the native-born. Yet "the well-being of immigrants and their descendants is highly dependent on immigrant starting points and on the segment of American society—the racial and ethnic groups, the legal status, the social class, and the geographic area—into which they integrate."[4] The economic conditions, hierarchies, and bureaucratic structures in place that immigrants encounter (oftentimes regrettably) can interrupt or even prevent integration.

Integration is commonly mistakenly conflated with assimilation and acculturation, but these are all distinct concepts. *Acculturation* refers to the process of learning about the culture of the new place of residence and becoming culturally fluent. While, over time, there will be dissimilation—immigrants becoming culturally different from people in their hometowns who have no migration experience[5]—immigrants can acculturate while maintaining many of their native traditions and culture. As it is used here, social integration denotes equality in rights and opportunities while respecting cultural differences. It is an ideal, given that few places provide this reality for all immigrants and ethno-racial or religious minorities.

Assimilation

Early Chicago School sociologists and the 1952 book *The Uprooted* by the historian Oscar Handlin compared immigrants to abruptly transplanted plants that lacked the native terroir to nurture and ground them properly. Their uprooting and transplantation to new lands led to malaise, degradation, alcoholism, and proclivity to crime. Immigrants outside their culture were assumed to have lost their moral compass. In the view of these white scholars, some of them having Jewish or white immigrant backgrounds themselves, the goal was *Americanization*: assimilation into American culture without any ethnic traces beyond a few symbols like

St. Patrick's Day for the Irish.[6] Therefore, in previous decades, the way to measure immigrant success was to compare immigrants to the native-born and see how similarly they fared and behaved. At the turn of the twentieth century, leaders of the progressive era like Jane Addams established settlement houses to welcome and house immigrants, an effort now referred to as the social settlement movement. Addams and the members of the Hull House in Chicago focused on building community via diversity, believing that each immigrant brought something unique and valuable to the table.[7] According to Robert Carlson, Addams took an integrative approach and not an assimilationist one, although she thought that just living in the United States would Americanize immigrants for better or worse.[8] On the other hand, some members of the social settlement movement emphasized Americanization in order to turn foreign-born individuals quickly into people they considered to be ideal "Americans."

Academic work on immigration during most of the twentieth century used the term *assimilation* to describe the process through which immigrants became *similar* or practically identical to locals. It is a process that prioritizes the receiving society's cultures, norms, and values as better or of higher moral standing than those of any immigrants or minorities. Thus, for early scholars, to study immigration meant to study and theorize on assimilation. During this period, *integration* was a term often used to discuss African American culture and to stand in opposition to segregation and cultural differentiation.[9]

The assimilation of immigrants and minorities was seen as a mutually beneficial goal. In theory, it would decrease the uprootedness that stressed immigrants and the cultural differences that worried natives. Americanization was somewhat beneficial—but only for very few. As Gordon described, learning English and local norms helped ameliorate discrimination and exclusion, allowing ethnically white immigrants to access higher levels of education and better jobs and even to intermarry with established immigrants. This was the process that Italian, Irish, and Polish Americans went through in the Midwest and on the East Coast of the United States.[10] Nevertheless, this path was not as feasible for Black immigrants from the Caribbean or Brown immigrants from Mexico—the color line proved to be durable.[11] Asian Americans and immigrants also did not reap the full benefits of Americanization and suffered from recurrent stereotypes.[12]

Legal Enforcement of Symbolically Violent Policies Assimilation is a form of ethnocentrism, cultural discrimination, and epistemic or symbolic violence[13] because it accepts and enforces the idea that the local culture is superior to that of newcomers. As a result, an immigrant is expected to completely depart from their home culture in their efforts to adopt the traditions, religious practices, language, and values of the dominant local culture of their new place of residence. While individuals should be able to preserve facets of their native cultural practices and identity, social and political forces can coax or force immigrants to abandon them.

Assimilation efforts did not end in the twentieth century: recent examples of legally enforced assimilation can be seen in France, the Netherlands, Denmark, and Austria. One clear example is how these governments have banned women from wearing niqabs and burqas in the name of national security, secularism, and adherence to social norms. The United Nations Human Rights Committee ruled that the sweeping ban on Islamic face and body coverings in France is a violation of human rights for the minority of women who choose to wear them, yet these countries still uphold these bans.[14] Similarly, Canada's Quebec Province issued a ban on all veils and headscarves, as well as yarmulkes and turbans, in public schools.[15] In this way, assimilation operates on a foundation of intolerance for identities that diverge from the dominant and often Eurocentric culture.

In the United States, assimilation has historically revolved around the belief that success is achieved only when foreign-born people adopt white cultural ideals and practices. This has long been an expectation for immigrants, although it is now being challenged extensively as being inherently racist, discriminatory, and xenophobic. The genocide of Native Americans by European settlers and their descendants was perhaps the first instance of the exclusion of and violence toward people on the North American continent who do not fit an Anglo-Saxon or Eurocentric mold. Incongruously, the U.S. Supreme Court ruled that Native Americans were encroaching on U.S. territory as "alien nations . . . with whom the United States might and habitually did deal, as they thought fit."[16] Indigenous lands were stolen, and the lives of the surviving future generations of Native Americans were impoverished, partly under the pretense of white supremacy and the belief that Christianity gave Europeans the right to settle in lands inhabited by non-Christians. Boarding schools were used by the federal government as tools of mass cultural extermination, erasing the languages, cultures, and pride of Native American children beginning around 1879. In Canada, these schools would employ force and violence, which resulted in the deaths of many Native minors. To this day, mass graves cradling the bones of children and adolescents are being found across North America.[17] Many of these schools were closed only because the 1953 Indian Termination Act granted all Native Americans formal

U.S. citizenship, but the act also allowed the United States to absorb Native lands and relabel them as reservations. Today Indigenous communities in North America and other colonized and resettled regions of the world still face the impact of genocide and forced assimilation. They have lower life expectancies and exhibit disproportionately high rates of suicide and mental health and substance use disorders.[18]

Le Droit a la Différence The unattainable expectation to fit into an exclusionary white culture remains a strong undertone in the experiences of immigrants today. For example, a 2019 article published in the *Washington Examiner* equated celebrating diversity and providing bilingual education with an "impractical desire for political correctness" that restricted immigrants' abilities and desires to become truly American.[19] Those who are not perceived to have assimilated or made an effort to do so are deemed a threat. Furthermore, the pressures to assimilate sometimes alienate or disillusion minoritized individuals (those affected by processes that reduce the opportunities for those who are members of a numerical minority in a larger group), causing them to limit their interactions to small and ethnically homogenous enclaves.

Nonetheless, any one culture is not better than another—it is simply different. Throughout history, people from all types of cultures and subcultures have always coexisted. Many places have embraced the value of cultural tolerance, or what some French activists refer to as *le droit a la différence* (the right to be different).[20] Some scholars and policymakers refer to this principle as *interculturalism*, achieved in practice when different ethnic or cultural groups within the same political unit or territory have the same respect, rights, and representation. This goal has to be intentional with policies that back it up and that, to a large degree, create something approximating this arrangement.

Integration Is Not a Blueprint for Whiteness

While assimilation and those who tout it are not gone for good, things changed in the 1960s when assimilation fell from favor following the civil rights movement. Since then, many scholars in the social sciences have used terms such as *integration* and *political incorporation* to discuss immigrants' abilities to succeed and fully participate in their new communities without the normative expectation that they forget their previous lives and cultural heritages as soon as they cross a sea or a political border. Integration embraces cultural duality wherein immigrants retain their home culture while also developing fluency in the dominant culture; integrating and preserving connections with the country of origin can happen simultaneously. Being a part of any culture is not mutually exclusive.

Integration is defined and understood differently depending on the intent and professional field in which it is being discussed. The complex theoretical interpretations of integration are often lost when the concept is operationalized in research because the "successes" and "failures" of immigrants are typically based on the average performance of native-born people in a host country.[21] Successful members of the majority group are seen as the baseline, or "normal," and integration is framed as a process that immigrants undergo in order to eventually overcome their "abnormal" status. In predominantly Eurocentric and white environments, this expectation is especially salient for immigrants of color. They are told to strive for the white standard, which they can never truly meet because it functions to exclude people based on their skin color, physical appearance, culture, religion, or ethnic identification. For an immigrant of color, trying to achieve success as it relates to whiteness is like being offered a seat at the table only to have your hands tied to the chair so you are unable to eat.

The assimilationist framing of immigrant success and the use of integration in the operationalization of some social science research are inadequate and discriminatory. For example, an immigrant who earns the same average salary as a native-born person may feel less a part of their new society than a different immigrant who earns less, but the higher earner is considered "better integrated" by some research standards and integration indexes. The comparison is often normative: for instance, when the economic integration or success of immigrants in Canada is measured by how close they come to earning the same amount as the average native-born Canadian.[22] An individual's unique identity and motivations for migrating are also not accounted for when integration is defined by the characteristics of average native-born people of a region. Furthermore, native-born people are not a blueprint that immigrants need to follow in order to cultivate a sense of belonging. Integration is not a process of fitting in but one of acknowledging and overcoming obstacles in different realms of life that block someone from their pursuits in their host country. An equally problematic expectation is that immigrants, to prove their worth and their place, must go above and beyond in their education and career, becoming exceptional entrepreneurs, innovative inventors, gifted artists, brilliant academics, skilled athletes, high school valedictorians, successful college students, or active members of the Armed Forces (in the case of the DREAMers and DACA recipients).[23]

Biculturalism

According to Larissa Remennick, "Effective integration requires diverse personal resources: languages, education, social skills, and the ability to adapt to different roles."[24] This causes people to believe that assimilation is a simpler route: they think that adjustment will be easier if an immigrant does not need to juggle multiple cultures. However, it is an illusion that immigrants and their children are culturally dynamic; neither can they change who they are and what they know with one snap of their fingers. Learning a new culture is complicated and takes time, but it is not impossible. In fact, much like bilingualism, learning a new culture does not subtract from someone's native culture, and people who are fluent in more than one culture can benefit from their bi- or multicultural identity (see chapter 4). That is not to say that it does not present challenges: different social expectations sometimes create confusion and conflict in a person's life. What is important is that immigrants *themselves* are the ones who choose when, where, why, how, and to what degree they wish to integrate into their new country.

Integration can be made difficult by oppressive immigration policies as well as exclusionary social narratives and linguistic and cultural barriers. In eastern Europe and West Asia, a fair share of countries approach integration in a conservative and restrictive way, especially in terms of education, citizenship, and a collective political voice.[25] Many countries, including the United States, have integration policies that fall short of providing proper support. Although all immigration systems have flaws, the members of the international community will hopefully learn from one another's errors.[26] Nonetheless, learning cannot begin without first acknowledging the damage that has been done. The histories of assimilation in different world regions recount cultural erasure, language death, systematic social exclusion, and genocide.[27] Because of the mistakes that governments have made in the past in forcing immigrants to subdue or relinquish their identities and lives, it is essential that from now on, policies that impact foreign-born communities weigh just as heavily on a country's native-born population. Immigrants are equally as valuable to the social fabric as native-born people.

Collective National Identities

National philosophies regarding identity and citizenship influence policies and attitudes toward immigrants and integration. Comparative research in Europe typically emphasizes national models of immigrant integration, although they are not the be-all and end-all explanations for a nation's policies and practices. For example, assimilation is more heavily encouraged in France than in the Netherlands, as the uniting identity in France is a shared political and social philosophy that centers the republic.[28] Nationality defines citizenship in France, whereas the United Kingdom and the Netherlands have historically encouraged a multicultural and transethnic view, albeit fluctuating, of what makes someone a citizen. Therefore, an immigrant's ability to integrate is partially determined by the host country's environment, attitudes toward immigrants, and national ideology.[29]

Immigrant Integration in Cities

Integration takes place not at the national level but in certain cities that are popular destinations. An estimated 95 percent of immigrants that the United States received in 2012 put down new roots in urban areas like New York, Chicago, San Francisco, Boston, Los Angeles, Houston, and Miami.[30] Although more and more foreign-born people are moving into the suburban outskirts of larger metropolitan areas, cities remain primary immigrant-receiving regions. They are also the spaces that thus far have adopted the most practical and welcoming immigrant integration policies in North America because of the economic and social benefits they experience from social diversity and immigrant labor.

The contexts in which immigrants and refugees are received vary around the world with different degrees of success. In the United States, over one hundred sanctuary states, counties, and cities have taken the initiative to lower the number of deportations by restricting compliance with federal immigration authorities, like U.S. Immigration and Customs Enforcement, within their jurisdictions.[31] The following section examines the actions that cities take to integrate immigrants into the social, economic, political, and cultural fabric of a region as well as immigrants' resilience throughout the demanding process of establishing themselves in a new place.

CULTIVATING BELONGING IN A NEW PLACE

Recent scholarship on immigration has studied the lived experiences of immigrants and their descendants, moving beyond the emphasis on tracing trajectories of assimilation, integration, or incorporation and instead grappling more fully with questions of inclusion, exclusion, and belonging.[32] Increasingly, authors have explored the concept of belonging.[33] Building on the work of the Dutch sociologist Jan Willem Duyvendak, Castañeda defines *belonging* as feeling "at home" when conducting day-to-day routines, regardless of immigrant status, or "the opposite of feeling excluded or like an outsider" not only in their homes but also in public spaces.[34] Thus, belonging is influenced by others' sentiments toward an immigrant and their ethnic group as well as that immigrant's subjective perception of their daily experiences. More specifically, Castañeda characterizes *urban belonging* as "a subjective feeling of belonging that responds to real social integration that includes economic, political, and institutional integration"[35] into a neighborhood, city, or metropolitan area. This concept could also be expanded to encompass a person's sense of belonging to a country, a region, or the world. For instance, *cosmopolitanism* refers to feeling like a citizen of the world or feeling at home in many places, despite being bureaucratically constrained to one place of birth and limited countries of citizenship.

The concept of integration embodies a deeply emotional experience that is simultaneously rooted in a broader context. Keith Banting and Stuart Soroka write that integration "reflects the person's sense of attachment to the country, but it also reflects the extent to which that person feels accepted by other denizens of the place."[36] A person's sense of belonging might differ from what others believe it to be based on external measures of integration, like language proficiency and length of time spent in the new place. These indicators are used by most researchers to interpret immigrants' experiences but may not align with an immigrant's internal relationship with their new home.

Existing structures shape two distinct indicators of immigrant integration: objective data—e.g., socioeconomic and health outcomes, policies, inclusion on paper—and subjective data—e.g., the perception of discrimination and feeling part of a community. The subjective, more personal information is gathered by asking immigrants basic questions about their experiences and perceived integration levels, which are partly informed by premigration expectations as well as fresher assessments of the host country's state, society, and work experiences and opportunities. Assessments of immigrant integration typically focus on a standard battery of outcomes, such as employment, educational and residential attainment, legal inclusion, and access to resources and services, but it is useful to examine these objective conditions alongside immigrants' subjective feelings of belonging. Nevertheless, it is important to realize that immigrants can simultaneously experience fluctuating degrees of inclusion and exclusion, and their feelings of belonging to a place do not always coincide with the expectations of researchers who pay attention only to the broader structural contexts of migration.[37] Focusing beyond traditional objective measures of immigrant incorporation allows us to fuse macro and micro levels of analysis to emphasize the importance of feeling at home where one lives. Next, we expand on the importance of social context and place when examining an immigrant's holistic integration experience by referencing New York City, Paris, and Barcelona, as in Castañeda's monograph *A Place to Call Home*.

INTEGRATION IN NEW YORK CITY, PARIS, AND BARCELONA

Contextual Factors Affecting Belonging

Varying contexts of reception within combinations of cities, countries, cultures, and policies produce different outcomes for different immigrants. The context of reception is often nested in smaller and larger units with different degrees of support for immigrants. Within the United States, New York is friendlier to undocumented Mexican workers than Maricopa County, Arizona. Paris is more hostile to North African immigrants than Marseille. There are also particularities at the block, neighborhood, school, and organization levels.[38]

   Places around the world with different historical legacies, or even regions with claims for political independence, have developed explicit multicultural models that they apply to themselves and extend to new arrivals. The most prominent examples of this are French-speaking Quebec Province within English-speaking

Canada, Catalonia vis-à-vis Spain,[39] and the Netherlands, which created a pillar system to accommodate different religious affiliations.

The historical context of racial and ethnic relations and stratification in an immigrant-receiving country impacts how new immigrant groups integrate. In the United States, the legacy of racism, white supremacy, and Black-white inequality and segregation shapes the context in which new immigrants, particularly immigrants of color, are received. In intensely prejudiced societies, immigrants' subjective sense of belonging and objective markers of integration suffer. As Jean Beaman asked, "How much can someone feel at home or included while also subject to racism and discrimination?"[40] The legacies of colonialism and slavery still influence the relationships and disparities between immigrants and native-born individuals. For example, many Algerian Muslims are still resentful of the French colonial rule of their homeland, and many French still perceive their culture as superior to that of North Africa. It is not enough for immigrants to want to integrate if the context does not permit it.[41] Therefore, it is important to consider objective and subjective indicators of integration together with what immigration literature calls contexts of reception—building on the work of Alejandro Portes, Rubén Rumbaut, and Alex Stepick.[42]

The factors shaping the context of immigrant reception include locals' attitudes about immigration and race, locals' tolerance for other cultures, economic incorporation and opportunities, the history of migration, the feasibility of life as an undocumented migrant, and avenues for collective action and political voice through migrant and ethnic group organizations, minority spokespeople, and elected representatives. These factors are not easily quantified, and their sway in fostering a sense of belonging is not easily measured. This blend of factors is weighed in the balance of individual perceptions and feelings and in the possibility of daily life in a society that does not limit immigrants to chronic unemployment, incarceration, or the figurative prison of the four walls of a public housing unit in the banlieues of Paris.[43]

In Paris, individuals' desire to integrate, formal laws that determine legal status, and national philosophies, such as France's civic discourse of equality, are insufficient to foster integration, given the exclusion, racism, and ethnocentrism that immigrants of color often face there. In contrast, in Barcelona and New York, immigrants may be excluded legally through restrictive immigration policies, but they can feel integrated when other mechanisms that foster their social and economic integration are in place. Social interactions, cultural practices, and experiences are key to integration, and these factors are shaped by broader socioeconomic and political contexts of reception.[44]

Sense of Belonging in Urban Spaces

In New York City, the distinction between local and foreigner is more blurred than in other urban places. Its laissez-faire mode of integration, high level of religious tolerance, strong legitimacy accorded to ethnic-group-based claims, and large percentage of foreign-born residents make New York a relatively inclusive space that enables urban belonging for all types of people.[44]

Mexicans and other Latin immigrants living in New York City who are sometimes legally and socially excluded still identify as New Yorkers and feel a sense of belonging. Social mobility and economic integration—living out the American dream—play a significant role in the connection Mexican immigrants feel to New York, as many can find jobs or situate themselves in diverse ethnic communities.[45] People of other nationalities and the children of immigrants in New York feel similarly.[46] While grappling with undocumented status and legal recognition, immigrants find themselves socially connected to the city through social movements to better their living situations.[47] An important factor that promotes the inclusion of immigrants and their children is the civil rights reforms, which ironically enabled better academic and work outcomes for immigrants compared to their U.S.-born Black and Puerto Rican counterparts. Many immigrant groups across the United States have enjoyed social mobility partly by adopting anti-Black attitudes and segregationist practices.[48] Belonging is often related to race or nationality, so legal status is not the only thing that contributes to systematic exclusion.

These characteristics foster a sense of multiculturalism, meaning that immigrants can add to rather than replace the identities they had when they arrived. It is also common in New York City for immigrants and their descendants to share a sense of pride in their countries of origin, which does not prevent them from contributing to the United States. Available jobs and a dynamic organizational infrastructure that can make claims on behalf of immigrant groups help mitigate some of the considerable material differences between the high-earning and low-earning labor markets in this global city.[49] Overall, immigrants of all statuses feel comparatively less pressure to erase their native cultural identities in this environment, even amid struggles with legal status, policing, working conditions, and social mobility.[50]

However, the environment for immigrants in Paris is very different than that in New York City. Expectations related to assimilation and French citizenship are more rigid than in New York, pressuring immigrants to follow a linear process of becoming French through developing language proficiency, adopting the cultural norms of Parisian elites, and acquiring political rights as individuals instead of as members of an ethno-racial group. North African immigrants are expected to shed their home cultures and identities to engage in society properly.[51] Most self-identify as French, despite their exclusion, and simultaneously participate in protests and other forms of resistance against the state. In France, relying on identities based on ethnicity, race, and religion as the basis for friendships or for community or political organizing is frowned on and derogatively called *communautarisme*.[52] Furthermore, France's history of *laïcité*, the policy of private religious practice, renders the possibility of immigrants articulating a collective identity in Paris very low. Also, several realities coexist in Paris, each with a different set of practices and constellation of relationships.[53] Paris can be both home and nonhome. The Parisian banlieues are home to some migrants who feel like outsiders in other parts of the city reserved for elites. Some can be and feel Français while also experiencing exclusion. In addition, belonging is expressed precisely in practices that connect a person with a place and make them part of the national community.[54]

France's republican, secularist, and assimilationist culture, as well as its fixation on national identity, rarely produces feelings of belonging among both immigrant and native-born minorities. North Africans in France face the most severe exclusion.[55] As one North African respondent told Castañeda, "People always make you feel like a foreigner."[56] This is worsened by the political under-representation of racial and ethnic minorities, the low legitimacy accorded to group-based claims, and a general lack of tolerance for religious freedom in Paris. Algerian immigrants and their descendants are still searching for the type of urban belonging that immigrants in New York City experience. Segregated from middle-class Parisian neighborhoods and urban centers, they do not have opportunities to grow and succeed.[57] Whereas immigrants in New York are met with challenges regarding their undocumented immigration status, immigrants in Paris grapple with postcolonial animosity and liberal political ideals that obstruct claims making at the group level. Even though most of the Algerians with whom Castañeda spoke had or sought French citizenship and wanted to be treated as French citizens, their communities were barred from employment opportunities and often subject to heavy police surveillance. Due to this, they felt excluded from their new home, even though they were recognized by the government as legal residents and supported through social welfare programs.

In Barcelona, the largest municipality in northeastern Spain's Catalonia region, North African immigrants feel a strong sense of urban belonging because of ample job opportunities, supportive public programs, and a general acceptance of immigrants. However, racial and ethnic stigmatization still occurs. Moroccans have social clubs, friendship networks within and across national groups, and a moderate political voice as city residents. They rely on certain spokespeople to prevent stigmatization of Muslims in the media, and the Catalan government has instituted several policies and programs to include newcomers from Morocco while respecting and protecting their cultural differences. Public religious fervor is seen as problematic in France and is used as an excuse to criticize and attack Muslim immigrants. Nonetheless, religious institutions often support their social incorporation, mutual aid, and pride. The Catholic Church is a long-established transnational institution in the Global North, especially in Spain, and tradition-ally welcomes migrants and the poor. In contrast, Islam has religious institutions that are relatively new in the Global North and not as visible.[58] Thus, Islamic institutions are not as accepted culturally in Christian-dominant countries, and people participating in Islam are not celebrated or viewed the same as those participating in Catholicism.

Political Integration and Representation

Local governments and organizations have an influential role in integration. Immigrant organizations offer services and sometimes a public voice. Repre-sentatives, government officials, and immigrant electoral influence can push cities further away from restrictive national policies and closer to a welcoming environment.[59] Local political opportunity structures can take many forms,[60] such as top-down modes of representation like in Barcelona or more bot-tom-up modes like in New York City. Citywide immigrant movements and campaigns can be important to bring actors across national and regional spaces, but local political units like the neighborhood, barrio, and *mairie* are crucial settings for some contentious politics, even in France with its cen-tralized state.[61] Nevertheless, even after the decentralization reforms of the 1980s first diluted the national state, the control over associations' funding by prefects in Paris has prevented the immigrant associations from engaging directly in contentious politics.[62]

After Spain entered the European Union in 1986, the number of international migrants, tourists, and British and European retirees living there increased. This rapid influx of people spurred economic growth that slowed only temporarily during the 2007 financial crisis. Since the late 1990s, Barcelona has been one of the most popular destinations for international migrants. The city's immigrant population jumped from just 3.5 percent in 2000 to over 25 percent by 2018.[63] Spain's integration policies emphasize immigrant participation and interculturalism as a two-way process. Integration policies openly recognize the importance of immigrant organizations in formulating and successfully implementing immigration policies.[64] In addition, there is institutionalized support for immigrant integration into society and labor markets through dedicated local programming, often in the immigrants' native language.[65]

As Spain grew in popularity among migrants and visitors, the national government increasingly delegated immigrant integration initiatives to local governments. In 1993, Catalonia developed its First Interdepartmental Immigration Plan with corresponding offices and a budget. Over four hundred immigrant, ethnic, and neighborhood associations and labor unions were consulted in planning the 2008–2011 Immigration Plan.[66] In 1989, the Barcelona City Council created SAIER (Servicio de Atención a Inmigrantes Extranjeros y Refugiados), which coordinated a set of urban social services offered to immigrants that included information about housing, employment, and legal matters. It also offered free Spanish and Catalan classes to approximately twenty-five thousand people per year.[67] Building on these policies, the Barcelona municipal government has hired immigrants as functionaries and advisers working on minority policies and has dedicated considerable funds to financing immigrant-led events and initiatives. The number and richness of immigrant organizations in Barcelona reflect the city government's goal to be proactive with immigrant integration that allows immigrants to retain and even celebrate their respective cultures. Indeed, Laura Morales and Laia Jorba write that in Barcelona, "immigrant integration is viewed as a 'natural' process that will emerge from immigrants' equal access to all social welfare services, which are based on the same principles and requirements [as] for pre-existing residents."[68] The availability of social services and a high level of political representation work together to create a winning formula for immigrant integration.[69]

Combining Objective and Subjective Indicators of Immigration

Comparing objective indicators of integration with immigrants' subjective expectations and assessments is important because both shape the sense of belonging. Barcelona provides a valuable example where both types of data are helpful in expressing immigrants' integration levels and experiences. Spanish immigration laws and local interviewees openly prefer Latin American immigrants over Moroccans, which indicates that North Africans might feel more socially excluded. Nevertheless, Castañeda discovered that Moroccan immigrants' premigration expectations powerfully shaped their sense of belonging, possibly even more so than perceived discrimination.[70] Moroccans anticipated a hard time adapting and being accepted into Catalan society due to historical tensions and cultural differences between Spain and Morocco, but in general, most experienced a relatively positive reception. On the other hand, immigrants from Latin America had different expectations. They considered Spain as their best option for integration because of their presumed cultural similarities. However, upon arrival, they found that linguistic and cultural differences were more of a shock than they anticipated. Despite Catalonians and Latin Americans typically being able to communicate in Spanish, the manner of speaking and some vocabulary words are different in Spain, and these are seen as markers of difference. Furthermore, Catalonian culture is distinct from that of mainstream Spain, and the region speaks its own language of Catalan. Therefore, Latin American immigrants needed a couple of years to adapt and change some of their speaking patterns, which certain highly educated Latin American professionals resented.

These premigration expectations and postmigration letdowns are the reason why Latin individuals in Barcelona have more objective integration options but struggle to feel like they belong. The inverse occurs among Moroccans: they experience more exclusion on all fronts and yet feel "at home" comparatively quickly. Neither of these, however, is an ideal outcome. Also, given the barriers to integration that immigrants in Paris experience, formal legal citizenship in any context is incomplete if immigrants are not simultaneously experiencing economic, cultural, and political inclusion. To achieve optimal well-being and peaceful cohabitation for natives and immigrants alike, comprehensive structural integration and palpable respect for cultural and religious differences must be accompanied by job opportunities, access to social services, and the safety net and political rights of legal citizenship. In this environment, immigrants'

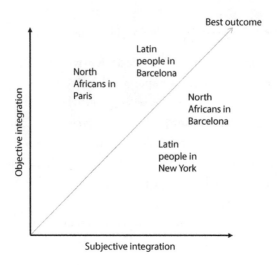

10.1 Relative belonging

Source: Castañeda, *A Place to Call Home,* 142.

objective and subjective feelings of integration will thrive together. None of the three cities we discuss in this chapter provides all these ideal conditions (see figure 10.1).[71]

Conclusions from Comparing New York City, Paris, and Barcelona

There is no fixed interpretation of belonging because it is different for everyone. Immigrants' integration experiences are defined by the complexities of their personal experiences, feelings, and outcomes in a new place. Most immigrants living in New York City, Paris, Barcelona, and other parts of the world do not undergo an easy transition to social mobility or a seamless integration into the local social fabric of a host region.[72] Gradually, through social interaction and cultural experience, immigrants become familiar with their new social context. Still, this subjective adaptation also responds to objective conditions, including the receptivity of locals in the new context in which they live. While the legal stipulations upon arrival establish objective opportunities for employment, schooling, language instruction, social and political rights, naturalization, and the like, a personal sense of membership is contingent on the host society's dominant attitude and level of openness. Even when immigrants want to integrate, the receiving society and state must provide a welcoming, tolerant context for

TABLE 10.1 Key dimensions of social context: New York, El Paso, Paris, and Barcelona

Dimension	New York	El Paso	Paris	Barcelona
Integration model	Laissez-faire, de facto multicultural	Americanization	Civic republicanism, assimilationist	Intercultural
Basis for the legitimate organization of civil society	Race/ethnicity	Identity	Class	Culture
Levels of policymaking and implementation	State and local	State and local	Central and local	Central, federal, regional, and local
Legitimacy of minority religious and cultural practices in public	High	High	Low	Medium
Legitimacy of claims based on ethnicity	High	Medium	Low	High
Legitimacy of ethnic organizations	High	High	Low	High
Legitimacy of immigrant organizations	High	Medium	Medium	High
Funding	Some public funding is available, but most organizations receive grants from private foundations/ donations	Some public funding is available, but most organizations receive grants from private foundations/ donations	Mainly state funding; very little private funding for ethnic organizations	Public funding for organizations

Source: Castañeda, "Urban Contexts and Immigrant Organizations."

El Paso's population is over 80 percent Hispanic, and most immigrants are from Mexico and Latin America. Still, does the Hispanic population feel a sense of belonging? Belonging varies depending on different social positions (table 10.2).

About 70 percent of Hispanic people who attended a religious institution felt that they belonged to a community compared to 53.3 percent of those who did not attend religious gatherings. Spending time with people of the same religion or in a sacred religious space strengthened Hispanic people's senses of community and belonging. Hispanic people who voted were 9.1 percent more likely to feel like a part of their community than those who did not regularly vote.

Given the demographics of El Paso, people with all or mostly Hispanic friends felt they were a part of a community (63 percent) (table 10.3). However, the people who most felt they were a part of a community were those whose friends consisted of roughly equal shares of Hispanics and non-Hispanics (68.6 percent). Hispanic people who were friends with only or mainly non-Hispanic people were less likely to feel a sense of belonging to a community (33.3 percent).

TABLE 10.2 Feeling of belonging to a community

Overall	63.9%
Men	62.1%
Women	65.3%
U.S.-born	63%
Foreign-born	65.3%
First generation	60.8%
1.5 generation	70.3%
Second generation	66.1%
Third generation	53.5%
More than third	60.8%
Visa	78.9%
Citizen	64.1%
Resident	60.6%
Undocumented	62.7%
Goes to religious institution	69.5%
Doesn't go to religious institution	53.3%
Votes	69%
Doesn't vote	59.9%

TABLE 10.3 Circle of friends

All Hispanics	31.7%
More Hispanics than non-Hispanics	44.9%
About half and half	19.8%
More non-Hispanics than Hispanics	1.7%
All non-Hispanics	0.4%
Other	1.6%
Total	100%

Source: Self-reported friend ethnicity in El Paso, the population of which is over 83 percent Hispanic.

cultural differences. An intercultural model makes it easier to accommodate linguistic, cultural, and religious differences and paradoxically serves to further integrate immigrants into the mainstream.[73]

METHODOLOGICAL NATIONALISM AND ETHNIC COMMUNITIES ABROAD

One of the main causes of anti-immigrant sentiment comes from nationalism and what many have been taught about governments representing one national group residing in a corresponding territory. Starting our analysis taken nation-states as the eternal bases of social groups should be question reflexive because otherwise constitutes "methodological nationalism" which means defining research questions and collecting data along national lines. A problem in much immigration research and policy, as well as in popular media discussions, is the focus on the largest immigrant group in a place. The members of that group are described and discussed as one homogenous population while other immigrant groups are ignored. For instance, Hispanics and Muslims are frequent categorical groupings used to talk about "problematic" immigrants in the United States and Europe, but these populations are actually comprised of individuals of varying classes, genders, skin tones, immigrant generations, and national origins. It is not simply that what happens in "elsewheres" beyond the sending and receiving places affects the immigrant experience directly, as the sociologist Tahseen Shams argues,[74] but also that the stereotypes politicians and people use include categorical groups from different parts of the world, so the geopolitics and negative actions of a few members of the category can affect all. This is indeed the case for Bangladeshi Muslim professionals who are as stigmatized as Afghani Taliban or suicide bombers just because they are put in the same categorical basket, although most of these people are neither fanatical nor especially political. The same goes for an Argentinian professional of European origin who, when abroad, is put in the same group as an Indigenous farmer from Bolivia. Categorical labels are simplifications that betray and harm many individual intersectional identities.[75]

Similarly, the social sciences and everyday conversation should move away from using the term *community* to talk about supposed racial or ethnic groups because it uses the boundaries of nation-states or racism premises to assume the culture and history of *all* people from any given place. Political divides drawn through communities do not separate people's lives on the ground, nor do they fuse them into one binary set of norms, institutions, customs, or experiences.[76] The term *community* is overused in sociology and politics. Community should be used to refer to either neighborhoods rich in social capital or categorical networks that actually engage in collective action, as Tilly argues in his relational understanding of sociology.[77]

Political Discourse, Public Opinion, and Racism

It is clear that people's preexisting impressions of immigrant groups influence the extent to which such immigrants are able to integrate. If the general public begrudgingly accepts immigrant groups who are linked to negative stereotypes, fewer opportunities for integration are provided. In this context, immigrants remain excluded from mainstream society, especially when they are perceived as a threat to locals' safety. Native-born people in host countries who feel threatened by immigrants more often assume that immigrants must not want to integrate into the local society. In contrast, locals who feel neutral or welcoming toward foreigners are less likely to make such assumptions. Stephen Croucher found that public opinions about terrorism affect Muslim immigrants' integration levels in Europe. Compared to other European countries, more native-born citizens of France and the UK perceive Muslim immigrants and Islam as dangerous and are generally opposed to integration. Both nations also exhibit very high rates of immigrant unemployment, xenophobic sentiment, and state conflict with Muslim-majority countries.[78]

National leaders have even engaged in anti-immigrant fearmongering. Former UK prime minister Tony Blair condemned immigrants who could not speak English, claiming they refused to "share and support the values that sustain the British way of life."[79] He came out with this statement after four British Muslims committed a series of suicide bombings in London in July 2005. In doing so, he sent a hostile message about immigrants that some in the general public learned to mimic, and he created a national enemy, even though he later backtracked and clarified that Muslims around the world equally "deplore these acts of terrorism."[80] Ariane Chebel d'Appollonia and Simon Reich highlight that Blair's reaction was indicative of the ignorance that many politicians exhibit regarding the postimmigration process of integration.[81] The reality is that integration is the best defense against extremism.[82]

Racist Undertones in Research on Mental Health and Integration in Norway

Social integration informs an immigrant's mental health and well-being, a connection that led Odd Steffen Dalgard and Suraj Bahadur Thapa to examine the
different experiences of immigrants in Oslo, Norway, to determine the extent
of the relationship between their level of social integration and their mental
health. After surveying approximately 2,500 immigrants with origins in Europe,
the Americas, Asia, and Africa, they found that an immigrant's income, web
of social support, proficiency in Norwegian, and neighborly relationships with
Norwegians proved to protect against psychological distress. Those who considered themselves well integrated in these regards had lower levels of stress.[83]

However, distress levels and degrees of integration varied between groups. On
average, immigrants from the Americas and western Europe were more likely to
consider themselves socially integrated and revealed lower levels of psychological
distress than their eastern European, Asian, and African counterparts. Immigrants
who were more distressed had trouble getting work, finding social support, and
negotiating new sociocultural norms.[84] Additionally, stress manifested differently
across gender. Non-Western migrant women exhibited the highest average level of
distress in the entire study, and their negative emotions could not be explained by
employment, social networks, or language barriers. Social integration was associated with improved mental health for men, but women did not reap the same
benefits. Discrimination, xenophobia, and racism were not addressed as possible
moderators between distress and integration or mentioned when discussing possible explanations for gender differences; neither was segregated housing.[85]

The information provided by this study is valuable in its strengths and weak-
nesses. It helps us understand the obstacles that certain immigrant groups face
in the integration process. However, ignoring structural inequalities that create
additional stress for immigrants only perpetuates the problem and contradicts
the purpose of the research. Indirectly and unintentionally, this type of research
sidesteps and consequently normalizes racism.[86] The closest the authors come
to the topic of discrimination occurs in a brief discussion of assimilation that
pushes immigrants to "adjust rather quickly to Norwegian society."[87] While traditional cultural intricacies of social behavior are important to consider, Dalgard
and Thapa make the mistake of grouping immigrants from three different countries into one category and drawing generalizations based on their non-Western identities. For example, the finding that immigrant women feel less socially

integrated in Norway is tenuously attributed to "negative sanctions from men of their own ethnic group," who are said to prefer that they remain separate from Norwegian culture.[88] Making an assumption like this is dangerous, as the authors stereotype non-Western men as conservative and intolerant of women practicing their agency. Moving forward, it is crucial that researchers address macrolevel constraints related to integration and consider them while searching for potential explanations for certain integration outcomes.

Economic Integration in Sweden

In Sweden, 5 percent of the population consists of non-EU immigrants, many of whom come from Syria, Somalia, and Eritrea. The Swedish government established the Ministry of Integration and implemented a strategy called Empowerment Against Exclusion to foster equality in the sphere of education and to integrate arriving immigrants into the Swedish labor market. A €200 million budget increase to pay for this initiative was passed in 2016, and these funds are now primarily put toward integration programs like Swedish language courses, civic education, and vocational training. These changes came about even after 2015, when a rise in conservatism spread across Europe. During this time, Sweden repealed policies that had previously helped immigrants find employment, so Empowerment Against Exclusion aimed to make up for these repeals. Despite rising right-wing favoritism, Sweden is a hot spot for nongovernmental organizations that facilitate immigrant integration. The European Social Fund donated over €723 million to Sweden between 2014 and 2020 to support immigrant inclusion in the labor market.[89] Thus, although Sweden has retracted some of its progressive immigration policies in recent years, it has some fairly supportive economic integration programs.

What Other Factors Influence Immigrants' Abilities to Integrate?

Age First-generation immigrants who arrive in a new country at, for example, seventy years of age are bound to integrate differently than seven-year-olds. A person typically becomes more integrated as they are exposed to life in their new country and spend more time becoming familiar with its culture.[90] In Israel, more than 800,000 Russian Jews immigrated in the 1990s, leaving behind the collapse of the Soviet Union and rebellions for independence that spread throughout the former Soviet republics.[91] One study surveyed a thousand Russian immigrants about their integration experiences after living in Israel for six to ten years. This immigrant community was granted citizenship upon arrival and was considered exceptionally well educated and high skilled. Despite this, it was challenging for them to integrate into Israeli society. Adult and older Russians cited their lack of Hebrew as a social and economic obstacle, and some struggled financially. Younger immigrants, especially those who migrated before adulthood, were more likely to have a better grasp of the language.[92]

This is a prime example of the importance of providing both high-quality and long-term integration services that consider individuals' well-being as well as that of the entire nation. In the case of Israel, obtaining citizenship did not guarantee an immigrant any sense of security or belonging. Furthermore, older immigrants faced certain hurdles that younger ones did not. As a result, they were more ethnically isolated, had fewer job opportunities, and found it challenging to communicate in their host language. Comprehensive integration support can help immigrants close the gap between themselves and their new home that other policies do not acknowledge.

Labor Markets and Employment Opportunities Among the most important elements of settling into a new place is finding employment, which is the reason that most people migrate in the first place. For immigrants, a job is also a way to learn social practices and cues of the host country's dominant culture. Spending time in a work environment among native-born and immigrant coworkers builds cultural capital, creates new social ties, and can foster a sense of community and belonging. However, a new workplace also holds its own challenges. Work cultures—reflecting how people understand and carry their jobs—can differ greatly among regions of the world, a situation that is especially true for the United States. Immigrants may have to accustom themselves to new social and behavioral expectations and conventions.[93]

Fostering a welcoming environment for immigrants also enhances the economy, so integration in economic contexts is a mutually beneficial process. Community programs that help immigrants find employment and learn skills needed by certain sectors of their local job markets are the basic building blocks of integration support. Because of these programs, immigrants reduce labor shortages in vital areas of the economy, like agriculture, transportation, and customer service.[94]

Immigrant Generation Each generation of immigrants is more acculturated than their predecessors and spends more time in school.[95] For instance, on average, first-generation Mexican and Central American immigrants in the United States have not studied past the tenth grade. In Maryland, 13 percent of parents from Mexico were reported to have attended college in 2010.[96] On the other hand, second-generation immigrants have better access to education and related opportunities compared to their foreign-born counterparts. In the United States, children of immigrants almost always receive more education, earn higher wages, have a better grasp of English, and own more real estate than their parents. Second- and third-generation immigrants also marry outside their own races and ethnicities more often.[97] Of course, these statistics are not the reality for *all* Mexican and Central American immigrants—many are highly educated and experience considerable social mobility. We must be careful not to make generalizations and apply stereotypes of a group to any particular individual.

The Importance of Integration in Growing Immigrant Populations

Some regions of the world look to their immigrant communities to grow their populations and help raise the next generation of citizens. Countries across North America, Europe, and Asia are seeing their birth rates drop every year, and they worry that their future workforces and global presences will dwindle if the pattern continues. The U.S. population has been slowing down since 2015, and the birth rate is decreasing, too.[98] In 2020, its population growth was at its lowest point since 1930.[99] Similar trends are unfolding in Europe. People living in the EU represent only 6.9 percent of the global population, which also has a slowing birth rate.[100] The death rate in the EU was estimated to exceed the birth rate by 500,000 in 2019.[101] This decline in population has only been exacerbated by the COVID-19 pandemic. Successful immigrant integration policies are vital for these nations because they depend on immigrant communities, who initially tend to have higher average birth rates, to erase the birth deficits and ensure that their populations remain stable or grow.

The U.S. cities of Detroit, Cleveland, and Pittsburgh may no longer attract the large populations of immigrants that they once did, but they offer valuable lessons on the benefits of nurturing a welcoming environment for immigrant communities.[102] Thanks to an influx of immigrants, all three cities' economies rose out of a rut and were strengthened by the participation of younger, working-age people.[103] Maryland is a good example of a state where immigration is helping to boost the economy. The state saw massive growth in its workforce and population numbers as a result of immigration. The state's number of children with a foreign-born parent skyrocketed by 132,000 between 1990 and 2006; most of these children were born on U.S. soil. Native-born Americans had a growth rate of 6 percent during this period compared to 19 percent for immigrant parents.[104] Without its immigrant communities, Maryland would have likely experienced a drop in its overall child population and birth rate. However, policies are rarely perfect, and Maryland's integration policies are no exception. In 2006, highly educated and skilled immigrants living in Maryland were likely to earn the same wages as those with less education and skills.[105] Nevertheless, in order for a state to grow its population, it has to be ready and willing to assist immigrants via social, economic, and political integration programs. The population spike and resulting benefits in Maryland show the positive effects that local and state policies supportive of immigrants can have on the local economy and on all residents' lives.

Canada also depends on contemporary immigration for continued population growth, but Banting and Soroka express concern with the way that the Canadian government handles immigrant integration. They draw attention to the fact that "the realities of immigrant integration on the ground are deeply conditioned by the historic forms of ethnic diversity within each country."[106] While tolerant of cultural differences, Canada still maintains Franco-Saxon and Anglo-Saxon cultural references. These undertones become apparent when the fine print of Canadian policies is dissected. Integration laws are said to emphasize "shared values," and yet such values are not in fact shared by all native-born people. They are displayed to the public as shared to foster a false sense of sameness in the national population and ensure that the dominant white cultural standards remain the baseline for integrative success, which we outlined earlier in the section "Integration Is Not a Blueprint for Whiteness." Furthermore, some argue that because immigrants have *chosen* to move to their host country—even though some do not choose freely or do so under the influence of a history of imperialism and war—they have no right to push against the social and cultural norms of their new community. Peter Li considers this an "unspoken 'social contract'" between a nation and its foreign-born population. Violating this contract would mean that immigrants were endorsing "alternative norms, values and behaviors" and would no longer be welcome in the country.[107] From the perspective of native-born Canadians, immigrants' belonging is conditional, based on their willingness and ability to uphold their end of the social contract. In exchange for acceptance, immigrants are expected to assimilate.

MOVING FORWARD

Migration is a geographically and socially dislocating process. For an individual and their family, the integration process takes time, and for ethnic groups, it takes generations. There is no fixed interpretation as to when this process is finished because arriving at a feeling of belonging is different for everyone. An immigrant may never feel fully socially, economically, or politically integrated in their lifetime.[108] Their experiences are defined by the complexities of their personal feelings and outcomes in a new place. Most immigrants do not undergo an easy transition to social mobility or a seamless integration into the broader local social fabric.[109] Gradually, with the accumulation of time, social interaction, and cultural experience, immigrants become familiar with their new homes. However, this subjective belonging also responds to objective conditions, including receptivity of the new context and locals' sentiments toward immigrant groups. Even when immigrants want to integrate, the receiving society and state must provide a welcoming and tolerant context for cultural differences.

There are some common flaws across immigration systems that hinder integration. For example, national governments sit back and encourage immigrants to engage and participate in the local community. They fail to understand the challenges that immigrants face in doing so, like legal eligibility for those who wish to vote and discriminatory homeownership rules that segregate neighborhoods.[110] A successful integration system allows immigrants the same social mobility as native-born residents. Ideally, an immigration system accounts for overlooked bureaucratic barriers. In 2019, some of the top-rated cities in terms of the prospects and treatment of immigrants were in California, New Jersey, New York, Illinois, and Maryland.[111] Andrew Lim rated one hundred cities in the United States based on their treatment of immigrants and the socioeconomic outcomes of their foreign-born communities.[112] Various aspects were considered, like free access to translation services for migrants and exclusionary political rhetoric or anti-immigrant sentiments. According to this methodology, in 2019, the top ten

U.S. cities for immigrants were (in descending order): Chula Vista, CA; Jersey City, NJ; New York City, NY; Chicago, IL; Baltimore, MD; Newark, NJ; San Francisco, CA; Detroit, MI; San Jose, CA; and Atlanta, GA.[113]

The Salvadoran population in the United States began to increase during a bloody civil war in El Salvador, cutting short many lives and displacing many others. Due to the United States' official stance on the Salvadoran civil war, the Reagan administration refused to label Salvadorans as refugees, calling them economic migrants instead.[114] Many had to come to the country without papers because they knew their asylum claims would be denied. Here is a case of exclusion where the government said an entire population was not fleeing violence but rather was seeking economic opportunity. Even so, many who did make it to the United States felt as though they belonged, and they began to craft communities that now exist in many major U.S. cities—notably, Los Angeles, Houston, New York City, and the Washington, D.C., area.[115] The visibility of Salvadoran, Central American, and Latin parades and public events on the Washington Mall and in other parts of the D.C. metropolitan area help increase the pride of immigrants and their children and subsequently their feelings of belonging.[116]

In the earlier comparative discussion on New York City, Paris, and Barcelona, we analyzed how social context and place matter for immigrant integration. In Paris, immigrants are characterized by low levels of social integration and urban belonging due to limits placed on their political representation and social mobility. Despite some French immigrants' economic security, access to welfare benefits, and legal French citizenship, they felt excluded from mainstream society and did not often feel like they belonged, unlike immigrants in New York City and Barcelona, who enjoyed high levels of social integration and urban belonging.[117]

The United States has a lot to learn about integration. Despite its large immigrant population, the country still has no national integration program or federal policies specifically addressing integration support. Migrants are expected to undergo the process alone, with the help of their community, or with the assistance of community organizations or refugee resettlement agencies. While the U.S. government focuses much of its attention and resources on the southern border and restrictive immigration laws, it turns its back on the needs of those who are already living within its borders. For immigrants to reach their highest potential, federal policies must be developed with the explicit intention "to help immigrants achieve the greater social inclusion, economic mobility, and civic and political voice that their contributions to American society warrant."[118]

Over the years, some states have created offices for this purpose, like the Massachusetts Office for Refugees and Immigrants (1985), the New York State Office for New Americans (2012), and the Michigan Office for New Americans (2014).[119] Other cities and states are working toward opening similar offices. Those offices tend to be small, understaffed and under-resourced. Still, the national government remains reluctant to extend an olive branch to immigrants in this regard by allocating serious funds for welcoming and integrating immigrants and asylum-seekers in an on-going basis.

Integration is a multifaceted process that requires partnerships among local, state, and national entities across the private and public sectors. Cities and civil organizations working on philanthropy, education, faith, and community development have provided integration services for centuries. They have already built a foundation for further collaboration between the state governments and the national actors with which they are beginning to work. In response to the lack of federal action, different states have enacted laws to integrate immigrants. As of 2017, fifteen states offered civic education classes to help immigrants pass their naturalization examination, while twenty-seven funded English learning programs. Fewer states have passed legislation that recognizes credentials granted by foreign institutions. Some, like Iowa and Washington, have done so to ensure that immigrants with professional licenses can continue working in their professions. California, Illinois, and Rhode Island have appointed task forces specialized in immigrant assistance and integration.[120]

Common arguments against integration revolve around fabrications intended to criminalize immigrants and render them unworthy of belonging in a new place. Around the world, false narratives claim that immigrants access welfare more than native-born citizens, steal jobs, and lower wages, all of which we have continuously refuted throughout the book. The U.S. government has been reluctant for decades to reimagine immigration policies because of these myths and any potential pushback from the public. Integration bears fruit when the rights and contributions of immigrants are respected and valued by local mainstream society. While regions with policies that do so intentionally and well were few and far between more localities are supporting immigrant reception centers and programs and they can learn from the triumphs and errors of New York City, Paris, and Barcelona.

NOTES

INTRODUCTION: IMMIGRATION AS A HISTORY OF EXCLUSION AND HOMEMAKING

1. Castañeda and Shemesh, "Overselling Globalization," 21; McGhee White, "Out of Many, One."
2. Kaufmann and Goodwin, "The Diversity Wave."
3. Castañeda, "Introduction to 'Reshaping the World.'"
4. Castañeda, *Building Walls*.
5. Dietz, Li, and Castañeda, "Keeping in Motion or Staying Put."
6. Cornelius, "My Odyssey"; Portes, "America and Its Immigrants"; Massey and Waters, "Scientific Versus Public Debates"; Massey, "Immigration Policy Mismatches and Counterproductive Outcomes."
7. Levy, Pisarevskaya, and Scholten, "Between Fragmentation and Institutionalisation."
8. The book format is inspired by Charles Tilly's influential book *Big Structures, Large Processes, Huge Comparisons*, which challenges eight "pernicious postulates" in the social sciences.
9. Chavez, *The Latino Threat*; Shapira, *Waiting for José*.
10. Castañeda and Heyman, "Is the Southwestern Border Really Unsafe?"; Castaneda, "Is the Border Safe?"; Castañeda and Chiappetta, "Border Residents' Perceptions of Crime and Security in El Paso, Texas."
11. Castañeda, "Building Walls, Excluding People, and Terrorizing Minorities."
12. Dear, *Why Walls Won't Work*; Castañeda, "Review of Michael Dear's *Why Walls Won't Work*."
13. López, "Gran Encuesta Revela Que en la Frontera de Estados Unidos y México No Quieren el Muro de Trump."
14. MacDonald and Saunders, "Are Immigrant Youth Less Violent?"; Rumbaut and Ewing, *The Myth of Immigrant Criminality and the Paradox of Assimilation*.
15. Castañeda and Heyman, "Is the Southwestern Border Really Unsafe?"
16. MacDonald and Sampson, "The World in a City"; Martinez, Stowell, and Lee, "Immigration and Crime in an Era of Transformation."
17. Loza, Castañeda, and Diedrich, "Substance Use by Immigrant Generation in a U.S.-Mexico Border City."

18. Zolberg and Woon, "Why Islam Is Like Spanish."

19. Portes and Rumbaut, *Immigrant America.*

20. Van Hook and Bean, "Explaining Mexican Immigrant Welfare Behaviors "; Fox, *Three Worlds of Relief.*

21. Hernandez and Coutin, "Remitting Subjects"; Bakker, *Migrating Into Financial Markets.*

22. Rodriguez, "The Emergence of Labor Brokerage."

23. U.S. Census Bureau, Interactive Population Map; U.S. Census Bureau: "QuickFacts: El Paso County."

24. Castañeda, Morales, and Ochoa, "Transnational Behavior in Comparative Perspective"; Loza, Castañeda, and Diedrich, "Substance Use by Immigrant Generation in a U.S.-Mexico Border City"; Castañeda and Chiappetta, "Border Residents' Perceptions of Crime and Security in El Paso, Texas."

1. THE SOUTHERN BORDER IS SAFE, BUT BORDER ENFORCEMENT MAKES IT UNSAFE FOR MANY

1. Contreras, "FBI Stats Show Border Cities Are Among the Safest"; Nowrasteh, "Crime Along the Mexican Border Is Lower Than in the Rest of the Country."

2. Lind, "The Border Is in Crisis"; Semple, "Migrants in Mexico Face Kidnappings and Violence While Awaiting Immigration Hearings in U.S."; Jordan, "Father and Son Abducted in Mexico Are Allowed Into the U.S."

3. Meierotto, *Introduction.*

4. Ngai, *Impossible Subjects*; Castañeda, *Building Walls.*

5. Domínguez and Castro, *The United States and Mexico.*

6. Castañeda, Danielson, and Rathod, "Fortress North America."

7. Heyman, "A Border That Divides," 79.

8. Heyman, "Constructing a Virtual Wall."

9. Heyman, "Constructing a Virtual Wall," 305.

10. Velasco Ortiz and Contreras, "The Border as a Life Experience."

11. Golash-Boza, *Deported.*

12. Velasco Ortiz and Contreras, "The Border as a Life Experience"; Frank-Vitale, "Leave If You're Able."

13. Miller, *Border Patrol Nation*, 41.

14. Miroff, "U.S. Customs Agency Is So Short-Staffed, It's Sending Officers from Airports to the Mexican Border."

15. Kladzyk, "From Detroit to El Paso"; Kocherga, "The COVID-19 Pandemic Is Crushing Retailers Who Rely on Cross-Border Shoppers for Holiday Sales."

16. Heyman, "A Border That Divides," 81.

17. Fuentes and Peña, "Globalization and Its Effects on the Urban Socio-spatial Structure of a Transfrontier Metropolis."

18. Ampudia Ruedas and Gutiérrez Casas, "Empleo y Estructura Económica en el Contexto de la Crisis en Juárez, 1999–2004."

19. Heyman, "A Border That Divides," 81.

20. Orrenius, "Benefits of Immigration Outweigh the Costs."

21. Heyman, "A Border That Divides."

22. Castillo-Villar, "Destination Image Restoration Through Local Gastronomy."

23. Aguirre and Simmers, "Mexican Border Crossers," 99.

24. J. Chavez, "Frequent Crossers of U.S.-Mexico Border Fret Over Threatened Shutdown"; Mark, "Closing the Border Would Put the US Economy at a 'Standstill' and Actually Worsen Illegal Border Crossings."

25. West, "Thousands of Students Cross the Southern Border Every Day to Go to College."

26. Herrington and Baselice, "One Way to Tank Markets and the U.S. Economy?"

27. Mark, "Closing the Border Would Put the US Economy at a 'Standstill' and Actually Worsen Illegal Border Crossings."

28. Castañeda, "Introduction to 'Reshaping the World.'"

29. Mark, "Closing the Border Would Put the US Economy at a 'Standstill' and Actually Worsen Illegal Border Crossings"; West, "Thousands of Students Cross the Southern Border Every Day to Go to College."

30. Alden, "Is Border Enforcement Effective?."

31. West, "Thousands of Students Cross the Southern Border Every Day to Go to College."

32. West, "Thousands of Students Cross the Southern Border Every Day."

33. Alden, "Is Border Enforcement Effective?."

34. H. Campbell, *Drug War Zone.*

35. Mark, "Closing the Border Would Put the US Economy at a 'Standstill' and Actually Worsen Illegal Border Crossings."

36. Heyman, "A Border That Divides."

37. *El Paso Times,* "El Paso Ranked in 'Top 10 Safest Metro Cities' in U.S."; A. Garcia, "El Paso, TX"; Woody, "Here's How Mexican Cartels Actually Operate in the United States"; CQ Press, "City Crime Rankings 2013."

38. Castañeda and Chiappetta, "Border Residents' Perceptions of Crime and Security in El Paso, Texas."

39. L. Chavez, *The Latino Threat;* Hirschfeld Davis, "Trump Calls Some Unauthorized Immigrants 'Animals' in Rant"; Scott, "Trump's Most Insulting—and Violent—Language Is Often Reserved for Immigrants."

40. Bier and Nowrasteh, "45,000 'Special Interest Aliens' Caught Since 2007, but No U.S. Terrorist Attacks from Illegal Border Crossers."

41. Robertson, "Misleading Border Crime Statistic."

42. Robertson, "Misleading Border Crime Statistic."

43. John T. Sherwood, *Building the Wall: The Efficacy of a US-Mexico Border Fence* (n.p., Biblioscholar, 2012).

44. Bier and Nowrasteh, "45,000 'Special Interest Aliens' Caught Since 2007, but No U.S. Terrorist Attacks from Illegal Border Crossers."

45. Kanno-Youngs, "Trump Administration Adds Six Countries to Travel Ban."

46. Sherwood, "Building the Wall."

47. Bier and Nowrasteh, "45,000 'Special Interest Aliens' Caught Since 2007, but No U.S. Terrorist Attacks from Illegal Border Crossers."

48. Bier and Nowrasteh; Dear, "5 Problems 'the Wall' Won't Solve."

49. Nowrasteh, "Terrorism and Immigration."

50. Robertson, "Misleading Border Crime Statistic."
51. Anti-Defamation League, "Murder and Extremism in the United States in 2019."
52. Anti-Defamation League, "Murder and Extremism in the United States in 2019."
53. *Al Jazeera*, "Mexico Urges Tighter US Gun Control After Deadly El Paso Shooting"; Arango, Bogel-Burroughs, and Benner, "Minutes Before El Paso Killing, Hate-Filled Manifesto Appears Online."
54. *Al Jazeera*, "Mexico Urges Tighter US Gun Control After Deadly El Paso Shooting."
55. Keith and Naylor, "'Hate Has No Place' in America, Trump Says After El Paso and Dayton Shootings."
56. Horton, "Trump Keeps Calling the Southern Border 'Very Dangerous.'"
57. McAllen Police Department, *Crime in McAllen 2018*; Papenfuss, "Border Towns 'Safer Than Any City Trump Has Lived In,' Says Texas Congressman."
58. Cruz, "Border Towns Are Among the Safest in the United States."
59. Nowrasteh, "Crime Along the Mexican Border Is Lower Than in the Rest of the Country."
60. U.S. Sentencing Commission, *Statistical Information Packet: Fiscal Year 2019, Southern District of Texas*, 1.
61. Velázquez Vargas and Martínez Canizales, "La Inseguridad En Ciudad Juárez Desde La Percepción de Los Ciudadanos," 73, 75.
62. Martínez Toyes and Arellano Quiroga, "Movilidad Poblacional: Efecto de La Violencia e Inseguridad En Ciudad Juárez."
63. For more details, see D. Martínez, Heyman, and Slack, *Border Enforcement Developments Since 1993 and How to Change CBP*.
64. McGuire and Georges, "Undocumentedness and Liminality as Health Variables," 192.
65. Horton, "Trump Keeps Calling the Southern Border 'Very Dangerous.'"
66. Whitaker, "Mexican Deaths in the Arizona Desert."
67. Alden, "Is Border Enforcement Effective?"
68. Urrea, *The Devil's Highway*; see also Aguirre and Simmers, "Mexican Border Crossers," 99
69. Holmes, "–'Is It Worth Risking Your Life?,'" 153.
70. Meneses, "Human Rights and Undocumented Migration Along the Mexican-U.S. Border"; Eschbach et al., "Death at the Border."
71. *Asia News Monitor*, "United States/Mexico."
72. Eschbach et al., "Death at the Border."
73. Massey, Durand, and Malone, *Beyond Smoke and Mirrors*.
74. Slack, *Deported to Death*.
75. Whitaker, "Mexican Deaths in the Arizona Desert."
76. Soto and Martínez, "The Geography of Migrant Death," 75.
77. U.S. Government Accountability Office, *Illegal Immigration*, 16.
78. Hampton, "Zero Protection."
79. Slack, *Deported to Death*, 71.
80. Slack, *Deported to Death*.
81. Castañeda and Jenks, *Reunited*; Root, "At a Crowded Mexican Shelter, Migrants Wait Months to Claim Asylum."
82. Lind, "The Border Is in Crisis."
83. Meneses, "Human Rights and Undocumented Migration Along the Mexican-U.S. Border," 268.

84. Eschbach et al., "Death at the Border."

85. Hampton, "Zero Protection."

86. Hampton, "Zero Protection."

87. Cheng, "Justice for José Antonio, a 16-Year-Old Boy Killed by U.S. Border Patrol."

88. Adlerstein, "A Not-Guilty Verdict Absolves Border Patrol of Cross-Border Killing."

89. Miller, *Border Patrol Nation*, 15.

90. Miller, *Border Patrol Nation*, 16; ACLU New Mexico, Know Your Rights in the 100 Mile Border Zone, accessed May 13, 2024, https://www.aclu-nm.org/en/know-your-rights/know-your-rights-100-mile-border-zone.

91. Agerholm, "US Border Patrol Exposed Kicking Over Water Bottles Left for Migrants."

92. Hampton, "Zero Protection."

93. Hampton, "Zero Protection."

94. Castañeda and Jenks, *Reunited.*

95. Cheatham, "U.S. Detention of Child Migrants."

96. U.S. CBP, "U.S. Border Patrol Southwest Border Apprehensions by Sector"; see also Coulter et al., "A Study and Analysis of the Treatment of Mexican Unaccompanied Minors by Customs and Border Protection"; Cheatham, "U.S. Detention of Child Migrants";

97. Burnett, "'I Want To Be Sure My Son Is Safe.'"

98. Burnett, "'I Want To Be Sure My Son Is Safe.'"

99. Cheatham, "U.S. Detention of Child Migrants."

100. Kids in Need of Defense, "Blocked from Safety."

101. National Immigration Forum, "Trafficking Victims Protection Reauthorization Act Safeguards Children"; United Nations High Commissioner for Refugees, Convention and Protocol Relating to the Status of Refugees.

102. Coulter et al., "A Study and Analysis of the Treatment of Mexican Unaccompanied Minors by Customs and Border Protection," 4.

103. Kids in Need of Defense, "Blocked from Safety," 1–2.

104. Kids in Need of Defense, "Blocked from Safety," 2.

105. Coulter et al., "A Study and Analysis of the Treatment of Mexican Unaccompanied Minors by Customs and Border Protection," 7–8.

106. ACLU, "Neglect & Abuse of Unaccompanied Children by U.S. Customs and Border Protection," 11.

107. ACLU, "Neglect & Abuse of Unaccompanied Children by U.S. Customs and Border Protection," 13.

108. Warren, "Reverse Migration to Mexico Led to US Undocumented Population Decline."

109. E. Jensen, "Apprehensive About 'Apprehensions' (and 'Crisis' and 'Record')"; Miller, *Border Patrol Nation*, 220.

110. The Conversation, November 8, 2022, https://theconversation.com/why-the-number-of-encounters-at-the-southern-u-s-border-does-not-mean-what-the-gop-says-it-means-191144; The Conversation, May 11, 2023, https://theconversation.com/despite-the-end-of-title-42-restrictions-on-asylum-seekers-are-expected-to-continue-under-biden-administration-205343

111. Bray, "Inadmissibility."

112. Bray, "Inadmissibility"; National Immigration Forum, "Trafficking Victims Protection Reauthorization Act Safeguards Children."

113.   National Immigration Forum, "Trafficking Victims Protection Reauthorization Act Safeguards Children."

114.   Coulter et al., "A Study and Analysis of the Treatment of Mexican Unaccompanied Minors by Customs and Border Protection"; Kids in Need of Defense, "Blocked from Safety"; National Immigration Forum, "Trafficking Victims Protection Reauthorization Act Safeguards Children."

115.   Gündoğdu, "Statelessness and the Right to Have Rights."

116.   United Nations High Commissioner for Refugees, Convention and Protocol Relating to the Status of Refugees, 3.

117.   Kanno-Youngs, "Squalid Conditions at Border Detention Centers, Government Report Finds."

118.   Kanno-Youngs, "Squalid Conditions at Border Detention Centers, Government Report Finds."

119.   Irwin, "Federal Court Finds Conditions in Customs and Border Protection Detention Facilities Unconstitutional."

120.   Macías-Rojas, "Immigration and the War on Crime."

121.   ACLU, "Neglect & Abuse of Unaccompanied Children by U.S. Customs and Border Protection"; E. Cohen, Illegal, 21.

122.   Acevedo, "Why Are Migrant Children Dying in U.S. Custody?"

123.   Kanno-Youngs, "Squalid Conditions at Border Detention Centers, Government Report Finds."

124.   Kanno-Youngs, "Squalid Conditions at Border Detention Centers, Government Report Finds; U.S. Customs and Border Protection, "United States Border Patrol Southwest Family Unit Subject and Unaccompanied Alien Children Apprehensions Fiscal Year 2016"; Viñas, "Immigrant Detainees Say They Were Sexually Abused in CBP Custody"; Wright, "Necropolitics, Narcopolitics, and Femicide."

125.   A. Alba and Guzmán, Making a Killing.

126.   Wright, "Necropolitics, Narcopolitics, and Femicide."

127.   Leyva-Flores et al., "Migrants in Transit Through Mexico to the US."

128.   Carmona López, Gómez Caballero, and Castro Rodríguez, "Feminicide in Latin America in the Movement for Women's Human Rights."

129.   Wright, "Necropolitics, Narcopolitics, and Femicide."

130.   Albuquerque and Vemala, "A Statistical Evaluation of Femicide Rates in Mexican Cities Along the US-Mexico Border."

131.   Wright, "Necropolitics, Narcopolitics, and Femicide."

132.   International Labor Organization, "Global Estimates of Modern Slavery."

133.   Walters and Davis, "Human Trafficking, Sex Tourism, and Child Exploitation on the Southern Border."

134.   Walters and Davis, "Human Trafficking, Sex Tourism, and Child Exploitation on the Southern Border."

135.   Kara, Modern Slavery, 134.

136.   Vogt, "Crossing Mexico," 774.

137.   Kara, Modern Slavery, 134.

138.   Kara, Modern Slavery, 130.

139. Lachica, Castañeda, and McDonald, Poverty, Place, and Health Along the US-Mexico Border.
140. Fanning, "One Man Thinks El Paso's Long-Distance Relationship with Texas Should End in Divorce."
141. S. Wallace, "Papers Please"; Romero, "Are Your Papers in Order?"
142. Johnson and Trujillo, Immigration Law and the U.S.–Mexico Border; S. Wallace, "Papers Please."
143. Miller, Border Patrol Nation, 115–50.
144. Aguirre and Simmers, "Mexican Border Crossers."

2. BORDER WALLS DO NOT KEEP IMMIGRANTS OUT OF A COUNTRY

The chapter epigraph comes from the preface to Payan, The Three U.S.-Mexico Border Wars, xiii.

1. Holland and Cowan, "Backing Down, Trump Agrees to End Shutdown Without Border Wall Money."
2. Baker, "Trump Declares a National Emergency, and Provokes a Constitutional Clash."
3. Cruz, "Border Towns Are Among the Safest in the United States."
4. Cruz, "Border Towns Are Among the Safest in the United States."
5. White House, Proclamation on the Termination of Emergency with Respect to the Southern Border of the United States and Redirection of Funds Diverted to Border Wall Construction.
6. Horton, "Trump Keeps Calling the Southern Border 'Very Dangerous.'"
7. Deeds and Whiteford, "The Social and Economic Costs of Trump's Wall."
8. Cornelius, "Death at the Border"; Slack, Deported to Death, 42; Dunn, The Militarization of the U.S.-Mexico Border, 1978–1992; Dunn, Blockading the Border and Human Rights; Andreas, Border Games.
9. U.S. Department of Justice, "An Investigation of Travel Reimbursements in Connection with the INS's Operation Safeguard"; Miller, Border Patrol Nation, 59–60; Orraca Romano and Corona Villavicencio, "Risk of Death and Aggressions Encountered While Illegally Crossing the U.S.-Mexico Border"; Slack, Deported to Death, 42; Slack, Martinez, and Whiteford, The Shadow of the Wall.
10. Cheathan, Felter, and Laub, "How the U.S. Patrols Its Borders."
11. Passel and Cohn, "Mexicans Decline to Less Than Half the U.S. Unauthorized Immigrant Population for the First Time"; Passel, Cohn, and Gonzalez-Barrera, "Net Migration from Mexico Falls to Zero—and Perhaps Less."
12. R. C. Jones, "The Decline of International Migration as an Economic Force in Rural Areas."
13. Castañeda, "Introduction to 'Reshaping the World.'"
14. Horton, "Trump Keeps Calling the Southern Border 'Very Dangerous'"; Massey, Durand, and Malone, Beyond Smoke and Mirrors.
15. E. Cohen, Illegal.
16. Lachica, Castañeda, and McDonald, "Poverty, Place, and Health Along the US-Mexico Border."
17. San Pedro River Valley, "San Pedro River Ecology."

18. U. S. Customs and Border Protection, "Border Wall Status."

19. De León, *The Land of Open Graves.*

20. MSNBC, *Fence Not Needed at Parts of Mexico Border.*

21. Business Insider, *What It's Really Like at the US-Mexico Border.*

22. Miller, *Border Patrol Nation,* 57, 68.

23. E. Cohen, *Illegal,* 107; K. Hernandez, *Migra!.*

24. E. Cohen, *Illegal,* 97–107; Miller, *Border Patrol Nation,* 128.

25. U.S. Customs and Border Protection, "CBP Border Security Report: Fiscal Year 2018."

26. Nuñez-Neto, "Border Security, 40."

27. Argueta, "Border Security."

28. Copp, "2,100 Mostly Unarmed Guard Troops on Border as Trump Vows to Send More to Stop Migrant Caravan"; Gutierrez, "Sent by Trump, Soldiers Arrive at Border as Migrant Caravan in Mexico Pushes North."

29. Chomsky, *Undocumented,* 14, 119.

30. United Nations High Commissioner for Refugees, Convention and Protocol Relating to the Status of Refugees.

31. Meissner, Hipsman, and Aleinikoff, *The U.S. Asylum System in Crisis.*

32. Kahn, "'Remain in Mexico' Policy's End Brings Renewed Hope to Asylum Seekers"; Cheathan, Felter, and Laub, "How the U.S. Patrols Its Borders."

33. INA 208(b)(1)(A), 8 U.S.C. § 1158(b)(1)(A). The Convention and Protocol Relating to the Status of Refugees issued by the United Nations High Commissioner for Refugees defines a *refugee* as "someone who is unable or unwilling to return to their country of origin owing to a well-founded fear of being persecuted for reasons of race, religion, nationality, membership of a particular social group, or political opinion" (3).

34. INA 208(b)(2), 8 U.S.C. § 1158(b)(2); 8 C.F.R. 1240.8(d).

35. INA 101(a)(42)(A), 8 U.S.C. § 1101(a)(42)(A); United Nations High Commissioner for Refugees, Convention and Protocol Relating to the Status of Refugees, 3.

36. United Nations High Commissioner for Refugees, Convention and Protocol Relating to the Status of Refugees; Cheathan, Felter, and Laub, "How the U.S. Patrols Its Borders."

37. Slack, *Deported to Death,* 180.

38. 84 Fed. Reg. 33,829.

39. Isacson, Meyer, and Hite, "New 'Migrant Protection Protocols' Ignore U.S. Legal Obligations to Asylum Seekers and Exacerbate Humanitarian Border Crisis."

40. Lind, "The Border Is in Crisis."

41. Galli, "Humanitarian Capital"; Chomsky, *Undocumented,* 159.

42. Harvard Law Review, "American Courts and the U.N. High Commissioner for Refugees."

43. Holmes, ""Is It Worth Risking Your Life?"; Holmes, *Fresh Fruit, Broken Bodies*; Massey, Durand, and Malone, *Beyond Smoke and Mirrors.*

44. Chomsky, *Undocumented,* 74.

45. Chomsky, *Undocumented,* 11.

46. Donato, Durand, and Massey, "Stemming the Tide?"

47. Miller, *Border Patrol Nation,* 214.

48. Miller, *Border Patrol Nation,* 214.

49. U.S. Immigration and Customs Enforcement, "Form I-9 Inspection."

50. W. Lopez, *Separated*; Mathews, "The Community Caretaker Role."

51. Boyce, "The Neoliberal Underpinnings of Prevention Through Deterrence and the United States Government's Case Against Geographer Scott Warren."

52. U.S. Border Patrol, "Border Patrol Strategic Plan 1994 and Beyond"; Boyce, "The Neoliberal Underpinnings of Prevention Through Deterrence and the United States Government's Case Against Geographer Scott Warren"; Slack et al., "The Geography of Border Militarization."

53. Aguirre and Simmers, "Mexican Border Crossers"; Heyman, "A Border That Divides"; U.S. Department of Homeland Security, "FY 2021: Budget in Brief."

54. Allen, de Castro Dobbin, and Morten, "Border Walls"; E. Cohen, *Illegal*, 32.

55. Aguirre and Simmers, "Mexican Border Crossers."

56. U.S. Government Accountability Office, "Border Security."

57. Orraca Romano and Corona Villavicencio, "Risk of Death and Aggressions Encountered While Illegally Crossing the U.S.-Mexico Border"; Slack, Martinez, and Whiteford, *The Shadow of the Wall*.

58. Cornelius, "Death at the Border."

59. Cheathan, Felter, and Laub, "How the U.S. Patrols Its Borders."

60. E. Cohen, *Illegal*, 17.

61. U.S. Department of Homeland Security, "FY 2021: Budget in Brief."

62. U.S. Department of Homeland Security, "FY 2021: Budget in Brief."

63. U.S. House of Representatives, "Examining Challenges and Wasted Taxpayer Dollars in Modernizing Border Security IT Systems."

64. White House, "Fact Sheet: Department of Defense and Department of Homeland Security Plans for Border Wall Funds."

65. U.S. Department of Homeland Security, "FY 2021: Budget in Brief."

66. Orraca Romano and Corona Villavicencio, "Risk of Death and Aggressions Encountered While Illegally Crossing the U.S.-Mexico Border."

67. Viñas, "Immigrant Detainees Say They Were Sexually Abused in CBP Custody."

68. Slack, Martinez, and Whiteford, *The Shadow of the Wall*.

69. 8 C.F.R. Part 287—Field Officers Powers and Duties.

70. Rubio Goldsmith et al., "Ethno-racial Profiling and State Violence in a Southwest Barrio"; Sabo et al., "Everyday Violence, Structural Racism and Mistreatment at the US–Mexico Border."

71. Southern Border Communities Coalition, "Fatal Encounters with CBP."

72. K. R. Johnson and Trujillo, *Immigration Law and the U.S.-Mexico Border*, 185–86.

73. Thompson, "Border Patrol Has a Long History of Agent Misconduct"

74. E. Cohen, *Illegal*, 26–27; Miller, *Border Patrol Nation*, 273–76.

75. R. Jones, "Borders and Walls."

76. E. Cohen, *Illegal*, 202.

77. Glied and Pap, "The 'Christian Fortress of Hungary.'"

78. Heyman, "Constructing a Virtual Wall."

79. Warren, "Reverse Migration to Mexico Led to US Undocumented Population Decline," 34.

80. Frazee and Barajas, "Trump Says Walls Work"

81. Poston, "Here's Why Trump's Border Wall Won't Work."

82.   *Asia News Monitor*, "United States/Mexico"; Holmes, "'Is It Worth Risking Your Life?'"

83.   Meneses, "Human Rights and Undocumented Migration Along the Mexican-U.S. Border"; Whitaker, "Mexican Deaths in the Arizona Desert."

84.   De León, *The Land of Open Graves*, 63.

85.   Stephen, "Hemispheric and Transborder Perspectives."

86.   Orraca Romano and Corona Villavicencio, "Risk of Death and Aggressions Encountered While Illegally Crossing the U.S.-Mexico Border."

87.   Barros, "Summer Turns Deadly for US-Bound Migrants Braving Scorching Desert Heat."

88.   Barros, "Summer Turns Deadly for US-Bound Migrants Braving Scorching Desert Heat."

89.   U.S. Department of Homeland Security, "FY 2021: Budget in Brief."

90.   Guerette, "Immigration Policy, Border Security, and Migrant Deaths."

91.   Lind, "The Border Is in Crisis."

92.   Warren, "Reverse Migration to Mexico Led to US Undocumented Population Decline."

93.   Warren, 34.

94.   Warren, 37.

95.   MSNBC, *Fence Not Needed at Parts of Mexico Border*.

96.   MSNBC, *Fence Not Needed at Parts of Mexico Border*.

97.   Heyman, "A Border That Divides."

98.   Frazee and Barajas, "Trump Says Walls Work"; Lind, "The Border Is in Crisis."

99.   Poston, "Here's Why Trump's Border Wall Won't Work."

100. Poston, "Here's Why Trump's Border Wall Won't Work."

101. Horton, "Trump Keeps Calling the Southern Border 'Very Dangerous.'"

102. Horton, "Trump Keeps Calling the Southern Border 'Very Dangerous.'"

103. Heyman, "A Border That Divides."

104. E. Flores, "Two Countries and One Headless Body."

105. E. Flores, "Two Countries and One Headless Body."

106. Miroff, "U.S. Customs Agency Is So Short-Staffed, It's Sending Officers from Airports to the Mexican Border."

107. Lind, "The Border Is in Crisis."

108. J. Chavez, "Frequent Crossers of U.S.-Mexico Border Fret Over Threatened Shutdown."

109. J. Chavez, "Frequent Crossers of U.S.-Mexico Border Fret Over Threatened Shutdown."

110. Villagran, "US Customs and Border Protection Chief Mark Morgan Tours New Border Wall Area Near El Paso."

111. B. McEwen, "Protective and Damaging Effects of Stress Mediators."

112. B. Lee, Renwick, and Cara Labrador, "Mexico's Long War."

113. Felbab-Brown, "The Wall."

114. Felbab-Brown, "The Wall"; Nixon, "Border Wall Could Cost 3 Times Estimates, Senate Democrats' Report Says."

115. U.S. Government Accountability Office, "Border Security," 12.

116. Slack, Martinez, and Whiteford, *The Shadow of the Wall*.

117. American Immigration Council, "The Cost of Immigration Enforcement and Border Security."

118. Allen, de Castro Dobbin, and Morten, "Border Walls."

119. Muller, "Unsafe at Any Speed?"

120. R. Peters et al., "Nature Divided, Scientists United."
121. McCallum, Rowcliffe, and Cuthill, "Conservation on International Boundaries."
122. Owens, "Trump's Border-Wall Pledge Threatens Delicate Desert Ecosystems."
123. Eriksson and Taylor, "The Environmental Impacts of the Border Wall Between Texas and Mexico."
124. E. Cohen, *Illegal*, 202.
125. Stephen, "Towards a Transborder Perspective."
126. Forster-Cox et al., "The Environmental Health/Home Safety Education Project."
127. Cappellano and Makkonen, "Cross-Border Regional Innovation Ecosystems."
128. Ramos, "The Positive Steps Made in Making Our Southern Border Safer."

3. IMMIGRANTS COMMIT LESS CRIME THAN NATIVE-BORN PEOPLE

1. Gomez, "No . . . Immigrants Don't Commit More Crimes than U.S.-Born People."
2. Misra, "For the Last Time, Here's the Real Link Between Immigration and Crime."
3. R. Flores and Schachter, "Who Are the 'Illegals'?"
4. Budiman, "Key Findings About U.S. Immigrants."
5. Gonzalez O'Brien, Collingwood, and El-Khatib, "The Politics of Refuge."
6. Wadsworth, "Is Immigration Responsible for the Crime Drop?"
7. Budiman, "Key Findings About U.S. Immigrants."
8. Sampson, "Open Doors Don't Invite Criminals"; Stowell et al., "Immigration and the Recent Violent Crime Drop in the United States."
9. Butcher and Piehl, "Cross-City Evidence on the Relationship Between Immigration and Crime"; Chalfin, "The Long-Run Effect of Mexican Immigration on Crime in US Cities"; Ousey and Kubrin, "Exploring the Connection Between Immigration and Violent Crime Rates in U.S. Cities, 1980–2000"; MacDonald and Saunders, "Are Immigrant Youth Less Violent?"
10. Butcher and Piehl, "Cross-City Evidence on the Relationship Between Immigration and Crime"; Olson et al., "Immigration and Violent Crime"; Light and Miller, "Does Undocumented Immigration Increase Violent Crime?"
11. Flagg, "Is There a Connection Between Undocumented Immigrants and Crime?"
12. R. Martinez, Stowell, and Iwama, "The Role of Immigration."
13. Ferraro, "Immigration and Crime in the New Destinations, 2000–2007."
14. Sampson, "Open Doors Don't Invite Criminals."
15. A. Velazquez and Kempf-Leonard, "Mexican Immigration."
16. Salas-Wright, Vaughn, and Goings, "Immigrants from Mexico Experience Serious Behavioral and Psychiatric Problems at Far Lower Rates than US-Born Americans."
17. Krogstad, Stepler, and Lopez, "English Proficiency on the Rise Among Latinos."
18. Nowrasteh, "Crime Along the Mexican Border Is Lower than in the Rest of the Country."
19. Macrotrends, "El Paso TX Murder/Homicide Rate 1999–2018."
20. Cross, "El Paso Police Release Murder Statistics from 1960 to 2018."
21. Gomez, "No . . . Immigrants Don't Commit More Crimes than U.S.-Born People."
22. Budiman, "Key Findings About U.S. Immigrants."
23. Chalfin, "The Long-Run Effect of Mexican Immigration on Crime in US Cities."

24. Ewing, Martínez, and Rumbaut, *The Criminalization of Immigration in the United States*; Light, He, and Robey, "Comparing Crime Rates Between Undocumented Immigrants, Legal Immigrants, and Native-Born US Citizens in Texas."

25. U.S. Census Bureau, "QuickFacts: Texas."

26. American Immigration Council, "The Cost of Immigration Enforcement and Border Security."

27. Nowrasteh, "Criminal Immigrants in Texas."

28. Texas Department of Public Safety, "Crime in Texas, 2019," Austin, Texas, https://www.dps.texas.gov/sites/default/files/documents/crimereports/19/cit2019.pdf.

29. Ingraham, "Two Charts Demolish the Notion That Immigrants Here Illegally Commit More Crime"; Nowrasteh, "Criminal Immigrants in Texas."

30. Nowrasteh, "Criminal Immigrants in Texas."

31. Edwards, Esposito, and Lee, "Risk of Police-Involved Death by Race/Ethnicity and Place, United States, 2012–2018"; Jenks and Cataneda, "Defunding the Police Is an Immigrants' Rights Issue, Too."

32. A. Velazquez and Kempf-Leonard, "Mexican Immigration."

33. Vargas and Scrivener, "Why Latino Youth (Don't) Call Police."

34. Andrews, *Undocumented Politics.*

35. Bernat, "Immigration and Crime."

36. M. Morales, Delgado, and Curry, "Variations in Citizenship Profiling by Generational Status"; Lauren Villagran, "Sector Chief Gloria Chavez Readies El Paso Border Patrol for End of Title 42, Return of Asylum," *El Paso Times*, April 22, 2022, https://www.elpasotimes.com/story/news/2022/04/22/el-paso-border-patrol-cbp-title-42-asylum-immigration-migrants/7355068001/; Jack Herrera, "If All the Officers Assigned to the Texas-Mexico Border Stood Side By Side, How Far Apart Would They Be?," *Texas Monthly*, May 10, 2023, https://www.texasmonthly.com/news-politics/texas-border-agents-title-42/.

37. Castañeda, *A Place to Call Home.*

38. Aoki and Todo, "Are Immigrants More Likely to Commit Crimes?"; Castañeda, *A Place to Call Home.*

39. Aoki and Todo, "Are Immigrants More Likely to Commit Crimes?," 1540.

40. P. Simon, "French National Identity and Integration: Who Belongs to the National Community?"; Castañeda, *A Place to Call Home.*

41. R. Simon and Sikich, "Public Attitudes Toward Immigrants and Immigration Policies Across Seven Nations"; Wortley, "The Immigration-Crime Connection."

42. Svensson and Hagquist, "Adolescent Alcohol and Illicit Drug Use Among First- and Second-Generation Immigrants in Sweden."

43. Castañeda, *A Place to Call Home.*

44. B. Lee, Renwick, and Cara Labrador, "Mexico's Long War."

45. Gutiérrez-Romero, "Estimating the Impact of Mexican Drug Cartels and Drug-Related Homicides on Crime and Perceptions of Safety."

46. Gutiérrez-Romero, "Estimating the Impact of Mexican Drug Cartels and Drug-Related Homicides on Crime and Perceptions of Safety"; Beittel, *Mexico*; Flores Nández, *La Farsa.*

47. Luhnow, "Latin America Is the Murder Capital of the World"; Instituto Nacional de Estadística y Geografía, "Datos Preliminares Revelan que en 2016 Se Registraron 23 Mil 174 Homicidios"; B. Lee, Renwick, and Cara Labrador, "Mexico's Long War."

48. Woody, "Here's How Mexican Cartels Actually Operate in the United States."

49. Ospina, Tinajero, and Jelsma, "Poppies, Opium, and Heroin Production in Colombia and Mexico."

50. Magis-Rodríguez et al., "HIV Prevalence and Correlates of Receptive Needle Sharing Among Injection Drug Users in the Mexican-U.S. Border City of Tijuana."

51. Pacurucu-Castillo et al., "World Opioid and Substance Use Epidemic."

52. U.S. Federal Bureau of Investigation, "Crime on the Southwest Border."

53. Brophy, *Mexico*; Lybecker et al., "Do New Media Support New Policy Narratives?"

54. Mercille, "Violent Narco-Cartels or US Hegemony?"

55. Weisheit, "Cannabis Cultivation in the United States," 145.

56. Campoy and Rohrlich, "Immigrants Are Being Denied US Citizenship for Smoking Legal Pot."

57. R. Flores, "Living in the Eye of the Storm."

58. Bier, "77 Percent of Drug Traffickers Are U.S. Citizens, Not Illegal Immigrants."

59. Sanchez and Zhang, "Rumors, Encounters, Collaborations, and Survival."

60. Kara, *Modern Slavery*; Horton, "Trump Keeps Calling the Southern Border 'Very Dangerous.'"

61. Miller, *Border Patrol Nation*.

62. Sanchez and Zhang, "Rumors, Encounters, Collaborations, and Survival."

63. Cottam and Marenin, "The Management of Border Security in NAFTA."

64. Sherman, "Nixon's Drug War, an Excuse to Lock Up Blacks and Protesters, Continues."

65. Perry, "The Shocking Story Behind Richard Nixon's 'War on Drugs' That Targeted Blacks and Anti-War Activists."

66. Hussey et al., "Sexual Behavior and Drug Use Among Asian and Latino Adolescents."

67. Lassiter, "Impossible Criminals."

68. Salas-Wright, Vaughn, and Goings, "Immigrants from Mexico Experience Serious Behavioral and Psychiatric Problems at Far Lower Rates than US-Born Americans"; Salas-Wright et al., "Substance Use Disorders Among First- and Second-Generation Immigrant Adults in the United States."

69. Salas-Wright et al., "Substance Use Disorders Among First- and Second-Generation Immigrant Adults in the United States."

70. Ojeda, Patterson, and Strathdee, "The Influence of Perceived Risk to Health and Immigration-Related Characteristics on Substance Use Among Latino and Other Immigrants"; Salas-Wright, Vaughn, and Goings, "Immigrants from Mexico Experience Serious Behavioral and Psychiatric Problems at Far Lower Rates than US-Born Americans."

71. Hussey et al., "Sexual Behavior and Drug Use Among Asian and Latino Adolescents."

72. Blake et al., "Recency of Immigration, Substance Use, and Sexual Behavior Among Massachusetts Adolescents."

73. S. Garcia, "What Happens to Immigrants Who Face Addiction."

74. Borges et al., "Mexican Immigration to the U.S. and Alcohol and Drug Use Opportunities."

75. Salas-Wright et al., "Substance Use Disorders Among First- and Second-Generation Immigrant Adults in the United States."

76. Finch et al., "Contextual Effects of Acculturation on Perinatal Substance Exposure Among Immigrant and Native-Born Latinas."

77. Borges et al., "Mexican Immigration to the U.S. and Alcohol and Drug Use Opportunities."

78. S. Wallace, Mendez-Luck, and Castañeda, "Heading South"; S. Garcia, "What Happens to Immigrants Who Face Addiction."

79. Ojeda, Patterson, and Strathdee, "The Influence of Perceived Risk to Health and Immigration-Related Characteristics on Substance Use Among Latino and Other Immigrants," 864.

80. Loza, Castañeda, and Diedrich, "Substance Use by Immigrant Generation in a U.S.-Mexico Border City."

81. Substance Abuse and Mental Health Services Administration, *Results from the 2012 National Survey on Drug Use and Health: Summary of National Findings*; Substance Abuse and Mental Health Services Administration, "Key Substance Use and Mental Health Indicators in the United States: Results from the 2017 National Survey on Drug Use and Health."

82. Immigrant Legal Resource Center, "Controlled Substances"; National Association of Criminal Defense Lawyers, "Understanding Immigration Consequences of Drug Offenses."

83. Light, "Does Undocumented Immigration Increase Drug and Alcohol Problems?"; R. Cohen, "Undocumented Immigrants Less Likely to Be Arrested for Drugs, Alcohol."

84. Light, Miller, and Kelly, "Undocumented Immigration, Drug Problems, and Driving Under the Influence in the United States, 1990–2014."

85. Burnett, "Illegal Immigration Does Not Increase Violent Crime, 4 Studies Show."

86. Kulig et al., "'Bad Hombres' at the Southern US Border?"

87. Hagan and Palloni, "Sociological Criminology and the Mythology of Hispanic Immigration and Crime."

88. MacDonald, Hipp, and Gill, "The Effects of Immigrant Concentration on Changes in Neighborhood Crime Rates"; Warner, "The Social Construction of the Criminal Alien in Immigration Law, Enforcement Practice and Statistical Enumeration."

89. Wortley, "The Immigration-Crime Connection."

90. Wortley, "The Immigration-Crime Connection."

91. St. Martin, "Do More Broken Windows Mean More Crime?"

92. Fagan and Davies, "Street Stops and Broken Windows."

93. Howell, "Broken Lives from Broken Windows," 274.

94. J. Fox, "'Broken Windows' Theory Was Right . . . About the Windows"; Stuster, "Albuquerque Police Department's Safe Streets Program"; White, "Ethnic Diversity and Differential Policing in Australia."

95. Wortley, "The Immigration-Crime Connection."

96. Wong, *Transpacific Attachments*; Chan, "The Exclusion of Chinese Women, 1870–1943."

97. Ngai, *Impossible Subjects*; E. Lee, "The Chinese Exclusion Example."

98. Morenoff and Astor, "Immigrant Assimilation and Crime."

99. Moehling and Piehl, "Immigration, Crime, and Incarceration in Early Twentieth-Century America."

100. Gonzalez O'Brien, Collingwood, and El-Khatib, "The Politics of Refuge."

101. Moehling and Piehl, "Immigration, Crime, and Incarceration in Early Twentieth-Century America."

102. De Genova, "The Legal Production of Mexican/Migrant 'Illegality.'"

103. Cornelius, "Controlling 'Unwanted' Immigration."
104. Macías-Rojas, "Immigration and the War on Crime."
105. Perla and Coutin, "Legacies and Origins of the 1980s US–Central American Sanctuary Movement."
106. Villazor, "What Is a Sanctuary."
107. Walker and Leitner, "The Variegated Landscape of Local Immigration Policies in the United States."
108. Lasch et al., "Understanding 'Sanctuary Cities.'"
109. Martínez-Schuldt and Martínez, "Immigrant Sanctuary Policies and Crime-Reporting Behavior."
110. Yee, "Judge Blocks Trump Effort to Withhold Money from Sanctuary Cities."
111. Kittrie, "Federalism, Deportation and Crime Victims Afraid to Call the Police"; Gonzalez O'Brien, Collingwood, and El-Khatib, "The Politics of Refuge."
112. Martínez-Schuldt and Martínez, "Sanctuary Policies and City-Level Incidents of Violence, 1990 to 2010."
113. Awan, "Global Terror and the Rise of Xenophobia/Islamophobia"; Hervik, "Xenophobia and Nativism."
114. Rubio Goldsmith et al., "Ethno-racial Profiling and State Violence in a Southwest Barrio"; Sabo et al., "Everyday Violence, Structural Racism and Mistreatment at the US-Mexico Border."
115. E. Cohen, Illegal; Peralta, "You Say You're an American, but What If You Had to Prove It or Be Deported?"
116. Peralta, "You Say You're an American, but What If You Had to Prove It or Be Deported?"
117. Zoghlin, "Draconian Discrimination."
118. Flynn, "U.S. Citizen Freed After Nearly a Month in Immigration Custody, Family Says."
119. Zoghlin, "Draconian Discrimination."
120. National Immigrant Justice Center, "Access to Counsel"; Ryo, "Representing Immigrants."
121. Eagly and Shafer, "A National Study of Access to Counsel in Immigration Court."
122. "An immigration detainer is a notice that DHS issues to federal, state, and local law enforcement agencies (LEAs) to inform the LEA that ICE intends to assume custody of an individual in the LEA's custody." Immigration and Customs Enforcement, "ICE Detainers."
123. Warner, "The Social Construction of the Criminal Alien in Immigration Law, Enforcement Practice and Statistical Enumeration," 59.
124. Stevens, "U.S. Government Unlawfully Detaining and Deporting U.S. Citizens as Aliens"; Finnegan, "The Deportation Machine"; Coll, "When ICE Tries to Deport Americans, Who Defends Them?"
125. Castañeda, "Places of Stigma."
126. American Immigration Council, Two Systems of Justice.
127. Armenta, "Racializing Crimmigration"; Golash-Boza, Deported.
128. Macías-Rojas, "Immigration and the War on Crime." We thank reviewer 3 for this explanation. For more, see Abrego et al., "Making Immigrants Into Criminals."
129. Hagan and Palloni, "Sociological Criminology and the Mythology of Hispanic Immigration and Crime," 619.

130. E. Cohen, *Illegal*, 81.

131. Warner, "The Social Construction of the Criminal Alien in Immigration Law, Enforcement Practice and Statistical Enumeration."

132. Warner, "The Social Construction of the Criminal Alien in Immigration Law, Enforcement Practice and Statistical Enumeration"; J. X. Dowling and Inda, *Governing Immigration Through Crime*; Hagan, Levi, and Dinovitzer, "The Symbolic Violence of the Crime-Immigration Nexus."

133. Light, He, and Robey, "Comparing Crime Rates Between Undocumented Immigrants, Legal Immigrants, and Native-Born US Citizens in Texas."

134. Loza, Castañeda, and Diedrich, "Substance Use by Immigrant Generation in a U.S.-Mexico Border City."

135. Flórez et al., "Acculturation and Drug Use Stigma Among Latinos and African Americans."

136. R. Flores and Schachter, "Who Are the 'Illegals'? "; Wei, López, and Wu, "The Role of Language in Anti-Immigrant Prejudice"; Pearson, "How 'Undocumented Workers' and 'Illegal Aliens' Affect Prejudice Toward Mexican Immigrants."

137. Cervantes, "'Looking Mexican.'"

4. IMMIGRANTS WANT TO, AND DO, LEARN THE LOCAL LANGUAGE

1. Camarota and Zeigler, "One in Five U.S. Residents Speaks Foreign Language at Home."

2. Tse, *"Why Don't They Learn English?"*

3. Budiman, "Key Findings About U.S. Immigrants."

4. Hill, "English Proficiency of Immigrants."

5. Mario Alberto V. Espinoza-Kulick, Maura Fennelly, Kevin Beck, and Ernesto Castañeda, "Ethnic Enclaves."

6. Wolfman-Arent, "Research Shows Spanish Speakers Take Longer to Learn English"; Zong and Batalova, "The Limited English Proficient Population in the United States in 2013."

7. Budiman, "Key Findings About U.S. Immigrants."

8. Lowell and Suro, "The Improving Educational Profile of Latino Immigrants"; Schneider, Martinez, and Ownes, "Barriers to Educational Opportunities for Hispanics in the United States."

9. Piller, "The Real Problem with Linguistic Shirkers."

10. Piller, "The Real Problem with Linguistic Shirkers"; Toppelberg and Collins, "Language, Culture, and Adaptation in Immigrant Children."

11. Cain, Oakhill, and Elbro, "The Ability to Learn New Word Meanings from Context by School-Age Children with and Without Language Comprehension Difficulties."

12. Wiley, "Accessing Language Rights in Education."

13. Tse, *"Why Don't They Learn English?"*

14. J. A. Dowling, Ellison, and Leal, "Who Doesn't Value English?"; Tummala-Narra, "The Fear of Immigrants."

15. Neal et al., "Community and Conviviality?"

16. J. A. Dowling, Ellison, and Leal, "Who Doesn't Value English?"; Espenshade and Fu, "An Analysis of English-Language Proficiency Among U.S. Immigrants."

17. Waters and Pineau, *The Integration of Immigrants Into American Society*.
18. Fang, "GOP Candidates Say Immigrants Don't Learn English, but Report Proves Them Wrong."
19. Ammon, "World Languages."
20. Krogstad, Stepler, and Lopez, "English Proficiency on the Rise Among Latinos."
21. Tse, *"Why Don't They Learn English?,"* 9.
22. J. A. Dowling, Ellison, and Leal, "Who Doesn't Value English?," 373.
23. Gorman, "Immigrants' Children Grow Fluent in English, Study Says."
24. S. Kim, Ehrich, and Ficorilli, "Perceptions of Settlement Well-Being, Language Proficiency, and Employment."
25. Krogstad, Stepler, and Lopez, "English Proficiency on the Rise Among Latinos."
26. U.S. Census Bureau, "Detailed Languages Spoken at Home and Ability to Speak English for the Population 5 Years and Over: 2009–2013."
27. Tse, *"Why Don't They Learn English?,"* 53.
28. Antoniou, "The Advantages of Bilingualism Debate."
29. United Nations Office of the High Commissioner for Human Rights, International Covenant on Civil and Political Rights.
30. L. G., "Immigrants Do Not Need to Speak English Before They Arrive."
31. Anderson, "Immigrants and English"; Wilkerson and Salmons, "'GOOD Old Immigrants of Yesteryear,' Who Didn't Learn English."
32. United Nations Office of the High Commissioner for Human Rights, International Covenant on Civil and Political Rights.
33. U.S. Census Bureau, "Close to Half of New Immigrants Report High English-Language Speaking Ability, Census Bureau Reports."
34. U.S. Census Bureau, "Close to Half of New Immigrants Report High English-Language Speaking Ability, Census Bureau Reports."
35. Jones Gast, Okamoto, and Feldman, "'We Only Speak English Here'"; Mouw and Xie, "Bilingualism and the Academic Achievement of First- and Second-Generation Asian Americans."
36. Tse, *"Why Don't They Learn English?"*
37. Beckhusen et al., "Living and Working in Ethnic Enclaves."
38. Fennelly and Palasz, "English Language Proficiency of Immigrants and Refugees in the Twin Cities Metropolitan Area." 101.
39. Jang et al., "Health Vulnerability of Immigrants with Limited English Proficiency."
40. Norton Peirce, "Identity and Second Language Acquisition"; Trofimovich and Turuseva, "Ethnic Identity and Second Language Learning."
41. Menard-Warwick, *Gendered Identities and Immigrant Language Learning*.
42. Menard-Warwick, *Gendered Identities and Immigrant Language Learning*.
43. Espinosa and Massey, "Determinants of English Proficiency Among Mexican Migrants to the United States"; Carliner, "The Language Ability of U.S. Immigrants."
44. Bialystok and Hakuta, "Confounded Age"; DeKeyser and Larson-Hall, "What Does the Critical Period Really Mean?"
45. Fennelly and Palasz, "English Language Proficiency of Immigrants and Refugees in the Twin Cities Metropolitan Area."

46. Bleakley and Chin, "Age at Arrival, English Proficiency, and Social Assimilation Among US Immigrants." Immigrant children are typically more fluent English speakers than their parents and elders, and they often serve as conduits with wider U.S. society, particularly its bureaucratic and administrative features, in such areas as healthcare, insurance, and taxes.

47. De Gregorio and Lee, "Education and Income Inequality."

48. Orrenius and Zavodny, "Do Immigrants Work in Riskier Jobs?"

49. Zong and Batalova, "The Limited English Proficient Population in the United States in 2013."

50. National Immigration Forum, "Engaging Business for Immigrant Integration"; Community College Consortium for Immigrant Education, "CCCIE Community College Consortium for Immigrant Education."

51. National Immigration Forum, "English Language Programs Help Immigrants Prepare for Jobs."

52. Hill, "English Proficiency of Immigrants."

53. Fennelly and Palasz, "English Language Proficiency of Immigrants and Refugees in the Twin Cities Metropolitan Area."

54. G. Kim et al., "Vulnerability of Older Latino and Asian Immigrants with Limited English Proficiency."

55. Wolfman-Arent, "Research Shows Spanish Speakers Take Longer to Learn English."

56. Mouw and Xie, "Bilingualism and the Academic Achievement of First- and Second-Generation Asian Americans."

57. Krogstad and Gonzalez-Barrera, "A Majority of English-Speaking Hispanics in the U.S. Are Bilingual."

58. Massey, "Migration and Categorical Inequality."

59. A. Portes and Armony, *The Global Edge*.

60. Fennelly and Palasz, "English Language Proficiency of Immigrants and Refugees in the Twin Cities Metropolitan Area."

61. Beckhusen et al., "Living and Working in Ethnic Enclaves."

62. Iceland and Scopilliti, "Immigrant Residential Segregation in U.S. Metropolitan Areas, 1990–2000."

63. Espinoza-Kulick, Fennelly, Beck, and Castañeda, "Ethnic Enclaves."

64. Wolfman-Arent, "Research Shows Spanish Speakers Take Longer to Learn English."

65. Norton Peirce, "Social Identity, Investment, and Language Learning."

66. Hubenthal, "Older Russian Immigrants' Experiences in Learning English."

67. Dávila, "Language and Opportunity in the 'Land of Opportunity.'"

68. Dávila, "Language and Opportunity in the 'Land of Opportunity.'"

69. Olsen, "Learning English and Learning America."

70. Norton Peirce, "Social Identity, Investment, and Language Learning."

71. Gorman, "Immigrants' Children Grow Fluent in English, Study Says"; Hakimzadeh and Cohn, "English Usage Among Hispanics in the United States."

72. Nkimbeng et al., "'All I Know Is That There Is a Lot of Discrimination.'"

73. Schildkraut, "Official-English and the States."

74. L. G., "Immigrants Do Not Need to Speak English Before They Arrive."

75. Ernesto Castañeda, Michael Danielson, and Jayesh Rathod, "Fortress North America: Theorizing a Regional Approach to Migration Management."
76. English Language Unity Act of 2019, H.R. 997, 116th Cong. (2019–2020).
77. Pew Research Center, "Shifting Public Views on Legal Immigration Into the U.S."
78. Jones Gast, Okamoto, and Feldman, "'We Only Speak English Here.'"
79. Larota, "Immigrants Learning English in a Time of Anti-Immigrant Sentiment."
80. Wong Fillmore and Snow, "What Teachers Need to Know About Language," 27, 38.
81. Gerber, "Caucasians Are Made and Not Born."
82. N. Flores and Rosa, "Undoing Appropriateness."
83. N. Flores, Tseng, and Subtirelu, *Bilingualism for All?*
84. Gardner-Chloros, "Code-Switching in Community, Regional and National Repertoires."
85. Zarate, "'You Don't Look Like You Speak English.'"
86. Rubin, "Nonlanguage Factors Affecting Undergraduates' Judgments of Nonnative English-Speaking Teaching Assistants."
87. Leeman, "Investigating Language Ideologies in Spanish as a Heritage Language"; Tseng, "'Qué Barbaridad, Son Latinos y Deberían Saber Español Primero.'"
88. J. Garrett and Holcomb, "Meeting the Needs of Immigrant Students with Limited English Ability."
89. Gonzalez and Ayala-Alcantar, "Critical Caring."
90. Guo, "The Biggest Ideas Underpinning the Anti-Immigration Movement Aren't Backed Up by Data"; U.S. Government Accountability Office, *Teacher Preparation*."
91. Hutchinson, "Bridging the Gap"; Ek, Sánchez, and Quijada Cerecer, "Linguistic Violence, Insecurity, and Work."
92. Quintero and Hansen, "English Learners and the Growing Need for Qualified Teachers."
93. Master et al., "Different Skills?"
94. Olsen, "Learning English and Learning America."
95. Daoud and Quiocho, "I Can't See You If I Don't Know You."
96. Tropp and Molina, "Intergroup Processes."
97. Macswan, "The Threshold Hypothesis, Semilingualism, and Other Contributions to a Deficit View of Linguistic Minorities"; A. Sullivan, "Disproportionality in Special Education Identification and Placement of English Language Learners."
98. Olsen, "Learning English and Learning America."198.
99. A. Portes and Hao, "E Pluribus Unum."
100. A. Portes and Rumbaut, *Legacies*; Trofimovich and Turuseva, "Ethnic Identity and Second Language Learning."
101. A. Portes and Hao, "The Price of Uniformity"; Tseng, "'Qué Barbaridad, Son Latinos y Deberían Saber Español Primero.'"
102. Hakimzadeh and Cohn, "English Usage Among Hispanics in the United States."
103. Snipper, "Real Americans Don't Speak Spanish." 13.
104. Mirici, Galleano, and Torres, "Immigrant Parent vs. Immigrant Children."
105. Jeon, "Korean EFL Teachers' Beliefs of English-Only Instruction."
106. Fillmore, "When Learning a Second Language Means Losing the First."
107. Toppelberg and Collins, "Language, Culture, and Adaptation in Immigrant Children."
108. Toppelberg and Collins, "Language, Culture, and Adaptation in Immigrant Children."

109. Tseng, "'Qué Barbaridad, Son Latinos y Deberían Saber Español Primero.'"
110. Fillmore, "When Learning a Second Language Means Losing the First," 342.
111. Nesteruk and Marks, "Grandparents Across the Ocean."
112. Krogstad, Stepler, and Lopez, "English Proficiency on the Rise Among Latinos."
113. C. Brown, "Maintaining Heritage Language."
114. Krogstad, Stepler, and Lopez, "English Proficiency on the Rise Among Latinos."
115. Mahdi, "Ethnic Identity Among Second-Generation Iranians in the United States,"86.
116. Mouw and Xie, "Bilingualism and the Academic Achievement of First- and Second-Generation Asian Americans."
117. Alba et al., "Only English by the Third Generation?"
118. Ebaugh and Chafetz, "Dilemmas of Language in Immigrant Congregations."
119. Tseng and Hinrichs, "Mobility and the English Language."
120. Fought, *Chicano English in Context*; Slomanson and Newman, "Peer Group Identification and Variation in New York Latino English Laterals."
121. Tseng, "Vowel Variation, Style, and Identity Construction in the English of Latinos in Washington, D.C."
122. Tseng, "Bilingualism, Ideological Recentering, and New Latinx Identity Construction in the Global City."
123. L. G., "Immigrants Do Not Need to Speak English Before They Arrive."
124. Kouritzin, "Immigrant Mothers Redefine Access to ESL Classes."
125. National Center for Education Statistics, "English Language Learners in U.S. Schools."
126. Escamilla, "The False Dichotomy Between ESL and Transitional Bilingual Education Programs."
127. Cervantes-Soon, "A Critical Look at Dual Language Immersion in the New Latin@ Diaspora."
128. Valdés, "Dual-Language Immersion Programs."
129. Guo, "The Biggest Ideas Underpinning the Anti-Immigration Movement Aren't Backed Up by Data."
130. Gándara and Aldana, "Who's Segregated Now?"
131. Gándara and Aldana, "Who's Segregated Now?," 739.
132. Powers and Patton, "Between *Mendez* and *Brown*."
133. Villegas et al., "Preparing Future Mainstream Teachers to Teach English Language Learners."
134. Orellana, Ek, and Hernandez, "Bilingual Education in an Immigrant Community."
135. Roberts, "Bilingual Education Program Models."
136. Orellana, Ek, and Hernandez, "Bilingual Education in an Immigrant Community."
137. Wolfman-Arent, "Research Shows Spanish Speakers Take Longer to Learn English."
138. G. Kim et al., "Vulnerability of Older Latino and Asian Immigrants with Limited English Proficiency."
139. Okafor et al., "The Relationship of Language Acculturation (English Proficiency) to Current Self-Rated Health Among African Immigrant Adults."
140. G. Kim et al., "Vulnerability of Older Latino and Asian Immigrants with Limited English Proficiency"; Zhang et al., "Limited English Proficiency and Psychological Distress Among Latinos and Asian Americans."
141. Rhee, "Korean Immigrant Older Adults Residing in Non-Korean Ethnic Enclaves."

142. Christmas and Barker, "The Immigrant Experience."

143. A. Portes and Hao, "E Pluribus Unum"; Ando, "Bidimensional Acculturation and Psychosocial Adaptation Among First-Generation Japanese Immigrants."

144. Gibson, *El Norte*.

145. Heimlich, "Acadians."

5. IMMIGRANTS DO NOT DEPEND ON WELFARE PROGRAMS MORE THAN NATIVE-BORN PEOPLE

1. Simon, "Immigrants, Taxes, and Welfare in the United States"; A. Campbell, "Poor Immigrants Are the Least Likely Group to Use Welfare, Despite Trump's Claims."

2. Gamboa, "Income Test Under Trump Proposal Places Tougher Hurdles for Families to Get Green Cards."

3. Narea, "A Federal Judge Blocked Trump's Rule Creating a Wealth Test for Immigrants."

4. Gamboa, "Income Test Under Trump Proposal Places Tougher Hurdles for Families to Get Green Cards."

5. Feinstein and Jackson Lewis P.C., "Dropping Public Charge Rule, DHS Announces Return to Previous Policy to Determine Admissibility"; Van Voris, "Biden Review of Immigration 'Wealth Test' Halts Legal Challenge."

6. Gelatt, "The RAISE Act."

7. A. Campbell, "Poor Immigrants Are the Least Likely Group to Use Welfare, Despite Trump's Claims."

8. Cave, "Verify: Are Most Immigrants on Welfare?"

9. Tobias, "Are 55 Percent of Immigrants in California on Welfare?"

10. Marinari, *Unwanted*.

11. Blau, "The Use of Transfer Payments by Immigrants"; Tienda and Jensen, "Immigration and Public Assistance Participation"; L. Jensen, "Patterns of Immigration and Public Assistance Utilization, 1970–1980."

12. Borjas and Trejo, "Immigrant Participation in the Welfare System."

13. Hao and Kawano, "Immigrants' Welfare Use and Opportunity for Contact with Co-ethnics."

14. Bean, Van Hook, and Glick, "Country of Origin, Type of Public Assistance, and Patterns of Welfare Recipiency Among U.S. Immigrants and Natives"; Borjas, "National Origin and the Skills of Immigrants in the Postwar Period"; Hu, "Elderly Immigrants on Welfare"; Ono and Becerra, "Race, Ethnicity and Nativity, Family Structure, Socioeconomic Status and Welfare Dependency."

15. Uwaifo Oyelere and Oyolola, "Do Immigrant Groups Differ in Welfare Usage?"

16. M. Perez, "Colonialism, Americanization, and Indigenous Identity."

17. Uwaifo Oyelere and Oyolola, "Do Immigrant Groups Differ in Welfare Usage?"

18. Broder, Lessard, and Moussavian, "Overview of Immigrant Eligibility for Federal Programs."

19. Nam, "Welfare Reform and Elderly Immigrants' Health Insurance Coverage."

20. Haider et al., "Immigrants, Welfare Reform, and the Economy."

21. Amuedo-Dorantes, Averett, and Bansak, "Welfare Reform and Immigrant Fertility"; Broder, Lessard, and Moussavian, "Overview of Immigrant Eligibility for Federal Programs."

22. National Immigration Forum, "Fact Sheet: Immigrants and Public Benefits"; A. Campbell, "Poor Immigrants Are the Least Likely Group to Use Welfare, Despite Trump's Claims."

23. Passel and Cohn, "Mexicans Decline to Less Than Half the U.S. Unauthorized Immigrant Population for the First Time."

24. Ortega et al., "Health Care Access, Use of Services, and Experiences Among Undocumented Mexicans and Other Latinos."

25. Kaiser Family Foundation, "Key Facts on Health Coverage of Immigrants."

26. Fix, Capps, and Kaushal, "Immigrants and Welfare."

27. Fix, Capps, and Kaushal, "Immigrants and Welfare."

28. Haider et al., "Immigrants, Welfare Reform, and the Economy."

29. Potochnick, "Reversing Welfare Reform?"; Nam, "Welfare Reform and Elderly Immigrants' Health Insurance Coverage."

30. Fix and Haskins, "Welfare Benefits for Non-citizens"; Haider et al., "Immigrants, Welfare Reform, and the Economy."

31. Kropf, Nackerud, and Gorokhovski, "Social Work Practice with Older Soviet Immigrants."

32. Haskins, "Limiting Welfare Benefits for Noncitizens"; Fix, Capps, and Kaushal, "Immigrants and Welfare."

33. Kropf, Nackerud, and Gorokhovski, "Social Work Practice with Older Soviet Immigrants."

34. Haider et al., "Immigrants, Welfare Reform, and the Economy."

35. Kullgren, "Restrictions on Undocumented Immigrants' Access to Health Services."

36. Haider et al., "Immigrants, Welfare Reform, and the Economy."

37. Potochnick, "Reversing Welfare Reform?"

38. National Immigration Forum, "Fact Sheet: Immigrants and Public Benefits."

39. Potochnick, "Reversing Welfare Reform?"

40. Haider et al., "Immigrants, Welfare Reform, and the Economy"; Fix, Capps, and Kaushal, "Immigrants and Welfare."

41. Nowrasteh and Orr, "Immigration and the Welfare State."

42. Perreira et al., "Barriers to Immigrants' Access to Health and Human Services Programs."

43. Nam and Kim, "Welfare Reform and Elderly Immigrants' Naturalization"; Haider et al., "Immigrants, Welfare Reform, and the Economy."

44. Lowrey, "Are Immigrants a Drain on Government Resources?"

45. U.S. Citizenship and Immigration Services, "Public Charge."

46. U.S. Citizenship and Immigration Services, "Immigration and Public Charge."

47. Holder, "How Rule Changes About Public Benefits Could Affect Immigrants."

48. Orrenius and Zavodny, "Do Immigrants Work in Riskier Jobs?"; Zavodny, "Do Immigrants Work in Worse Jobs than U.S. Natives?"

49. New American Economy, "How the 'Public Charge' Rule Change Could Impact Immigrants and U.S. Economy."

50. U.S. Citizenship and Immigration Services, "Public Charge Provisions of Immigration Law."

51. U.S. Citizenship and Immigration Services, "Public Charge Provisions of Immigration Law."

52. Hirota, *Expelling the Poor*, 2.

53. U.S. Department of Homeland Security, "Inadmissibility and Deportability on Public Charge Grounds."

54. Bernstein, "Immigrants Receiving Welfare Could Be Denied Citizenship Under New DHS Rule."

55. Bernstein, "Immigrants Receiving Welfare Could Be Denied Citizenship Under New DHS Rule."

56. Kaushal and Kaestner, "Welfare Reform and Health Insurance of Immigrants."

57. Amuedo-Dorantes, Averett, and Bansak, "Welfare Reform and Immigrant Fertility," 767.

58. Boonstra, "Welfare Law and the Drive to Reduce 'Illegitimacy.'"

59. Boonstra.

60. Boonstra.

61. Camardelle, "Repeal Georgia's Cap on Kids."

62. Guttmacher Institute, "Regulating Insurance Coverage of Abortion."

63. Barrett and McCarthy, "Immigrants and Welfare Programmes."

64. Ku and Bruen, "Poor Immigrants Use Public Benefits at a Lower Rate than Poor Native-Born Citizens," 4.

65. Balistreri, "Welfare and the Children of Immigrants."

66. Nowrasteh and Orr, "Immigration and the Welfare State."

67. Nowrasteh and Orr, "Immigration and the Welfare State."

68. Cave, "Verify: Are Most Immigrants on Welfare?"; Ku and Bruen, "Poor Immigrants Use Public Benefits at a Lower Rate than Poor Native-Born Citizens."

69. Zavodny, "Welfare and the Locational Choices of New Immigrants"; Castañeda, *Immigration and Categorical Inequality*; Zavodny, "Determinants of Recent Immigrants' Locational Choices."

70. Cammett, "Welfare Queens Redux."

71. Cammett, "Welfare Queens Redux," 378.

72. Perry, "Stop Blaming Black Parents for Underachieving Kids."

73. S. Lee, "Reflecting Again on the Model Minority"; S. Lee, Wong, and Alvarez, "The Model Minority and the Perpetual Foreigner."

74. G. Li, "Other People's Success."

75. D. Sullivan and Ziegert, "Hispanic Immigrant Poverty."

76. Budiman et al., "Facts on U.S. Immigrants, 2018."

77. Ku and Pillai, "The Economic Mobility of Immigrants."

78. Kropf, Nackerud, and Gorokhovski, "Social Work Practice with Older Soviet Immigrants."

79. Gusmano and Okma, "Population Aging and the Sustainability of the Welfare State"; P. Jensen and Lolle, "The Fragmented Welfare State."

80. Hao and Kawano, "Immigrants' Welfare Use and Opportunity for Contact with Co-ethnics."

81. Hu, "Elderly Immigrants on Welfare."

82. Nam and Kim, "Welfare Reform and Elderly Immigrants' Naturalization."

83. Jakobsen and Pedersen, "Poverty Risk Among Older Immigrants in a Scandinavian Welfare State."

84. M. Johnson, "The Social Ecology of Acculturation."

85. M. Johnson, "The Social Ecology of Acculturation."

86. Dettlaff, Earner, and Phillips, "Latino Children of Immigrants in the Child Welfare System."
87. BBC News, "US-Mexico Border."
88. Alvarez, "Parents of 391 Migrant Children Separated at Border Under Trump Still Have Not Been Found, Court Filing Says."
89. Perreira et al., "Barriers to Immigrants' Access to Health and Human Services Programs."
90. S. Velazquez and Dettlaff, "Immigrant Children and Child Welfare in the United States."
91. Amuedo-Dorantes, Averett, and Bansak, "Welfare Reform and Immigrant Fertility"; Watson, "Inside the Refrigerator."
92. S. Velazquez and Dettlaff, "Immigrant Children and Child Welfare in the United States."
93. Alulema and Pavilon, *Immigrants' Use of New York City Programs, Services, and Benefits.*
94. Javier et al., "Children with Special Health Care Needs."
95. Gee et al., "Undocumented Immigrants' State & Local Tax Contributions."
96. Budiman, "Key Findings About U.S. Immigrants."
97. Zallman et al., "Immigrants Pay More in Private Insurance Premiums than They Receive in Benefits."
98. Zallman et al., "Immigrants Pay More in Private Insurance Premiums Than They Receive in Benefits."
99. Ku and Pillai, "The Economic Mobility of Immigrants."
100. Barrett and Maître, "Immigrant Welfare Receipt Across Europe."
101. Government of Ireland, "Habitual Residence Condition."
102. Citizens Information, "The Habitual Residence Condition."
103. gov.ie, "Operational Guidelines."
104. Government of Ireland, "Habitual Residence Condition"; Citizens Information, "The Habitual Residence Condition."
105. Barrett, Joyce, and Maître, "Immigrants and Welfare Receipt in Ireland."
106. Barrett, Joyce, and Maître, "Immigrants and Welfare Receipt in Ireland."
107. Dagilytė and Greenfields, "United Kingdom Welfare Benefit Reforms in 2013–2014."
108. Gustafsson, "Social Assistance Among Immigrants and Natives in Sweden."
109. Hansen and Lofstrom, "Immigrant Assimilation and Welfare Participation"
110. Jakobsen and Pedersen, "Poverty Risk Among Older Immigrants in a Scandinavian Welfare State."
111. Jakobsen and Pedersen, "Poverty Risk Among Older Immigrants in a Scandinavian Welfare State."
112. Jakubowicz, "The State and the Welfare of Immigrants in Australia."
113. Mills and Klein, "Affective Technologies of Welfare Deterrence in Australia and the United Kingdom," 400.
114. Khoo, "Correlates of Welfare Dependency Among Immigrants in Australia."
115. Cortina, *Aporophobia: Why We Reject the Poor Instead of Helping Them.*

6. REMITTANCES DO NOT DRAIN HOST COUNTRIES' ECONOMIES AND ARE NOT LIKE FOREIGN AID

1. Castañeda, "Remittances"; Castañeda, "Living in Limbo"; Castañeda and Buck, "Remittances, Transnational Parenting, and the Children Left Behind."

2. Barry and Overland, "Why Remittances to Poor Countries Should Not Be Taxed."

3. United Nations News, "Remittances Matter."

4. D. Yang, "Migrant Remittances."

5. D. Yang, "Migrant Remittances."

6. J. Cohen, "Migration, Remittances, and Household Strategies"; Castañeda and Buck, "Remittances, Transnational Parenting, and the Children Left Behind"; Castañeda and Buck, "A Family of Strangers"; Castañeda et al., "Symptoms of PTSD and Depression Among Central American Immigrant Youth"; Castañeda, "Living in Limbo"; Castañeda and Jenks, *Reunited*.

7. North, "Another Good Reason to Limit the $68 Billion in Remittances—Covid-19"; O'Brien, Raley, and Ryan, "The United States Loses $150 Billion Annually in Remittances."

8. Beaubien, "A Proposed New Tax, Mainly on Latinos, to Pay for Trump's Border Wall."

9. United Nations News, "Remittances Matter"; Castañeda, Aguilar, and Turkington, "Migration as a Driver of Economic Growth."

10. Chami et al., "Macroeconomic Consequences of Remittances."

11. World Bank, "Defying Predictions, Remittance Flows Remain Strong During COVID-19 Crisis."

12. Budiman and Connor, "Immigrants Sent a Record Amount of Money Home to Sub-Saharan African Countries in 2017."

13. World Bank, "Migration and Remittances Data."

14. World Bank Group, KNOMAD, "Leveraging Diaspora Finances for Private Capital Mobilization."

15. International Monetary Fund, *Balance of Payments and International Investment Position Manual*, 272.

16. Page and Plaza, "Migration Remittances and Development."

17. Young, Shinnar, and Cho, "Financial Behaviors Among Hispanic Immigrants."

18. Castañeda, Morales, and Ochoa, "Transnational Behavior in Comparative Perspective"; Cooray, "Who Remits?"; Niimi, Ozden, and Schiff, "Remittances and the Brain Drain."

19. Duany, "To Send or Not to Send," 214.

20. Duany, "To Send or Not to Send."

21. Organisation for Economic Co-operation and Development, *International Migration Outlook*, 146–47; Bishal Bhakta Kasu, Ernesto Castañeda, and Guangqing Chi. 2018. "Remittance-driven Migration in spite of Microfinance? The Case of Nepalese Households."

22. Amuedo-Dorantes and Pozo, "Remittances as Insurance."

23. D. Yang and Choi, "Are Remittances Insurance?"

24. Levitt and Waters, *The Changing Face of Home*; Castañeda, "Transnationalism in the Lives of Migrants"; Castañeda, Morales, and Ochoa, "Transnational Behavior in Comparative Perspective."

25. Castañeda, "Asking Immigrants for Money."

26. Castañeda, "Understanding Inequality, Migration, Race, and Ethnicity from a Relational Perspective."

27. Beaubien, "A Proposed New Tax, Mainly on Latinos, to Pay for Trump's Border Wall."

28. Beaubien, "A Proposed New Tax, Mainly on Latinos, to Pay for Trump's Border Wall."

29. K. Johnson, "Many Happy Returns"; Beaubien, "A Proposed New Tax, Mainly on Latinos, to Pay for Trump's Border Wall"; Ratha, De, and Schuettler, "Why Taxing Remittances Is a Bad Idea."

30. Young, Shinnar, and Cho, "Financial Behaviors Among Hispanic Immigrants."

31. Beaubien, "A Proposed New Tax, Mainly on Latinos, to Pay for Trump's Border Wall"; Ratha, De, and Schuettler, "Why Taxing Remittances Is a Bad Idea."

32. United Arab Emirates, "Value Added Tax (VAT)."

33. Deloitte Global, "Saudi Arabia Highlights 2020."

34. Navarrette, "Remittance Taxes Could Curb Illegal Immigration from Mexico"; O'Brien, Raley, and Ryan, "The United States Loses $150 Billion Annually in Remittances."

35. Pew Research Center, "Remittance Flows Worldwide in 2017."

36. Beaubien, "A Proposed New Tax, Mainly on Latinos, to Pay for Trump's Border Wall."

37. Amuedo-Dorantes and Pozo, "Remittances as Insurance."

38. K. Johnson, "Many Happy Returns."

39. K. Johnson, 6.

40. K. Johnson, 7.

41. Castañeda, Aguilar, and Turkington, "Migration as a Driver of Economic Growth."

42. Ratha, De, and Schuettler, "Why Taxing Remittances Is a Bad Idea."

43. Ratha, De, and Schuettler.

44. Ratha, De, and Schuettler.

45. Ratha, De, and Schuettler.

46. Ratha, De, and Schuettler; Orozco, "Globalization and Migration."

47. Swing, "How Migrants Who Send Money Home Have Become a Global Economic Force."

48. Niimi, Ozden, and Schiff, "Remittances and the Brain Drain"; Cooray, "Who Remits?"

49. Castañeda, Morales, and Ochoa, "Transnational Behavior in Comparative Perspective."

50. Faini, "Remittances and the Brain Drain."

51. Blocher, "Why Funding a US/Mexico Wall with a 'Remittance Tax' Is a Recipe for Disaster"; Henderson, "Immigrant Remittances Are Private Foreign Aid"; Karagöz, "Workers' Remittances and Economic Growth."

52. Stevenson, "Recovering Lost Tax Revenue Through Taxation of Transnational Households."

53. Blocher, "Why Funding a US/Mexico Wall with a 'Remittance Tax' Is a Recipe for Disaster"; Lowery and Ramachandran, *Unintended Consequences of Anti–Money Laundering Policies for Poor Countries.*

54. Castañeda, "Asking Immigrants for Money"; Castañeda, "Remittances."

55. Karagöz, "Workers' Remittances and Economic Growth."

56. S. Brown, "Can Remittances Spur Development?"

57. Xpress Money, "Formal Versus Informal Remittance Channels."

58. Castañeda, "Development Experts and the Framing of Remittances as a Development Tool."

59. Sirkeci, Cohen, and Ratha, "Migration and Remittances During the Global Financial Crisis and Beyond."

60. Ratha and Mohapatra, "Remittances and Development."

61. Swing, "How Migrants Who Send Money Home Have Become a Global Economic Force."

62. Conway and Cohen, "Consequences of Migration and Remittances for Mexican Transnational Communities."

63. Durand, Parrado, and Massey, "Migradollars and Development"; Massey, Goldring, and Durand, "Continuities in Transnational Migration."

64. Conway and Cohen, "Consequences of Migration and Remittances for Mexican Transnational Communities"; Castañeda and Jenks, *Reunited*.

65. Cocco et al., "Remittances."

66. Cocco et al., "Remittances."

67. Blocher, "Why Funding a US/Mexico Wall with a 'Remittance Tax' Is a Recipe for Disaster."

68. Cocco et al., "Remittances."

69. Orozco, "Globalization and Migration," 41.

70. Orozco, "Globalization and Migration."

71. Kapur, *Remittances*.

72. Acosta et al., "What Is the Impact of International Remittances on Poverty and Inequality in Latin America?"; Meyer and Shera, "The Impact of Remittances on Economic Growth."

73. Al-Assaf and Al-Malki, "Modelling the Macroeconomic Determinants of Workers' Remittances," 522.

74. Blocher, "Why Funding a US/Mexico Wall with a 'Remittance Tax' Is a Recipe for Disaster"; Page and Plaza, "Migration Remittances and Development"; United Nations News, "Remittances Matter."

75. Sirkeci, Cohen, and Ratha, "Migration and Remittances During the Global Financial Crisis and Beyond"; D. Yang, "Migrant Remittances."

76. D. Yang, "Migrant Remittances."

77. World Bank, "Defying Predictions, Remittance Flows Remain Strong During COVID-19 Crisis."

78. World Bank.

79. World Bank.

80. Suro, "Remittance Senders and Receivers."

81. United Nations News, "Remittances Matter."

82. United Nations News, "Remittances Matter."

83. Ratha and Mohapatra, "Remittances and Development."

84. Ratha, "Leveraging Remittances for Development."

85. Blocher, "Why Funding a US/Mexico Wall with a 'Remittance Tax' Is a Recipe for Disaster."

86. Henderson, "Immigrant Remittances Are Private Foreign Aid."

87. Henderson, "Immigrant Remittances Are Private Foreign Aid."

88. Ratha and Mohapatra, "Remittances and Development."

89. United Nations News, "Remittances Matter."

90. Blocher, "Why Funding a US/Mexico Wall with a 'Remittance Tax' Is a Recipe for Disaster."

91. Page and Plaza, "Migration Remittances and Development"; Blocher, "Why Funding a US/Mexico Wall with a 'Remittance Tax' Is a Recipe for Disaster"; United Nations News, "Remittances Matter."

92. Castañeda, "Development Experts and the Framing of Remittances as a Development Tool."

93. Chami et al., "Macroeconomic Consequences of Remittances," 3.
94. Alcaraz, Chiquiar, and Salcedo, "Remittances, Schooling, and Child Labor in Mexico."
95. Alcaraz, Chiquiar, and Salcedo, "Remittances, Schooling, and Child Labor in Mexico."
96. Levitt, "Social Remittances," 927.
97. Levitt.
98. Levitt, 927.
99. Levitt.
100. W. Roth, *Race Migrations*.
101. Escribà-Folch, Meseguer, and Wright, "Remittances and Democratization."
102. Abdih et al., "Remittances and Institutions"; Tyburski, "The Resource Curse Reversed?"
103. Ahmed, "The Perils of Unearned Foreign Income."
104. Castañeda, "Charles Tilly's Elegant Theories About the Origins of European Nation-States, Social Movements, Contentious Politics, and Democracy"; Tilly, Castañeda, and Wood, *Social Movements, 1768–2018*; Castañeda and Jenks, "January 6th and De-democratization in the United States."
105. Castañeda and Jenks, "January 6th and De-democratization in the United States."
106. Faini, "Remittances and the Brain Drain"; Mendoza, "Examining the Risk of Brain Drain and Lower Remittances."
107. K. Johnson, "Many Happy Returns."

7. THERE IS NO REFUGEE CRISIS

1. Chalabi, "What Happened to History's Refugees?"
2. United Nations High Commissioner for Refugees, Convention and Protocol Relating to the Status of Refugees.
3. Del Mundo, "2001 Global Refugee Statistics"; United Nations High Commissioner for Refugees, "Refugee Statistics."
4. Esses, Hamilton, and Gaucher, "The Global Refugee Crisis"; United Nations High Commissioner for Refugees, "Global Trends—Forced Displacement in 2019."
5. Trilling, "Five Myths About the Refugee Crisis."
6. Phillips, "Asylum Seekers and Refugees."
7. United Nations High Commissioner for Refugees, "Spain."
8. Uyghur Human Rights Project, *Weaponized Passports*.
9. McKenna and Hobman, "Problems and Solutions to the International Migrant Crisis."
10. United Nations High Commissioner for Refugees, "Global Trends—Forced Displacement in 2019."
11. United Nations High Commissioner for Refugees, "Global Trends—Forced Displacement in 2019."
12. Aleinikoff, "Reflections on the Worldwide Refugee Crisis"; Igielnik and Krogstad, "Where Refugees to the U.S. Come From."
13. U.S. Department of State, "Refugee Admissions."
14. European Commission, "First Population Estimates: EU Population Up to 508.2 Million at 1 January 2015," 2.
15. Trines, "The State of Refugee Integration in Germany in 2019."

16. K. Roth, "The Refugee Crisis That Isn't."

17. European Commission, "First Population Estimates: EU Population in 2020."

18. Miles, "U.N. View on the European Migrant Crisis?" See also Martin, "The Global Refugee Crisis."

19. Miles, "U.N. View on the European Migrant Crisis?"

20. Miles, "U.N. View on the European Migrant Crisis?"

21. Bourgois, "Insecurity, the War on Drugs, and Crimes of the State"; Morgan, "Behind the Secret U.S. War in Africa."

22. Rao, "'Neocolonialism' or 'Globalization'?"

23. Nwachuku, "Neo-colonialism."

24. Rao, "'Neocolonialism' or 'Globalization'?," 169.

25. Vine et al., "Creating Refugees."

26. K. Coleman, *A Camera in the Garden of Eden.*

27. Castañeda and Jenks, *Reuniting Families.*

28. Yazgan, Utku, and Sirkeci, "Syrian Crisis and Migration." See also U.S. Commission on International Religious Freedom, "Syria's Refugee Crisis and Its Implications."

29. United Nations High Commissioner for Refugees, "Global Trends—Forced Displacement in 2015."

30. Here we are talking about UNHCR-mandated refugees who have been granted formal refugee status as well as UNHCR-mandated displaced people and asylum seekers, so many of the official figures do not include people who have not been counted in UNHCR refugee camps, by governments, or by other resettlement or aid agencies. Still, there is a moral imperative to help them, and their undercounted, undocumented, informal situation does not render them less deserving of protection.

31. Esses, Hamilton, and Gaucher, "The Global Refugee Crisis."

32. United Nations High Commissioner for Refugees, "Global Trends—Forced Displacement in 2020."

33. Ostrand, "The Syrian Refugee Crisis."

34. United Nations High Commissioner for Refugees, "Global Trends—Forced Displacement in 2016."

35. United Nations High Commissioner for Refugees, "Global Trends—Forced Displacement in 2019"; United Nations High Commissioner for Refugees, "Global Trends—Forced Displacement in 2018."

36. United Nations High Commissioner for Refugees, "Global Trends—Forced Displacement in 2020."

37. Aleinikoff, "Reflections on the Worldwide Refugee Crisis."

38. O. Brown, *Migration and Climate Change.*

39. Biermann and Boas, "Protecting Climate Refugees."

40. United Nations High Commissioner for Refugees, "Desperate Journeys."

41. Kallergis, "Pushbacks"; Tondo, "'It's a Day Off'"; United Nations News, "Italy Failed to Rescue Over 200 Migrants in 2013 Mediterranean Disaster, UN Rights Body Finds."

42. Amnesty International, "8 Ways to Solve the World Refugee Crisis."

43. United Nations News, "UN Rights Office Concerned Over Migrant Boat Pushbacks in the Mediterranean."

44. Siegfried, "The Refugee Brief—10 September 2021."

45. Amnesty International, "8 Ways to Solve the World Refugee Crisis."

46. Greenhill, "Open Arms Behind Barred Doors."

47. Greenhill, "Open Arms Behind Barred Doors."

48. Ruëgger, "Refugees, Ethnic Power Relations, and Civil Conflict in the Country of Asylum."

49. Esses, Hamilton, and Gaucher, "The Global Refugee Crisis"; Greussing and Boomgaarden, "Shifting the Refugee Narrative?"; Trilling, "Five Myths About the Refugee Crisis."

50. Amnesty International, "8 Ways to Solve the World Refugee Crisis."

51. Aleinikoff, "Reflections on the Worldwide Refugee Crisis."

52. Martin, "The Global Refugee Crisis."

53. Aleinikoff, "Reflections on the Worldwide Refugee Crisis."

54. Bertoli, Brücker, and Fernández-Huertas Moraga, "The European Crisis and Migration to Germany"; Rommel, "'We Are the People.'"

55. Greussing and Boomgaarden, "Shifting the Refugee Narrative?," 1751.

56. Greussing and Boomgaarden, "Shifting the Refugee Narrative?"

57. Braithwaite, Salehyan, and Savun, "Refugees, Forced Migration, and Conflict."

58. Holmes and Castañeda, "Representing the 'European Refugee Crisis' in Germany and Beyond," 12.

59. Holmes and Castañeda, "Representing the 'European Refugee Crisis' in Germany and Beyond," 21.

60. Castañeda, *Building Walls*, 147.

61. K. Jensen, *The Color of Asylum*, 2.

62. Noh et al., "Perceived Racial Discrimination, Depression, and Coping."

63. Hadley and Patil, "Perceived Discrimination Among Three Groups of Refugees Resettled in the USA."

64. Willis and Nkwocha, "Health and Related Factors for Sudanese Refugees in Nebraska."

65. Hadley and Patil, "Perceived Discrimination Among Three Groups of Refugees Resettled in the USA."

66. Crawley and Skleparis, "Refugees, Migrants, Neither, Both."

67. Ansems de Vries, Carrera, and Guild, "Documenting the Migration Crisis in the Mediterranean."

68. Esses, Hamilton, and Gaucher, "The Global Refugee Crisis."

69. Ansems de Vries, Carrera, and Guild, "Documenting the Migration Crisis in the Mediterranean," 3.

70. Esses, Hamilton, and Gaucher, "The Global Refugee Crisis."

71. Albert and Maizland, "The Rohingya Crisis."

72. López-Farjeat and Coronado-Angulo, "Group Asylum, Sovereignty, and the Ethics of Care"; Camacho-Beltrán, "Legitimate Exclusion of Would-Be Immigrants"; J. X. Dowling and Inda, *Governing Immigration Through Crime*.

73. T. Garrett, "The Security Apparatus, Federal Magistrate Courts, and Detention Centers as Simulacra."

74. Frej, "One Year Since Trump's First Travel Ban, Many Refugees Left with Only Hellish Options."

75. Al Jazeera, "Trump Considering Significantly Slashing Refugee Cap—Again."

76. Armenta, "Racializing Crimmigration"; J. X. Dowling and Inda, *Governing Immigration Through Crime.*

77. Misra, "For the Last Time, Here's the Real Link Between Immigration and Crime."

78. Bendixsen, "The Refugee Crisis."

79. Kampf, "How to Fix America's Refugee Policy."

80. Afkhami, "Can Academic Medicine Lead the Way in the Refugee Crisis?"

81. Holmes et al., "Deservingness."

82. Bendixsen, "The Refugee Crisis."

83. Ostrand, "The Syrian Refugee Crisis."

84. Martin, "The Global Refugee Crisis."

85. A. Yang and Saffer, "NGOs' Advocacy in the 2015 Refugee Crisis."

86. Gulland, "The Refugee Crisis," 1.

87. Ostrand, "The Syrian Refugee Crisis."

88. Fijnaut, "The Refugee Crisis," 826.

89. Bendixsen, "The Refugee Crisis."

90. Bojadžijev and Mezzadra, "'Refugee Crisis' or Crisis of European Migration Policies?"

91. Davis, "Syria's Refugee Crisis."

92. Sipsma et al., "Violence Against Congolese Refugee Women in Rwanda and Mental Health."

93. Castañeda et al., "Symptoms of PTSD and Depression Among Central American Immigrant Youth."

94. Hovil and Lomo, "Forced Displacement and the Crisis of Citizenship in Africa's Great Lakes Region," 47.

8. GLOBALIZATION AND MIGRATION ARE INDEPENDENT PROCESSES

1. Dietz, Li, and Castañeda, "Keeping in Motion or Staying Put."

2. Castañeda, "The Indignados of Spain"; Castañeda, "Challenging the 1 Percent."

3. Castles and Miller, *The Age of Migration.*

4. Koser, *International Migration*, 25.

5. Castells, *The Rise of the Network Society.*

6. Czaika and de Haas, "The Globalization of Migration."

7. Tilly, "Globalization Threatens Labor's Rights"; Castañeda and Shemesh, "Overselling Globalization."

8. Greenwald and Kahn, *Globalization.*

9. Castañeda and Shemesh, "Overselling Globalization."

10. United Nations, *International Migration Report 2017*, 1.

11. Boundless, "Immigration and Globalization."

12. Donnan and Leatherby, "Globalization Isn't Dying, It's Just Evolving."

13. Castles, *Ethnicity and Globalization.*

14. Piketty and Saez, "Income Inequality in the United States, 1913–1998"; Killewald, Pfeffer, and Schachner, "Wealth Inequality and Accumulation"; Case and Deaton, *Deaths of Despair and the Future of Capitalism*; Keister, "The One Percent."

15. Alvaredo et al., "The Top 1 Percent in International and Historical Perspective," 4.

16. Horowitz, Igielnik, and Kochhar, "Trends in Income and Wealth Inequality."

17. Castañeda and Shemesh, "Overselling Globalization."

18. *Politico*, "Full Transcript: Donald Trump's Jobs Plan Speech."

19. Hoban, "Do Immigrants 'Steal' Jobs from American Workers?"

20. Felbab-Brown, "The Wall."

21. R. W. Jones, "Immigration vs. Outsourcing."

22. Koser, *International Migration*.

23. Goodman, *The Deportation Machine*.

24. Martin, "Heavy Traffic."

25. Shangquan, "Economic Globalization."

26. Correnti, "Outsourcing Overseas and Its Effect on the U.S. Economy"; Stalker, *Workers Without Frontiers*.

27. *Economist*, "The Third Wave of Globalisation May Be the Hardest," 2.

28. Castañeda and Shemesh, "Overselling Globalization."

29. Boundless, "Immigration and Globalization."

30. Liu, *The Silk Road in World History*; M. Peters, "The Ancient Silk Road and the Birth of Merchant Capitalism."

31. Castañeda, Díaz-Cepeda, and Andrade, "Social Movements in Contemporary Mexico," 99–100.

32. Castañeda, Díaz-Cepeda, and Andrade, "Social Movements in Contemporary Mexico."

33. Segal, "Globalization, Migration, and Ethnicity."

34. Czaika and de Haas, "The Globalization of Migration."

35. Keating and Fischer-Baum, "How U.S. Immigration Has Changed."

36. Keating and Fischer-Baum, "How U.S. Immigration Has Changed."

37. Parreñas, *Children of Global Migration*; Kordes, Pütz, and Rand, "Analyzing Migration Management."

38. Benería, Diana Deere, and Kabeer, "Gender and International Migration."

39. Skeldon, "Globalization, Skilled Migration and Poverty Alleviation."

40. Benería, Diana Deere, and Kabeer, "Gender and International Migration."

9. BREXIT DID NOT AND WILL NOT HALT IMMIGRATION TO THE UNITED KINGDOM

1. Dunin-Wascowicz, "The Referendums of 1975 and 2016 Illustrate the Continuity and Change in British Euroscepticism."

2. Guárdia, "How Brexit Vote Broke Down"; Yeung, "'Worst Situation You Can Ever Be in.'"

3. Hayes, *Gringolandia*.

4. J. Portes, "Immigration After Brexit."

5. Rzepnikowska, "Racism and Xenophobia Experienced by Polish Migrants in the UK Before and After Brexit Vote"; Virdee and McGeever, "Racism, Crisis, Brexit."

6. Hobolt, "The Brexit Vote."

7. Hobolt, "The Brexit Vote"; T. Wadsworth, "Is Immigration Responsible for the Crime Drop?"

8. Hobolt, "The Brexit Vote."

9.   Hobolt, "The Brexit Vote."

10. Goodwin and Heath, "The 2016 Referendum, Brexit and the Left Behind."

11. Glencross, "Why a British Referendum on EU Membership Will Not Solve the Europe Question."

12. BBC, "Brexit"; McBride, "What Brexit Means"; Pruitt, "The History Behind Brexit"; N. Walker, "Brexit Timeline."

13. European Union, Treaty of Amsterdam Amending the Treaty on European Union, the Treaties Establishing the European Communities and Certain Related Acts, 8.

14. D. Coleman, "A Demographic Rationale for Brexit"; Mauldin, "3 Reasons Brits Voted for Brexit."

15. Conservative Home, "Boris Johnson's Speech on the EU Referendum"; Virdee and McGeever, "Racism, Crisis, Brexit."

16. Dagilytė, "Brexit and Benefits."

17. Dustmann and Frattini, "The Fiscal Effects of Immigration to the UK."

18. Dagilytė and Greenfields, "United Kingdom Welfare Benefit Reforms in 2013–2014."

19. Tilford, "Britain, Immigration and Brexit."

20. Christensen, Hussein, and Ismail, "Migrants' Decision-Process Shaping Work Destination Choice."

21. Alfano, Dustmann, and Frattini, "Immigration and the UK."

22. Springford, *Is Immigration a Reason for Britain to Leave the EU?*

23. Dinan, Nugent, and Paterson, *The European Union in Crisis.*

24. Bale, "Policy, Office, Votes—and Integrity."

25. Usherwood, "Some Trade, Not Much Cooperation."

26. Usherwood, "Some Trade, Not Much Cooperation."

27. R. Chanda and Betai, "Implications of Brexit for Skilled Migration from India to the UK."

28. R. Chanda and Betai, "Implications of Brexit for Skilled Migration from India to the UK."

29. GOV.UK, "The UK's Points-Based Immigration System."

30. J. Portes, "Immigration and the UK Economy After Brexit."

31. R. Chanda and Betai, "Implications of Brexit for Skilled Migration from India to the UK."

32. Barnard and Costello, "Settled Status Deadline."

33. GOV.UK, "Apply to the EU Settlement Scheme (Settled and Pre-settled Status)."

34. J. Portes, "Immigration and the UK Economy After Brexit"; GOV.UK, "Apply to the EU Settlement Scheme (Settled and Pre-settled Status)."

35. Barnard and Costello, "Settled Status Deadline."

36. Barnard and Costello, "Settled Status Deadline."

37. GOV.UK, "Apply to the EU Settlement Scheme (Settled and Pre-settled Status)."

38. GOV.UK, "Apply to the EU Settlement Scheme (Settled and Pre-settled Status)."

39. *Law Society Gazette,* "CJEU Issues Opinion in UK Discrimination Case."

40. Garavoglia, "What Brexit Means for Migration Policy."

41. Gietel-Basten, "Why Brexit?"

42. Spencer, "Multi-level Governance of an Intractable Policy Problem."

43. Spencer, "Multi-level Governance of an Intractable Policy Problem."

44. Gherson, "Family Reunion in the UK Post-Brexit."

45. Gherson, "Family Reunion in the UK Post-Brexit."

46. Yeo, "Refugee Family Reunion."

47. Yeo, "Refugee Family Reunion."

48. Alper, "Briefing."

49. Barnard and Costello, "Settled Status Deadline."

50. Tims and O'Carroll, "130,000 EU Citizens on UK Benefits Yet to Apply for Settled Status, Leak Suggests."

51. Serhan, "Brexit Has Triggered Britain's Most Ambitious Migration Exercise Ever."

52. Edgington and Morris, "Brexit"; BBC News, "Brexit: Animal-Based Food Checks at Ports Suspended."

53. BBC News, "EU Referendum: Scotland Backs Remain as UK Votes Leave."

54. BBC News, "EU Referendum: Scotland Backs Remain as UK Votes Leave"; Dombey, "Brexit, Scotland and the UN Security Council."

55. Castle, "Of Brexit and Boris."

56. N. McEwen and Murphy, "Brexit and the Union," 9.

57. King and Flynn, "Brexit and the Future of Immigration in the UK and EU"; Serhan, "Brexit Has Triggered Britain's Most Ambitious Migration Exercise Ever."

58. GOV.UK, "Living in Europe."

59. Confederation of British Industry, Open and Controlled.

60. J. Wadsworth et al., "Brexit and the Impact of Immigration on the UK."

61. Office for National Statistics, "Migration Statistics Quarterly Report."

62. Giles, "The Effects of EU Migration on Britain in 5 Charts."

63. J. Wadsworth et al., "Brexit and the Impact of Immigration on the UK."

64. Valverde and Latorre, "The Economic Impact of Potential Migration Policies in the UK After Brexit."

65. Sumption, "Labour Immigration After Brexit."

66. Staton, "Employers 'Simply Not Ready' for Post-Brexit Immigration Regime."

67. GOV.UK, "The UK's Points-Based Immigration System."

68. R. Chanda and Betai, "Implications of Brexit for Skilled Migration from India to the UK."

69. R. Chanda and Betai, "Implications of Brexit for Skilled Migration from India to the UK."

70. Dagilytė and Greenfields, "United Kingdom Welfare Benefit Reforms in 2013–2014."

71. Vargas-Silva and Rienzo, "Migrants in the UK."

72. Miliken, "Immigration to Britain Falls to Five-Year Low Ahead of Brexit"; Office for National Statistics, "Migration Statistics Quarterly Report."

73. Office for National Statistics, "Migration Statistics Quarterly Report."

74. Vargas-Silva and Rienzo, "Migrants in the UK."

75. Vargas-Silva and Rienzo, "Migrants in the UK."

76. Office for National Statistics, "Migration Statistics Quarterly Report."

77. Office for National Statistics, "Migration Statistics Quarterly Report."

78. Blinder, "Non-EU Labour Migration to the UK."

79. Bale, "Policy, Office, Votes—and Integrity"; Miliken, "Immigration to Britain Falls to Five-Year Low Ahead of Brexit."

80. Dagilytė and Greenfields, "United Kingdom Welfare Benefit Reforms in 2013–2014."

10. IMMIGRANTS CAN INTEGRATE WHILE MAINTAINING THEIR IDENTITIES

1. Castañeda, "Urban Contexts and Immigrant Organizations."
2. Gordon, *Assimilation in American Life*, 71.
3. Waters and Pineau, *The Integration of Immigrants Into American Society*, 2.
4. Waters and Pineau, *The Integration of Immigrants Into American Society*, 3.
5. Jiménez and Fitzgerald, "Mexican Assimilation."
6. Gans, "Symbolic Ethnicity."
7. M. Brown and Starnaman, "'Unless We Americanize Them They Will Foreignize Us.'"
8. Carlson, "Americanization as an Early Twentieth-Century Adult Education Movement."
9. Morris, *The Scholar Denied*.
10. R. Alba and Nee, *Remaking the American Mainstream*.
11. Itzigsohn, "The Racial Blinders of Assimilation Theory."
12. S. Lee, Wong, and Alvarez, "The Model Minority and the Perpetual Foreigner."
13. Bourdieu, *Language and Symbolic Power*.
14. Miles, "French Ban on Full-Face Islamic Veil Violates Human Rights: U.N. Panel."
15. Syed, "Forced Assimilation Is an Unhealthy Policy Intervention."
16. Piccard, "Death by Boarding School."
17. Associated Press, "751 Bodies Found Buried at Indigenous School In Canada, Leaders Say."
18. Brown-Rice, "Examining the Theory of Historical Trauma Among Native Americans"; Clifford, Doran, and Tsey, "A Systematic Review of Suicide Prevention Interventions Targeting Indigenous Peoples in Australia, United States, Canada and New Zealand."
19. McGhee White, "Out of Many, One."
20. Kastoryano and Escafré-Dublet, "Tolerance and Cultural Diversity Discourses in France."
21. P. Li, "Deconstructing Canada's Discourse of Immigrant Integration."
22. P. Li, "Deconstructing Canada's Discourse of Immigrant Integration."
23. Tilly, Castañeda, and Wood, *Social Movements, 1768–2018*.
24. Remennick, "What Does Integration Mean?," 27.
25. Pasetti, "Configurations of Immigrant Integration Policies in Europe," 46.
26. Quoctrung and Dickerson, "What Can the U.S. Learn from How Other Countries Handle Immigration?"
27. Cengel, "The Reintegration of Rwandan Ex-Combatants."
28. Bertossi, "National Models of Integration in Europe."
29. Geddes and Scholten, *The Politics of Migration and Immigration in Europe*; Heckmann and Schnapper, *The Integration of Immigrants in European Societies*; Penninx, "Integration"; Penninx and Martiniello, "Integration Processes and Policies"; Bertossi, "National Models of Integration in Europe."
30. Singer, *Practice to Policy*.
31. K. Walker and Leitner, "The Variegated Landscape of Local Immigration Policies in the United States."
32. Beaman, "A Place to Call Home," 217.
33. Yuval-Davis, "Belonging and the Politics of Belonging"; Çaglar and Schiller, *Migrants and City-Making*.

34. Castañeda, *A Place to Call Home*, 6.
35. Castañeda, *A Place to Call Home*, 5–6.
36. Banting and Soroka, "Minority Nationalism and Immigrant Integration in Canada," 163.
37. Chernysheva, "Ernesto Castañeda. A Place to Call Home."
38. Golash-Boza and Valdez, "Nested Contexts of Reception: Undocumented Students at the University of California, Central"; N. Perez, "Nested Contexts of Reception"; Ruszczyk, "Non-state Actors in the Regularisation of Undocumented Youths"; Nicholls, "The Uneven Geographies of Politicisation."
39. Tilly, Castañeda, and Wood, *Social Movements, 1768–2018*, 208–19.
40. Beaman, "A Place to Call Home," 218.
41. Beaman, "A Place to Call Home," 217.
42. A. Portes and Rumbaut, *Legacies*; A. Portes and Rumbaut, *Immigrant America*; Stepick and Dutton Stepick, "Diverse Contexts of Reception and Feelings of Belonging"; Castañeda, *A Place to Call Home*; Castañeda, "Urban Contexts and Immigrant Organizations."
43. Castañeda, "Places of Stigma"; Castañeda, "Banlieue."
44. Ruszczyk, "Inclusion in the Nation Via the City."
45. Castañeda, *A Place to Call Home*, 41, 45; Silver, "Book Review."
46. Kasinitz et al., *Inheriting the City*.
47. Castañeda, *A Place to Call Home*, 37.
48. Ruszczyk, "Inclusion in the Nation Via the City," 789; Ignatiev, *How the Irish Became White*.
49. Sassen, *The Global City*.
50. Ruszczyk, "Inclusion in the Nation Via the City."
51. Beaman, *Citizen Outsider*.
52. Castañeda, "Urban Contexts and Immigrant Organizations"; Bouamama, *Communautarisme*; Bérengère Bocquillon, "« Expliquez-nous »."
53. Pinçon and Pinçon-Charlot, *Sociologie de Paris*; Pinçon and Pinçon-Charlot, *Les Ghettos du Gotha*; Latour and Hermant, "Paris."
54. Chernysheva, "Ernesto Castañeda. A Place to Call Home."
55. Castañeda, *A Place to Call Home*; Beauchemin, Hamel, and Simon, *Trajectories and Origins*.
56. Castañeda, *A Place to Call Home*, 61.
57. Castañeda, *A Place to Call Home*, 47.
58. Silver, "Book Review," 733.
59. de Graauw, *Making Immigrant Rights Real*.
60. Penninx and Martiniello, "Integration Processes and Policies."
61. Ruszczyk, "Local Governance of Immigrant Incorporation."
62. Nicholls and Uitermark, *Cities and Social Movements*, 118–19.
63. Ajuntament de Barcelona, "La Població Estrangera a Barcelona."
64. Aragón Medina et al., *Las Políticas Locales para la Integración de los Inmigrantes y la Participación de los Agentes Sociales*, 22–23.
65. Bezunartea, López, and Tedesco, "Muslims in Spain and Islamic Religious Radicalism."
66. Aragón Medina et al., *Las Políticas Locales para la Integración de los Inmigrantes y la Participación de los Agentes Sociales*, 22–23.

67. Aragón Medina et al., *Las Políticas Locales para la Integración de los Inmigrantes y la Participación de los Agentes Sociales*, 22–23.

68. L. Morales and Jorba, "Transnational Links and Practices of Migrants' Organisations in Spain," 272.

69. The preceding section is adapted from Castañeda, "Urban Contexts and Immigrant Organizations," 125.

70. Castañeda, *A Place to Call Home*.

71. Castañeda, *A Place to Call Home*, 142; Silver, "Book Review."

72. Ruszczyk, "Inclusion in the Nation Via the City."

73. Castañeda, *A Place to Call Home*, 144; Silver, "Book Review."

74. Tahseen Shams, *Here, There, and Elsewhere: The Making of Immigrant Identities in a Globalized World*.

75. Castañeda, *Immigration and Categorical Inequality*; Tilly, *Durable Inequality*.

76. Çaglar and Schiller, *Migrants and City-Making*.

77. Tilly, *Big Structures, Large Processes, Huge Comparisons*; Castañeda, "Understanding Inequality, Migration, Race, and Ethnicity from a Relational Perspective."

78. Croucher, "Integrated Threat Theory and Acceptance of Immigrant Assimilation."

79. Croucher, "Integrated Threat Theory and Acceptance of Immigrant Assimilation."

80. Cowell, "After Coordinated Bombs, London Is Stunned, Bloodied and Stoic."

81. d'Appollonia and Reich, *Immigration, Integration, and Security*.

82. Castañeda, *A Place to Call Home*; Miller-Idriss, *Hate in the Homeland*.

83. Dalgard and Thapa, "Immigration, Social Integration and Mental Health in Norway, with Focus on Gender Differences."

84. Dalgard and Thapa, "Immigration, Social Integration and Mental Health in Norway, with Focus on Gender Differences."

85. Vang, "The Limits of Spatial Assimilation for Immigrants' Full Integration."

86. Gudrun Jensen, Weibel, and Vitus, "'There Is No Racism Here.'"

87. Dalgard and Thapa, "Immigration, Social Integration and Mental Health in Norway, with Focus on Gender Differences."

88. Dalgard and Thapa, "Immigration, Social Integration and Mental Health in Norway, with Focus on Gender Differences."

89. European Commission, "Governance of Migrant Integration in Sweden."

90. Harder et al., "Multidimensional Measure of Immigrant Integration."

91. Remennick, "What Does Integration Mean?"

92. Remennick, "What Does Integration Mean?

93. Remennick, "What Does Integration Mean?"

94. Zavodny, "Do Immigrants Work in Worse Jobs than U.S. Natives?."

95. Waters and Pineau, *The Integration of Immigrants Into American Society*.

96. Fortuny et al., "The Integration of Immigrants and Their Families in Maryland."

97. Jiménez, *Replenished Ethnicity*.

98. U.S. Census Bureau, "Nation's Population Growth Slowed This Decade."

99. Frey, "Census 2020."

100. Kiss et al., *Demographic Outlook for the European Union 2020*.

101. European Commission, "Excess Mortality—Statistics."

102. Singer, *Practice to Policy*.

103. Huang, "Do Local Immigrant-Welcoming Efforts Increase Immigration?"; Huang and Liu, "Welcoming Cities"; Warf and Holly, "The Rise and Fall and Rise of Cleveland"; Ross, "Serving the Urban Poor in Turn-of-the-Century Cleveland."
104. Vericker et al., *Effects of Immigration on WIC and NSLP Caseloads.*
105. Capps and Fortuny, "The Integration of Immigrants in Maryland's Growing Economy."
106. Banting and Soroka, "Minority Nationalism and Immigrant Integration in Canada," 156–57.
107. Li, "Deconstructing Canada's Discourse of Immigrant Integration," 321.
108. Silver, "Book Review."
109. Ruszczyk, "Inclusion in the Nation Via the City."
110. Frey, "Neighborhood Segregation Persists for Black, Latino or Hispanic, and Asian Americans"; Vang, "The Limits of Spatial Assimilation for Immigrants' Full Integration"; Carter, Polevychok, and Friesen, "Winnipeg's Inner City."
111. New American Economy, "NAE Cities Index"; Lim, "Ranked."
112. Lim, "Ranked."
113. New American Economy, "NAE Cities Index."
114. Menjívar, *Fragmented Ties*; Scallen, "The Bombs That Drop in El Salvador Explode in Mt. Pleasant."
115. Mahler, *American Dreaming.*
116. Castañeda and Jenks, *Reunited.*
117. Castañeda, *A Place to Call Home*; Silver, "Book Review."
118. de Graauw, "Rolling Out the Welcome Mat."
119. de Graauw and Bloemraad, "Working Together."
120. I. Chanda, "State Efforts to Help Immigrants Integrate."

REFERENCES

Abdih, Yasser, Ralph Chami, Jihad Dagher, and Peter Montiel. "Remittances and Institutions: Are Remittances a Curse?" *World Development* 40, no. 4 (2012): 657–66. https://doi.org/10.1016/j.worlddev.2011.09.014.

Abrego, Leisy, Mat Coleman, Daniel E. Martínez, Cecilia Menjívar, and Jeremy Slack. "Making Immigrants Into Criminals: Legal Processes of Criminalization in the Post-IIRIRA Era." *Journal on Migration and Human Security* 5, no. 3 (2017): 694–715.

Acevedo, Nicole. "Why Are Migrant Children Dying in U.S. Custody?" NBC News, May 29, 2019. https://www.nbcnews.com/news/latino/why-are-migrant-children-dying-u-s-custody-n1010316.

ACLU. "Know Your Rights in the 100 Mile Border Zone." ACLU New Mexico. Accessed May 13, 2024. https://www.aclu-nm.org/en/know-your-rights/know-your-rights-100-mile-border-zone.

ACLU. "Neglect & Abuse of Unaccompanied Children by U.S. Customs and Border Protection." ACLU of San Diego and Imperial Counties, May 23, 2018. https://www.aclusandiego.org/en/news/neglect-abuse-unaccompanied-children-us-customs-and-border-protection.

Acosta, Pablo, Cesar Calderón, Pablo Fajnzylber, and Humberto Lopez. "What Is the Impact of International Remittances on Poverty and Inequality in Latin America?" *World Development* 36, no. 1 (2008): 89–114. https://doi.org/10.1016/j.worlddev.2007.02.016.

Adlerstein, Ana. "A Not-Guilty Verdict Absolves Border Patrol of Cross-Border Killing." NPR, November 25, 2018. https://www.npr.org/2018/11/25/670668243/a-not-guilty-verdict-absolves-border-patrol-of-cross-border-killing.

Afkhami, Amir A. "Can Academic Medicine Lead the Way in the Refugee Crisis?" *Academic Medicine: Journal of the Association of American Medical Colleges* 91, no. 12 (2016): 1595–97. https://doi.org/10.1097/ACM.0000000000001427.

Agerholm, Harriet. "US Border Patrol Exposed Kicking Over Water Bottles Left for Migrants." Independent, January 18, 2018. https://www.independent.co.uk/news/world/americas/us-border-patrol-mexico-water-bottles-video-migrants-kick-over-video-illegals-mexicans-hispanics-a8165591.html.

Aguirre, Adalberto, Jr., and Jennifer K. Simmers. "Mexican Border Crossers: The Mexican Body in Immigration Discourse." *Social Justice* 35, no. 4 (2008): 99–106.

Ahmed, Faisal Z. "The Perils of Unearned Foreign Income: Aid, Remittances, and Government Survival." *American Political Science Review* 106, no. 1 (2012): 146–65.

Ajuntament de Barcelona. "La Població Estrangera a Barcelona. La Població de Barcelona Nascuda a l'estranger." Barcelona: Departament d'Estadísticai Difusió de Dades, 2018. https://www.bcn.cat/estadistica/catala/dades/inf/pobest/pobest18/pobest18.pdf.

Al-Assaf, Ghazi, and Abdullah M. Al-Malki. "Modelling the Macroeconomic Determinants of Workers' Remittances: The Case of Jordan." *International Journal of Economics and Financial Issues* 4, no. 3 (2014): 514–26.

Alba, Alicia Gaspar de, and Georgina Guzmán. *Making a Killing: Femicide, Free Trade, and La Frontera.* Austin: University of Texas Press, 2010.

Alba, Richard D., John Logan, Amy Lutz, and Brian Stults. "Only English by the Third Generation? Loss and Preservation of the Mother Tongue Among the Grandchildren of Contemporary Immigrants." *Demography* 39, no. 3 (2002): 467–84. https://doi.org/10.1353/dem.2002.0023.

Alba, Richard D., and Victor Nee. *Remaking the American Mainstream: Assimilation and Contemporary Immigration.* Cambridge, MA: Harvard University Press, 2003.

Albert, Eleanor, and Lindsay Maizland. "The Rohingya Crisis." Council on Foreign Relations, January 23, 2020. https://www.cfr.org/backgrounder/rohingya-crisis.

Albuquerque, Pedro H., and Prasad Vemala. "A Statistical Evaluation of Femicide Rates in Mexican Cities Along the US-Mexico Border." Social Science Research Network, 2008. https://papers.ssrn.com/sol3/papers.cfm?abstract_id=1112308.

Alcaraz, Carlo, Daniel Chiquiar, and Alejandrina Salcedo. "Remittances, Schooling, and Child Labor in Mexico." *Journal of Development Economics* 97, no. 1 (2012): 156–65. https://doi.org/10.1016/j.jdeveco.2010.11.004.

Alden, Edward. "Is Border Enforcement Effective? What We Know and What It Means." *Journal of Migration and Human Security* 5, no. 2 (2017): 481–90. https://doi.org/10.1177/233150241700500213.

Aleinikoff, T. Alexander. "Reflections on the Worldwide Refugee Crisis." *UCLA Journal of International Law and Foreign Affairs* 21, no. 1 (2017): 1–9.

Alfano, Mark, Christian Dustmann, and Tommaso Frattini. "Immigration and the UK: Reflections After Brexit." In *Refugees and Economic Migrants: Facts, Policies and Challenges*, ed. Francesco Fasani, 55–79. London: CEPR Press, 2016. http://giovanniperi.ucdavis.edu/uploads/5/6/8/2/56826033/refugees_and_economic_migrants.pdf#page=65.

Al Jazeera. "Mexico Urges Tighter US Gun Control After Deadly El Paso Shooting." August 5, 2019. https://www.aljazeera.com/news/2019/8/5/mexico-urges-tighter-us-gun-control-after-deadly-el-paso-shooting.

——. "Trump Considering Significantly Slashing Refugee Cap—Again." September 7, 2019. https://www.aljazeera.com/news/2019/9/7/trump-considering-significantly-slashing-refugee-cap-again.

Allen, Treb, Cauê de Castro Dobbin, and Melanie Morten. "Border Walls." Social Science Research Network, November 1, 2018. https://papers.ssrn.com/abstract=3286888.

Alper, Lucy. "Briefing: How Brexit Leaves Refugee Families Stranded in Greece." Free Movement, February 11, 2021. http://www.freemovement.org.uk/briefing-how-brexit-leaves-refugee-families-stranded-in-greece/.

Alulema, Daniela, and Jacquelyn Pavilon. *Immigrants' Use of New York City Programs, Services, and Benefits: Examining the Impact of Fear and Other Barriers to Access.* New York: Center for Migration Studies, January 2022. https://cmsny.org/publications/nyc-programs-services-and-benefits-report-013122/.

Alvarez, Priscilla. "Parents of 391 Migrant Children Separated at Border Under Trump Still Have Not Been Found, Court Filing Says." CNN, May 19, 2021. https://www.cnn.com/2021/05/19/politics/ms-l-children-reunited/index.html.

Alvaredo, Facundo, Anthony B. Atkinson, Thomas Piketty, and Emmanuel Saez. "The Top 1 Percent in International and Historical Perspective." *Journal of Economic Perspectives* 27, no. 3 (2013): 3–20.

American Immigration Council. "The Cost of Immigration Enforcement and Border Security." January 20, 2021. https://www.americanimmigrationcouncil.org/research/the-cost-of-immigration-enforcement-and-border-security.

——. *Two Systems of Justice: How the Immigration System Falls Short of American Ideals of Justice.* Washington DC: AIC, March 19, 2013. https://www.americanimmigrationcouncil.org/research/two-systems-justice-how-immigration-system-falls-short-american-ideals-justice.

Ammon, U. "World Languages: Trends and Futures." In *The Handbook of Language and Globalization,* ed. Nikolas Coupland, 101–22. Hoboken, NJ: Blackwell, 2010.

Amnesty International. "8 Ways to Solve the World Refugee Crisis." 2015. https://www.amnesty.org/en/latest/campaigns/2015/10/eight-solutions-world-refugee-crisis/.

Ampudia Ruedas, Lourdes, and Luis Enrique Gutiérrez Casas. "Empleo y Estructura Económica en el Contexto de la Crisis en Juárez, 1999–2004." In *Seguridad y Violencia en Ciudad Juárez, México,* ed. Myrna Limas Hernández. Ciudad Juárez, Chihuahua: Universidad Autónoma de Ciudad Juárez, 2012.

Amuedo-Dorantes, Catalina, Susan L. Averett, and Cynthia A. Bansak. "Welfare Reform and Immigrant Fertility." *Journal of Population Economics* 29, no. 3 (2016): 757–79. https://doi.org/10.1007/s00148-016-0584-1.

Amuedo-Dorantes, Catalina, and Susan Pozo. "Remittances as Insurance: Evidence from Mexican Immigrants." *Journal of Population Economics* 19, no. 2 (2006): 227–54.

Anderson, Stuart. "Immigrants and English." *Immigration Reform Bulletin,* October 2010.

Ando, Sachi. "Bidimensional Acculturation and Psychosocial Adaptation Among First-Generation Japanese Immigrants." *Journal of Theory Construction & Testing* 18 (January 1, 2014): 17–21.

Andreas, Peter. *Border Games: Policing the U.S.-Mexico Divide.* 2nd ed. Ithaca, NY: Cornell University Press, 2009.

Andrews, Abigail Leslie. *Undocumented Politics: Place, Gender, and the Pathways of Mexican Migrants.* Oakland: University of California Press, 2018.

Ansems de Vries, Leonie, Sergio Carrera, and Elspeth Guild. "Documenting the Migration Crisis in the Mediterranean: Spaces of Transit, Migration Management and Migrant Agency." Social Science Research Network, September 13, 2016. https://papers.ssrn.com/abstract=2859431.

Anti-Defamation League. "Murder and Extremism in the United States in 2019." February 25, 2020. https://www.adl.org/resources/report/murder-and-extremism-united-states-2019.

Antoniou, Mark. "The Advantages of Bilingualism Debate." *Annual Review of Linguistics* 5, no. 1 (2019): 395–415. https://doi.org/10.1146/annurev-linguistics-011718-011820.

Aoki, Yu, and Yasuyuki Todo. "Are Immigrants More Likely to Commit Crimes? Evidence from France." *Applied Economics Letters* 16, no. 15 (2009): 1537–41.

Appollonia, Ariane Chebel d', and Simon Reich, eds. *Immigration, Integration, and Security: America and Europe in Comparative Perspective.* Pittsburgh: University of Pittsburgh Press, 2008.

Aragón Medina, Jorge, Alba Artiaga Leiras, Mohammed A. Haidour, Alicia Martínez Poza, and Fernando Rocha Sánchez. *Las Políticas Locales para la Integración de los Inmigrantes y la Participación de los Agentes Sociales.* Madrid: Catarata, 2009.

Arango, Tim, Nicholas Bogel-Burroughs, and Katie Benner. "Minutes Before El Paso Killing, Hate-Filled Manifesto Appears Online." *New York Times,* August 4, 2019. https://www.nytimes.com/2019/08/03/us/patrick-crusius-el-paso-shooter-manifesto.html.

Argueta, Carla N. *Border Security: Immigration Enforcement Between Ports of Entry.* Washington, DC: Congressional Research Service, 2016. http://fedweb.com/wp-content/uploads/2017/08/CRS-Border-Security-Immigration-Enforcement-Between-Ports-of-Entry.pdf.

Armenta, Amada. "Racializing Crimmigration: Structural Racism, Colorblindness, and the Institutional Production of Immigrant Criminality." *Sociology of Race and Ethnicity* 3, no. 1 (2017): 82–95. https://doi.org/10.1177/2332649216648714.

Asia News Monitor. "United States/Mexico: The US-Mexico Border—A Dangerous Place with or Without a Wall." January 27, 2017. http://www.proquest.com/docview/1861934243/citation/CCC2257D60FD45CFPQ/1.

Associated Press. "751 Bodies Found Buried at Indigenous School in Canada, Leaders Say." *HuffPost,* June 24, 2021. https://www.huffpost.com/entry/751-bodies-found-buried-at-indigenous-school-in-canada-leaders-say_n_60d4ac37e4b052e474ff5ad8.

Awan, Muhammad Safeer. "Global Terror and the Rise of Xenophobia/Islamophobia: An Analysis of American Cultural Production Since September 11." *Islamic Studies* 49, no. 4 (2010): 521–37.

Baker, Peter. "Trump Declares a National Emergency, and Provokes a Constitutional Clash." *New York Times,* February 5, 2019. https://www.nytimes.com/2019/02/15/us/politics/national-emergency-trump.html.

Bakker, Matt. *Migrating Into Financial Markets: How Remittances Became a Development Tool.* Oakland: University of California Press, 2015.

Bale, Tim. "Policy, Office, Votes—and Integrity. The British Conservative Party, Brexit, and Immigration." *Journal of Ethnic and Migration Studies* 48, no. 2 (2022): 482–501. https://doi.org/10.1080/1369183X.2020.1853909.

Balistreri, Kelly Stamper. "Welfare and the Children of Immigrants: Transmission of Dependence or Investment in the Future?" *Population Research and Policy Review* 29, no. 5 (2010): 715–43. https://doi.org/10.1007/s11113-009-9169-y.

Banting, Keith, and Stuart Soroka. "Minority Nationalism and Immigrant Integration in Canada." *Nations and Nationalism* 18, no. 1 (2012): 156–76. https://doi.org/10.1111/j.1469-8129.2011.00535.x.

Barnard, Catherine, and Fiona Costello. "Settled Status Deadline: What's Next for EU Citizens in the UK?" *Conversation,* June 30, 2021. http://theconversation.com/settled-status-deadline-whats-next-for-eu-citizens-in-the-uk-163673.

Barrett, Alan, Corona Joyce, and Bertrand Maître. "Immigrants and Welfare Receipt in Ireland." *International Journal of Manpower* 34, no. 2 (2013): 142–54. https://doi.org/10.1108/01437721311320663.

Barrett, Alan, and Bertrand Maître. "Immigrant Welfare Receipt Across Europe." *International Journal of Manpower* 34, no. 1 (2013): 8–23. https://doi.org/10.1108/01437721311319629.

Barrett, Alan, and Yvonne McCarthy. "Immigrants and Welfare Programmes: Exploring the Interactions Between Immigrant Characteristics, Immigrant Welfare Dependence, and

Welfare Policy." *Oxford Review of Economic Policy* 24, no. 3 (2008): 542–59. https://doi.org/10.1093/oxrep/grn026.

——. "Immigrants in a Booming Economy: Analysing Their Earnings and Welfare Dependence." *Labour* 21, no. 4–5 (2007): 789–808. https://doi.org/10.1111/j.1467-9914.2007.00389.x.

Barros, Aline. "Summer Turns Deadly for US-Bound Migrants Braving Scorching Desert Heat." *Voice of America*, July 29, 2021. https://www.voanews.com/usa/immigration/summer-turns-deadly-us-bound-migrants-braving-scorching-desert-heat.

Barry, Christian, and Gerhard Overland. "Why Remittances to Poor Countries Should Not Be Taxed." *New York University Journal of International Law and Politics* 42 (2010): 1180–1207.

BBC. "Brexit: A Brief History of Britain and the EU." January 31, 2020. https://www.bbc.co.uk/newsround/50166269.

BBC News. "Brexit: Animal-Based Food Checks at Ports Suspended." February 2, 2021. https://www.bbc.com/news/uk-northern-ireland-55895276.

——. "EU Referendum: Scotland Backs Remain as UK Votes Leave." May 24, 2016. https://www.bbc.com/news/uk-scotland-scotland-politics-36599102.

——. "US-Mexico Border: Parents of 545 Separated Children Still Not Found." October 21, 2020. https://www.bbc.com/news/world-us-canada-54636223.

Beaman, Jean. *Citizen Outsider: Children of North African Immigrants in France.* Oakland: University of California Press, 2017.

——. "A Place to Call Home: Immigrant Exclusion and Urban Belonging in New York, Paris, and Barcelona." *Contemporary Sociology* 50, no. 3 (2021): 217–19. https://doi.org/10.1177/00943061211006085d.

Bean, Frank D., Jennifer V. W. Van Hook, and Jennifer E. Glick. "Country of Origin, Type of Public Assistance, and Patterns of Welfare Recipiency Among U.S. Immigrants and Natives." *Social Science Quarterly* 78, no. 2 (1997): 432–51.

Beaubien, Jason. "A Proposed New Tax, Mainly on Latinos, to Pay for Trump's Border Wall." NPR, May 25, 2017. https://www.npr.org/sections/goatsandsoda/2017/05/25/529507199/a-proposed-new-tax-mainly-on-latinos-to-pay-for-trumps-border-wall.

Beauchemin, Cris, Christelle Hamel, and Patrick Simon, eds. *Trajectories and Origins: Survey on the Diversity of the French Population.* Cham, Switzerland: Springer, 2019.

Beckhusen, Julia, J. G. M. Raymond, Thomas de Graff, Jacques Poot, and Brigitte Waldorf. "Living and Working in Ethnic Enclaves: Language Proficiency of Immigrants in U.S. Metropolitan Areas." *Papers in Regional Science* 92, no. 1 (2013), 305–29.

Beittel, June S. *Mexico: Organized Crime and Drug Trafficking Organizations.* Washington, DC: Congressional Research Service, 2020. https://sgp.fas.org/crs/row/R41576.pdf.

Bendixsen, Synnøve K. N. "The Refugee Crisis: Destabilizing and Restabilizing European Borders." *History and Anthropology* 27, no. 5 (2016): 536–54. https://doi.org/10.1080/02757206.2016.1221407.

Benería, Lourdes, Carmen Diana Deere, and Naila Kabeer. "Gender and International Migration: Globalization, Development, and Governance." *Feminist Economics* 18, no. 2 (2012): 1–33. https://doi.org/10.1080/13545701.2012.688998.

Bernat, Frances. "Immigration and Crime." *Oxford Research Encyclopedia of Criminology and Criminal Justice*, April 26, 2017. https://doi.org/10.1093/acrefore/9780190264079.013.93.

Bernstein, Leandra. "Immigrants Receiving Welfare Could Be Denied Citizenship Under New DHS Rule." Center for Law and Social Policy, September 25, 2018. https://www.clasp.org /press-room/news-clips/immigrants-receiving-welfare-could-be-denied-citizenship-under -new-dhs-rule.

Bertoli, Simone, Herbert Brücker, and Jesús Fernández-Huertas Moraga. "The European Crisis and Migration to Germany." *Regional Science and Urban Economics* 60 (September 1, 2016): 61–72. https://doi.org/10.1016/j.regsciurbeco.2016.06.012.

Bertossi, Christophe. "National Models of Integration in Europe: A Comparative and Critical Analysis." *American Behavioral Scientist* 55, no. 12 (2011): 1561–80. https://doi.org/10.1177/000276 4211409560.

Bezunartea, Patricia, José Manuel López, and Laura Tedesco. "Muslims in Spain and Islamic Religious Radicalism." In *Ethno-religious Conflict in Europe*, ed. Michael Emerson, 136–58. Brussels: Centre for European Policy Studies, 2009.

Bialystok, Ellen, and Kenji Hakuta. "Confounded Age: Linguistic and Cognitive Factors in Age Differences for Second Language Acquisition." In *Second Language Acquisition and the Critical Period Hypothesis*, ed. D. Birdsong, 161–81. Mahwah, NJ: Erlbaum, 1999.

Bier, David J. "77 Percent of Drug Traffickers Are U.S. Citizens, Not Illegal Immigrants." Cato Institute, July 3, 2019. https://www.cato.org/blog/77-drug-traffickers-are-us-citizens-not -illegal-immigrants.

Bier, David J., and Alex Nowrasteh. "45,000 'Special Interest Aliens' Caught Since 2007, but No U.S. Terrorist Attacks from Illegal Border Crossers." Cato at Liberty, December 17, 2018. https://www.cato.org/blog/45000-special-interest-aliens-caught-2007-no-us-terrorist -attacks-illegal-border-crossers.

Biermann, Frank, and Ingrid Boas. "Protecting Climate Refugees: The Case for a Global Protocol." *Environment: Science and Policy for Sustainable Development* 50, no. 6 (2008): 8–16.

Bishal Bhakta Kasu, Ernesto Castañeda, and Guangqing Chi. "Remittance-driven Migration in Spite of Microfinance? The Case of Nepalese Households." In *Immigration and Categorical Inequality: Migration to Cities and the Birth of Race and Ethnicity*, ed. Ernesto Castañeda, 171–96. New York: Routledge, 2018.

Blake, Susan M., Rebecca Ledsky, Carol Goodenow, and Lydia O'Donnell. "Recency of Immigration, Substance Use, and Sexual Behavior Among Massachusetts Adolescents." *American Journal of Public Health* 91, no. 5 (2001): 794–98.

Blau, Francine D. "The Use of Transfer Payments by Immigrants." *Industrial and Labor Relations Review* 37, no. 2 (1984): 222–39. https://doi.org/10.1177/001979398403700205.

Bleakley, Hoyt, and Aimee Chin. "Age at Arrival, English Proficiency, and Social Assimilation Among US Immigrants." *American Economic Journal: Applied Economics* 2, no. 1 (2010): 165–92. https://doi.org/10.1257/app.2.1.165.

Blinder, Scott. "Non-EU Labour Migration to the UK." Migration Observatory, April 4, 2017. http://migrationobservatory.ox.ac.uk/wp-content/uploads/2017/04/Briefing-Non-European -Labour-Migration17-1.pdf.

Blocher, Julia. "Why Funding a US/Mexico Wall with a 'Remittance Tax' Is a Recipe for Disaster." *Our World*, June 16, 2017. https://ourworld.unu.edu/en/why-funding-a-us-mexico-wall-with-a -remittance-tax-is-a-recipe-for-disaster.

Bocquillon, Bérengère. "« Expliquez-nous »: communautarisme, où en est-on en France?" RMC, February 18, 2020. https://rmc.bfmtv.com/emission/expliquez-nous-communautarisme-ou-en -est-on-en-france-1860096.html.

Bojadžijev, Manuela, and Sandro Mezzadra. " 'Refugee Crisis' or Crisis of European Migration Policies?" *Focaal Blog*, November 12, 2015. http://www.focaalblog.com/2015/11/12/manuela -bojadzijev-and-sandro-mezzadra-refugee-crisis-or-crisis-of-european-migration-policies/.

Boonstra, Heather D. "Welfare Law and the Drive to Reduce 'Illegitimacy.' " *Guttmacher Policy Review* 3, no. 6 (2000): 7–10. https://www.guttmacher.org/gpr/2000/12/welfare-law-and-drive-reduce -illegitimacy.

Borges, Guilherme, Claudia Rafful, Corina Benjet, Daniel J. Tancredi, Naomi Saito, Sergio Aguilar -Gaxiola, Maria Elena Medina-Mora, and Joshua Breslau. "Mexican Immigration to the U.S. and Alcohol and Drug Use Opportunities: Does It Make a Difference in Alcohol and /or Drug Use?" *Drug and Alcohol Dependence* 125, no. 1 (2012): S4–11. https://doi.org/10.1016/j .drugalcdep.2012.05.007.

Borjas, George J. "National Origin and the Skills of Immigrants in the Postwar Period." In *Immigration and the Work Force: Economic Consequences for the United States and Source Areas*, ed. George J. Borjas and Richard B. Freeman, 17–47. Chicago: University of Chicago Press, 1992.

Borjas, George J., and Stephen J. Trejo. "Immigrant Participation in the Welfare System." *Industrial and Labor Relations Review* 44, no. 2 (1991): 195–211. https://doi.org/10.1177/001979399104400201.

Bouamama, Saïd. *Communautarisme: "un spectre hante la France."* Paris: La Découverte, 2020. https://doi.org/10.3917/dec.slaou.2020.01.0249.

Boundless. "Immigration and Globalization." December 8, 2017. https://www.boundless.com /blog/globalization/.

Bourdieu, Pierre. *Language and Symbolic Power.* Cambridge, MA: Harvard University Press, 1991.

Bourgois, Philippe. "Insecurity, the War on Drugs, and Crimes of the State: Symbolic Violence in the Americas." In *Violence at the Urban Margins*, ed. Javier Auyero, Philippe Bourgois, and Nancy Scheper-Hughes, 305–21. Oxford: Oxford University Press, 2015. https://www.academia .edu/34279651/Bourgois_2015_Insecurity_the_war_on_drugs_and_crimes_of_the_state_pdf.

Boyce, Geoffrey Alan. "The Neoliberal Underpinnings of Prevention Through Deterrence and the United States Government's Case Against Geographer Scott Warren." *Journal of Latin American Geography* 18, no. 3 (2019): 192–201.

Braithwaite, Alex, Idean Salehyan, and Burcu Savun. "Refugees, Forced Migration, and Conflict: Introduction to the Special Issue." *Journal of Peace Research* 56, no. 1 (2019): 5–11. https://doi.org /10.1177/0022343318814128.

Bray, Llona. "Inadmissibility: When the U.S. Can Keep You Out." Nolo, 2020. https://www.nolo .com/legal-encyclopedia/us-deny-entry-inadmissibility-reasons-29715.html.

Broder, Tanya, Gabrielle Lessard, and Avideh Moussavian. "Overview of Immigrant Eligibility for Federal Programs." National Immigration Law Center, July 2021. https://www.nilc.org /issues/economic-support/overview-immeligfedprograms/.

Brophy, Stephanie. "Mexico: Cartels, Corruption and Cocaine; A Profile of the Gulf Cartel." *Global Crime* 9, no. 3 (2008): 248–61. https://doi.org/10.1080/17440570802254353.

Brown, Clara Lee. "Maintaining Heritage Language: Perspectives of Korean Parents," *Multicultural Education* 19, no. 1 (2011): 31–37.

Brown, Matthew J, and Sabrina Starnaman. " 'Unless We Americanize Them They Will Foreignize Us': Pragmatism, Progressivism, and Americanization." n.d.

Brown, Oli. *Migration and Climate Change*. Geneva: International Organization for Migration, February 2008.

Brown, Stuart S. "Can Remittances Spur Development? A Critical Survey." *International Studies Review* 8, no. 1 (2006): 55–75. https://doi.org/10.1111/j.1468-2486.2006.00553.x.

Brown-Rice, Kathleen. "Examining the Theory of Historical Trauma Among Native Americans." *Professional Counselor* 3, no. 3 (2013): 117–30.

Budiman, Abby. "Key Findings About U.S. Immigrants." Pew Research Center, August 20, 2020. https://www.pewresearch.org/fact-tank/2020/08/20/key-findings-about-u-s-immigrants/.

Budiman, Abby, and Phillip Connor. "Immigrants Sent a Record Amount of Money Home to Sub-Saharan African Countries in 2017." Pew Research Center, April 3, 2019. https://www.pewresearch.org/fact-tank/2019/04/03/immigrants-sent-a-record-amount-of-money-home-to-sub-saharan-african-countries-in-2017/.

Budiman, Abby, Christine Tamir, Lauren Mora, and Luis Noe-Bustamante. "Facts on U.S. Immigrants, 2018: Statistical Portrait of the Foreign-Born Population in the United States." Pew Research Center, August 20, 2020. https://www.pewresearch.org/hispanic/2020/08/20/facts-on-u-s-immigrants/.

Burnett, John. " 'I Want To Be Sure My Son Is Safe': Asylum-Seekers Send Children Across Border Alone." NPR, November 27, 2019. https://www.npr.org/2019/11/27/783360378/i-want-to-be-sure-my-son-is-safe-asylum-seekers-send-children-across-border-alon.

——. "Illegal Immigration Does Not Increase Violent Crime, 4 Studies Show." National Public Radio, May 2, 2018. https://www.npr.org/2018/05/02/607652253/studies-say-illegal-immigration-does-not-increase-violent-crime.

Business Insider. *What It's Really Like at the US-Mexico Border*. 2019. https://www.youtube.com/watch?v=rLZB_EkgFBQ.

Butcher, Kristin F., and Anne Morrison Piehl. "Cross-City Evidence on the Relationship Between Immigration and Crime." *Journal of Policy Analysis and Management* 17, no. 3 (1998): 457–93.

Çaglar, Ayse, and Nina Glick Schiller. *Migrants and City-Making: Dispossession, Displacement, and Urban Regeneration*. Durham, NC: Duke University Press, 2018.

Cain, Kate, Jane Oakhill, and Carsten Elbro. "The Ability to Learn New Word Meanings from Context by School-Age Children with and Without Language Comprehension Difficulties." *Journal of Child Language* 30, no. 3 (2003): 681–94. https://doi.org/10.1017/S0305000903005713.

Camacho-Beltrán, Enrique. "Legitimate Exclusion of Would-Be Immigrants: A View from Global Ethics and the Ethics of International Relations." *Social Sciences* 8, no. 8 (2019): art. 238. https://doi.org/10.3390/socsci8080238.

Camardelle, Alex. "Repeal Georgia's Cap on Kids." Georgia Budget and Policy Institute, February 3, 2020. https://gbpi.org/repeal-georgias-cap-on-kids/.

Camarota, Steven A, and Karen Zeigler. "One in Five U.S. Residents Speaks Foreign Language at Home." Center for Immigration Studies, October 5, 2015.

Cammett, Ann. "Welfare Queens Redux: Criminalizing Black Mothers in the Age of Neoliberalism." *Southern California Interdisciplinary Law Journal* 25 (April 8, 2016): 363–94.

Campbell, Alexia Fernández. "Poor Immigrants Are the Least Likely Group to Use Welfare, Despite Trump's Claims." Vox, 2017. https://www.vox.com/policy-and-politics/2017/8/4/16094684/trump-immigrants-welfare.

Campbell, Howard. *Drug War Zone: Frontline Dispatches from the Streets of El Paso and Juárez.* Austin: University of Texas Press, 2009.

Campoy, Ana, and Justin Rohrlich. "Immigrants Are Being Denied US Citizenship for Smoking Legal Pot." Quartz, April 20, 2019. https://qz.com/1600262/immigrants-are-being-denied-us-citizenship-for-smoking-legal-pot/.

Cappellano, Francesco, and Teemu Makkonen. "Cross-Border Regional Innovation Ecosystems: The Role of Non-profit Organizations in Cross-Border Cooperation at the US-Mexico Border." *GeoJournal* 85, no. 6 (2020): 1515–28. https://doi.org/10.1007/s10708-019-10038-w.

Capps, Randy, and Karina Fortuny. "The Integration of Immigrants in Maryland's Growing Economy." Urban Institute, 2008. https://doi.org/10.1037/e722552011-001.

Carliner, Geoffrey. "The Language Ability of U.S. Immigrants: Assimilation and Cohort Effects." *International Migration Review* 34, no. 1 (2000): 158–82. https://doi.org/10.1177/019791830003400107.

Carlson, Robert A. "Americanization as an Early Twentieth-Century Adult Education Movement." *History of Education Quarterly* 10, no. 4 (1970): 440–64. https://doi.org/10.2307/367410.

Carmona López, Adriana, Alma Gómez Caballero, and Lucha Castro Rodríguez. "Feminicide in Latin America in the Movement for Women's Human Rights." In *Terrorizing Women: Feminicide in the Americas*, ed. Rosa-Linda Fregoso and Cynthia Bejarano. Durham, NC: Duke University Press, 2010.

Case, Anne, and Angus Deaton. *Deaths of Despair and the Future of Capitalism.* Princeton, NJ: Princeton University Press, 2020.

Castañeda, Ernesto. "Asking Immigrants for Money: Marketing Remittances Services Around the World." *Independent Social Research Foundation Bulletin*, no. 23 (May 21, 2021): 47–61.

——. "Banlieue." In *Encyclopedia of Urban Studies*, ed. Ray Hutchison. Thousand Oaks, CA: SAGE, n.d. https://doi.org/10.4135/9781412971973.

——. *Building Walls: Excluding Latin People in the United States.* Lanham, MD: Lexington Books, 2019.

——. "Building Walls, Excluding People, and Terrorizing Minorities." Center for the Study of Immigrant Integration, 2020.

——. "Challenging the 1 Percent: The Indignados and Occupy Movements." In *Social Movements, 1768–2018*, ed. Charles Tilly, Ernesto Castañeda, and Lesley J. Wood, 194–207. 4th ed. New York: Routledge, 2020.

——. "Charles Tilly's Elegant Theories About the Origins of European Nation-States, Social Movements, Contentious Politics, and Democracy." *American Behavioral Scientist*, August 30, 2023. https://doi.org/10.1177/00027642231194871.

——. "Despite the end of Title 42, restrictions on asylum seekers are expected to continue under Biden administration." *The Conversation*, May 11, 2023. https://theconversation.com/despite-the-end-of-title-42-restrictions-on-asylum-seekers-are-expected-to-continue-under-biden-administration-205343.

——. "Development Experts and the Framing of Remittances as a Development Tool." Center for Latin American and Latino Studies Working Paper.

——. *Immigration and Categorical Inequality: Migration to the City and the Birth of Race and Ethnicity*. New York: Routledge, 2018.

——. "The Indignados of Spain: A Precedent to Occupy Wall Street." *Social Movement Studies* 11, no. 3–4 (2012): 309–19. https://doi.org/10.1080/14742837.2012.708830.

——. "Introduction to 'Reshaping the World: Rethinking Borders.'" *Social Sciences* 9, no. 11 (2020): art. 214. https://doi.org/10.3390/socsci9110214.

——. "Is the Border Safe? Border Residents' Perceptions of Crime and Security." *Contexts* (blog), September 5, 2016. https://contexts.org/blog/is-the-border-safe-border-residents-perceptions -of-crime-and-security/.

——. "Living in Limbo: Transnational Households, Remittances and Development." *International Migration* 51, no. s1 (2013): 13–35. https://doi.org/10.1111/j.1468-2435.2012.00745.x.

——. "Places of Stigma: Ghettos, Barrios and Banlieues." In *The Ghetto: Contemporary Global Issues and Controversies*, ed. Ray Hutchison and Bruce D. Haynes, 159–90. Boulder, CO: Westview Press, 2012.

——. *A Place to Call Home: Immigrant Exclusion and Urban Belonging in New York, Paris, and Barcelona*. Stanford, CA: Stanford University Press, 2018.

——. "Remittances." In *The Palgrave Dictionary of Transnational History*, ed. Akira Iriye and Pierre-Yves Saunier, 904–7. Basingstoke, UK: Palgrave Macmillan, 2009.

——. "Review of Michael Dear's *Why Walls Won't Work*: Repairing the US-Mexico Divide." *AAG Review of Books* 3, no. 3 (2015): 125–27.

——. "Transnationalism in the Lives of Migrants: The Relevance of Znaniecki's Work to Understand Contemporary Migrant Life." In *Contemporary Migrations in the Humanistic Coefficient Perspective: Florian Znaniecki's Thought in Today's Science*, ed. Jacek Kubera and Łukasz Skoczylas. Frankfurt: Peter Lang, 2017.

——. "Understanding Inequality, Migration, Race, and Ethnicity from a Relational Perspective." In *Immigration and Categorical Inequality: Migration to the City and the Birth of Race and Ethnicity*, ed. Ernesto Castañeda. New York: Routledge, 2018.

——. "Urban Contexts and Immigrant Organizations: Differences in New York, El Paso, Paris, and Barcelona." *Annals of the American Academy of Political and Social Science* 690, no. 1 (2020): 117–35. https://doi.org/10.1177/0002716220938043.

——. "Why the Number of Encounters at the Southern U.S. Border Does Not Mean What the GOP Says It Means." *The Conversation*, November 8, 2022. https://theconversation.com /why-the-number-of-encounters-at-the-southern-u-s-border-does-not-mean-what-the -gop-says-it-means-191144.

Castañeda, Ernesto, and Lesley Buck. "A Family of Strangers: Transnational Parenting and the Consequences of Family Separation due to Undocumented Migration." In *Hidden Lives and Human Rights in America: Understanding the Controversies and Tragedies of Undocumented Immigration*, ed. Lois Ann Lorentzen. Santa Barbara, CA: Praeger, 2014.

——. "Remittances, Transnational Parenting, and the Children Left Behind: Economic and Psychological Implications." *Latin Americanist* 55, no. 4 (2011): 85–110. https://doi.org/10.1111/j.1557 -203X.2011.01136.x.

Castañeda, Ernesto, Edgar Aguilar, and Natalie Turkington. 2024. "Migration as a Driver of Economic Growth: Increasing Productivity and Filling the Labor Gaps." Immigration Lab and CLALS. Working paper Series #47. February 26. https://papers.ssrn.com/sol3/papers.cfm ?abstract_id=4740925.

Castañeda, Ernesto, and Casey Chiappetta. "Border Residents' Perceptions of Crime and Security in El Paso, Texas." *Social Sciences* 9, no. 3 (2020): art. 24.

Castañeda, Ernesto, Michael Danielson, and Jayesh Rathod. "Fortress North America: Theorizing a Regional Approach to Migration Management." In *North American Regionalism: Stagnation, Decline, or Renewal?*, ed. Eric Hershberg and Eric Long. Albuquerque: University of New Mexico Press, 2023.

Castañeda, Ernesto, Luis Rúben Díaz-Cepeda, and Kara Andrade. "Social Movements in Contemporary Mexico." In *Social Movements, 1768–2018*, ed. Charles Tilly, Ernesto Castañeda, and Lesley J. Wood, 99–127. 4th ed. New York: Routledge, 2020.

Castañeda, Ernesto, and Josiah M. Heyman. "Is the Southwestern Border Really Unsafe?" Scholars Strategy Network, 2012. http://www.scholarsstrategynetwork.org/sites/default/files/ssn_basic_facts_castaneda_and_heymann_on_border_safety.pdf.

Castañeda, Ernesto, and Daniel Jenks. "January 6th and De-democratization in the United States." *Social Sciences* 12, no. 4 (2023): art. 238. https://doi.org/10.3390/socsci12040238.

——. *Reunited: Family Separation and Central American Youth Migration*. New York: Russell Sage Foundation, 2024.

Castañeda, Ernesto, Daniel Jenks, Jessica Chaikof, Carina Cione, SteVon Felton, Isabella Goris, Lesley Buck, and Eric Hershberg. "Symptoms of PTSD and Depression Among Central American Immigrant Youth." *Trauma Care* 1, no. 2 (2021): 99–118. https://doi.org/10.3390/traumacare1020010.

Castañeda, Ernesto, Maria Cristina Morales, and Olga Ochoa. "Transnational Behavior in Comparative Perspective: The Relationship Between Immigrant Integration and Transnationalism in New York, El Paso, and Paris." *Comparative Migration Studies* 2, no. 3 (2014): 305–33. https://doi.org/10.5117/CMS2014.3.CAST.

Castañeda, Ernesto, and Amber Shemesh. "Overselling Globalization: The Misleading Conflation of Economic Globalization and Immigration, and the Subsequent Backlash." *Social Sciences* 9, no. 5 (2020): art. 61.

Castells, Manuel. *The Rise of the Network Society*. Vol. 1 of *The Information Age: Economy, Society, and Culture*. Oxford: Blackwell, 1986.

Castillo-Villar, Fernando Rey. "Destination Image Restoration Through Local Gastronomy: The Rise of Baja Med Cuisine in Tijuana." *International Journal of Culture, Tourism and Hospitality Research* 14, no. 4 (2020): 507–23. https://doi.org/10.1108/IJCTHR-03-2019-0054.

Castle, Stephen. "Of Brexit and Boris: What's Driving the Call for Scottish Independence." *New York Times*, May 8, 2021. https://www.nytimes.com/2021/05/08/world/europe/brexit-scotland-independence.html.

Castles, Stephen. *Ethnicity and Globalization: From Migrant Worker to Transnational Citizen*. London: SAGE, 2000. https://doi.org/10.4135/9781446217733.

Castles, Stephen, and Mark J. Miller. *The Age of Migration: International Population Movements in the Modern World*. 4th ed. New York: Guilford Press, 2009. http://www.loc.gov/catdir/toc/fy0903/2008040916.html.

Cave, Anthony. "Verify: Are Most Immigrants on Welfare?" Center for Law and Social Policy, August 16, 2017. https://www.clasp.org/press-room/news-clips/verify-are-most-immigrants-welfare.

Cengel, Katya. "The Reintegration of Rwandan Ex-Combatants." Al Jazeera, February 25, 2016. http://america.aljazeera.com/articles/2016/2/25/a-long-road-to-reintegration-for-rwandan-ex-combatants.html.

Cervantes, Andrea Gómez. "'Looking Mexican': Indigenous and Non-Indigenous Latina/o Immigrants and the Racialization of Illegality in the Midwest." *Social Problems* 68, no. 1 (2021): 100–117. https://academic.oup.com/socpro/article-abstract/68/1/100/5651092.

Cervantes-Soon, Claudia G. "A Critical Look at Dual Language Immersion in the New Latin@ Diaspora." *Bilingual Research Journal* 37, no. 1 (2014): 64–82. https://doi.org/10.1080/15235882 .2014.893267.

Chalabi, Mona. "What Happened to History's Refugees?" *Guardian*, July 25, 2013. https://www .theguardian.com/news/datablog/interactive/2013/jul/25/what-happened-history-refugees.

Chalfin, Aaron. "The Long-Run Effect of Mexican Immigration on Crime in US Cities: Evidence from Variation in Mexican Fertility Rates." *American Economic Review* 105, no. 5 (2015): 220–25.

Chami, Ralph, Adolfo Barajas, Thomas Cosimano, Connel Fullenkamp, M. Gapen, and P. Montiel. *Macroeconomic Consequences of Remittances*. IMF Occasional Paper 259. Washington, DC: International Monetary Fund, 2008.

Chan, Sucheng. "The Exclusion of Chinese Women, 1870–1943." In *Entry Denied: Exclusion and the Chinese Community in America, 1882–1943*, 95–147. Philadelphia: Temple University Press, 1991. https://www.lcsc.org/cms/lib/MN01001004/Centricity/Domain/81/TAH%202.pdf.

Chanda, Ishanee. "State Efforts to Help Immigrants Integrate." *National Conference of State Legislatures* 25, no. 45 (2017).

Chanda, Rupa, and Neha Vinod Betai. "Implications of Brexit for Skilled Migration from India to the UK." *Foreign Trade Review* 56, no. 3 (2021): 289–300. https://doi.org/10.1177 /00157325211012207.

Chavez, Julio-Cesar. "Frequent Crossers of U.S.-Mexico Border Fret Over Threatened Shutdown." Reuters, March 30, 2019. https://www.reuters.com/article/us-usa-immigration-trump-reaction -idUSKCN1RB0IW.

Chavez, Leo R. *The Latino Threat: Constructing Immigrants, Citizens, and the Nation*. Stanford, CA: Stanford University Press, 2008.

Cheatham, Amelia. "U.S. Detention of Child Migrants." Council on Foreign Relations, May 4, 2021. https://www.cfr.org/backgrounder/us-detention-child-migrants.

Cheathan, Amelia, Claire Felter, and Zachary Laub. "How the U.S. Patrols Its Borders." Council on Foreign Relations, April 12, 2021. https://www.cfr.org/backgrounder/how-us -patrols-its-borders.

Cheng, Amrit. "Justice for José Antonio, a 16-Year-Old Boy Killed by U.S. Border Patrol." ACLU, 2017. https://www.aclu.org/blog/immigrants-rights/ice-and-border-patrol-abuses /justice-jose-antonio-16-year-old-boy-killed-us.

Chernysheva, Liubov. "Ernesto Castañeda. A Place to Call Home: Immigrant Exclusion and Urban Belonging in New York, Paris, and Barcelona. Stanford, CA: Stanford University Press, 2018." *Laboratorium: Russian Review of Social Research* 12, no. 1 (2020): 208–10. https:// doi.org/10.25285/2078-1938-2020-12-1-208-210.

Chomsky, Aviva. *Undocumented: How Immigration Became Illegal*. Boston: Beacon Press, 2014. https://www.amazon.com/Undocumented-How-Immigration-Became-Illegal/dp /0807001678.

Christensen, Karen, Shereen Hussein, and Mohamed Ismail. "Migrants' Decision-Process Shaping Work Destination Choice: The Case of Long-Term Care Work in the United Kingdom and Norway." *European Journal of Ageing* 14, no. 3 (2017): 219–32. https://doi.org/10.1007/s10433-016-0405-0.

Christmas, Christine N., and Gina G. Barker. "The Immigrant Experience: Differences in Acculturation, Intercultural Sensitivity, and Cognitive Flexibility Between the First and Second Generation of Latino Immigrants." *Journal of International and Intercultural Communication* 7, no. 3 (2014): 238–57. https://doi.org/10.1080/17513057.2014.929202.

Citizens Information. "The Habitual Residence Condition." July 29, 2020. https://www.citizens information.ie/en/social_welfare/irish_social_welfare_system/social_assistance_payments /residency_requirements_for_social_assistance_in_ireland.html.

Clifford, Anton C., Christopher M. Doran, and Komla Tsey. "A Systematic Review of Suicide Prevention Interventions Targeting Indigenous Peoples in Australia, United States, Canada and New Zealand." *BMC Public Health* 13, no. 1 (): art. 463. https://doi.org/10.1186/1471-2458-13-463.

Cocco, Federica, Jonathan Wheatly, Jane Pong, David Blood, and Ændrew Rininsland. "Remittances: The Hidden Engine of Globalisation." Financial Times, September 28, 2019. https://ig.ft.com/remittances-capital-flow-emerging-markets/.

Cohen, Elizabeth F. *Illegal*. New York: Basic Books, 2020.

Cohen, Jeffrey H. "Migration, Remittances, and Household Strategies." *Annual Review of Anthropology* 40 (2011): 103–14.

Cohen, Ronnie. "Undocumented Immigrants Less Likely to Be Arrested for Drugs, Alcohol." Reuters, August 8, 2017. https://www.reuters.com/article/us-health-crime-immigrants /undocumented-immigrants-less-likely-to-be-arrested-for-drugs-alcohol-idUSKBN1AO2EC.

Coleman, David. "A Demographic Rationale for Brexit." *Population and Development Review* 42, no. 4 (2016): 681–92.

Coleman, Kevin. *A Camera in the Garden of Eden: The Self-Forging of a Banana Republic*. Austin: University of Texas Press, 2016.

Coll, Steve. "When ICE Tries to Deport Americans, Who Defends Them?" *New Yorker*, March 21, 2018. https://www.newyorker.com/news/daily-comment/when-ice-tries-to-deport-americans -who-defends-them.

Community College Consortium for Immigrant Education. "CCCIE Community College Consortium for Immigrant Education," 2015. https://www.presidentsalliance.org/press /community-college-consortium-for-immigrant-education-integrates-key-resources-and -initiatives-into-the-presidents-alliance/.

Confederation of British Industry. *Open and Controlled: A New Approach to Immigration After Brexit*. August 2018. https://www.cbi.org.uk/media/1230/open-and-controlled.pdf.

Conservative Home. "Boris Johnson's Speech on the EU Referendum." May 9, 2016. https://www .conservativehome.com/parliament/2016/05/boris-johnsons-speech-on-the-eu-referendum -full-text.html.

Contreras, Russell. "FBI Stats Show Border Cities Are Among the Safest." Axios, December 1, 2020. https://www.axios.com/border-cities-safest-fbi-data-4133476d-5056-477e-9194-a09169 2045a9.html.

Conway, Dennis, and Jeffrey H. Cohen. "Consequences of Migration and Remittances for Mexican Transnational Communities." *Economic Geography* 74, no. 1 (1998): 26–44.

Cooray, Arusha. "Who Remits? An Examination of Emigration by Education Level and Gender." *World Economy* 37, no. 10 (2014): 1441–53. https://doi.org/10.1111/twec.12154.

Copp, Tara. "2,100 Mostly Unarmed Guard Troops on Border as Trump Vows to Send More to Stop Migrant Caravan." *Military Times*, October 23, 2018. https://www.militarytimes.com /news/your-military/2018/10/23/2000-unarmed-guard-troops-on-border-as-trump-vows -to-send-more-to-stop-migrant-caravan/.

Cornelius, Wayne A. "Controlling 'Unwanted' Immigration: Lessons from the United States, 1993–2004." *Journal of Ethnic and Migration Studies* 31, no. 4 (2005): 775–94. https://doi.org /10.1080/13691830500110017.

——. "Death at the Border: Efficacy and Unintended Consequences of US Immigration Control Policy." *Population and Development Review* 27 (December 1, 2001): 661–85. https://doi.org /10.1111/j.1728-4457.2001.00661.x.

——. "My Odyssey." *Forum for Social Economics* 51, no. 2 (2020): 5–10.

Correnti, Madison. "Outsourcing Overseas and Its Effect on the U.S. Economy." National Customs Brokers & Forwarders Association of America. Accessed August 31, 2021. https://www .ncbfaa.org/Scripts/4Disapi.dll/4DCGI/cms/review.html?Action=CMS_Document&DocID =14050&MenuKey=pubs.

Cortina, Adela. *Aporophobia: Why We Reject the Poor Instead of Helping Them*. Princeton, NJ: Princeton University Press, 2022.

Cottam, Martha L., and Otwin Marenin. "The Management of Border Security in NAFTA: Imagery, Nationalism, and the War on Drugs." *International Criminal Justice Review* 15, no. 1 (2005): 5–37. https://doi.org/10.1177%2F1057567705275669.

Coulter, Kiera, Samantha Sabo, Daniel Martínez, Katelyn Chisholm, Kelsey Gonzalez, Sonia Bass Zavala, Edrick Villalobos, Diego Garcia, Taylor Levy, and Jeremy Slack. "A Study and Analysis of the Treatment of Mexican Unaccompanied Minors by Customs and Border Protection." *Journal on Migration and Human Security* 8, no. 2 (2020): 96–110. https://doi.org /10.1177/2331502420915898.

Cowell, Allen. "After Coordinated Bombs, London Is Stunned, Bloodied and Stoic." *New York Times*, 2005. https://www.nytimes.com/2005/07/07/international/europe/after-coordinated -bombs-london-is-stunned-bloodied-and.html.

CQ Press. "City Crime Rankings 2013." 2013. http://os.cqpress.com/citycrime/2012/City Crime2013_CityCrimeRankingsFactSheet.pdf.

Crawley, Heaven, and Dimitris Skleparis. "Refugees, Migrants, Neither, Both: Categorical Fetishism and the Politics of Bounding in Europe's 'Migration Crisis.' " *Journal of Ethnic and Migration Studies* 44, no. 1 (2018): 48–64. https://doi.org/10.1080/1369183X.2017.1348224.

Cross, David. "El Paso Police Release Murder Statistics from 1960 to 2018." KFOX14, January 16, 2019. https://kfoxtv.com/news/local/police-murders-in-el-paso-see-slight-increase-after-steel -border-fence-construction.

Croucher, Stephen M. "Integrated Threat Theory and Acceptance of Immigrant Assimilation: An Analysis of Muslim Immigration in Western Europe." *Communication Monographs* 80, no. 1 (2013): 46–62. https://doi.org/10.1080/03637751.2012.739704.

Cruz, Melissa. "Border Towns Are Among the Safest in the United States." Immigration Impact, February 12, 2019. https://immigrationimpact.com/2019/02/12/border-towns-safest-in-united -states/#.YSESHtNKj_Q.

Czaika, Mathias, and Hein de Haas. "The Globalization of Migration: Has the World Become More Migratory?" *International Migration Review* 48, no. 2 (2014): 283–323. https://doi.org /10.1111/imre.12095.

Dagilytė, Egle. "Brexit and Benefits: Why Leaving the EU Won't Solve Britain's Migration Issues." *Conversation*, June 21, 2016. https://theconversation.com/brexit-and-benefits-why-leaving -the-eu-wont-solve-britains-migration-issues-60916.

Dagilytė, Egle, and Margaret Greenfields. "United Kingdom Welfare Benefit Reforms in 2013–2014: Roma Between the Pillory, the Precipice and the Slippery Slope." *Journal of Social Welfare and Family Law* 37, no. 4 (2015): 476–95. https://doi.org/10.1080/09649069.2015 .1121954.

Dalgard, Odd Steffen, and Suraj Bahadur Thapa. "Immigration, Social Integration and Mental Health in Norway, with Focus on Gender Differences." *Clinical Practice and Epidemiology in Mental Health* 3, no. 1 (2007): art. 24. https://doi.org/10.1186/1745-0179-3-24.

Daoud, Annette M., and Alice M. L. Quiocho. "I Can't See You If I Don't Know You: How Students Create Inequality." *Multicultural Perspectives* 7, no. 4 (2005): 3–12. https://doi.org /10.1207/s15327892mcp0704_2.

Dávila, Liv T. "Language and Opportunity in the 'Land of Opportunity': Latina Immigrants' Reflections on Language Learning and Professional Mobility." *Journal of Hispanic Higher Education* 7, no. 4 (2008): 356–70. https://doi.org/10.1177/1538192708321652.

Davis, Rochelle. "Syria's Refugee Crisis." In *Great Decisions 2015*, 65–76. New York: Foreign Policy Association, 2015.

Dear, Michael J. "5 Problems 'the Wall' Won't Solve." *Politico*, February 28, 2017. https://www .politico.com/magazine/story/2017/02/trump-wall-mexico-problems-immigration-214837.

——. *Why Walls Won't Work: Repairing the US-Mexico Divide*. New York: Oxford University Press, 2013.

Deeds, Colin, and Scott Whiteford. "The Social and Economic Costs of Trump's Wall." *Voices of Mexico*, no. 102 (2016): 5.

De Genova, Nicholas. "The Legal Production of Mexican/Migrant 'Illegality.'" *Latino Studies* 2004, no. 2 (2004): 160–85.

de Graauw, Els. "Rolling Out the Welcome Mat: State and City Immigrant Affairs Offices in the United States," *IdeAs* 6 (2015) December 2015. http://journals.openedition.org/ideas/1293; DOI: https://doi.org/10.4000/ideas.1293.

De Gregorio, José, and Jong-Wha Lee. "Education and Income Inequality: New Evidence from Cross-Country Data." *Review of Income and Wealth* 48, no. 3 (2002): 395–416. https://doi.org /10.1111/1475-4991.00060.

DeKeyser, Robert, and Jenifer Larson-Hall. "What Does the Critical Period Really Mean?" In *Handbook of Bilingualism: Psycholinguistic Approaches*, ed. Judith F. Kroll and Annette M. B. de Groot. New York: Oxford University Press, 2009.

De León, Jason. *The Land of Open Graves: Living and Dying on the Migrant Trail*. Oakland: University of California Press, 2015.

Deloitte Global. "Saudi Arabia Highlights 2020," 2020. https://pdf4pro.com/fullscreen/saudi -arabia-highlights-2020-deloitte-74441c3.html.

Dettlaff, Alan J., Ilze Earner, and Susan D. Phillips. "Latino Children of Immigrants in the Child Welfare System: Prevalence, Characteristics, and Risk." *Children and Youth Services Review* 31, no. 7 (2009): 775–83. https://doi.org/10.1016/j.childyouth.2009.02.004.

Dietz, Joshua, Bulin Li, and Ernesto Castañeda. "Keeping in Motion or Staying Put: Internal Migration in the United States and China." *Societies* 13, no. 7 (July 2023): art. 162. https://doi.org /10.3390/soc13070162.

Dinan, Desmond, Neill Nugent, and William E. Paterson. *The European Union in Crisis*. New York: Macmillan International, 2017.

Dombey, Norman. "Brexit, Scotland and the UN Security Council." *Survival* 62, no. 6 (2020): 103–12. https://doi.org/10.1080/00396338.2020.1851089.

Domínguez, Jorge I., and Rafael Fernández de Castro. *The United States and Mexico: Between Partnership and Conflict*. 2nd ed. New York: Routledge, 2009.

Donato, Katharine M., Jorge Durand, and Douglas S. Massey. "Stemming the Tide? Assessing the Deterrent Effects of the Immigration Reform and Control Act." *Demography* 29, no. 2 (1992): 139–57. https://doi.org/10.2307/2061724.

Donnan, Shawn, and Lauren Leatherby. "Globalization Isn't Dying, It's Just Evolving." Bloomberg, July 23, 2019. https://www.bloomberg.com/graphics/2019-globalization/.

Dowding, Jillian, and Farinaz Razi. "A Call to Action: Leading the Way to Successful Immigrant Integration." In *Our Diverse Cities*, ed. J. S. Frideres, 163–68. Toronto: Metropolis, 2006.

Dowling, Jonathan Xavier, and Julie A. Inda, eds. *Governing Immigration Through Crime: A Reader*. Stanford, CA: Stanford University Press, 2013.

Dowling, Julie A., Christopher G. Ellison, and David L. Leal. "Who Doesn't Value English? Debunking Myths About Mexican Immigrants' Attitudes Toward the English Language." *Social Science Quarterly* 93, no. 2 (2012): 356–78.

Duany, Jorge. "To Send or Not to Send: Migrant Remittances in Puerto Rico, the Dominican Republic, and Mexico." *Annals of the American Academy of Political and Social Science* 630, no. 1 (2010): 205–23. https://doi.org/10.1177/0002716210368111.

Dunin-Wascowicz, Roch. "The Referendums of 1975 and 2016 Illustrate the Continuity and Change in British Euroscepticism." *LSE Brexit* (blog), July 31, 2017. https://blogs.lse.ac.uk/brexit/2017/07/31/the-referendums-of-1975-and-2016-illustrate-the-continuity-and-change-in-british-euroscepticism/.

Dunn, Timothy J. *Blockading the Border and Human Rights: The El Paso Operation That Remade Immigration Enforcement*. Austin: University of Texas Press, 2009.

——. *The Militarization of the U.S.-Mexico Border, 1978–1992: Low-Intensity Conflict Doctrine Comes Home*. Austin: CMAS Books, University of Texas at Austin, 1996.

Durand, Jorge, Emilio A. Parrado, and Douglas S. Massey. "Migradollars and Development: A Reconsideration of the Mexican Case." *International Migration Review* 30, no. 2 (1996): 423–44.

Dustmann, Christian, and Tommaso Frattini. "The Fiscal Effects of Immigration to the UK." *Economic Journal* 124, no. 580 (2014): F593–643. https://doi.org/10.1111/ecoj.12181.

Eagly, Ingrid V., and Steven Shafer. "A National Study of Access to Counsel in Immigration Court." *University of Pennsylvania Law Review* 164, no. 1 (2015): 1–91.

Ebaugh, Helen Rose, and Janet Saltzman Chafetz. "Dilemmas of Language in Immigrant Congregations: The Tie That Binds or the Tower of Babel?" *Review of Religious Research* 41, no. 4 (2000): 432–52. https://doi.org/10.2307/3512314.

Economist. "The Third Wave of Globalisation May Be the Hardest." November 19, 2016. https://www.economist.com/books-and-arts/2016/11/19/the-third-wave-of-globalisation-may-be-the-hardest.

Edgington, Tom, and Tamara Kovacevic. "Brexit: What's the Northern Ireland Protocol?" BBC News, 2 February 2024. https://www.bbc.com/news/explainers-53724381.

Edwards, Frank, Michael H. Esposito, and Hedwig Lee. "Risk of Police-Involved Death by Race /Ethnicity and Place, United States, 2012–2018." *American Journal of Public Health* 108, no. 9 (2018): 1241–48. https://doi.org/10.2105/ajph.2018.304559.

Ek, Lucila D., Patricia Sánchez, and Patricia D. Quijada Cerecer. "Linguistic Violence, Insecurity, and Work: Language Ideologies of Latina/o Bilingual Teacher Candidates in Texas." *International Multilingual Research Journal* 7, no. 3 (2013): 197–219. https://doi.org/10.1080 /19313152.2013.768144.

El Paso Times. "El Paso Ranked in 'Top 10 Safest Metro Cities' in U.S." April 24, 2019. https://www .elpasotimes.com/story/news/local/el-paso/2019/04/24/el-paso-ranked-top-10-safest-metro -cities-u-s/3556070002/.

English Language Unity Act of 2019. H.R. 997, 116th Cong. (2019–2020). https://www.congress .gov/bill/116th-congress/house-bill/997/text.

Eriksson, Lindsay, and Melinda Taylor. "The Environmental Impacts of the Border Wall Between Texas and Mexico." University of Texas School of Law. Accessed September 2, 2021. https://law.utexas.edu/humanrights/borderwall/analysis/briefing-The-Environmental -Impacts-of-the-Border-Wall.pdf.

Escamilla, Kathy. "The False Dichotomy Between ESL and Transitional Bilingual Education Programs: Issues That Challenge All of Us." *Educational Considerations* 26 (April 1, 1999). https://doi.org/10.4148/0146-9282.1343.

Eschbach, Karl, Jacqueline Hagan, Nestor Rodriguez, Rubén Hernández-León, and Stanley Bailey. "Death at the Border." *International Migration Review* 33, no. 2 (1999): 430–54. https://doi.org/10.1177/019791839903300206.

Escribà-Folch, Abel, Covadonga Meseguer, and Joseph Wright. "Remittances and Democratization." *International Studies Quarterly* 59, no. 3 (2015): 571–86. https://doi.org/10.1111/isqu.12180.

Espenshade, Thomas J., and Haishan Fu. "An Analysis of English-Language Proficiency Among U.S. Immigrants." *American Sociological Review* 62, no. 2 (1997): 288–305. https://doi.org /10.2307/2657305.

Espinosa, Kristin E., and Douglas S. Massey. "Determinants of English Proficiency Among Mexican Migrants to the United States." *International Migration Review* 31, no. 1 (1997): 28–50. https://doi.org/10.1177/019791839703100102.

Espinoza-Kulick, Mario Alberto V., Maura Fennelly, Kevin Beck, and Ernesto Castañeda. "Ethnic Enclaves." *Oxford Bibliographies in Sociology*. Ed. Lynette Spillman. New York: Oxford University Press, 2021.

Esses, Victoria M., Leah K. Hamilton, and Danielle Gaucher. "The Global Refugee Crisis: Empirical Evidence and Policy Implications for Improving Public Attitudes and Facilitating Refugee Resettlement." *Social Issues and Policy Review* 11, no. 1 (2017): 78–123. https://doi.org /10.1111/sipr.12028.

European Commission. "Excess Mortality—Statistics." Eurostat, September 13, 2021. https:// ec.europa.eu/eurostat/statistics-explained/index.php?title=Excess_mortality_-_statistics.

——. "First Population Estimates: EU Population in 2020: Almost 448 Million." Eurostat news release, 2020. https://ec.europa.eu/eurostat/documents/2995521/11081093/3-10072020-AP-EN .pdf/d2f799bf-4412-05cc-a357-7b49b93615f1.

——. "First Population Estimates: EU Population Up to 508.2 Million at 1 January 2015." Eurostat news release, 2015. https://ec.europa.eu/eurostat/documents/2995521/6903510/3-10072015 -AP-EN.pdf/d2bfb01f-6ac5-4775-8a7e-7b104c1146d0.

——. "Governance of Migrant Integration in Sweden." European Web Site on Integration, September 7, 2021. https://ec.europa.eu/migrant-integration/governance/sweden.

European Union. Treaty of Amsterdam Amending the Treaty on European Union, the Treaties Establishing the European Communities and Certain Related Acts, 1997. https://eur-lex.europa.eu/legal-content/EN/TXT/?uri=CELEX:11997D/TXT.

Ewing, Walter, Daniel E. Martínez, and Rúben G. Rumbaut. *The Criminalization of Immigration in the United States.* Washington, DC: American Immigration Council, July 13, 2015. https://www.americanimmigrationcouncil.org/research/criminalization-immigration-united-states.

Fagan, Jeffrey, and Garth Davies. "Street Stops and Broken Windows: Terry, Race, and Disorder in New York City." *Fordham Urban Law Journal* 28, no. 2 (2000): 457–504.

Faini, Riccardo. "Remittances and the Brain Drain: Do More Skilled Migrants Remit More?" *World Bank Economic Review* 21, no. 2 (2007): 177–91.

Fang, Marina. "GOP Candidates Say Immigrants Don't Learn English, but Report Proves Them Wrong." HuffPost, September 23, 2015. https://www.huffpost.com/entry/gop-immigration-learning-english_n_56o315ace4bofde8bod124ea.

Fanning, Rhonda. "One Man Thinks El Paso's Long-Distance Relationship with Texas Should End in Divorce." KUT Radio, October 12, 2018. https://www.kut.org/texas/2018-10-12/one-man-thinks-el-pasos-long-distance-relationship-with-texas-should-end-in-divorce.

Feinstein, Jessica, and Jackson Lewis P.C. "Dropping Public Charge Rule, DHS Announces Return to Previous Policy to Determine Admissibility." JD Supra, March 12, 2021. https://www.jdsupra.com/legalnews/dropping-public-charge-rule-dhs-3376831/.

Felbab-Brown, Vanda. "The Wall: The Real Costs of a Barrier Between the United States and Mexico." Brookings Institution, August 22, 2017. https://www.brookings.edu/essay/the-wall-the-real-costs-of-a-barrier-between-the-united-states-and-mexico/.

Fennelly, Kathrine, and Nicole Palasz. "English Language Proficiency of Immigrants and Refugees in the Twin Cities Metropolitan Area." *International Migration* 41, no. 5 (2003): 93–125. https://doi.org/10.1111/j.0020-7985.2003.00262.x.

Ferraro, Vincent. "Immigration and Crime in the New Destinations, 2000–2007: A Test of the Disorganizing Effect of Migration." *Journal of Quantitative Criminology* 32, no. 1 (2016): 23–45. https://doi.org/10.1007/s10940-015-9252-y.

Fijnaut, Cyrille. "The Refugee Crisis: The End of Schengen?" In *The Containment of Organised Crime and Terrorism*, 825–41. Leiden, Netherlands: Brill Nijhoff, 2016. https://doi.org/10.1163/9789004281943_047.

Fillmore, Lily Wong. "When Learning a Second Language Means Losing the First." *Early Childhood Research Quarterly* 6, no. 3 (1991): 323–46. https://doi.org/10.1016/S0885-2006(05)80059-6.

Finch, Brian Karl, Jason D. Boardman, Bohdan Kolody, and William Armando Vega. "Contextual Effects of Acculturation on Perinatal Substance Exposure Among Immigrant and Native-Born Latinas." *Social Science Quarterly* 81, no. 1 (2000): 421–39.

Finnegan, William. "The Deportation Machine." *New Yorker*, April 22, 2013. https://www.newyorker.com/magazine/2013/04/29/the-deportation-machine.

Fix, Michael E., Randy Capps, and Neeraj Kaushal. "Immigrants and Welfare: Overview." In *Immigrants and Welfare: The Impact of Welfare Reform on America's Newcomers*, ed. Michael E. Fix, 1–36. New York: Russell Sage Foundation, 2009. https://www.jstor.org/stable/10.7758/9781610446228.

Fix, Michael E., and Ron Haskins. "Welfare Benefits for Non-citizens." Brookings Institution, February 2, 2002. https://www.brookings.edu/research/welfare-benefits-for-non-citizens/.

Flagg, Anna. "Is There a Connection Between Undocumented Immigrants and Crime?" Marshall Project, May 13, 2019. https://www.themarshallproject.org/2019/05/13/is-there-a-connection-between-undocumented-immigrants-and-crime.

Flores, Esteban. "Two Countries and One Headless Body: An Analysis of Border Corruption." *Harvard International Review* 38, no. 2 (2017): 10–12.

Flores, Nelson, and Jonathan Rosa. "Undoing Appropriateness: Raciolinguistic Ideologies and Language Diversity in Education." *Harvard Educational Review* 85, no. 2 (2015): 149–71. https://doi.org/10.17763/0017-8055.85.2.149.

Flores, Nelson, Amelia Tseng, and Nicholas Subtirelu. *Bilingualism for All?* Bristol, UK: Multilingual Matters, 2020.

Flores, Rene. "Living in the Eye of the Storm: How Did Hazleton's Restrictive Immigration Ordinance Affect Local Interethnic Relations?" *American Behavioral Scientist* 58, no. 13 (2014): 1743–63.

Flores, René D., and Ariela Schachter. "Who Are the 'Illegals'? The Social Construction of Illegality in the United States." *American Sociological Review* 83, no. 5 (2018): 839–68. https://doi.org/10.1177/0003122418794635.

Flores Nández, Nancy. *La Farsa: Detrás de la Guerra Contra el Narco*. Mexico City: Oceano, 2012.

Flórez, Karen R., Kathryn Pitkin Derose, Joshua Breslau, Beth Ann Griffin, Ann C. Haas, David E. Kanouse, Brian D. Stucky, and Malcolm V. Williams. "Acculturation and Drug Use Stigma Among Latinos and African Americans: An Examination of a Church-Based Sample." *Journal of Immigrant and Minority Health* 17, no. 6 (2015): 1607–14. https://doi.org/10.1007/s10903-015-0161-9.

Flynn, Meagan. "U.S. Citizen Freed After Nearly a Month in Immigration Custody, Family Says." *Washington Post*, June 24, 2019. https://www.washingtonpost.com/nation/2019/07/23/francisco-erwin-galicia-ice-cpb-us-citizen-detained-texas/.

Forster-Cox, Susan C., Thenral Mangadu, Benjamín Jacquez, and Lynne Fullerton. "The Environmental Health/Home Safety Education Project: A Successful and Practical U.S.-Mexico Border Initiative." *Health Promotion Practice* 11, no. 3 (2010): 325–31. https://doi.org/10.1177/1524839909341026.

Fortuny, Karina, Randy Capps, Ajay Chaudry, and Margaret Simms. "The Integration of Immigrants and Their Families in Maryland: A Look at Children of Immigrants and Their Families in Maryland." Urban Institute, June 2010. https://folio.iupui.edu/handle/10244/835.

Fought, Carmen. *Chicano English in Context*. New York: Palgrave Macmillan, 2003.

Fox, Cybelle. *Three Worlds of Relief: Race, Immigration, and the American Welfare State from the Progressive Era to the New Deal*. Princeton, NJ: Princeton University Press, 2012. https://doi.org/10.2307/j.ctt7sq50.

Fox, Justin. "'Broken Windows' Theory Was Right . . . About the Windows." *Lowell Sun*, October 20, 2019. https://www.lowellsun.com/2019/10/20/broken-windows-theory-was-right-about-the-windows/.

Frank-Vitale, Amelia. "Leave If You're Able: Migration, Survival, and the Everydayness of Deportation in Honduras." PhD diss., University of Michigan, 2021.

Frazee, Gretchen, and Joshua Barajas. "Trump Says Walls Work. It's Much More Complicated." *PBS News Hour*, January 9, 2019. https://www.pbs.org/newshour/nation/trump-says-walls-work -its-much-more-complicated.

Frej, Willa. "One Year Since Trump's First Travel Ban, Many Refugees Left with Only Hellish Options." HuffPost, January 27, 2018. https://www.huffpost.com/entry/one-year-travel-ban -refugees_n_5a65efa5e4b002283004bdaf.

Frey, William H. "Census 2020: First Results Show Near Historically Low Population Growth and a First-Ever Congressional Seat Loss for California." Brookings Institution, April 26, 2021. https://www.brookings.edu/research/census-2020-data-release/.

——. "Neighborhood Segregation Persists for Black, Latino or Hispanic, and Asian Americans." Brookings Institution, April 6, 2021. https://www.brookings.edu/research/neighborhood -segregation-persists-for-black-latino-or-hispanic-and-asian-americans/.

Fuentes, César M., and Sergio Peña. "Globalization and Its Effects on the Urban Socio-spatial Structure of a Transfrontier Metropolis: El Paso, TX–Ciudad Juárez, Chih.–-Sunland-Park, NM." In *Cities and Citizenship at the U.S.-Mexico Border: The Paso Del Norte Metropolitan Region*, ed. Kathleen Staudt, César M. Fuentes, and Julia E. Monárrez Fragoso, 93–117. New York: Palgrave Macmillan, 2010. https://doi.org/10.1057/9780230112919.

Galli, Chiara. "Humanitarian Capital: How Lawyers Help Immigrants Use Suffering to Claim Membership in the Nation-State." *Journal of Ethnic and Migration Studies* 46, no. 11 (2020): 2181–98. https://doi.org/10.1080/1369183X.2019.1582325.

Gamboa, Suzanne. "Income Test Under Trump Proposal Places Tougher Hurdles for Families to Get Green Cards." NBC News, October 10, 2018. https://www.nbcnews.com/news/latino /income-test-under-trump-proposal-places-tougher-hurdles-families-get-n917931.

Gándara, Patricia C., and Ursula S. Aldana. "Who's Segregated Now? Latinos, Language, and the Future of Integrated Schools." *Educational Administration Quarterly* 50, no. 5 (2014): 735–48. https://doi.org/10.1177/0013161X14549957.

Gans, Herbert J. "Symbolic Ethnicity: The Future of Ethnic Groups and Cultures in America." *Ethnic and Racial Studies* 2, no. 1 (1979): 1–20. https://doi.org/10.1080/01419870.1979.9993248.

Garavoglia, Matteo. "What Brexit Means for Migration Policy." Brookings Institution, September 26, 2016. https://www.brookings.edu/blog/order-from-chaos/2016/09/26/what -brexit-means-for-migration-policy/.

Garcia, Alexis. "El Paso, TX." U.S. News and World Report, 2020. https://realestate.usnews .com/places/texas/el-paso.

Garcia, Samuel. "What Happens to Immigrants Who Face Addiction." Forbes, October 15, 2018. https://www.forbes.com/sites/samuelgarcia/2018/10/15/what-happens-to-immigrants -who-face-addiction/?sh=62dadbb84745.

Gardner-Chloros, Penelope. "Code-Switching in Community, Regional and National Repertoires: The Myth of the Discreteness of Linguistic Systems." In *One Speaker, Two Languages: Cross-Disciplinary Perspectives on Code-Switching*, ed. Lesley Milroy and Pieter Muysken, 68–89. Cambridge: Cambridge University Press, 1995. https://doi.org/10.1017/CBO9780511620867.004.

Garrett, Jerry E, and Shannon Holcomb. "Meeting the Needs of Immigrant Students with Limited English Ability." *International Education* 35, no. 1 (2005): 49–64.

Garrett, Terence Michael. "The Security Apparatus, Federal Magistrate Courts, and Deten-tion Centers as Simulacra: The Effects of Trump's Zero Tolerance Policy on Migrants and

Refugees in the Rio Grande Valley." *Politics & Policy* 48, no. 2 (2020): 372–95. https://doi.org/10.1111/polp.12348.

Geddes, Andrew, and Peter Scholten. *The Politics of Migration and Immigration in Europe.* 2nd ed. London: SAGE, 2016. https://doi.org/10.4135/9781473982703.

Gee, Lisa Christensen, Matthew Gardner, Misha E. Hill, and Meg Wiehe. *Undocumented Immigrants' State & Local Tax Contributions.* Washington, DC: Institute on Taxation and Economic Policy, March 2017. https://itep.sfo2.digitaloceanspaces.com/ITEP-2017-Undocumented-Immigrants-State-and-Local-Contributions.pdf.

Gelatt, Julia. "The RAISE Act: Dramatic Change to Family Immigration, Less So for the Employment-Based System." Migration Policy Institute, August 4, 2017. https://www.migrationpolicy.org/news/raise-act-dramatic-change-family-immigration-less-so-employment-based-system.

Genesee, Fred, Kathryn Lindholm-Leary, William Saunders, and Donna Christian. "English Language Learners in U.S. Schools: An Overview of Research Findings," *Journal of Education for Students Placed at Risk* 10, no. 4 (November 2009). http://www.tandfonline.com/doi/abs/10.1207/s15327671espr1004_2.

Gerber, David A. "Caucasians Are Made and Not Born: How European Immigrants Became White People." *Reviews in American History* 27, no. 3 (1999): 437–43.

Gherson. "Family Reunion in the UK Post-Brexit." January 12, 2021. https://www.gherson.com/blog/family-reunion-uk-post-brexit.

Gibson, Carrie. *El Norte: The Epic and Forgotten Story of Hispanic North America.* New York: Grove Atlantic, 2020.

Gietel-Basten, Stuart. "Why Brexit? The Toxic Mix of Immigration and Austerity." *Population and Development Review* 42, no. 4 (2016): 673–80.

Giles, Chris. "The Effects of EU Migration on Britain in 5 Charts." Financial Times, September 18, 2018. https://www.ft.com/content/797f7b42-bb44-11e8-94b2-17176fbf93f5.

Glencross, Andrew. "Why a British Referendum on EU Membership Will Not Solve the Europe Question." *International Affairs* 91, no. 2 (2015): 303–17. https://doi.org/10.1111/1468-2346.12236.

Glied, Viktor, and Norbert Pap. "The 'Christian Fortress of Hungary'—The Anatomy of the Migration Crisis in Hungary." *Yearbook of Polish European Studies* 19 (2016): 133–49.

Golash-Boza, Tanya Maria. *Deported: Immigrant Policing, Disposable Labor, and Global Capitalism.* New York: New York University Press, 2015.

Golash-Boza, Tanya Maria, and Zulema Valdez. "Nested Contexts of Reception: Undocumented Students at the University of California, Central." *Sociological Perspectives* 61, no. 4 (2018): 535–52.

Gomez, Alan. "No . . . Immigrants Don't Commit More Crimes than U.S.-Born People." *USA Today*, August 23, 2018. https://www.pressreader.com/usa/usa-today-us-edition/20180823/281535111844709.

Gonzalez, Rosemary, and Christina U. Ayala-Alcantar. "Critical Caring: Dispelling Latino Stereotypes Among Preservice Teachers." *Journal of Latinos and Education* 7, no. 2 (2008): 129–43. https://doi.org/10.1080/15348430701828699.

Gonzalez O'Brien, Benjamin, Loren Collingwood, and Stephen Omar El-Khatib. "The Politics of Refuge: Sanctuary Cities, Crime, and Undocumented Immigration" 55, no. 1 (2017): 3–40.

Goodman, Adam. *The Deportation Machine: America's Long History of Expelling Immigrants.* Princeton, NJ: Princeton University Press, 2021.

Goodwin, Matthew J., and Oliver Heath. "The 2016 Referendum, Brexit and the Left Behind: An Aggregate-Level Analysis of the Result." *Political Quarterly* 87, no. 3 (2016): 323–32. https://doi.org/10.1111/1467-923X.12285.

Gordon, Milton Myron. *Assimilation in American Life: The Role of Race, Religion, and National Origins.* New York: Oxford University Press, 1964.

Gorman, Anna. "Immigrants' Children Grow Fluent in English, Study Says." *Los Angeles Times*, November 30, 2007. https://www.latimes.com/local/la-me-english30nov30-story.html.

Government of Ireland. "Habitual Residence Condition." September 3, 2019. https://www.gov.ie/en/publication/170e70-habitual-residence-condition/#exemption-from-the-habitual-residence-condition.

Gov.ie. "Operational Guidelines: For Deciding Officers and Designated Persons on the Determination of Habitual Residence." March 18, 2020. https://www.gov.ie/en/publication/fc9c5e-operational-guidelines-for-deciding-officers-on-the-determination-of/.

GOV.UK. "Apply to the EU Settlement Scheme (Settled and Pre-settled Status)." Accessed August 30, 2021. https://www.gov.uk/settled-status-eu-citizens-families/switch-from-presettled-status-to-settled-status.

——. "Living in Europe: Citizens' Rights If You Moved Before 1 January 2021." January 30, 2020. https://www.gov.uk/guidance/living-in-europe.

——. "The UK's Points-Based Immigration System: Policy Statement." February 19, 2020. https://www.gov.uk/government/publications/the-uks-points-based-immigration-system-policy-statement/the-uks-points-based-immigration-system-policy-statement.

Graauw, Els de. *Making Immigrant Rights Real: Nonprofits and the Politics of Integration in San Francisco.* Ithaca, NY: Cornell University Press, 2016.

Graauw, Els de, and Irene Bloemraad. "Working Together: Building Successful Policy and Program Partnerships for Immigrant Integration." *Journal on Migration and Human Security* 5, no. 1 (2017): 105–23.

Greenhill, Kelly M. "Open Arms Behind Barred Doors: Fear, Hypocrisy and Policy Schizophrenia in the European Migration Crisis." *European Law Journal* 22, no. 3 (2016): 317–32. https://doi.org/10.1111/eulj.12179.

Greenwald, Bruce C., and Judd Kahn. *Globalization: The Irrational Fear That Someone in China Will Take Your Job.* Hoboken, NJ: Wiley, 2008.

Greussing, Esther, and Hajo G. Boomgaarden. "Shifting the Refugee Narrative? An Automated Frame Analysis of Europe's 2015 Refugee Crisis." *Journal of Ethnic and Migration Studies* 43, no. 11 (2017): 1749–74. https://doi.org/10.1080/1369183X.2017.1282813.

Guárdia, Arnau. "How Brexit Vote Broke Down." *Politico*, June 24, 2016. https://www.politico.eu/article/graphics-how-the-uk-voted-eu-referendum-brexit-demographics-age-education-party-london-final-results/.

Gudrun Jensen, Tina, Kristina Weibel, and Kathrine Vitus. " 'There Is No Racism Here': Public Discourses on Racism, Immigrants and Integration in Denmark." *Patterns of Prejudice* 51, no. 1 (2017): 51–68. https://doi.org/10.1080/0031322X.2016.1270844.

Guerette, Rob T. "Immigration Policy, Border Security, and Migrant Deaths: An Impact Evaluation of Life-Saving Efforts Under the Border Safety Initiative." *Criminology & Public Policy* 6, no. 2 (2007): 245–66. https://doi.org/10.1111/j.1745-9133.2007.00433.x.

Gulland, Anne. "The Refugee Crisis: What Care Is Needed and How Can Doctors Help?" *BMJ* 351 (September 10, 2015): h4881. https://doi.org/10.1136/bmj.h4881.

Gündoğdu, Ayten. "Statelessness and the Right to Have Rights." In *Hannah Arendt*, ed. Patrick Hayden, 108–23. New York: Routledge, 2014.

Guo, Jeff. "The Biggest Ideas Underpinning the Anti-Immigration Movement Aren't Backed Up by Data." *Washington Post*, October 1, 2015. https://www.washingtonpost.com/news/wonk/wp/2015/10/01/these-common-beliefs-about-immigrants-are-all-wrong/.

Gusmano, Michael K., and Kieke G. H. Okma. "Population Aging and the Sustainability of the Welfare State." In "What Makes a Good Life in Late Life? Citizenship and Justice in Aging Societies." Supplement, *Hastings Center Report* 48, no. 53 (2018): S57–61. https://doi.org/10.1002/hast.915.

Gustafsson, Björn Anders. "Social Assistance Among Immigrants and Natives in Sweden." *International Journal of Manpower* 34, no. 2 (2013): 126–41. https://doi.org/10.1108/01437721311320654.

Gutierrez, Gabe. "Sent by Trump, Soldiers Arrive at Border as Migrant Caravan in Mexico Pushes North." NBC News, November 3, 2018. https://www.nbcnews.com/news/us-news/sent-trump-soldiers-arrive-border-migrant-caravan-pushes-north-n930751.

Gutiérrez-Romero, Roxana. "Estimating the Impact of Mexican Drug Cartels and Drug-Related Homicides on Crime and Perceptions of Safety." *Journal of Economic Geography* 16, no. 4 (2016): 941–73. https://doi.org/10.1093/jeg/lbv023.

Guttmacher Institute. "Regulating Insurance Coverage of Abortion." September 1, 2021. https://www.guttmacher.org/state-policy/explore/regulating-insurance-coverage-abortion.

Hadley, Craig, and Crystal Patil. "Perceived Discrimination Among Three Groups of Refugees Resettled in the USA: Associations with Language, Time in the USA, and Continent of Origin." *Journal of Immigrant and Minority Health* 11, no. 6 (2009): 505. https://doi.org/10.1007/s10903-009-9227-x.

Hagan, John, Ron Levi, and Ronit Dinovitzer. "The Symbolic Violence of the Crime-Immigration Nexus: Migrant Mythologies in the Americas." *Criminology & Public Policy* 7, no. 1 (2008): 95–112. https://doi.org/10.1111/j.1745-9133.2008.00493.x.

Hagan, John, and Alberto Palloni. "Sociological Criminology and the Mythology of Hispanic Immigration and Crime." *Social Problems* 46, no. 4 (1999): 617–32. https://doi.org/10.2307/3097078.

Haider, Steven J., Robert F. Schoeni, Yuhua Bao, and Caroline Danielson. "Immigrants, Welfare Reform, and the Economy." *Journal of Policy Analysis and Management* 23, no. 4 (2004): 745–64. https://doi.org/10.1177/000312240907400305.

Hakimzadeh, Shirin, and D'vera Cohn. "English Usage Among Hispanics in the United States." Pew Research Center, November 29, 2007. https://www.pewresearch.org/hispanic/2007/11/29/english-usage-among-hispanics-in-the-united-states/.

Hampton, Kathryn. "Zero Protection: How U.S. Border Enforcement Harms Migrant Safety and Health." Physicians for Human Rights, January 10, 2019. https://phr.org/our-work/resources/zero-protection-how-u-s-border-enforcement-harms-migrant-safety-and-health/.

Hansen, Jorgen, and Magnus Lofstrom. "Immigrant Assimilation and Welfare Participation: Do Immigrants Assimilate Into or out of Welfare?" *Journal of Human Resources* 38, no. 1 (2003): 74–98. https://doi.org/10.3368/jhr.XXXVIII.1.74.

Hao, Lingxin, and Yukio Kawano. "Immigrants' Welfare Use and Opportunity for Contact with Co-ethnics." *Demography* 38, no. 3 (2001): 375–89. https://doi.org/10.1353/dem.2001.0027.

Harder, Niklas, Lucila Figueroa, Rachel M. Gillum, Dominik Hangartner, David D. Laitin, and Jens Hainmueller. "Multidimensional Measure of Immigrant Integration." *Proceedings of the National Academy of Sciences* 115, no. 45 (2018): 11483–88. https://doi.org/10.1073/pnas.1808793115.

Harvard Law Review. "American Courts and the U.N. High Commissioner for Refugees: A Need for Harmony in the Face of a Refugee Crisis." 131, no. 1 (2018): 1399–1420.

Haskins, Ron. "Limiting Welfare Benefits for Noncitizens: Emergence of Compromises." In *Immigrants and Welfare: The Impact of Welfare Reform on America's Newcomers*, ed. Michael E. Fix, 39–68. New York: Russell Sage Foundation, 2009.https://www.jstor.org/stable/10.7758/9781610446228.

Hayes, Matthew. *Gringolandia: Lifestyle Migration Under Late Capitalism*. Minneapolis: University of Minnesota Press, 2018.

Heckmann, Friedrich, and Dominique Schnapper. *The Integration of Immigrants in European Societies: National Differences and Trends of Convergence*. Berlin: Walter de Gruyter, 2016.

Heimlich, Evan. "Acadians: History, Settlement Patterns, Internal Migration, Camps, Acculturation and Assimilation." World Culture Encyclopedia, 2022. https://www.everyculture.com/multi/A-Br/Acadians.html.

Henderson, David R. "Immigrant Remittances Are Private Foreign Aid." Hoover Institution, June 25, 2019. https://www.hoover.org/research/immigrant-remittances-are-private-foreign-aid.

Hernandez, Ester, and Susan Bibler Coutin. "Remitting Subjects: Migrants, Money and States." *Economy and Society* 35, no. 2 (2006): 185–208. https://doi.org/10.1080/03085140600635698.

Hernandez, Kelly Lytle. *Migra! A History of the U.S. Border Patrol*. Berkeley: University of California Press, 2010.

Herrington, Neil, and Jon Baselice. "One Way to Tank Markets and the U.S. Economy? Close the Border with Mexico." U.S. Chamber of Commerce, March 28, 2019. https://www.uschamber.com/series/above-the-fold/one-way-tank-markets-and-the-us-economy-close-the-border-mexico.

Hervik, Peter. "Xenophobia and Nativism." In *International Encyclopedia of the Social & Behavioral Sciences*, 25:796–801. 2nd ed. Oxford, UK: Elsevier, 2015. https://vbn.aau.dk/en/publications/xenophobia-and-nativism.

Heyman, Joe. "A Border That Divides. A Border That Joins." *Anthropology Now* 1, no. 3 (2009): 79–85.

——. "Constructing a Virtual Wall: Race and Citizenship in U.S.-Mexico Border Policing." *Journal of the Southwest* 50, no. 3 (2008): 305–33.

Hill, Laura. "English Proficiency of Immigrants." Public Policy Institute of California, March 2011. https://www.ppic.org/publication/english-proficiency-of-immigrants/.

Hirota, Hidetaka. *Expelling the Poor: Atlantic Seaboard States and the Nineteenth-Century Origins of American Immigration Policy*. New York: Oxford University Press, 2017.

Hirschfeld Davis, Julie. "Trump Calls Some Unauthorized Immigrants 'Animals' in Rant." *New York Times*, May 16, 2018. https://www.nytimes.com/2018/05/16/us/politics/trump-undocumented-immigrants-animals.html.

Hoban, Brennan. "Do Immigrants 'Steal' Jobs from American Workers?" Brookings Institution, August 24, 2017. https://www.brookings.edu/blog/brookings-now/2017/08/24/do-immigrants-steal-jobs-from-american-workers/.

Hobolt, Sara B. "The Brexit Vote: A Divided Nation, a Divided Continent." *Journal of European Public Policy* 23, no. 9 (2016): 1259–77. https://doi.org/10.1080/13501763.2016.1225785.

Holder, Sarah. "How Rule Changes About Public Benefits Could Affect Immigrants." Bloomberg CityLab, August 13, 2019. https://www.bloomberg.com/news/articles/2019-08-13/new-rules-to-scare-immigrants-off-public-services.

Holland, Steve, and Richard Cowan. "Backing Down, Trump Agrees to End Shutdown Without Border Wall Money." Reuters, January 25, 2019. https://www.reuters.com/article/us-usa-shutdown/backing-down-trump-agrees-to-end-shutdown-without-border-wall-money-idUSKCN1PJ126.

Holmes, Seth M. *Fresh Fruit, Broken Bodies: Migrant Farmworkers in the United States.* Berkeley: University of California Press, 2013.

——. " 'Is It Worth Risking Your Life?': Ethnography, Risk and Death on the U.S.-Mexico Border." *Social Science & Medicine* 99 (December 1, 2013): 153–61. https://doi.org/10.1016/j.socscimed.2013.05.029.

Holmes, Seth M., Ernesto Castañeda, Jeremy Geeraert, Heide Castañeda, Ursula Probst, Nina Zeldes, Sarah S. Willen et al. "Deservingness: Migration and Health in Social Context." *BMJ Global Health* 6, no. S1 (2021): e005107. https://doi.org/10.1136/bmjgh-2021-005107.

Holmes, Seth M., and Heide Castañeda. "Representing the 'European Refugee Crisis' in Germany and Beyond: Deservingness and Difference, Life and Death." *American Ethnologist* 43, no. 1 (2016): 12–24. https://doi.org/10.1111/amet.12259.

Horowitz, Juliana Menasce, Ruth Igielnik, and Rakesh Kochhar. "Trends in Income and Wealth Inequality." Pew Research Center, January 9, 2020. https://www.pewresearch.org/social-trends/2020/01/09/trends-in-income-and-wealth-inequality/.

Horton, Alex. "Trump Keeps Calling the Southern Border 'Very Dangerous.' It Is—but Not for Americans." *Washington Post*, January 20, 2018. https://www.washingtonpost.com/news/politics/wp/2018/01/17/trump-calls-the-u-s-mexico-border-extremely-dangerous-it-is-but-not-for-americans/.

Hovil, Lucy, and Zachary A. Lomo. "Forced Displacement and the Crisis of Citizenship in Africa's Great Lakes Region: Rethinking Refugee Protection and Durable Solutions." *Refuge* 31, no. 2 (2015): 39–50. https://refuge.journals.yorku.ca/index.php/refuge/article/view/40308.

Howell, K. Babe. "Broken Lives from Broken Windows: The Hidden Costs of Aggressive Order-Maintenance Policing." *NYU Review of Law and Social Change* 33 (2009): 271–329.

Hu, Wei-Yin. "Elderly Immigrants on Welfare." *Journal of Human Resources* 33, no. 3 (1998): 711–41. https://doi.org/10.2307/146339.

Huang, Xi. "Do Local Immigrant-Welcoming Efforts Increase Immigration? The Detroit Experience." *Urban Affairs Review* 58, no. 5 (2022): 1340–73. https://doi.org/10.1177/10780874211025214.

Huang, Xi, and Cathy Yang Liu. "Welcoming Cities: Immigration Policy at the Local Government Level." *Urban Affairs Review* 54, no. 1 (2018): 3–32. https://doi.org/10.1177/1078087416678999.

Hubenthal, Wendy. "Older Russian Immigrants' Experiences in Learning English: Motivation, Methods, and Barriers." *ProQuest* 14, no. 2 (2004): 104–26.

Hussey, Jon M., Denise D. Hallfors, Martha W. Waller, Bonita J. Iritani, Carolyn T. Halpern, and Danie J. Bauer. "Sexual Behavior and Drug Use Among Asian and Latino Adolescents: Association with Immigrant Status." *Journal of Immigrant Health* 9 (2007): 85–94. https://doi.org/10.1007/s10903-006-9020-z.

Hutchinson, Mary. "Bridging the Gap: Preservice Teachers and Their Knowledge of Working with English Language Learners." *TESOL Journal* 4, no. 1 (2013): 25–54.

Iceland, John, and Mellisa Scopilliti. "Immigrant Residential Segregation in U.S. Metropolitan Areas, 1990-2000." *Demography* 45, no. 1 (2008): 79–94.

Igielnik, Ruth, and Jens Manuel Krogstad. "Where Refugees to the U.S. Come From." Pew Research Center, February 3, 2017. https://www.pewresearch.org/fact-tank/2017/02/03/where-refugees-to-the-u-s-come-from/.

Ignatiev, Noel. *How the Irish Became White.* New York: Routledge, 1996. http://www.ilo.org/global/publications/books/WCMS_575479/lang—en/index.htm.

Immigrant Legal Resource Center. "Controlled Substances." March 2019. https://www.ilrc.org/sites/default/files/resources/n8_controlled_substance-032019.pdf.

Ingraham, Christopher. "Two Charts Demolish the Notion That Immigrants Here Illegally Commit More Crime." *Washington Post*, June 19, 2018. https://www.washingtonpost.com/news/wonk/wp/2018/06/19/two-charts-demolish-the-notion-that-immigrants-here-illegally-commit-more-crime/.

Instituto Nacional de Estadística y Geografía. "Datos Preliminares Revelan que en 2016 Se Registraron 23 Mil 174 Homicidios." June 30, 2018. https://www.inegi.org.mx/contenidos/saladeprensa/boletines/2018/EstSegPub/homicidios2017_07.pdf.

International Labor Organization. "Global Estimates of Modern Slavery: Forced Labour and Forced Marriage." September 19, 2017. http://www.ilo.org/global/publications/books/WCMS_575479/lang—en/index.htm.

International Monetary Fund. *Balance of Payments and International Investment Position Manual.* 6th ed. Washington: DC IMF, 2009.

Irwin, Richard. "Federal Court Finds Conditions in Customs and Border Protection Detention Facilities Unconstitutional." National Immigration Law Center, February 20, 2020. https://www.nilc.org/2020/02/19/cbp-detention-facility-conditions-unconstitutional/.

Isacson, Adam, Maureen Meyer, and Adeline Hite. "New 'Migrant Protection Protocols' Ignore U.S. Legal Obligations to Asylum Seekers and Exacerbate Humanitarian Border Crisis." WOLA, January 25, 2019. https://www.wola.org/analysis/trump-asylum-seekers-wait-in-mexico-border-crisis/.

Itzigsohn, José. "The Racial Blinders of Assimilation Theory." *Scatterplot* (blog), July 15, 2021. https://scatter.wordpress.com/2021/07/15/the-racial-blinders-of-assimilation-theory/.

Jakobsen, Vibeke, and Peder J. Pedersen. "Poverty Risk Among Older Immigrants in a Scandinavian Welfare State." *European Journal of Social Security* 19, no. 3 (2017): 242–62. https://doi.org/10.1177/1388262717725937.

Jakubowicz, Andrew. "The State and the Welfare of Immigrants in Australia." *Ethnic and Racial Studies* 12, no. 1 (1989): 1–35. https://doi.org/10.1080/01419870.1989.9993620.

Jang, Yuri, Hyunwoo Yoon, Nan Sook Park, and David A. Chiriboga. "Health Vulnerability of Immigrants with Limited English Proficiency: A Study of Older Korean Americans." *Journal of the American Geriatrics Society* 64, no. 7 (2016): 1498–1502. https://doi.org/10.1111/jgs.14199.

Javier, Joyce R., Lynne C. Huffman, Fernando S. Mendoza, and Paul H. Wise. "Children with Special Health Care Needs: How Immigrant Status Is Related to Health Care Access, Health Care Utilization, and Health Status." *Maternal and Child Health Journal* 14, no. 4 (2010): 567–79. http://dx.doi.org.proxyau.wrlc.org/10.1007/s10995-009-0487-9.

Jenks, Daniel, and Ernesto Castañeda. "Defunding the Police Is an Immigrants' Rights Issue, Too." Common Dreams, July 9, 2020. https://www.commondreams.org/views/2020/07/09/defunding-police-immigrants-rights-issue-too.

Jensen, Elizabeth. "Apprehensive About 'Apprehensions' (and 'Crisis' and 'Record')." NPR, April 16, 2019. https://www.npr.org/sections/publiceditor/2019/04/16/712872424/apprehensive-about-apprehensions-and-crisis-and-record.

Jensen, Katherine. *The Color of Asylum: The Racial Politics of Safe Haven in Brazil*. Chicago: University of Chicago Press, 2023.

Jensen, Leif. "Patterns of Immigration and Public Assistance Utilization, 1970–1980." *International Migration Review* 22, no. 1 (1998): 51–83. https://doi.org/10.1177/019791838802200103.

Jensen, Per H., and Henrik Lolle. "The Fragmented Welfare State: Variations in Services for Older People." *Journal of Social Policy* 42, no. 2 (2013): 349–70. https://doi.org/10.1017/S0047279412001006.

Jeon, In-Jae. "Korean EFL Teachers' Beliefs of English-Only Instruction." *English Teaching* 63, no. 3 (2008): 205–29.

Jiménez, Tomás R. *Replenished Ethnicity: Mexican Americans, Immigration, and Identity*. Berkeley: University of California Press, 2010.

Jiménez, Tomás R., and David Fitzgerald. "Mexican Assimilation: A Temporal and Spatial Reorientation." *Du Bois Review* 4, no. 2 (2007): 337–54. https://doi.org/10.1017/S1742058X07070191.

Johnson, Kevin R., and Bernard Trujillo. *Immigration Law and the U.S.–Mexico Border: ¿Sí Se Puede?* Tucson: University of Arizona Press, 2011.

Johnson, Kristin. "Many Happy Returns: Remittances and Their Impact." American Immigration Council, February 2010. https://www.americanimmigrationcouncil.org/sites/default/files/research/Remittances_021010.pdf.

Johnson, Michelle A. "The Social Ecology of Acculturation: Implications for Child Welfare Services to Children of Immigrants." *Children and Youth Services Review* 29, no. 11 (2007): 1426–38. https://doi.org/10.1016/j.childyouth.2007.06.002.

Jones, Reece. "Borders and Walls: Do Barriers Deter Unauthorized Migration?" Migration Policy Institute, October 4, 2016. https://www.migrationpolicy.org/article/borders-and-walls-do-barriers-deter-unauthorized-migration.

Jones, Richard C. "The Decline of International Migration as an Economic Force in Rural Areas: A Mexican Case Study." *International Migration Review* 48, no. 3 (2014): 728–61. https://doi.org/10.1111/imre.12085.

Jones, Ronald W. "Immigration Vs. Outsourcing: Effects on Labor Markets." *International Review of Economics & Finance* 14, no. 2 (2005): 105–14. https://doi.org/10.1016/j.iref.2004.08.004.

Jones Gast, Melanie, Dina G. Okamoto, and Valerie Feldman. "'We Only Speak English Here': English Dominance in Language Diverse, Immigrant After-School Programs." *Journal of Adolescent Research* 32, no. 1 (December 27, 2016): 94–121. https://doi.org/10.1177/0743558416674562.

Jordan, Miriam. "Father and Son Abducted in Mexico Are Allowed Into the U.S." *New York Times*, February 17, 2021. https://www.nytimes.com/2021/02/17/us/migrants-kidnapped-biden.html.

Kahn, Carrie. "'Remain In Mexico' Policy's End Brings Renewed Hope to Asylum Seekers." NPR, February 14, 2021. https://www.npr.org/2021/02/14/967807189/remain-in-mexico-policys-end-brings-renewed-hope-to-asylum-seekers.

Kaiser Family Foundation. "Key Facts on Health Coverage of Immigrants." KFF, September 17, 2023. https://www.kff.org/racial-equity-and-health-policy/fact-sheet/key-facts-on-health -coverage-of-immigrants/.

Kallergis, Kostas. "Pushbacks: Migrants Accuse Greece of Sending Them Back out to Sea." BBC News, December 12, 2020. https://www.bbc.com/news/world-europe-55231203.

Kampf, David. "How to Fix America's Refugee Policy." Center for Strategic Studies, July 12, 2018. https://sites.tufts.edu/css/how-to-fix-americas-refugee-policy/.

Kanno-Youngs, Zolan. "Squalid Conditions at Border Detention Centers, Government Report Finds." *New York Times*, 2019. https://www.nytimes.com/2019/07/02/us/politics/border-center -migrant-detention.html.

——. "Trump Administration Adds Six Countries to Travel Ban." *New York Times*, January 1, 2020. https://www.nytimes.com/2020/01/31/us/politics/trump-travel-ban.html.

Kapur, Devesh. *Remittances: The New Development Mantra.*" New York: United Nations, April 2004. https://unctad.org/publication/remittances-new-development-mantra.

Kara, Siddharth. *Modern Slavery: A Global Perspective.* New York: Columbia University Press, 2017.

Karagöz, Kadir. "Workers' Remittances and Economic Growth: Evidence from Turkey." *Journal of Yasar University*, 2009, 18.

Kasinitz, Philip, Mary Waters, John H. Mollenkopf, and Jennifer Holdaway. *Inheriting the City: The Children of Immigrants Come of Age.* New York: Russell Sage Foundation, 2009.

Kastoryano, Riva, and Angéline Escafré-Dublet. "Tolerance and Cultural Diversity Discourses in France." European University Institute, 2010.

Kaufmann, Eric, and Matthew J. Goodwin. "The Diversity Wave: A Meta-Analysis of the Native-Born White Response to Ethnic Diversity." *Social Science Research* 76 (November 2018): 120–31. https://doi.org/10.1016/j.ssresearch.2018.07.008.

Kaushal, Neeraj, and Robert Kaestner. "Welfare Reform and Health Insurance of Immigrants." *Health Services Research* 40, no. 3 (2005): 697–721. https://doi.org/10.1111/j.1475-6773.2005.00381.x.

Keating, Dan, and Reuben Fischer-Baum. "How U.S. Immigration Has Changed." *Washington Post*, January 12, 2018. https://www.washingtonpost.com/graphics/2018/national/immigra- tion-waves/.

Keister, Lisa A. "The One Percent." *Annual Review of Sociology* 40, no. 1 (2014): 347–67. https:// doi.org/10.1146/annurev-soc-070513-075314.

Keith, Tamara, and Brian Naylor. " 'Hate Has No Place' in America, Trump Says After El Paso and Dayton Shootings." NPR, August 5, 2019. https://www.npr.org/2019/08/05/748190808 /trump-calls-for-strong-background-checks-following-el-paso-and-dayton-shootings.

Khoo, Siew-Ean. "Correlates of Welfare Dependency Among Immigrants in Australia." *International Migration Review* 28, no. 1 (1994): 68–92. https://doi.org/10.1177/019791839402800104.

Kids in Need of Defense. "Blocked from Safety: Unaccompanied Children Along the U.S.- Mexico Border." 2019. https://supportkind.org/wp-content/uploads/2019/04/Blocked-From -Safety-KIND-Border-Report-4-29-19_FINAL.pdf.

Killewald, Alexandra, Fabian T. Pfeffer, and Jared N. Schachner. "Wealth Inequality and Accumulation." *Annual Review of Sociology* 43, no. 1 (2017): 379–404. https://doi.org/10.1146 /annurev-soc-060116-053331.

Kim, Giyeon, Courtney B. Worley, Rebecca S. Allen, Latrice Vinson, Martha R. Crowther, Patri- cia Parmelee, and David A. Chiriboga. "Vulnerability of Older Latino and Asian Immigrants with Limited English Proficiency." *Journal of the American Geriatrics Society* 59, no. 7 (2011): 1246–52. https://doi.org/10.1111/j.1532-5415.2011.03483.x.

Kim, Sun Hee Ok, John Ehrich, and Laura Ficorilli. "Perceptions of Settlement Well-Being, Language Proficiency, and Employment: An Investigation of Immigrant Adult Language Learners in Australia." *International Journal of Intercultural Relations* 36, no. 1 (2012): 41–52. https://doi.org/10.1016/j.ijintrel.2010.11.010.

King, Emily, and Aaron Flynn. "Brexit and the Future of Immigration in the UK and EU." *Financier Worldwide*, January 2018. https://www.financierworldwide.com/brexit-and-the -future-of-immigration-in-the-uk-and-eu.

Kiss, Monika, Tarja Laaninen, Vasileios Margaras, Ionel Zamfir, Marie-Laure Augére-Granier, and Nikolai Atanassov. *Demographic Outlook for the European Union 2020.* Luxembourg: European Union, 2020. https://data.europa.eu/doi/10.2861/999213.

Kittrie, Orde F. "Federalism, Deportation and Crime Victims Afraid to Call the Police." Social Science Research Network, September 6, 2006. https://papers.ssrn.com/abstract=926766.

Kladzyk, René. "From Detroit to El Paso: The Uneven Impacts of COVID-19 Border Travel Restrictions." *El Paso Matters* (blog), March 18, 2021. https://elpasomatters.org/2021/03/18 /from-detroit-to-el-paso-the-uneven-impacts-of-covid-19-border-travel-restrictions/.

Kocherga, Angela. "The COVID-19 Pandemic Is Crushing Retailers Who Rely on Cross-Border Shoppers for Holiday Sales." *El Paso Matters* (blog), December 21, 2020. https://elpasomatters .org/2020/12/21/the-covid-19-pandemic-is-crushing-retailers-who-rely-on-cross-border -shoppers-for-holiday-sales/.

Kordes, Jan, Robert Pütz, and Sigrid Rand. "Analyzing Migration Management: On the Recruitment of Nurses to Germany." *Social Sciences* 9, no. 2 (2020): art. 19. https://doi.org/10.3390 /socsci9020019.

Koser, Khalid. *International Migration: A Very Short Introduction.* 2nd ed. Oxford: Oxford University Press, 2016.

Kouritzin, Sandra. "Immigrant Mothers Redefine Access to ESL Classes: Contradiction and Ambivalence." *Journal of Multilingual and Multicultural Development*, no. 1 (March 29, 2010): 14–32. https://doi.org/10.1080/01434630008666391.

Krogstad, Jens Manuel, and Ana Gonzalez-Barrera. "A Majority of English-Speaking Hispanics in the U.S. Are Bilingual." Pew Research Center, March 24, 2015. https://www.pewresearch.org /fact-tank/2015/03/24/a-majority-of-english-speaking-hispanics-in-the-u-s-are-bilingual/.

Krogstad, Jens Manuel, Renee Stepler, and Mark Hugo Lopez. "English Proficiency on the Rise Among Latinos." Pew Research Center, May 12, 2015. https://www.pewresearch.org /hispanic/2015/05/12/english-proficiency-on-the-rise-among-latinos/.

Kropf, Nancy P., Larry Nackerud, and Inna Gorokhovski. "Social Work Practice with Older Soviet Immigrants." *Journal of Multicultural Social Work* 7, no. 1–2 (1999): 111–26. https://doi.org /10.1300/J285v07n01_07.

Ku, Leighton, and Brian Bruen. "Poor Immigrants Use Public Benefits at a Lower Rate than Poor Native-Born Citizens." *Cato Institute Economic Development Bulletin*, no. 17 (March 4, 2013). https://www.cato.org/publications/economic-development-bulletin/poor-immigrants -use-public-benefits-lower-rate-poor.

Ku, Leighton, and Drishti Pillai. "The Economic Mobility of Immigrants: Public Charge Rules Could Foreclose Future Opportunities." Social Science Research Network, November 15, 2018. https://doi.org/10.2139/ssrn.3285546.

Kulig, Teresa C., Amanda Graham, Francis T. Cullen, Alex R. Piquero, and Murat Haner. "'Bad Hombres' at the Southern US Border? White Nationalism and the Perceived Dangerousness of Immigrants." *Journal of Criminology* 54, no. 3 (2021): 283–304.

Kullgren, Jeffrey T. "Restrictions on Undocumented Immigrants' Access to Health Services: The Public Health Implications of Welfare Reform." *American Journal of Public Health* 93, no. 10 (2003): 1630–33. https://doi.org/10.2105/AJPH.93.10.1630.

Lachica, Josué, Ernesto Castañeda, and Yolanda McDonald. "Poverty, Place, and Health Along the US-Mexico Border." In *Poverty and Health: A Crisis Among America's Most Vulnerable.* Vol. 2, *The Importance of Place in Determining Their Future,* ed. Kevin M. Fitzpatrick, 87–104. Santa Barbara, CA: ABC-CLIO, 2013.

Larota, Clarena. "Immigrants Learning English in a Time of Anti-Immigrant Sentiment." *Adult Literacy Education* 1, no. 1 (2019): 53–58. https://doi.org/10.35847/CLarrotta.1.1.53.

Lasch, Christopher N., R. Linus Chan, Ingrid V. Eagly, Dina Francesca Haynes, Annie Lai, Elizabeth M. McCormick, and Juliet P. Stumpf. "Understanding 'Sanctuary Cities.'" *Boston College Law Review* 59, no. 4 (2018): 1703–74.

Lassiter, Mathew D. "Impossible Criminals: The Suburban Imperatives of America's War on Drugs." *Journal of American History* 102, no. 1 (2015): 126–40. https://doi.org/10.1093/jahist/jav243.

Latour, Bruno, and Emilie Hermant. "Paris: Invisible City," 2006. Paris: La Découverte-Les Empêcheurs de penser en rond. http://www.bruno-latour.fr/sites/default/files/downloads /viii_paris-city-gb.pdf.

Law Society Gazette. "CJEU Issues Opinion in UK Discrimination Case." June 24, 2021. https:// www.lawsociety.ie/gazette/top-stories/cjeu-issues-opinion-in-uk-discrimination-case/.

Lee, Brianna, Danielle Renwick, and Rocio Cara Labrador. "Mexico's Long War: Drugs, Crime, and the Cartels." Council on Foreign Relations, February 26, 2021. https://www.cfr.org /backgrounder/mexicos-long-war-drugs-crime-and-cartels.

Lee, Erika. "The Chinese Exclusion Example: Race, Immigration, and American Gatekeeping, 1882–1924." *Journal of American Ethnic History* 21, no. 3 (2002): 36–62.

Lee, Stacey J. "Reflecting Again on the Model Minority." In *Unraveling the "Model Minority" Stereotype: Listening to Asian American Youth.* 2nd ed. New York: Columbia University Teachers College Press, 1996. http://faculty.umb.edu/lawrence_blum/courses/CCT627_10/readings/lee _unraveling_model_minority_stereotype.pdf.

Lee, Stacey J., Nga-Wing Anjela Wong, and Alvin N. Alvarez. "The Model Minority and the Perpetual Foreigner: Stereotypes of Asian Americans." In *Asian American Psychology: Current Perspectives,* ed. Nita Tewari and Alvin Alvarez, 69–84. New York: Routledge, 2009.

Leeman, Jennifer. "Investigating Language Ideologies in Spanish as a Heritage Language." In *Spanish as a Heritage Language in the United States: The State of the Field,* ed. Sara M. Beaudrie and Marta Fairclough, 43–60. Washington, DC: Georgetown University Press, 2012. https:// www.jstor.org/stable/j.ctt2tt42d.

Levitt, Peggy. "Social Remittances: Migration Driven Local-Level Forms of Cultural Diffusion." *International Migration Review* 32, no. 4 (1998): 926–48. https://doi.org/10.2307/2547666.

Levitt, Peggy, and Mary C. Waters. *The Changing Face of Home: The Transnational Lives of the Second Generation.* New York: Russell Sage Foundation, 2002.

Levy, Nathan, Asya Pisarevskaya, and Peter Scholten. "Between Fragmentation and Institution-alisation: The Rise of Migration Studies as a Research Field." *Comparative Migration Studies* 8, no. 1 (2020): art. 24. https://doi.org/10.1186/s40878-020-00180-7.

Leyva-Flores, René, Cesar Infante, Juan Pablo Gutierrez, Frida Quintino-Perez, MariaJose Gómez-Saldivar, and Cristian Torres-Robles. "Migrants in Transit Through Mexico to the US: Experiences with Violence and Related Factors, 2009–2015." *PLOS One* 14, no. 8 (2019): e0220775. https://doi.org/10.1371/journal.pone.0220775.

L. G. "Immigrants Do Not Need to Speak English Before They Arrive." *Economist*, August 3, 2017. https://www.economist.com/democracy-in-america/2017/08/03/immigrants-do-not-need-to-speak-english-before-they-arrive.

Li, Guofang. "Other People's Success: Impact of the 'Model Minority' Myth on Underachieving Asian Students in North America." *KEDI Journal of Educational Policy* 2, no. 1 (2005): 69–86. https://www.proquest.com/openview/9ad1f810feoe328e705414ddd8848fa1/1?pq-origsite=gscholar&cbl=946348.

Li, Peter S. "Deconstructing Canada's Discourse of Immigrant Integration." *Journal of International Migration and Integration* 4, no. 3 (2003): 315–33. https://doi.org/10.1007/s12134-003-1024-0.

Light, Michael T. "Does Undocumented Immigration Increase Drug and Alcohol Problems?" *Public Health Post* (blog), November 9, 2017. https://www.publichealthpost.org/research/undocumented-immigration-increase-drug-alcohol-problems/.

Light, Michael T., Jingying He, and Jason P. Robey. "Comparing Crime Rates Between Undocumented Immigrants, Legal Immigrants, and Native-Born US Citizens in Texas." *Proceedings of the National Academy of Sciences* 117, no. 51 (2020): 32340–47.

Light, Michael T., and Ty Miller. "Does Undocumented Immigration Increase Violent Crime?" *Criminology* 56, no. 2 (2018): 370–401. https://doi.org/10.1111/1745-9125.12175.

Light, Michael T., Ty Miller, and Brian C. Kelly. "Undocumented Immigration, Drug Problems, and Driving Under the Influence in the United States, 1990–2014." *American Journal of Public Health* 107 (2017): 1448–54. https://doi.org/10.2105/AJPH.2017.303884.

Lim, Andrew. "Ranked: Where Do US Immigrants Integrate Best?" Apolitical, 2018. https://apolitical.co/solution-articles/en/ranked-where-in-the-us-do-immigrants-integrate-best.

Lind, Dara. "The Border Is in Crisis. Here's How It Got This Bad." Vox, April 11, 2019. https://www.vox.com/2019/4/11/18290677/border-immigration-illegal-asylum-central-america-mexico-trump.

Liu, Xinru. *The Silk Road in World History*. Oxford: Oxford University Press, 2010.

López, José Fernando and Luis Melgar. "Gran Encuesta Revela Que en la Frontera de Estados Unidos y México No Quieren el Muro de Trump," July 14, 2016. Univision Noticias. https://www.univision.com/noticias/amexica/gran-encuesta-revela-que-en-la-frontera-de-estados-unidos-y-mexico-no-quieren-el-muro-de-trump.

Lopez, William D. *Separated: Family and Community in the Aftermath of an Immigration Raid*. Baltimore: Johns Hopkins University Press, 2021.

López-Farjeat, Luis Xavier, and Cecilia Coronado-Angulo. "Group Asylum, Sovereignty, and the Ethics of Care." *Social Sciences* 9, no. 8 (2020): art. 142. https://doi.org/10.3390/socsci9080142.

Lowell, B. Lindsey, and Roberto Suro. "The Improving Educational Profile of Latino Immigrants." Pew Research Center, December 4, 2002. https://www.pewresearch.org/hispanic/2002/12/04/the-improving-educational-profile-of-latino-immigrants/.

Lowery, Clay, and Vijaya Ramachandran. *Unintended Consequences of Anti-Money Laundering Policies for Poor Countries*. Washington, DC: Center for Global Development, 2015.

Lowrey, Annie. "Are Immigrants a Drain on Government Resources?" *Atlantic*, September 29, 2018. https://www.theatlantic.com/ideas/archive/2018/09/are-immigrants-drain-government-resources/571582/.

Loza, Oralia, Ernesto Castañeda, and Brian Diedrich. "Substance Use by Immigrant Generation in a U.S.-Mexico Border City." *Journal of Immigrant and Minority Health* 19, no. 5 (2017):
1132–39. https://doi.org/10.1007/s10903-016-0407-1.

Luhnow, David. "Latin America Is the Murder Capital of the World." *Wall Street Journal*,
September 20, 2018.

Lybecker, Donna L., Mark K. McBeth, Maria A. Husmann, and Nicholas Pelikan. "Do New
Media Support New Policy Narratives? The Social Construction of the U.S.-Mexico Border
on YouTube." *Policy and Internet* 7, no. 4 (2015): 497–525. https://doi.org/10.1002/poi3.94.

MacDonald, John M., John R. Hipp, and Charlotte Gill. "The Effects of Immigrant Concentration on Changes in Neighborhood Crime Rates." *Journal of Quantitative Criminology* 29, no. 2
(2013): 191–215. https://doi.org/10.1007/s10940-012-9176-8.

MacDonald, John M., and Robert J. Sampson. "The World in a City: Immigration and America's
Changing Social Fabric." *Annals of the American Academy of Political and Social Science* 641,
no. 1 (2012): 6–15. https://doi.org/10.1177/0002716212438939.

MacDonald, John M., and Jessica Saunders. "Are Immigrant Youth Less Violent? Specifying the
Reasons and Mechanisms." *Annals of the American Academy of Political and Social Science* 641,
no. 1 (2012): 125–47. https://doi.org/10.1177/0002716211432279.

Macías-Rojas, Patrisia. "Immigration and the War on Crime: Law and Order Politics and the
Illegal Immigration Reform and Immigrant Responsibility Act of 1996." *Journal on Migration
and Human Security* 6, no. 1 (2018): 1–25. https://doi.org/10.1177/233150241800600101.

Macrotrends. "El Paso TX Murder/Homicide Rate 1999–2018." 2024. https://www.macrotrends
.net/cities/us/tx/el-paso/murder-homicide-rate-statistics.

Macswan, Jeff. "The Threshold Hypothesis, Semilingualism, and Other Contributions to a
Deficit View of Linguistic Minorities." *Hispanic Journal of Behavioral Sciences* 22, no. 1 (2000):
3–45. https://doi.org/10.1177/0739986300221001.

Magis-Rodríguez, Carlos, Kimberly C. Brouwer, Sonia Morales, Cecilia Gayet, Remedios Lozada,
Raul Ortiz-Mondragón, Erin P. Ricketts, and Steffanie A. Strathdee. "HIV Prevalence and
Correlates of Receptive Needle Sharing Among Injection Drug Users in the Mexican-U.S.
Border City of Tijuana." *Journal of Psychoactive Drugs* 37, no. 3 (2005): 333–39. https://doi.org
/10.1080/02791072.2005.10400528.

Mahdi, Ali Akbar. "Ethnic Identity Among Second-Generation Iranians in the United States."
Iranian Studies 13, no. 1 (1998): 77–95. https://doi.org/10.1080/00210869808701897.

Mahler, Sarah J. *American Dreaming: Immigrant Life on the Margins.* Princeton, NJ: Princeton University Press, 1995.

Marinari, M. *Unwanted: Italian and Jewish Mobilization Against Restrictive Immigration Laws,
1882–1965.* Chapel Hill, NC: University of North Carolina Press, 2019.

Mark, Michelle. "Closing the Border Would Put the US Economy at a 'Standstill' and Actually Worsen Illegal Border Crossings. Here's How It Would Affect Food Prices, Jobs, and
Americans' Everyday Lives." Business Insider, April 2, 2019. https://www.businessinsider.
com/us-mexico-border-closed-what-could-happen-2019-4.

Martin, Susan F. "The Global Refugee Crisis." *Georgetown Journal of International Affairs* 17,
no. 1 (2016): 5–11.

——. "Heavy Traffic: International Migration in an Era of Globalization." Brookings Institution,
September 1, 2001. https://www.brookings.edu/articles/heavy-traffic-international-migration
-in-an-era-of-globalization/.

Martínez, Daniel E., Josiah Heyman, and Jeremy Slack. *Border Enforcement Developments Since 1993 and How to Change CBP*. New York: Center for Migration Studies, 2020. https://cmsny .org/publications/border-enforcement-developments-since-1993-and-how-to-change-cbp/.

Martinez, Ramiro, Jacob I. Stowell, and Janice A. Iwama. "The Role of Immigration: Race/ Ethnicity and San Diego Homicides Since 1970." *Journal of Quantitative Criminology* 32, no. 3 (2016): 471–88. https://doi.org/10.1007/s10940-016-9294-9.

Martinez, Ramiro, Jacob I. Stowell, and Matthew T. Lee. "Immigration and Crime in an Era of Transformation: A Longitudinal Analysis of Homicides in San Diego Neighborhoods, 1980– 2000." *Criminology* 48, no. 3 (2010): 797–829. https://doi.org/10.1111/j.1745-9125.2010.00202.x.

Martínez-Schuldt, Ricardo D., and Daniel E. Martínez. "Immigrant Sanctuary Policies and Crime-Reporting Behavior: A Multilevel Analysis of Reports of Crime Victimization to Law Enforcement, 1980 to 2004." *American Sociological Review* 86, no. 1 (2021): 154–85.

——. "Sanctuary Policies and City-Level Incidents of Violence, 1990 to 2010." *Justice Quarterly* 36, no. 4 (2017): 567–93.

Martínez Toyes, Wilebaldo Lorenzo, and Jaime Alberto Arellano Quiroga. "Movilidad Poblacional: Efecto de la Violencia e Inseguridad en Ciudad Juárez." In *Inseguridad y Violencia en Ciudad Juárez, México*, ed. Myrna Limas Hernández. Ciudad Juárez, Chihuahua: Universidad Autónoma de Ciudad Juárez, 2012. https://www.researchgate.net/publication /275582903_Inseguridad_y_violencia_en_Ciudad_Juarez_Mexico.

Massey, Douglas S. "Immigration Policy Mismatches and Counterproductive Outcomes: Unauthorized Migration to the U.S. in Two Eras." *Comparative Migration Studies* 8, no. 1 (2020): art. 21. https://doi.org/10.1186/s40878-020-00181-6.

——. "Migration and Categorical Inequality." In *Immigration and Categorical Inequality: Migration to the City and the Birth of Race and Ethnicity*, ed. Ernesto Castañeda. New York: Routledge, 2018.

Massey, Douglas S., Jorge Durand, and Nolan J. Malone. *Beyond Smoke and Mirrors: Mexican Immigration in an Era of Economic Integration*. New York: Russell Sage Foundation, 2002.

Massey, Douglas S., Luin Goldring, and Jorge Durand. "Continuities in Transnational Migration: An Analysis of Nineteen Mexican Communities." *American Journal of Sociology* 99, no. 6 (1994): 1492–1533. https://doi.org/10.1086/230452.

Massey, Douglas S., and Mary C. Waters. "Scientific Versus Public Debates: A PNAS Case Study." *Proceedings of the National Academy of Sciences* 117, no. 31 (2020): 18135–36. https://doi.org /10.1073/pnas.2012328117.

Master, Benjamin, Susanna Loeb, Camille Whitney, and James Wyckoff. "Different Skills? Identifying Differentially Effective Teachers of English Language Learners." *Elementary School Journal* 117, no. 2 (2016): 261–84. https://doi.org/10.1086/688871.

Mathews, Nick. "The Community Caretaker Role: How Weekly Newspapers Shielded Their Communities While Covering the Mississippi ICE Raids." *Journalism Studies* 22, no. 5 (2021): 670–87. https://doi.org/10.1080/1461670X.2021.1897477.

Mauldin, John. "3 Reasons Brits Voted for Brexit." Forbes, July 5, 2016. https://www.forbes.com /sites/johnmauldin/2016/07/05/3-reasons-brits-voted-for-brexit/?sh=65d160761f9d.

McAllen Police Department. *Crime in McAllen 2018*. McAllen, TX: MPD, 2018. https://www .mcallen.net/docs/default-source/pd/crime-reports/2018-crime-in-mcallen-report.pdf.

McBride, James. "What Brexit Means." Council on Foreign Relations, July 22, 2019. https://www .cfr.org/backgrounder/what-brexit-means.

McCallum, Jamie W., J. Marcus Rowcliffe, and Innes C. Cuthill. "Conservation on International Boundaries: The Impact of Security Barriers on Selected Terrestrial Mammals in Four Protected Areas in Arizona, USA." *PLOS One* 9, no. 4 (2014): e93679. https://journals.plos.org/plosone/article?id=10.1371/journal.pone.0093679.

McEwen, Bruce S. "Protective and Damaging Effects of Stress Mediators." *New England Journal of Medicine* 338, no. 3 (1998): 171–79. https://doi.org/10.1056/NEJM199801153380307.

McEwen, Nicola, and Mary C Murphy. "Brexit and the Union: Territorial Voice, Exit and Re-entry Strategies in Scotland and Northern Ireland After EU Exit." *International Political Science Review* 43, no. 3 (2022): 374–389. https://doi.org/10.1177/0192512121990543.

McGhee White, Kaylee. "Out of Many, One: Immigration Requires Assimilation." *Washington Examiner*, July 15, 2019. https://www.washingtonexaminer.com/tag/donald-trump?source=%2Fopinion%2Fout-of-many-one-immigration-requires-assimilation.

McGuire, Sharon, and Jane Georges. "Undocumentedness and Liminality as Health Variables." *Advances in Nursing Science* 26, no. 3 (2003): 185–95.

McKenna, Chris, and Brennan Hobman. "Problems and Solutions to the International Migrant Crisis." Brookings Institution, December 18, 2017. https://www.brookings.edu/blog/brookings-now/2017/12/18/problems-and-solutions-to-the-international-migrant-crisis/.

Meierotto, Lisa. *Immigration, Environment, and Security on the U.S.-Mexico Border*. Cham, Switzerland: Springer, 2020. https://doi.org/10.1007/978-3-030-31814-7_1.

Meissner, Doris, Faye Hipsman, and T. Alexander Aleinikoff. *The U.S. Asylum System in Crisis: Charting a Way Forward*. Washington, DC: Migration Policy Institute, September 2018.

Menard-Warwick, Julia. *Gendered Identities and Immigrant Language Learning*. Bristol, UK: Multilingual Matters, 2009.

Mendoza, Ronald U. "Examining the Risk of Brain Drain and Lower Remittances." *Singapore Economic Review* 58, no. 1 (2013): art. 1350006. https://doi.org/10.1142/S0217590813500069.

Meneses, Guillermo Alonso. "Human Rights and Undocumented Migration Along the Mexican-U.S. Border." *UCLA Law Review* 51 (October 7, 2003): 267–81.https://www.uclalawreview.org/human-rights-and-undocumented-migration-along-the-mexican-u-s-border/.

Menjívar, Cecilia. *Fragmented Ties: Salvadoran Immigrant Networks in America*. Berkeley: University of California Press, 2000.

Mercille, Julien. "Violent Narco-Cartels or US Hegemony? The Political Economy of the 'War on Drugs' in Mexico." *Third World Quarterly* 32, no. 9 (2011): 1637–53. https://doi.org/10.1080/01436597.2011.619881.

Meyer, Dietmar, and Adela Shera. "The Impact of Remittances on Economic Growth: An Econometric Model." *EconomiA* 18, no. 2 (2017): 147–55. https://doi.org/10.1016/j.econ.2016.06.001.

Miles, Tom. "French Ban on Full-Face Islamic Veil Violates Human Rights: U.N. Panel." Reuters, October 23, 2018. https://www.reuters.com/article/us-france-islam-un/french-ban-on-full-face-islamic-veil-violates-human-rights-u-n-panel-idUSKCN1MX15K.

——. "U.N. View on the European Migrant Crisis? There Isn't One." Reuters, July 6, 2018. https://www.reuters.com/article/us-europe-migrants-un/u-n-view-on-the-european-migrant-crisis-there-isnt-one-idUSKBN1JW1Z5.

Miliken, David. "Immigration to Britain Falls to Five-Year Low Ahead of Brexit: ONS." Reuters, August 22, 2019. https://www.reuters.com/article/us-britain-eu-immigration-idUSKCN1VC0TW.

Miller, Todd. *Border Patrol Nation: Dispatches from the Front Lines of Homeland Security*. San Francisco: City Lights, 2014.

Miller-Idriss, Cynthia. *Hate in the Homeland: The New Global Far Right*. Princeton, NJ: Princeton University Press, 2020.

Mills, China, and Elise Klein. "Affective Technologies of Welfare Deterrence in Australia and the United Kingdom." *Economy and Society* 50, no. 3 (2021): 397–422. https://doi.org/10.1080/03085147.2021.1875692.

Mirici, Ismail Hakki, Rebecca Galleano, and Kelly Torres. "Immigrant Parent Vs. Immigrant Children: Attitudes Toward Language Learning in the U.S." *Novitas-Royal* 7, no. 2 (2013): 137–46.

Miroff, Nick. "U.S. Customs Agency Is So Short-Staffed, It's Sending Officers from Airports to the Mexican Border." *Washington Post*, January 19, 2018. https://www.washingtonpost.com/world/national-security/us-customs-agency-is-so-short-staffed-its-sending-officers-from-airports-to-the-mexican-border/2018/01/18/44420a94-fc77-11e7-a46b-a3614530bd87_story.html.

Misra, Tanvi. "For the Last Time, Here's the Real Link Between Immigration and Crime." Bloomberg CityLab, February 6, 2019. https://www.bloomberg.com/news/articles/2019-02-06/what-s-the-real-link-between-crime-and-immigration.

Moehling, Carolyn, and Anne Morrison Piehl. "Immigration, Crime, and Incarceration in Early Twentieth-Century America." *Demography* 46, no. 4 (2009): 739–63. https://doi.org/10.1353/dem.0.0076.

Morales, Laura, and Laia Jorba. "Transnational Links and Practices of Migrants' Organisations in Spain." In *Diaspora and Transnationalism: Concepts, Theories and Methods*, ed. Rainer Baubock and Thomas Faist. Amsterdam: Amsterdam University Press, 2010.

Morales, Maria Cristina, Denise Delgado, and Theodore Curry. "Variations in Citizenship Profiling by Generational Status: Individual and Neighborhood Characteristics of Latina/os Questioned by Law Enforcement About Their Legal Status." *Race and Social Problems* 10, no. 4 (2018): 293–305. https://doi.org/10.1007/s12552-018-9235-3.

Morenoff, Jeffrey D., and Avraham Astor. "Immigrant Assimilation and Crime: Generational Differences in Youth Violence in Chicago." In *Immigration and Crime: Race, Ethnicity, and Violence*. New York: NYU Press, 2006.

Morgan, Wesley. "Behind the Secret U.S. War in Africa." *Politico*, July 2, 2018. https://www.politico.com/story/2018/07/02/secret-war-africa-pentagon-664005.

Morris, Aldon D. *The Scholar Denied: W. E. B. Du Bois and the Birth of Modern Sociology*. Oakland: University of California Press, 2015.

Mouw, Ted, and Yu Xie. "Bilingualism and the Academic Achievement of First- and Second-Generation Asian Americans: Accommodation with or Without Assimilation?" *American Sociological Review* 64, no. 2 (1999): 232–52. https://doi.org/10.2307/2657529.

MSNBC. *Fence Not Needed at Parts of Mexico Border*. 2016. https://www.youtube.com/watch?v=4W192A7g5KY.

Muller, Benjamin J. "Unsafe at Any Speed? Borders, Mobility and 'Safe Citizenship.'" *Citizenship Studies* 14, no. 1 (2010): 75–88. https://doi.org/10.1080/13621020903466381.

Mundo, Fernando del. "2001 Global Refugee Statistics." United Nations High Commissioner for Refugees, June 18, 2002. https://www.unhcr.org/en-us/news/latest/2002/6/3d0f6dcb5/2001-global-refugee-statistics.html.

Nam, Yunju. "Welfare Reform and Elderly Immigrants' Health Insurance Coverage: The Roles of Federal and State Medicaid Eligibility Rules." *Journal of Gerontological Social Work* 54, no. 8 (2011): 819–36. https://doi.org/10.1080/01634372.2011.614679.

Nam, Yunju, and Wooksoo Kim. "Welfare Reform and Elderly Immigrants' Naturalization: Access to Public Benefits as an Incentive for Naturalization in the United States." *International Migration Review* 46, no. 3 (2012): 656–79.

Narea, Nicole. "A Federal Judge Blocked Trump's Rule Creating a Wealth Test for Immigrants." Vox, July 30, 2020. https://www.vox.com/policy-and-politics/2019/10/11/20899253/trump-public -charge-rule-immigrants-welfare-benefits.

National Association of Criminal Defense Lawyers. "Understanding Immigration Consequences of Drug Offenses." July 28, 2019. https://www.nacdl.org/Content/Understanding-Immigration -Consequences-of-Drug-Off.

National Conference of State Legislatures. "Immigration and Public Charge," March 11, 2021. https://www.ncsl.org/research/immigration/immigration-and-public-charge-dhs-proposes -new-definition.aspx.

National Immigrant Justice Center. "Access to Counsel." Accessed May 10, 2024. https://immigrant justice.org/issues/access-counsel.

National Immigration Forum. "Engaging Business for Immigrant Integration." Accessed August 24, 2021. https://immigrationforum.org/landing_page/engaging-business-for-immigrant-integration/.

——. "English Language Programs Help Immigrants Prepare for Jobs." September 19, 2017. https:// immigrationforum.org/article/english-language-programs-help-immigrants-prepare -jobs/.

——. "Fact Sheet: Immigrants and Public Benefits." August 21, 2018. https://immigrationforum .org/article/fact-sheet-immigrants-and-public-benefits/.

——. "Trafficking Victims Protection Reauthorization Act Safeguards Children." May 23, 2018. https://immigrationforum.org/article/trafficking-victims-protection-reauthorization-act -safeguards-children/.

Navarrette, Ruben. "Navarrette: Remittance Taxes Could Curb Illegal Immigration from Mexico." *IndyStar*, April 12, 2016. https://www.indystar.com/story/opinion/columnists/2016/04/12 /navarrette-remittances-curb-illegal-immigration-mexico/82907124/.

Neal, Sarah, Katy Bennet, Allan Cochrane, and Giles Mohan. "Community and Conviviality? Informal Social Life in Multicultural Places." *Sociology* 53, no. 1 (2019): 69–86. https://doi.org /10.1177/0038038518763518.

Nesteruk, Olena, and Loren Marks. "Grandparents Across the Ocean: Eastern European Immigrants' Struggle to Maintain Intergenerational Relationships." *Journal of Comparative Family Studies* 40, no. 1 (2009): 77–95. https://doi.org/10.3138/jcfs.40.1.77.

New American Economy. "How the 'Public Charge' Rule Change Could Impact Immigrants and U.S. Economy." October 31, 2018. https://research.newamericaneconomy.org/report/economic -impact-of-proposed-rule-change-inadmissibility-on-public-charge-grounds/.

——. "NAE Cities Index." 2021. https://www.newamericaneconomy.org/cities-index/.

Ngai, Mae M. *Impossible Subjects: Illegal Aliens and the Making of Modern America.* Updated ed. Princeton, NJ: Princeton University Press, 2014.

Nicholls, Walter J. "The Uneven Geographies of Politicisation: The Case of the Undocumented Immigrant Youth Movement in the United States." *Antipode* 53, no. 2 (2021): 465–85. https:// doi.org/10.1111/anti.12663.

Nicholls, Walter J., and Justus Uitermark. *Cities and Social Movements: Immigrant Rights Activism in the US, France, and the Netherlands, 1970–2015.* Hoboken, NJ: Wiley, 2016.

Niimi, Yoko, Caglar Ozden, and Maurice Schiff. "Remittances and the Brain Drain: Skilled Migrants Do Remit Less." *Annals of Economics and Statistics*, no. 97/98 (2010): 123–41. https://doi.org/10.2307/41219112.

Nixon, Ron. "Border Wall Could Cost 3 Times Estimates, Senate Democrats' Report Says." *New York Times*, April 18, 2017. https://www.nytimes.com/2017/04/18/us/politics/senate-democrats-border-wall-cost-trump.html.

Nkimbeng, Manka, Janiece L. Taylor, Laken Roberts, Peter J. Winch, Yvonne Commodore-Mensah, Roland J. Thorpe, Hae-Ra Han, and Sarah L. Szanton. " 'All I Know Is That There Is a Lot of Discrimination': Older African Immigrants' Experiences of Discrimination in the United States." *Geriatric Nursing* 42, no. 1 (2021): 196–204. https://doi.org/10.1016/j.gerinurse.2020.08.002.

Noh, Samuel, Morton Beiser, Violet Kaspar, Feng Hou, and Joanna Rummens. "Perceived Racial Discrimination, Depression, and Coping: A Study of Southeast Asian Refugees in Canada." *Journal of Health and Social Behavior* 40, no. 3 (1999): 193–207. https://doi.org/10.2307/2676348.

North, David. "Another Good Reason to Limit the $68 Billion in Remittances—Covid-19." Center for Immigration Studies, October 9, 2020. https://cis.org/North/Another-Good-Reason-Limit-68-Billion-Remittances-Covid19.

Norton Peirce, Bonny. "Identity and Second Language Acquisition." In *The Encyclopedia of Applied Linguistics*, ed. Carol A. Chapelle. Chichester, UK: Wiley-Blackwell, 2013.

——. "Social Identity, Investment, and Language Learning." *TESOL Quarterly* 29, no. 1 (1995): 9–31. https://doi.org/10.2307/3587803.

Nowrasteh, Alex. "Crime Along the Mexican Border Is Lower than in the Rest of the Country." Cato Institute, 2019. https://www.cato.org/blog/crime-along-mexican-border-lower-rest-country.

——. "Criminal Immigrants in Texas: Illegal Immigrant Conviction and Arrest Rates for Homicide, Sex Crimes, Larceny, and Other Crimes." Cato Institute, 2018. https://www.cato.org/sites/cato.org/files/pubs/pdf/irpb-4-updated.pdf.

——. "Terrorism and Immigration: A Risk Analysis." Cato Institute, September 13, 2016. https://www.cato.org/policy-analysis/terrorism-immigration-risk-analysis.

Nowrasteh, Alex, and Robert Orr. "Immigration and the Welfare State: Immigrant and Native Use Rates and Benefit Levels for Means-Tested Welfare and Entitlement Programs." Cato Institute, May 10, 2018. https://www.cato.org/immigration-research-policy-brief/immigration-welfare-state-immigrant-native-use-rates-benefit.

Nuñez-Neto, Blas. *Border Security: The Role of the U.S. Border Patrol.* Washington, DC: Congressional Research Service, May 10, 2005.

Nwachuku, Levi A. "Neo-colonialism." In *The Encyclopedia of Empire.* Hoboken, NJ: Wiley, 2016. https://doi.org/10.1002/9781118455074.wbeoe237.

O'Brien, Matthew, Spencer Raley, and Casey Ryan. "The United States Loses $150 Billion Annually in Remittances." Federation for American Immigration Reform, May 2019. https://www.fairus.org/issue/publications-resources/united-states-loses-150-billion-annually-remittances.

Office for National Statistics. "Migration Statistics Quarterly Report," February 2019. https://www.ons.gov.uk/peoplepopulationandcommunity/populationandmigration/internationalmigration/bulletins/migrationstatisticsquarterlyreport/february2019.

Ojeda, Victoria D., Thomas L. Patterson, and Steffanie A. Strathdee. "The Influence of Perceived Risk to Health and Immigration-Related Characteristics on Substance Use Among Latino and Other Immigrants." *American Journal of Public Health* 98, no. 5 (2008): 862–68. https://doi.org/10.2105/AJPH.2006.108142.

Okafor, Maria-Theresa C., Olivia D. Carter-Pokras, Sandra J. Picot, and Min Zhan. "The Relationship of Language Acculturation (English Proficiency) to Current Self-Rated Health Among African Immigrant Adults." *Journal of Immigrant and Minority Health* 15, no. 3 (2013): 499–509. https://doi.org/10.1007/s10903-012-9614-6.

Olsen, Laurie. "Learning English and Learning America: Immigrants in the Center of a Storm." *Theory Into Practice* 39, no. 4 (2000): 196–202.

Olson, Christa Polczynski, Minna K. Laurikkala, Lin Huff-Corzine, and Jay Corzine. "Immigration and Violent Crime: Citizenship Status and Social Disorganization." *Homicide Studies* 13, no. 3 (2009): 227–41. https://doi.org/10.1177%2F1088767909336202.

Ono, Hiromi, and Rosina M. Becerra. "Race, Ethnicity and Nativity, Family Structure, Socioeconomic Status and Welfare Dependency." *International Migration Review* 34, no. 3 (2000): 739–65. http://dx.doi.org.proxyau.wrlc.org/10.1177/019791830003400304.

Orellana, Marjorie Faulstich, Lucila Ek, and Arcelia Hernandez. "Bilingual Education in an Immigrant Community: Proposition 227 in California." *International Journal of Bilingual Education and Bilingualism* 2, no. 2 (1999): 114–30. https://doi.org/10.1080/13670059908667683.

Organisation for Economic Co-operation and Development. *International Migration Outlook: Annual Report 2006.* Paris: OECD, 2006.

Orozco, Manuel. "Globalization and Migration: The Impact of Family Remittances in Latin America." *Latin American Politics and Society* 44, no. 2 (2002): 41–66. https://doi.org/10.2307/3177094.

Orraca Romano, Pedro Paulo, and Francisco de Jesús Corona Villavicencio. "Risk of Death and Aggressions Encountered While Illegally Crossing the U.S.-Mexico Border." *Migraciones Internacionales* 7, no. 3 (2014): 9–41.

Orrenius, Pia M. "Benefits of Immigration Outweigh the Costs." *Catalyst*, no. 2 (Spring 2016). http://www.bushcenter.org/catalyst/north-american-century/benefits-of-immigration-outweigh-costs.html.

Orrenius, Pia M., and Madeline Zavodny. "Do Immigrants Work in Riskier Jobs?" *Demography* 46, no. 3 (2009): 535–51.

Ortega, Alexander N., Hai Fang, Victor H. Perez, John A. Rizzo, Olivia Carter-Pokras, Steven P. Wallace, and Lillian Gelberg. "Health Care Access, Use of Services, and Experiences Among Undocumented Mexicans and Other Latinos." *JAMA Internal Medicine* 167, no. 21 (2007): 2354–60. https://doi.org/10.1001/archinte.167.21.2354.

Ospina, Guillermo Andrés, Jorge Hernández Tinajero, and Martin Jelsma. *Poppies, Opium, and Heroin Production in Colombia and Mexico.* Amsterdam: Transnational Institute, 2018.

Ostrand, Nicole. "The Syrian Refugee Crisis: A Comparison of Responses by Germany, Sweden, the United Kingdom, and the United States." *Journal on Migration and Human Security* 3, no. 3 (2015): 255–79. https://doi.org/10.1177/233150241500300301.

Ousey, Graham C., and Charis E. Kubrin. "Exploring the Connection Between Immigration and Violent Crime Rates in U.S. Cities, 1980–2000." *Social Problems* 56, no. 3 (2009): 447–73. https://doi.org/10.1525/sp.2009.56.3.447.

Owens, Brian. "Trump's Border-Wall Pledge Threatens Delicate Desert Ecosystems." *Nature* 536, no. 7616 (2016): 260–61. https://doi.org/10.1038/536260a.

Pacurucu-Castillo, Saul Francisco, José Marcelo Ordóñez-Mancheno, Adrián Hernández-Cruz, and Renato D. Alarcón. "World Opioid and Substance Use Epidemic: A Latin American Perspective." *Psychiatric Research and Clinical Practice* 1, no. 1 (2019): 32–38. https://doi.org/10.1176/appi.prcp.20180009.

Page, John, and Sonia Plaza. "Migration Remittances and Development: A Review of Global Evidence." *Journal of African Economies* 15, no. S2 (2006): 245–336. https://doi.org/10.1093/jae/ejl035.

Papenfuss, Mary. "Border Towns 'Safer than Any City Trump Has Lived In,' Says Texas Congressman." HuffPost, February 12, 2019. https://www.huffpost.com/entry/vincent-gonzales -border-towns-safer-than-trump-cities_n_5c5f707de4b0eec79b24089a.

Parreñas, Rhacel Salazar. *Children of Global Migration: Transnational Families and Gendered Woes.* Stanford, CA: Stanford University Press, 2005. http://www.loc.gov/catdir/toc/ecip0420 /2004016220.html.

Pasetti, Francesco. "Configurations of Immigrant Integration Policies in Europe: An Exploratory Appraisal." *World Affairs* 182, no. 1 (2019): 35–60. https://doi.org/10.1177/0043820019825935.

Passel, Jeffrey S., and D'Vera Cohn. "Mexicans Decline to Less than Half the U.S. Unauthorized Immigrant Population for the First Time." Pew Research Center, June 12, 2019. https://www .pewresearch.org/fact-tank/2019/06/12/us-unauthorized-immigrant-population-2017/.

Passel, Jeffrey S., D'Vera Cohn, and Ana Gonzalez-Barrera. "Net Migration from Mexico Falls to Zero—and Perhaps Less." Pew Research Center, April 23, 2012. http://www.pewhispanic .org/2012/04/23/net-migration-from-mexico-falls-to-zero-and-perhaps-less/.

Patient Protection and Affordable Care Act, Pub. L. No. 111-148, H.R. 3590, § 1312, 42 U.S.C. § 18032 64 (2009). https://www.govinfo.gov/content/pkg/BILLS-111hr3590enr/pdf/BILLS -111hr3590enr.pdf.

Payan, Tony. *The Three U.S.-Mexico Border Wars: Drugs, Immigration, and Homeland Security.* Santa Barbara, CA: Praeger, 2006.

Pearson, Matthew R. "How 'Undocumented Workers' and 'Illegal Aliens' Affect Prejudice Toward Mexican Immigrants." *Social Influence* 5, no. 2 (2010): 118–32.

Penninx, Rinus. "Integration: The Role of Communities, Institutions, and the State." Migration Policy Institute, October 1, 2003. https://www.migrationpolicy.org/article/integration-role -communities-institutions-and-state.

Penninx, Rinus, and Marco Martiniello. "Integration Processes and Policies: State of the Art and Lessons." In *Citizenship in European Cities: Immigrants, Local Politics and Integration Policies*, ed. R. Penninx, K. Kraal, M. Martiniello, and S. Vertovec, 139–64. Aldershot, UK: Ashgate, 2004.

Peralta, Eyder. "You Say You're an American, but What If You Had to Prove It or Be Deported?" NPR, December 22, 2019. https://www.npr.org/sections/thetwo-way/2016/12/22/504031635 /you-say-you-re-an-american-but-what-if-you-had-to-prove-it-or-be-deported#foot2.

Perez, Michael P. "Colonialism, Americanization, and Indigenous Identity: A Research Note on Chamorro Identity in Guam." *Sociological Spectrum* 25 (2005): 571–91. https://doi.org/10.1080 /02732170500176138.

Perez, Nicole. "Nested Contexts of Reception: Latinx Identity Development Across a New Immigrant Community." *Ethnic and Racial Studies* 44, no. 11 (2021): 1995–2015. https://doi.org /10.1080/01419870.2020.1807036.

Perla, Hector, Jr., and Susan Bibler Coutin. "Legacies and Origins of the 1980s US–Central American Sanctuary Movement." In *Sanctuary Practices in International Perspectives: Migration, Citizenship, and Social Movements*, ed. Randy Lippert and Sean Rehaag, 73–91. New York: Routledge, 2012.

Perreira, Krista M., Robert Crosnoe, Karina Fortuny, Juan Pedroza, Kjersti Ulvestad, Christina Weiland, Hirokazu Yoshikawa, and Ajay Chaudry. "Barriers to Immigrants' Access to Health and Human Services Programs." Urban Institute, May 2012. http://webarchive.urban.org/UploadedPDF/413260-Barriers-to-Immigrants-Access-to-Health-and-Human-Services-Programs.pdf.

Perry, Andre M. "Stop Blaming Black Parents for Underachieving Kids." *Washington Post*, July 30, 2014. https://www.washingtonpost.com/posteverything/wp/2014/07/30/stop-blaming-black-parents-for-underachieving-kids/.

Perry, Mark J. "The Shocking Story Behind Richard Nixon's 'War on Drugs' That Targeted Blacks and Anti-War Activists." American Enterprise Institute, June 14, 2018. https://www.aei.org/carpe-diem/the-shocking-and-sickening-story-behind-nixons-war-on-drugs-that-targeted-blacks-and-anti-war-activists/.

Peters, Michael A. "The Ancient Silk Road and the Birth of Merchant Capitalism." *Educational Philosophy and Theory* 53, no. 10 (2021): 955–61. https://doi.org/10.1080/00131857.2019.1691481.

Peters, Robert, William J. Ripple, Christopher Wolf, Matthew Moskwik, Gerardo Carreón-Arroyo, Gerardo Ceballos, Ava Córdova et al. "Nature Divided, Scientists United: US-Mexico Border Wall Threatens Biodiversity and Binational Conservation." American Institute of Biological Sciences, June 2018. https://academic.oup.com/bioscience/article/68/10/740/5057517.

Pew Research Center. "Remittance Flows Worldwide in 2017." April 3, 2019. https://www.pewresearch.org/global/interactives/remittance-flows-by-country/.

——. "Shifting Public Views on Legal Immigration Into the U.S." June 28, 2018. https://www.pewresearch.org/politics/2018/06/28/shifting-public-views-on-legal-immigration-into-the-u-s/.

Phillips, Janet. "Asylum Seekers and Refugees: What Are the Facts?" Parliament of Australia, January 14, 2011. https://www.aph.gov.au/about_parliament/parliamentary_departments/parliamentary_library/pubs/rp/rp1415/asylumfacts.

Piccard, Ann. "Death by Boarding School: The Last Acceptable Racism and the United States' Genocide of Native Americans." *Gonzaga Law Review* 49 (2013–2014): 137.

Piketty, Thomas, and Emmanuel Saez. "Income Inequality in the United States, 1913–1998." *Quarterly Journal of Economics* 118, no. 1 (2003): 1–41. https://doi.org/10.1162/00335530360535135.

Piller, Ingrid. "The Real Problem with Linguistic Shirkers." Language on the Move, March 30, 2016. http://www.languageonthemove.com/the-real-problem-with-linguistic-shirkers/.

Pinçon, Michel, and Monique Pinçon-Charlot. *Les Ghettos du Gotha: Comment la Bourgeoisie Défend Ses Espaces*. Paris: Seuil, 2007.

——. *Sociologie de Paris*. Paris: Découverte, 2004.

Politico. "Full Transcript: Donald Trump's Jobs Plan Speech." June 28, 2016. https://www.politico.com/story/2016/06/full-transcript-trump-job-plan-speech-224891.

Portes, Alejandro. "America and Its Immigrants: A Game of Mirrors." *Proceedings of the American Philosophical Society* 155, no. 4 (2011): 418–32.

Portes, Alejandro, and Ariel C. Armony. *The Global Edge: Miami in the Twenty-First Century*. Oakland: University of California Press, 2018.

Portes, Alejandro, and Lingxin Hao. "E Pluribus Unum: Bilingualism and Loss of Language in the Second Generation." *Sociology of Education* 71, no. 4 (1998): 269–94. https://doi.org /10.2307/2673171.

——. "The Price of Uniformity: Language, Family and Personality Adjustment in the Immigrant Second Generation." *Ethnic and Racial Studies* 25, no. 6 (2002): 889–912. https://doi.org/10.1080 /0141987022000009368.

Portes, Alejandro, and Rubén G. Rumbaut. *Immigrant America: A Portrait.* 4th ed. Berkeley: University of California Press, 2014.

——. *Legacies: The Story of the Immigrant Second Generation.* Berkeley: University of California Press, 2001.

Portes, Jonathan. "Immigration After Brexit." *National Institute Economic Review* 238 (November 2016): R13–21. https://doi.org/10.1177/002795011623800111.

——. "Immigration and the UK Economy After Brexit." IZA (Institute of Labor Economics), May 2021. https://ftp.iza.org/dp14425.pdf.

Poston, Dudley L. "Here's Why Trump's Border Wall Won't Work." Associated Press, January 5, 2019. https://apnews.com/article/lifestyle-travel-immigration-56d7094f0b554925abbd3d81f-8ca74c8.

Potochnick, Stephanie. "Reversing Welfare Reform? Immigrant Restoration Efforts and Food Stamp Receipt Among Mexican Immigrant Families." *Social Science Research* 60 (November 1, 2016): 88–99. https://doi.org/10.1016/j.ssresearch.2016.03.001.

Powers, Jeanne M., and Lirio Patton. "Between *Mendez* and *Brown: 'Gonzales* v. *Sheely'* (1951) and the Legal Campaign Against Segregation." *Law and Social Inquiry* 33, no. 1 (2008): 127–71.

Pruitt, Sarah. "The History Behind Brexit." History, March 29, 2017. https://www.history.com /news/the-history-behind-brexit.

Quintero, Diana, and Michael Hansen. "English Learners and the Growing Need for Qualified Teachers." Brookings Institution, June 2, 2017. https://www.brookings.edu/blog/brown-center -chalkboard/2017/06/02/english-learners-and-the-growing-need-for-qualified-teachers/.

Quoctrung, Bui, and Caitlin Dickerson. "What Can the U.S. Learn from How Other Countries Handle Immigration?" *New York Times*, February 16, 2018. https://www.nytimes.com/interactive /2018/02/16/upshot/comparing-immigration-policies-across-countries.html.

Ramos, Kristian. "The Positive Steps Made in Making Our Southern Border Safer." Latinovations, February 11, 2011. http://www.latinovations.com/2011/02/11/guest-blogger-series-kristian-ramos -the-positive-steps-made-in-making-our-southern-border-safer/.

Rao, Nagesh. " 'Neocolonialism' or 'Globalization'? Postcolonial Theory and the Demands of Political Economy." *Interdisciplinary Literary Studies* 1, no. 2 (2000): 165–84.

Ratha, Dilip. "Leveraging Remittances for Development." In *Migration, Trade, and Development*, ed. James Hollifield, Pia M. Orrenius, and Thomas Osang. Dallas: Federal Reserve Bank of Dallas and Southern Methodist University, 2007.

Ratha, Dilip, Supriyo De, and Kristen Schuettler. "Why Taxing Remittances Is a Bad Idea." *World Bank Blogs*, March 24, 2017. https://blogs.worldbank.org/peoplemove/why-taxing -remittances-bad-idea.

Ratha, Dilip, and Sanket Mohapatra. "Remittances and Development." In *The Wiley-Blackwell Encyclopedia of Globalization.* Hoboken: NJ: Wiley, 2012. https://doi.org/10.1002/9780470670590 .wbeog494.

Remennick, Larissa. "What Does Integration Mean? Social Insertion of Russian Immigrants in Israel." *Journal of International Migration and Integration* 4, no. 1 (2003): 23–49. https://doi.org /10.1007/s12134-003-1018-y.

Rhee, Stephanie L. "Korean Immigrant Older Adults Residing in Non-Korean Ethnic Enclaves: Acculturation Strategies and Psychosocial Adaptation," *Journal of Human Behavior in the Social Environment* 29, no. 7 (2019): 861–73.

Roberts, Cheryl A. "Bilingual Education Program Models: A Framework for Understanding." *Bilingual Research Journal* 19, no. 3–4 (1995): 369–78. https://doi.org/10.1080/15235882.1995 .10162679.

Robertson, Lori. "Misleading Border Crime Statistic." FactCheck.org, January 8, 2019. https:// www.factcheck.org/2019/01/misleading-border-crime-statistic/.

Rodriguez, Robyn Magalit. "The Emergence of Labor Brokerage: U.S. Colonial Legacies in the Philippines." In *Migrants for Export: How the Philippine State Brokers Labor to the World*, ed. Robyn Magalit Rodriguez. Minneapolis: University of Minnesota Press, 2010. https://doi .org/10.5749/minnesota/9780816665273.003.0001.

Romero, Mary. "Are Your Papers in Order? Racial Profiling, Vigilantes, and America's Toughest Sheriff." *Harvard Latino Law Review* 14 (2011): 337.

Rommel, Inken. " 'We Are the People.' Refugee–'Crisis,' and the Drag-Effects of Social Habitus in German Society." *Historical Social Research/Historische Sozialforschung* 42, no. 4 (2017): 133–54.

Root, Jay. "At a Crowded Mexican Shelter, Migrants Wait Months to Claim Asylum. Some Opt to Cross the River Instead." *Texas Tribune*, July 1, 2019. https://www.texastribune.org /2019/07/01/crowded-mexican-shelter-migrants-are-waiting-months-claim-asylum/.

Ross, Brian. "Serving the Urban Poor in Turn-of-the-Century Cleveland." *OAH Magazine of History* 5, no. 2 (1990): 55–57.

Roth, Kenneth. "The Refugee Crisis That Isn't." Human Rights Watch, September 3, 2015. https://www.hrw.org/news/2015/09/03/refugee-crisis-isnt.

Roth, Wendy D. *Race Migrations: Latinos and the Cultural Transformation of Race.* Stanford, CA: Stanford University Press, 2012.

Rubin, Donald L. "Nonlanguage Factors Affecting Undergraduates' Judgments of Nonnative English-Speaking Teaching Assistants." *Research in Higher Education* 33, no. 4 (1992): 511–31.

Rubio Goldsmith, Pat, Mary Romero, Raquel Rubio Goldsmith, Manuel Escobedo, and Laura Khoury. "Ethno-racial Profiling and State Violence in a Southwest Barrio." *Aztlán: A Journal of Chicano Studies* 34, no. 1 (2009): 93–123.

Ruëgger, Seraina. "Refugees, Ethnic Power Relations, and Civil Conflict in the Country of Asylum." *Journal of Peace Research* 56, no. 1 (2019): 42–57. https://doi.org/10.1177%2F0022343318812935.

Rumbaut, Rubén G., and Walter A. Ewing. *The Myth of Immigrant Criminality and the Paradox of Assimilation: Incarceration Rates Among Native and Foreign-Born Men.* Washington, DC: Immigration Policy Center, American Immigration Council, 2007. http://www.immigrationpolicy .org/special-reports/myth-immigrant-criminality-and-paradox-assimilation.

Ruszczyk, Stephen P. "Inclusion in the Nation via the City: Assessing Immigrant Claims of Belonging." *Sociological Forum* 34, no. 3 (2019): 786–90. https://doi.org/10.1111/socf.12527.

——. "Local Governance of Immigrant Incorporation: How City-Based Organizational Fields Shape the Cases of Undocumented Youth in New York City and Paris." *Comparative Migration Studies* 6, no. 1 (2018): art. 32. https://doi.org/10.1186/s40878-018-0097-z.

——. "Non-state Actors in the Regularisation of Undocumented Youths: The Role of the 'Education Without Borders Network' in Paris." *Journal of Ethnic and Migration Studies* 45, no. 15 (2019): 3023–40. https://doi.org/10.1080/1369183X.2018.1495068.

Ryo, Emily. "Representing Immigrants: The Role of Lawyers in Immigration Bond Hearings." *Law and Society Review* 52, no. 2 (2018): 503–31.

Rzepnikowska, Alina. "Racism and Xenophobia Experienced by Polish Migrants in the UK Before and After Brexit Vote." *Journal of Ethnic and Migration Studies* 45, no. 1 (2019): 61–77. https://doi.org/10.1080/1369183X.2018.1451308.

Sabo, Samantha, Susan Shaw, Maia Ingram, Nicolette Teufel-Shone, Scott Carvajal, Jill Quernsey de Zapien, Cecilia Rosales, Flor Redondo, Gina Garcia, and Raquel Rubio-Goldsmith. "Everyday Violence, Structural Racism and Mistreatment at the US-Mexico Border." *Social Science & Medicine* 109 (2014): 66–74.

Salas-Wright, Christopher P., Michael G. Vaughn, Trenette T. Clark, Lauren D. Terzis, and David Córdova. "Substance Use Disorders Among First- and Second-Generation Immigrant Adults in the United States: Evidence of an Immigrant Paradox?" *Journal of Studies on Alcohol and Drugs* 75, no. 6 (2014): 958–67. https://doi.org/10.15288/jsad.2014.75.958.

Salas-Wright, Christopher P., Michael G. Vaughn, and Trenette Clark Goings. "Immigrants from Mexico Experience Serious Behavioral and Psychiatric Problems at Far Lower Rates than US-Born Americans." *Social Psychiatry and Psychiatric Epidemiology* 52 (October 1, 2017): 1325–28. https://doi.org/10.1007/s00127-017-1425-6.

Sampson, Robert. "Open Doors Don't Invite Criminals." *New York Times*, 2006. https://www.nytimes.com/2006/03/11/opinion/open-doors-dont-invite-criminals.html.

Sanchez, Gabriella E., and Sheldon X. Zhang. "Rumors, Encounters, Collaborations, and Survival: The Migrant Smuggling–Drug Trafficking Nexus in the U.S. Southwest." *Annals of the American Academy of Political and Social Science* 676, no. 1 (2018): 135–51. https://doi.org/10.1177%2F0002716217752331.

San Pedro River Valley. "San Pedro River Ecology." 2010. https://sanpedrorivervalley.org/.

Sassen, Saskia. *The Global City: New York, London, Tokyo.* 2nd ed. Princeton, NJ: Princeton University Press, 2001.

Scallen, Patrick D. "The Bombs That Drop in El Salvador Explode in Mt. Pleasant: From Cold War Conflagration to Immigrant Struggles in Washington, D.C., 1970–1995." PhD diss., Georgetown University, 2019. https://repository.library.georgetown.edu/handle/10822/1057308.

Schildkraut, Deborah J. "Official-English and the States: Influences on Declaring English the Official Language in the United States." *Political Research Quarterly* 54, no. 2 (2001): 445–57. https://doi.org/10.1177/106591290105400211.

Schneider, Barbara, Sylvia Martinez, and Ann Owens. "Barriers to Educational Opportunities for Hispanics in the United States." In *Hispanics and the Future of America*, ed. Marta Tienda and Faith Mitchell. Washington, DC: National Academies Press, 2006. https://www.ncbi.nlm.nih.gov/books/NBK19909/.

Scott, Eugene. "Trump's Most Insulting—and Violent—Language Is Often Reserved for Immigrants." *Washington Post*, October 2, 2019. https://www.washingtonpost.com/politics/2019/10/02/trumps-most-insulting-violent-language-is-often-reserved-immigrants/.

Segal, Uma A. "Globalization, Migration, and Ethnicity: Opportunities and Challenges." *European Journal of Public Health* 28, no. 1 (2018). https://doi.org/10.1093/eurpub/cky044.001.

Semple, Kirk. "Migrants in Mexico Face Kidnappings and Violence While Awaiting Immigration Hearings in U.S." *New York Times*, July 12, 2019. https://www.nytimes.com/2019/07/12/world/americas/mexico-migrants.html.

Serhan, Yasmeen. "Brexit Has Triggered Britain's Most Ambitious Migration Exercise Ever." *Atlantic*, March 23, 2019. https://www.theatlantic.com/international/archive/2019/03/brexit-britain-millions-eu-citizens/584959/.

Shams, Tahseen. *Here, There, and Elsewhere: The Making of Immigrant Identities in a Globalized World.* Stanford, CA: Stanford University Press, 2020.

Shangquan, Gao. "Economic Globalization: Trends, Risks, and Risk Prevention." In Committee for Development Policy, Background Paper no. 1, United Nations, 2000. https://www.un.org/en/development/desa/policy/cdp/cdp_background_papers/bp2000_1.pdf.

Shapira, Harel. *Waiting for José: The Minutemen's Pursuit of America.* Princeton, NJ: Princeton University Press, 2013.

Sherman, Erik. "Nixon's Drug War, an Excuse to Lock Up Blacks and Protesters, Continues." Forbes, March 23, 2016. https://www.forbes.com/sites/eriksherman/2016/03/23/nixons-drug-war-an-excuse-to-lock-up-blacks-and-protesters-continues/?sh=25d5f98242c8.

Sherwood, John T. "Building the Wall: The Efficacy of a US-Mexico Border Fence." Army Command and General Staff College, Fort Leavenworth, KS, 2008. https://apps.dtic.mil/sti/citations/ADA502097.

Siegfried, Kristy. "The Refugee Brief—10 September 2021." United Nations High Commissioner for Refugees, September 10, 2021. https://www.unhcr.org/refugeebrief/latest-issues/.

Silver, Hilary. "Book Review: A Place to Call Home: Immigrant Exclusion and Urban Belonging in New York, Paris, and Barcelona." *City & Community* 18, no. 2 (2019): 732–34. https://doi.org/10.1111/cico.12407.

Simon, Julian L. "Immigrants, Taxes, and Welfare in the United States." *Population and Development Review* 10, no. 1 (1984): 55–69. https://doi.org/10.2307/1973162.

Simon, Patrick. "French National Identity and Integration: Who Belongs to the National Community?" Washington, DC: Migration Policy Institute, May 2012. https://www.migrationpolicy.org/pubs/FrenchIdentity.pdf.

Simon, Rita J., and Keri W. Sikich. "Public Attitudes Toward Immigrants and Immigration Policies Across Seven Nations." *International Migration Review* 41, no. 4 (2007): 956–62. https://doi.org/10.1111/j.1747-7379.2007.00107.x.

Singer, Audrey. *Practice to Policy: Lessons from Local Leadership on Immigrant Integration.* Toronto: Maytree Foundation, 2012. https://central.bac-lac.gc.ca/.item?id=practice_to_policy_engl&op=pdf&app=Library.

Sipsma, H. L., K. L. Falb, T. Willie, E. H. Bradley, L. Bienkowski, N. Meerdink, and J. Gupta. "Violence Against Congolese Refugee Women in Rwanda and Mental Health: A Cross-Sectional Study Using Latent Class Analysis." *BMJ Open* 5, no. 4 (2015): e006299. https://doi.org/10.1136/bmjopen-2014-006299.

Sirkeci, Ibrahim, Jeffery H. Cohen, and Dilip Ratha. "Migration and Remittances During the Global Financial Crisis and Beyond." World Bank, 2012. https://documents1.worldbank.org/curated/en/701621468149081927/pdf/693130PUB0publ067926B09780821388266.pdf.

Skeldon, Ron. "Globalization, Skilled Migration and Poverty Alleviation: Brain Drains in Context." University of Sussex, November 2005. http://sro.sussex.ac.uk/id/eprint/11227/1/WP-T15.pdf.

Slack, Jeremy. *Deported to Death: How Drug Violence Is Changing Migration on the US-Mexico Border.* Oakland: University of California Press, 2019.

Slack, Jeremy, Daniel E. Martínez, Alison Elizabeth Lee, and Scott Whiteford. "The Geography of Border Militarization: Violence, Death and Health in Mexico and the United States." *Journal of Latin American Geography* 15, no. 1 (2016): 7–32.

Slack, Jeremy, Daniel Martinez, and Scott Whiteford, eds. *The Shadow of the Wall: Violence and Migration on the U.S.-Mexico Border.* Tucson: University of Arizona Press, 2018.

Slomanson, Peter, and Michael Newman. "Peer Group Identification and Variation in New York Latino English Laterals." *English World-Wide* 25, no. 2 (2004): 199–216. https://doi.org/10.1075/eww.25.2.03slo.

Snipper, Grace Capizzi. "Real Americans Don't Speak Spanish: Some Hispanic Parents' Views on Bilingual Education." *Bilingual Review/La Revista Bilingüe* 13, no. 3 (1986): 13–25.

Soto, Gabriella, and Daniel E. Martínez. "The Geography of Migrant Death: Implications for Policy and Forensic Sciences." In *Sociopolitics of Migrant Death and Repatriation*, ed. Krista E. Latham and Alyson J. O'Daniel, 67–82. Cham, Switzerland: Springer, 2018. https://www.academia.edu/34845336/The_Geography_of_Migrant_Death_Implications_for_Policy_and_Forensic_Sciences.

Southern Border Communities Coalition. "Fatal Encounters with CBP." June 11, 2021; updated February 1, 2024. https://www.southernborder.org/deaths_by_border_patrol.

Spencer, Sarah. "Multi-level Governance of an Intractable Policy Problem: Migrants with Irregular Status in Europe." *Journal of Ethnic and Migration Studies* 44, no. 12 (2017): 2034–52. https://doi.org/10.1080/1369183X.2017.1341708.

Springford, John. *Is Immigration a Reason for Britain to Leave the EU?* London: Centre for European Reform, October 2013.

Stalker, Peter. *Workers Without Frontiers: The Impact of Globalization on International Migration.* Geneva: International Labour Organization, 2000.

Staton, Bethan. "Employers 'Simply Not Ready' for Post-Brexit Immigration Regime." Financial Times, September 19, 2019. https://www.ft.com/content/1a3668ea-d965-11e9-8f9b-77216ebe1f17.

Stephen, Lynn. "Hemispheric and Transborder Perspectives: Racialization of Mexicans Through Time." *Konturen* 4 (January 12, 2013): 46–88. https://doi.org/10.5399/u0/konturen.4.0.3066.

——. "Towards a Transborder Perspective: U.S.-Mexico Relations." *Iberoamericana* 12, no. 48 (2012): 85–99.

Stepick, Alex, and Carol Dutton Stepick. "Diverse Contexts of Reception and Feelings of Belonging." *Forum Qualitative Sozialforschung/Forum: Qualitative Social Research* 10, no. 3 (2009): art. 15. http://nbn-resolving.de/urn:nbn:de:0114-fqs0903156.

Stevens, Jacqueline. "U.S. Government Unlawfully Detaining and Deporting U.S. Citizens as Aliens." *University of Virginia Journal of Social Policy and the Law* 18, no. 3 (2011): 606–720.

Stevenson, Ariel. "Recovering Lost Tax Revenue Through Taxation of Transnational Households." *Berkeley Journal of International Law* 34, no. 1 (2016): 100–156. https://doi.org/10.15779/Z384G3Z.

St. Martin, Greg. "Do More Broken Windows Mean More Crime?" News@Northeastern, May 15, 2019. https://news.northeastern.edu/2019/05/15/northeastern-university-researchers-find-little-evidence-for-broken-windows-theory-say-neighborhood-disorder-doesnt-cause-crime/.

Stowell, Jacob I., Steven F. Messner, Kelly F. McGeever, and Lawrence E. Raffalovich. "Immigration and the Recent Violent Crime Drop in the United States: A Pooled, Cross-Sectional

Time-Series Analysis of Metropolitan Areas." *Criminology* 47, no. 3 (2009): 889–928. https://doi.org/10.1111/j.1745-9125.2009.00162.x.

Stuster, Jack. "Albuquerque Police Department's Safe Streets Program." U.S. Department of Transportation, National Highway Traffic Safety Administration, June 2021. https://rosap.ntl.bts.gov/view/dot/1048.

Substance Abuse and Mental Health Services Administration, *Results from the 2012 National Survey on Drug Use and Health: Summary of National Findings*, NSDUH Series H-46, HHS Publication No. (SMA) 13-4795. Rockville, MD: Substance Abuse and Mental Health Services Administration, 2013. https://store.samhsa.gov/home.

Substance Abuse and Mental Health Services Administration. (2018). Key substance use and mental health indicators in the United States: Results from the 2017 National Survey on Drug Use and Health (HHS Publication No. SMA 18-5068, NSDUH Series H-53). Rockville, MD: Center for Behavioral Health Statistics and Quality, Substance Abuse and Mental Health Services Administration. Retrieved from https://www.samhsa.gov/data/.

Sullivan, Amanda L. "Disproportionality in Special Education Identification and Placement of English Language Learners." *Exceptional Children* 77, no. 3 (2011): 317–34. https://doi.org/10.1177/001440291107700304.

Sullivan, Dennis H., and Andrea L. Ziegert. "Hispanic Immigrant Poverty: Does Ethnic Origin Matter?" *Population Research and Policy Review* 27 (2008): 667–87. https://doi.org/10.1007/s11113-008-9096-3.

Sumption, Madeleine. "Labour Immigration After Brexit: Questions and Trade-Offs in Designing a Work Permit System for EU Citizens." *Oxford Review of Economic Policy* 33, no. S1 (2017): S45–53. https://doi.org/10.1093/oxrep/grx006.

Suro, Roberto. "Remittance Senders and Receivers." Pew Research Center, November 24, 2003. https://www.pewresearch.org/hispanic/2003/11/24/remittance-senders-and-receivers/.

Svensson, Mikael, and Curt Hagquist. "Adolescent Alcohol and Illicit Drug Use Among First- and Second-Generation Immigrants in Sweden." *Scandinavian Journal of Public Health* 38, no. 2 (2009): 184–91. https://doi.org/10.1177/1403494809353822.

Swing, William. "How Migrants Who Send Money Home Have Become a Global Economic Force." World Economic Forum, June 14, 2018. https://www.weforum.org/agenda/2018/06/migrants-remittance-global-economic-force/.

Syed, Iffath U. B. "Forced Assimilation Is an Unhealthy Policy Intervention: The Case of the Hijab Ban in France and Quebec, Canada." *International Journal of Human Rights* 17, no. 3 (2013): 428–40. https://doi.org/10.1080/13642987.2012.724678.

Texas Department of Public Safety. "Crime in Texas, 2019." Austin, Texas. https://www.dps.texas.gov/sites/default/files/documents/crimereports/19/cit2019.pdf.

Thompson, A. C. "Border Patrol Has a Long History of Agent Misconduct. Why Hasn't It Been Addressed?" *Pacific Standard*, June 24, 2019. https://psmag.com/social-justice/why-border-patrol-agents-are-not-held-accountable-for-wrongdoing.

Tienda, Marta, and Leif Jensen. "Immigration and Public Assistance Participation: Dispelling the Myth of Dependency." *Social Science Research* 15, no. 4 (1986): 372–400. https://doi.org/10.1016/0049-089X(86)90019-0.

Tilford, Simon. "Britain, Immigration and Brexit." *Center for European Reform Bulletin*, no. 105 (January 2016). https://www.cer.eu/sites/default/files/bulletin_105_st_article1.pdf.

Tilly, Charles. *Big Structures, Large Processes, Huge Comparisons*. New York: Russell Sage Foundation, 1984.

——. *Durable Inequality*. Berkeley: University of California Press, 1998.

——. "Globalization Threatens Labor's Rights." *International Labor and Working-Class History* 47 (1995): 1–23.

Tilly, Charles, Ernesto Castañeda, and Lesley J. Wood, eds. *Social Movements, 1768–2018*. 4th ed, New York: Routledge, 2020.

Tims, Anna, and Lisa O'Carroll. "130,000 EU Citizens on UK Benefits Yet to Apply for Settled Status, Leak Suggests." *Guardian*, June 21, 2021. https://www.theguardian.com/uk-news/2021/jun/21/130000-eu-citizens-on-uk-benefits-yet-to-apply-for-settled-status-leak-suggests.

Tobias, Manuela. "Are 55 Percent of Immigrants in California on Welfare? That's an Exaggeration." PolitiFact, January 29, 2018. https://www.politifact.com/factchecks/2018/jan/29/steve-cortes/are-55-percent-immigrants-california-welfare-s-exa/.

Tondo, Lorenzo. " 'It's a Day Off': Wiretaps Show Mediterranean Migrants Were Left to Die." *Guardian*, April 16, 2021. http://www.theguardian.com/world/2021/apr/16/wiretaps-migrant-boats-italy-libya-coastguard-mediterranean.

Toppelberg, Claudio O., and Brian A. Collins. "Language, Culture, and Adaptation in Immigrant Children." *Child and Adolescent Psychiatric Clinics of North America* 19, no. 4 (2010): 697–717. https://doi.org/10.1016/j.chc.2010.07.003.

Trilling, Daniel. "Five Myths About the Refugee Crisis." *Guardian*, June 5, 2018. http://www.theguardian.com/news/2018/jun/05/five-myths-about-the-refugee-crisis.

Trines, Stefan. "The State of Refugee Integration in Germany in 2019." World Education News + Reviews, August 8, 2019. https://wenr.wes.org/2019/08/the-state-of-refugee-integration-in-germany-in-2019.

Trofimovich, Pavel, and Larisa Turuseva. "Ethnic Identity and Second Language Learning." *Annual Review of Applied Linguistics* 35 (2015): 234–52.

Tropp, Linda R., and Ludwin E. Molina. "Intergroup Processes: From Prejudice to Positive Relations Between Groups." In *The Oxford Handbook of Personality and Social Psychology*. 2nd ed. London: Oxford University Press, 2018.

Tse, Lucy. *"Why Don't They Learn English?" Separating Fact from Fallacy in the U.S. Language Debate*. New York: Teachers College Press, 2001.

Tseng, Amelia. "Bilingualism, Ideological Recentering, and New Latinx Identity Construction in the Global City." *Latina/o Studies Association 3rd Biennial Conference, Latinx Studies Now: DC*. Washington, DC, 2018. https://scholar.google.com/citations?view_op=view_citation&hl=en&user=2hSNDFcAAAAJ&sortby=pubdate&citation_for_view=2hSNDFcAAAAJ:KlAtU1dfN6UC.

——. " 'Qué Barbaridad, Son Latinos y Deberían Saber Español Primero': Language Ideology, Agency, and Heritage Language Insecurity Across Immigrant Generations." *Applied Linguistics* 42, no. 1 (2021): 113–35. https://doi.org/10.1093/applin/amaa004.

——. "Vowel Variation, Style, and Identity Construction in the English of Latinos in Washington, D.C." PhD diss., Georgetown University, 2014.

Tseng, Amelia, and Lars Hinrichs. "Mobility and the English Language." In *The Handbook of English Linguistics*, 637–52. 2nd ed. Hoboken, NJ: Wiley, 2021. https://doi.org/10.1002/9781119540618.ch32.

Tummala-Narra, P. "The Fear of Immigrants." *APA PsychNet* 37, no. 1 (2020): 50–61.

Tyburski, Michael D. "The Resource Curse Reversed? Remittances and Corruption in Mexico." *International Studies Quarterly* 56, no. 2 (2012): 339–50. https://doi.org/10.1111/j.1468-2478.2012 .00721.x.

United Arab Emirates. "Value Added Tax (VAT)." August 17, 2021.

United Nations. *International Migration Report 2017.* New York: UN, 2017. https://www.un.org /en/development/desa/population/migration/publications/migrationreport/docs/Migration Report2017_Highlights.pdf.

United Nations High Commission for Refugees. Convention and Protocol Relating to the Status of Refugees. 2010. https://www.unhcr.org/protection/basic/3b66c2aa10/convention -protocol-relating-status-refugees.html.

——. *Desperate Journeys.* Geneva: UNHCR, 2018. https://www.unhcr.org/desperatejourneys/#.

——. "Global Trends—Forced Displacement in 2015." June 20, 2016. https://www.unhcr.org /statistics/unhcrstats/576408cd7/unhcr-global-trends-2015.html.

——. "Global Trends—Forced Displacement in 2016." June 19, 2017.

——. "Global Trends—Forced Displacement in 2018." June 20, 2019. https://www.unhcr.org /globaltrends2018/.

——. "Global Trends—Forced Displacement in 2019." June 18, 2020. https://www.unhcr.org /flagship-reports/globaltrends/globaltrends2019/?web=1&wdLOR=cF8CD8137-7BF7-4540 -B7A3-901D102E2ED5.

——. "Global Trends—Forced Displacement in 2020." June 18, 2021. https://www.unhcr.org /60b638e37/unhcr-global-trends-2020.

——. "Refugee Statistics: Provisional 2000 Data Released." May 11, 2001. https://www.unhcr.org /news/briefing/2001/5/3b0118db2/refugee-statistics-provisional-2000-data-released.html.

——. "Spain." September 12, 2021. https://data2.unhcr.org/en/country/esp.

United Nations News. "Italy Failed to Rescue Over 200 Migrants in 2013 Mediterranean Disaster, UN Rights Body Finds." January 27, 2021. https://news.un.org/en/story/2021/01/1083082.

——. "Remittances Matter: 8 Facts You Don't Know About the Money Migrants Send Back Home." June 15, 2019. https://news.un.org/en/story/2019/06/1040581.

——. "UN Rights Office Concerned Over Migrant Boat Pushbacks in the Mediterranean," May 8, 2020. https://news.un.org/en/story/2020/05/1063592.

United Nations Office of the High Commissioner for Human Rights. International Covenant on Civil and Political Rights. March 23, 1976. https://www.ohchr.org/en/professionalinterest /pages/ccpr.aspx.

Urrea, Luis Alberto. *The Devil's Highway: A True Story.* New York: Back Bay, 2004.

U.S. Border Patrol. "Border Patrol Strategic Plan 1994 and Beyond: National Strategy." 1994. https://www.hsdl.org/?view&did=721845.

U.S. Census Bureau. 2010 Census Interactive Population Map. http://2010.census.gov/2010census /popmap/.

——. "Close to Half of New Immigrants Report High English-Language Speaking Ability, Census Bureau Reports." June 10, 2014. https://www.census.gov/newsroom/archives/2014-pr /cb14-105.html.

——. "Detailed Languages Spoken at Home and Ability to Speak English for the Population 5 Years and Over: 2009–2013." October 2015. https://www.census.gov/data/tables/2013/demo /2009-2013-lang-tables.html.

——. "Nation's Population Growth Slowed This Decade." April 6, 2020. https://www.census.gov /library/stories/2020/04/nations-population-growth-slowed-this-decade.html.

——. "QuickFacts: El Paso County, Texas." Accessed May 16, 2024. https://www.census.gov /quickfacts/fact/table/elpasocountytexas,US/PST040222.

——. "QuickFacts: Texas." 2019. Accessed May 16, 2024. https://www.census.gov/quickfacts/TX.

U.S. Citizenship and Immigration Services. "Public Charge." August 19, 2021. https://www.uscis .gov/green-card/green-card-processes-and-procedures/public-charge.

U.S. Commission on International Religious Freedom. "Syria's Refugee Crisis and Its Implications." July 2013. https://permanent.access.gpo.gov/gpo39835/Syria%20Factsheet%20-%20July %2018(2).pdf.

U.S. Customs and Border Protection. "Border Wall Status." January 8, 2021. https://interactive .khou.com/pdfs/CBPBorderWallStatusPaper_asof01082021.pdf.

——. "CBP Border Security Report: Fiscal Year 2018." March 2019. https://www.cbp.gov/sites /default/files/assets/documents/2019-Mar/CBP-Border-Security-Report-FY2018.pdf.

——. "United States Border Patrol Southwest Family Unit Subject and Unaccompanied Alien Children Apprehensions Fiscal Year 2016." 2023. https://www.cbp.gov/newsroom/stats /southwest-border-unaccompanied-children/fy-2016.

——. "U.S. Border Patrol Southwest Border Apprehensions by Sector." August 26, 2021. https:// www.cbp.gov/print/365977.

U.S. Department of Homeland Security. "FY 2021: Budget in Brief." 2021. https://www.dhs.gov /sites/default/files/publications/fy_2021_dhs_bib_web_version.pdf.

——. "Inadmissibility and Deportability on Public Charge Grounds." 64 Fed. Reg. 28676–88 (May 26, 1999).

U.S. Department of Justice. "An Investigation of Travel Reimbursements in Connection with the INS's Operation Safeguard." Office of the Inspector General, 2002. https://oig.justice .gov/sites/default/files/archive/special/0301/main.htm.

U.S. Department of State. "Refugee Admissions." Accessed September 7, 2021. https://www .state.gov/refugee-admissions/.

U.S. Federal Bureau of Investigation. *Crime on the Southwest Border*. Accessed August 21, 2021. https://www.fbi.gov/video-repository/newss-crime-on-the-southwest-border/view.

U.S. Government Accountability Office. *Border Security: Progress and Challenges with the Use of Technology, Tactical Infrastructure, and Personnel to Secure the Southwest Border*. Washington, DC: GAO, 2018. https://www.gao.gov/products/gao-18-397t.

——. *Illegal Immigration: Border Crossing Deaths Have Doubled Since 1995; Border Patrol's Efforts to Prevent Deaths Have Not Been Fully Evaluated*. Washington, DC: GAO, 2006. https://www.gao .gov/new.items/d06770.pdf.

——. *Teacher Preparation: Multiple Federal Education Offices Support Teacher Preparation for Instructing Students with Disabilities and English Language Learners but Systematic Departmentwide Coordination Could Enhance This Assistance*. Washington, DC: GAO, 2009. https://www.legistorm.com /reports/view/gao/39708/Multiple_Federal_Education_Offices_Support_Teacher_Preparation _for_Instructing_Students_with_Disabilities_and_English_Language_Learners_but_Systematic _Departmentwide_Coordination_Could_Enhance_This_Assistance.html.

U.S. House of Representatives. "Examining Challenges and Wasted Taxpayer Dollars in Modernizing Border Security IT Systems." Hearing Before the Subcommittee on Oversight and Management

Efficiency of the Committee on Homeland Security, 113th Congress, February 6, 2014. https://www.govinfo.gov/content/pkg/CHRG-113hhrg88024/html/CHRG-113hhrg88024.htm.

U.S. Immigration and Customs Enforcement. "Form I-9 Inspection." August 7, 2023. https://www.ice.gov/factsheets/i9-inspection.

——. "ICE Detainers: Frequently Asked Questions." December 28, 2011. https://www.ice.gov/identify-and-arrest/detainers/ice-detainers-frequently-asked-questions.

U.S. Sentencing Commission. *Statistical Information Packet: Fiscal Year 2019, Southern District of Texas.* Washington, DC: U.S. Sentencing Commission, 2020. https://www.ussc.gov/sites/default/files/pdf/research-and-publications/federal-sentencing-statistics/state-district-circuit/2019/txs19.pdf.

Usherwood, Simon. "Some Trade, Not Much Cooperation: The Hard Brexit Deal." *Political Insight* 12, no. 1 (2021): 26–28. https://doi.org/10.1177/20419058211001000.

Uwaifo Oyelere, Ruth, and Maharouf Oyolola. "Do Immigrant Groups Differ in Welfare Usage? Evidence from the U.S." *Atlantic Economic Journal* 39, no. 3 (2011): 231–47. https://doi.org/10.1007/s11293-011-9279-x.

Uyghur Human Rights Project. *Weaponized Passports: The Crisis of Uyghur Statelessness.* Washington, DC: UHRP, April 2020. https://docs.uhrp.org/pdf/Weaponized_Passports.pdf.

Valdés, Guadalupe. "Dual-Language Immersion Programs: A Cautionary Note Concerning the Education of Language-Minority Students." *Harvard Educational Review* 67, no. 3 (1997): 391–429. https://doi.org/10.17763/haer.67.3.n5q175qp86120948.

Valverde, Gabriela Ortiz, and María C. Latorre. "The Economic Impact of Potential Migration Policies in the UK After Brexit." *Contemporary Social Science* 14, no. 2 (2019): 208–25. https://doi.org/10.1080/21582041.2018.1558278.

Vang, Zoua M. "The Limits of Spatial Assimilation for Immigrants' Full Integration: Emerging Evidence from African Immigrants in Boston and Dublin." *Annals of the American Academy of Political and Social Science* 641, no. 1 (2012): 220–46. https://doi.org/10.1177/0002716211432280.

Van Hook, Jennifer, and Frank D. Bean. "Explaining Mexican Immigrant Welfare Behaviors: The Importance of Employment-Related Cultural Repertoires." *American Sociological Review* 74, no. 3 (2009): 423–44.

Van Voris, Bob. "Biden Review of Immigration 'Wealth Test' Halts Legal Challenge." Bloomberg CityLab, February 10, 2021. https://www.bloomberg.com/news/articles/2021-02-10/biden-review-of-immigration-wealth-test-halts-legal-challenge.

Vargas, Robert, and Lee Scrivener. "Why Latino Youth (Don't) Call Police." *Race and Justice* 11, no. 1 (2018): 47–64. https://doi.org/10.1177%2F2153368718776056.

Vargas-Silva, Carlos, and Cinzia Rienzo. "Migrants in the UK: An Overview." Migration Observatory, August 2, 2022. https://migrationobservatory.ox.ac.uk/resources/briefings/migrants-in-the-uk-an-overview/.

Velasco Ortiz, Laura, and Oscar F. Contreras. "The Border as a Life Experience: Identities, Asymmetry and Border Crossing Between Mexico and the United States." *Frontera Norte* 26, no. 3e (2014): 37–56.

Velazquez, Adrian M., and Kimberly Kempf-Leonard. "Mexican Immigration: Insiders' Views on Crime, Risks, and Victimization." *Journal of Ethnicity in Criminal Justice* 8, no. 2 (2009). https://doi.org/10.1080/15377931003761045.

Velazquez, Sonia C., and Alan J. Dettlaff. "Immigrant Children and Child Welfare in the United States: Demographics, Legislation, Research, Policy, and Practice Impacting Public Services." *Child Indicators Research* 4, no. 4 (2011): 679–95. https://doi.org/10.1007/s12187-011-9111-9.

Velázquez Vargas, María del Socorro, and Georgina Martínez Canizales. "La Inseguridad en Ciudad Juárez Desde la Percepción de los Ciudadanos." In *Inseguridad y Violencia en Ciudad Juárez, México*, ed. Myrna Limas Hernández. Ciudad Juárez, Chihuahua: Universidad Autónoma de Ciudad Juárez, 2012.

Vericker, Tracy, Karina Fortuny, Kenneth Finegold, and Sevgi Bayram Ozdemir. *Effects of Immigration on WIC and NSLP Caseloads*. Washington, DC: Urban Institute, 2010. https://www.urban.org/research/publication/effects-immigration-wic-and-nslp-caseloads.

Villagran, Lauren. "US Customs and Border Protection Chief Mark Morgan Tours New Border Wall Area Near El Paso." *El Paso Times*, August 26, 2020. https://www.elpasotimes.com/story/news/immigration/2020/08/26/cbp-leader-mark-morgan-tours-new-30-foot-steel-us-mexico-border-wall-section-east-el-paso/3436687001/.

Villazor, Rose Cuison. "What Is a Sanctuary." *SMU Law Review* 61, no. 1 (2008): 133–56.

Villegas, Ana Maria, Kit Saizdelamora, Adrian D. Martin, and Tammy Mills. "Preparing Future Mainstream Teachers to Teach English Language Learners: A Review of the Empirical Literature." *Educational Forum* 82, no. 2 (2018): 138–55.

Viñas, Silvia. "Immigrant Detainees Say They Were Sexually Abused in CBP Custody." NPR, March 24, 2019. https://www.npr.org/2019/03/24/706295417/immigrant-detainees-say-they-were-sexually-abused-in-cbp-custody.

Vine, David, Cala Coffman, Katalina Khoury, Madison Lovasz, Helen Bush, Rachael Leduc, and Jennifer Walkup. "Creating Refugees: Displacement Caused by the United States' Post-9/11 Wars." Watson Institute for International & Public Affairs, September 21, 2020. https://watson.brown.edu/costsofwar/files/cow/imce/papers/2020/Displacement_Vine%20et%20al_Costs%20of%20War%202020%2009%2008.pdf.

Virdee, Satnam, and Brendan McGeever. "Racism, Crisis, Brexit." *Ethnic and Racial Studies* 41, no. 10 (2018): 1802–19. https://doi.org/10.1080/01419870.2017.1361544.

Vogt, Wendy A. "Crossing Mexico: Structural Violence and the Commodification of Undocumented Central American Migrants." *American Ethnologist* 40, no. 4 (2013): 764–80. https://doi.org/10.1111/amet.12053.

Wadsworth, Johnathan, Swati Dhingra, Gianmarco Ottaviano, and Van Reenen. "Brexit and the Impact of Immigration on the UK." Center for Economic Performance, May 11, 2016. https://cep.lse.ac.uk/_new/publications/abstract.asp?index=5053.

Wadsworth, Tim. "Is Immigration Responsible for the Crime Drop? An Assessment of the Influence of Immigration on Changes in Violent Crime Between 1990 and 2000." *Social Science Quarterly* 91, no. 2 (2010): 531–53.

Walker, Kyle E., and Helga Leitner. "The Variegated Landscape of Local Immigration Policies in the United States." *Urban Geography* 32, no. 2 (2011): 156–78. https://doi.org/10.2747/0272-3638.32.2.156.

Walker, Nigel. "Brexit Timeline: Events Leading to the UK's Exit from the European Union." House of Commons Library, January 6, 2021. https://commonslibrary.parliament.uk/research-briefings/cbp-7960/.

Wallace, Sophia. "Papers Please: State-Level Anti-Immigrant Legislation in the Wake of Arizona's SB 1070." *Political Science Quarterly* 129, no. 2 (2014): 261–91.

Wallace, Steven P., Carolyn Mendez-Luck, and Xóchitl Castañeda. "Heading South: Why Mexican Immigrants in California Seek Health Services in Mexico." *Medical Care* 47, no. 6 (2009): 662–69. https://doi.org/10.1097/MLR.0b013e318190cc95.

Walters, Jim, and Patricia H. Davis. "Human Trafficking, Sex Tourism, and Child Exploitation on the Southern Border." *Journal of Applied Research on Children* 2, no. 1 (2011): art. 6.

Warf, Barney, and Brian Holly. "The Rise and Fall and Rise of Cleveland." *Annals of the American Academy of Political and Social Science* 551 (May 1, 1997): 208–21. https://doi.org/10.1177/0002 716297551001015.

Warner, Judith Ann. "The Social Construction of the Criminal Alien in Immigration Law, Enforcement Practice and Statistical Enumeration: Consequences for Immigrant Stereotyping." *Journal of Social and Ecological Boundaries* 1, no. 2 (2005): 56–80.

Warren, Robert. "Reverse Migration to Mexico Led to US Undocumented Population Decline: 2010 to 2018." *Journal on Migration and Human Security* 8, no. 1 (2020): 32–41. https://doi.org /10.1177/2331502420906125.

Waters, Mary C., and Marisa Gerstein Pineau. *The Integration of Immigrants Into American Society.* Washington, DC: National Academies Press, 2015.

Watson, Tara. "Inside the Refrigerator: Immigration Enforcement and Chilling Effects in Medicaid Participation." *American Economic Journal: Economic Policy* 6, no. 3 (2014): 313–38. https://doi.org/10.1257/pol.6.3.313.

Wei, Kai, Daniel Jacobson López, and Shiyou Wu. "The Role of Language in Anti-Immigrant Prejudice: What Can We Learn from Immigrants' Historical Experiences?" *Social Sciences* 8, no. 3 (2019): 93.

Weisheit, Ralph A. "Cannabis Cultivation in the United States." In *World Wide Weed: Global Trends in Cannabis Cultivation and Its Control*, ed. Tom Decorte, Gary Potter, and Martin Bouchard, 145–61. Farnham, UK: Ashgate, 2011.

West, Charlotte. "Thousands of Students Cross the Southern Border Every Day to Go to College." Hechinger Report, June 19, 2019. http://hechingerreport.org/thousands-of-students -cross-the-southern-border-every-day-to-go-to-college/.

Whitaker, Julie. "Mexican Deaths in the Arizona Desert: The Culpability of Migrants, Humanitarian Workers, Governments, and Businesses." *Journal of Business Ethics* 88, no. 2 (2009): 365–76. https://doi.org/10.1007/s10551-009-0283-x.

White House. "Fact Sheet: Department of Defense and Department of Homeland Security Plans for Border Wall Funds." June 11, 2021. https://www.whitehouse.gov/omb/briefing -room/2021/06/11/fact-sheet-department-of-defense-and-department-of-homeland-security -plans-for-border-wall-funds/.

——. Proclamation on the Termination of Emergency with Respect to the Southern Border of the United States and Redirection of Funds Diverted to Border Wall Construction. January 20, 2021. https://www.whitehouse.gov/briefing-room/presidential-actions/2021/01/20/proclamation -termination-of-emergency-with-respect-to-southern-border-of-united-states-and -redirection-of-funds-diverted-to-border-wall-construction/.

White, Rob. "Ethnic Diversity and Differential Policing in Australia: The Good, the Bad and the Ugly." *Journal of International Migration and Integration* 10, no. 4 (2009): 359–75. https://doi.org /10.1007/s12134-009-0111-2.

Wiley, Terrence G. "Accessing Language Rights in Education: A Brief History of the U.S. Context." In *Bilingual Education: An Introductory Reader*, ed. Ofelia García and Colin Baker, 89–107. Clevedon, UK: Multilingual Matters, 2007.

Wilkerson, Miranda E., and Joseph Salmons. "'GOOD Old Immigrants of Yesteryear,' Who Didn't Learn English: Germans in Wisconsin." *American Speech* 83, no. 3 (2008): 259–83. https://doi.org/10.1215/00031283-2008-020.

Willis, Mary S., and Onyema Nkwocha. "Health and Related Factors for Sudanese Refugees in Nebraska." *Journal of Immigrant and Minority Health* 8, no. 1 (2006): 19–33. https://doi.org/10.1007/s10903-006-6339-9.

World Bank Group, KNOMAD. Leveraging Diaspora Finances for Private Capital Mobilization. Migration and Development Brief 39. December 2023. https://www.knomad.org/sites/default/files/publication-doc/migration_development_brief_39_0.pdf.

Wolfman-Arent, Avi. "Research Shows Spanish Speakers Take Longer to Learn English. Why?" NPR, September 15, 2017. https://www.npr.org/sections/ed/2017/09/15/545629043/research-shows-spanish-speakers-take-longer-to-learn-english-why.

Wong, Lily. *Transpacific Attachments: Sex Work, Media Networks, and Affective Histories of Chineseness.* New York: Columbia University Press, 2018.

Wong Fillmore, Lily, and Catherine E. Snow. "What Teachers Need to Know About Language." In *What Teachers Need to Know about Language*, ed. Carolyn Temple Adger, Catherine E. Snow, and Donna Christian. 2nd ed. Bristol, UK: Multilingual Matters, 2018.

Woody, Christopher. "Here's How Mexican Cartels Actually Operate in the United States." Business Insider, September 27, 2017. https://www.businessinsider.com/what-are-mexican-cartels-doing-in-the-us-2017-4.

World Bank. "Defying Predictions, Remittance Flows Remain Strong During COVID-19 Crisis." May 12, 2021. https://www.worldbank.org/en/news/press-release/2021/05/12/defying-predictions-remittance-flows-remain-strong-during-covid-19-crisis.

——. "Migration and Remittances Data." November 16, 2017. https://www.worldbank.org/en/topic/migrationremittancesdiasporaissues/brief/migration-remittances-data.

Wortley, Scot. "The Immigration-Crime Connection: Competing Theoretical Perspectives." *Journal of International Migration and Integration* 10 (2009): 349. https://doi.org/10.1007/s12134-009-0117-9.

Wright, Melissa W. "Necropolitics, Narcopolitics, and Femicide: Gendered Violence on the Mexico-U.S. Border." *Signs* 36, no. 3 (2011): 707–31. https://doi.org/10.1086/657496.

Xpress Money. "Formal Versus Informal Remittance Channels: An Overview." January 23, 2020. https://www.xpressmoney.com/blog/industry/formal-versus-informal-remittance-channels-an-overview/.

Yang, Aimei, and Adam Saffer. "NGOs' Advocacy in the 2015 Refugee Crisis: A Study of Agenda Building in the Digital Age." *American Behavioral Scientist* 62, no. 4 (2018): 421–39. https://doi.org/10.1177/0002764218759578.

Yang, Dean. "Migrant Remittances." *Journal of Economic Perspectives* 25, no. 3 (2011): 129–52. https://doi.org/10.1257/jep.25.3.129.

Yang, Dean, and HwaJung Choi. "Are Remittances Insurance? Evidence from Rainfall Shocks in the Philippines." *World Bank Economic Review* 21, no. 2 (2007): 219–48. https://doi.org/10.1093/wber/lhm003.

Yazgan, Pinar, Deniz Eroglu Utku, and Ibrahim Sirkeci. "Syrian Crisis and Migration." *Migration Letters* 12, no. 3 (2015): 181–92. https://doi.org/10.33182/ml.v12i3.273.

Yee, Vivian. "Judge Blocks Trump Effort to Withhold Money from Sanctuary Cities." *New York Times*, April 25, 2017. https://www.nytimes.com/2017/04/25/us/judge-blocks-trump-sanctuary-cities.html.

Yeo, Colin. "Refugee Family Reunion: A User's Guide." Free Movement, March 20, 2019. https://www.freemovement.org.uk/refugee-family-reunion-a-users-guide/.

Yeung, Peter. " 'Worst Situation You Can Ever Be In': What Gen Z Thinks of Brexit." Al Jazeera, January 4, 2021. https://www.aljazeera.com/features/2021/1/4/brexit-generation-zs-view-on-the-uk-eu-divorce.

Young, Cheri A., Rachel S. Shinnar, and Seonghee Cho. "Financial Behaviors Among Hispanic Immigrants." *Journal of Personal Finance* 8 (2009): 147–69.

Yuval-Davis, Nira. "Belonging and the Politics of Belonging." *Patterns of Prejudice* 40, no. 3 (2006): 197–214. https://doi.org/10.1080/00313220600769331.

Zallman, Leah, Steffie Woolhandler, Sharon Touw, David U. Himmelstein, and Karen E. Finnegan. "Immigrants Pay More in Private Insurance Premiums Than They Receive in Benefits." *Health Affairs* 37, no. 10 (2018): 1663–68. https://doi.org/10.1377/hlthaff.2018.0309.

Zarate, Adanari. " 'You Don't Look Like You Speak English': Raciolinguistic Profiling and Latinx Youth Agency." In *Feeling It: Language, Race, and Affect in Latinx Youth Learning*, ed. Mary Bucholtz, Dolores Inés Casillas, and Jin Sook Lee. Oxfordshire, UK: Routledge, 2018.

Zavodny, Madeline. "Determinants of Recent Immigrants' Locational Choices." *International Migration Review* 33, no. 4 (1999): 1014–30. https://doi.org/10.1177/019791839903300408.

——. "Do Immigrants Work in Worse Jobs than U.S. Natives? Evidence from California." *Industrial Relations* 54, no. 2 (2015): 276–93. https://doi.org/10.1111/irel.12087.

——. "Welfare and the Locational Choices of New Immigrants." *Economic and Financial Policy Review*, no. Q II (1997): 2–10.

Zhang, Wei, Seunghye Hong, David T. Takeuchi, and Krysia N. Mossakowski. "Limited English Proficiency and Psychological Distress Among Latinos and Asian Americans." *Social Science & Medicine* 75, no. 6 (2012): 1006–14. https://doi.org/10.1016/j.socscimed.2012.05.012.

Zoghlin, Rachel. "Draconian Discrimination: One Man's Battle with U.S. Immigration Law for Fairness, Justice, and American Citizenship." *Modern American* 8, no. 2 (2012): 72–74.

Zolberg, Aristide R., and Long Litt Woon. "Why Islam Is Like Spanish: Cultural Incorporation in Europe and the United States." *Politics and Society* 27, no. 1 (1999): 5–38.

Zong, Jie, and Jeanne Batalova. "The Limited English Proficient Population in the United States in 2013." Migration Policy Institute, July 7, 2015. https://www.migrationpolicy.org/article/limited-english-proficient-population-united-states-2013.

INDEX

Printed in the USA
CPSIA information can be obtained
at www.ICGtesting.com
CBHW021107061224
18551CB00043B/262

9 780231 203753